P9-ECM-472

Table of Contents

by
Osamu Tezuka

translation
Frederik L. Schodt

lettering and retouch
Sno Cone Studios

Dark Horse Manga™

publisher
Mike Richardson

editor
Chris Warner

consulting editor
Toren Smith for **Studio Proteus**

collection designers
David Nestelle and **Lani Schreibstein**

English-language version produced by **Dark Horse Comics** and **Studio Proteus**

Astro Boy® Volume 21

The artwork of this volume has been produced as a mirror-image of the original Japanese edition to conform to English-language standards.

Published by
Dark Horse Manga
A division of Dark Horse Comics, Inc.
10956 SE Main Street
Milwaukie, OR 97222

www.darkhorse.com

To find a comics shop in your area, call the Comic Shop Locator Service toll-free at 1-888-266-4226.

First edition: November 2003
ISBN: 1-56971-902-0

10 9 8 7 6 5 4 3 2 1
Printed in Canada

A NOTE TO READERS

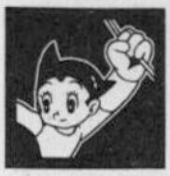

Many non-Japanese, including people from Africa and Southeast Asia, appear in Osamu Tezuka's works. Sometimes these people are depicted very differently from the way they actually are today, in a manner that exaggerates a time long past or shows them to be from extremely undeveloped lands. Some feel that such images contribute to racial discrimination, especially against people of African descent. This was never Osamu Tezuka's intent, but we believe that as long as there are people who feel insulted or demeaned by these depictions, we must not ignore their feelings.

We are against discrimination, in all its forms, and intend to continue to work for its elimination. Nonetheless, we do not believe it would be proper to revise these works. Tezuka is no longer with us, and we cannot erase what he has done, and to alter his work would only violate his rights as a creator. More importantly, stopping publication or changing the content of his work would do little to solve the problems of discrimination that exist in the world.

We are presenting Osamu Tezuka's work as it was originally created, without changes. We do this because we believe it is also important to promote the underlying themes in his work, such as love for mankind and the sanctity of life. We hope that when you, the reader, encounter this work, you will keep in mind the differences in attitudes, then and now, toward discrimination, and that this will contribute to an even greater awareness of such problems.

— Tezuka Productions and Dark Horse Comics

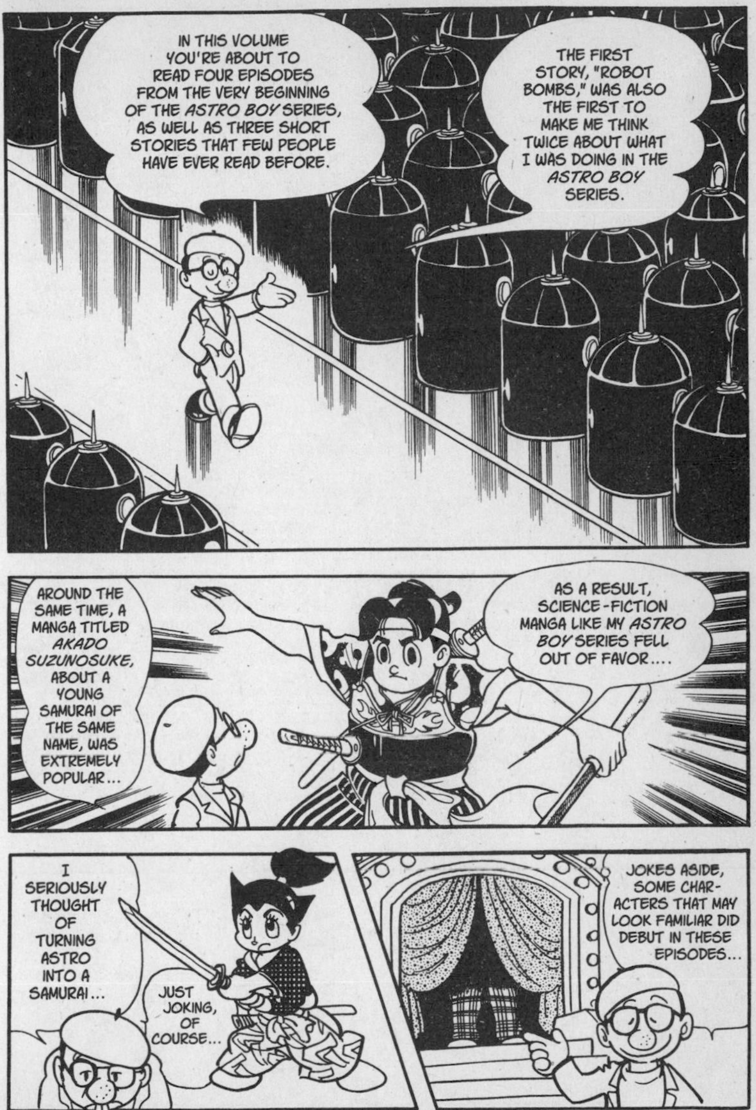
IN THIS VOLUME YOU'RE ABOUT TO READ FOUR EPISODES FROM THE VERY BEGINNING OF THE *ASTRO BOY* SERIES, AS WELL AS THREE SHORT STORIES THAT FEW PEOPLE HAVE EVER READ BEFORE.
THE FIRST STORY, "ROBOT BOMBS," WAS ALSO THE FIRST TO MAKE ME THINK TWICE ABOUT WHAT I WAS DOING IN THE *ASTRO BOY* SERIES.
AROUND THE SAME TIME, A MANGA TITLED *AKADO SUZUNOSUKE*, ABOUT A YOUNG SAMURAI OF THE SAME NAME, WAS EXTREMELY POPULAR...
AS A RESULT, SCIENCE-FICTION MANGA LIKE MY *ASTRO BOY* SERIES FELL OUT OF FAVOR....
I SERIOUSLY THOUGHT OF TURNING ASTRO INTO A SAMURAI...
JUST JOKING, OF COURSE...
JOKES ASIDE, SOME CHARACTERS THAT MAY LOOK FAMILIAR DID DEBUT IN THESE EPISODES...

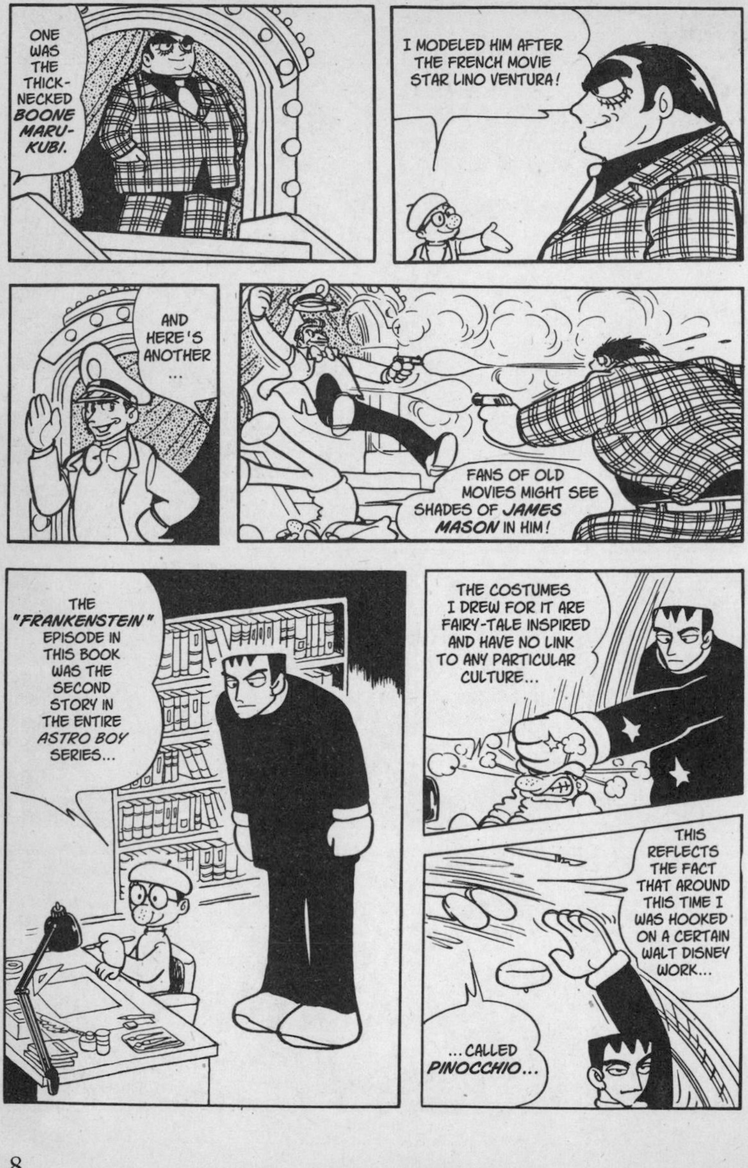
ONE WAS THE THICK-NECKED BOONE MARU-KUBI.
I MODELED HIM AFTER THE FRENCH MOVIE STAR LINO VENTURA!
AND HERE'S ANOTHER ...
FANS OF OLD MOVIES MIGHT SEE SHADES OF JAMES MASON IN HIM!
THE "FRANKENSTEIN" EPISODE IN THIS BOOK WAS THE SECOND STORY IN THE ENTIRE ASTRO BOY SERIES...
THE COSTUMES I DREW FOR IT ARE FAIRY-TALE INSPIRED AND HAVE NO LINK TO ANY PARTICULAR CULTURE...
THIS REFLECTS THE FACT THAT AROUND THIS TIME I WAS HOOKED ON A CERTAIN WALT DISNEY WORK...
...CALLED PINOCCHIO...

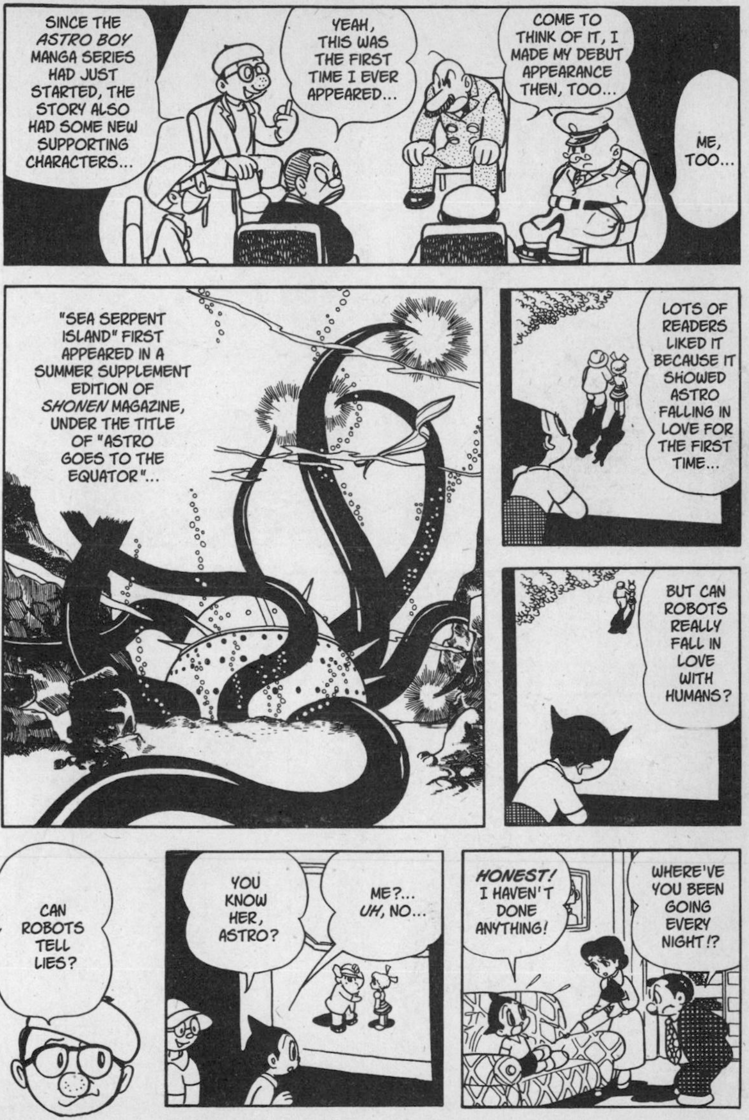
SINCE THE *ASTRO BOY* MANGA SERIES HAD JUST STARTED, THE STORY ALSO HAD SOME NEW SUPPORTING CHARACTERS...
YEAH, THIS WAS THE FIRST TIME I EVER APPEARED...
COME TO THINK OF IT, I MADE MY DEBUT APPEARANCE THEN, TOO...
ME, TOO...
"SEA SERPENT ISLAND" FIRST APPEARED IN A SUMMER SUPPLEMENT EDITION OF *SHONEN* MAGAZINE, UNDER THE TITLE OF "ASTRO GOES TO THE EQUATOR"...
LOTS OF READERS LIKED IT BECAUSE IT SHOWED ASTRO FALLING IN LOVE FOR THE FIRST TIME...
BUT CAN ROBOTS REALLY FALL IN LOVE WITH HUMANS?
CAN ROBOTS TELL LIES?
YOU KNOW HER, ASTRO?
ME?... *UH*, NO...
HONEST! I HAVEN'T DONE ANYTHING!
WHERE'VE YOU BEEN GOING EVERY NIGHT!?

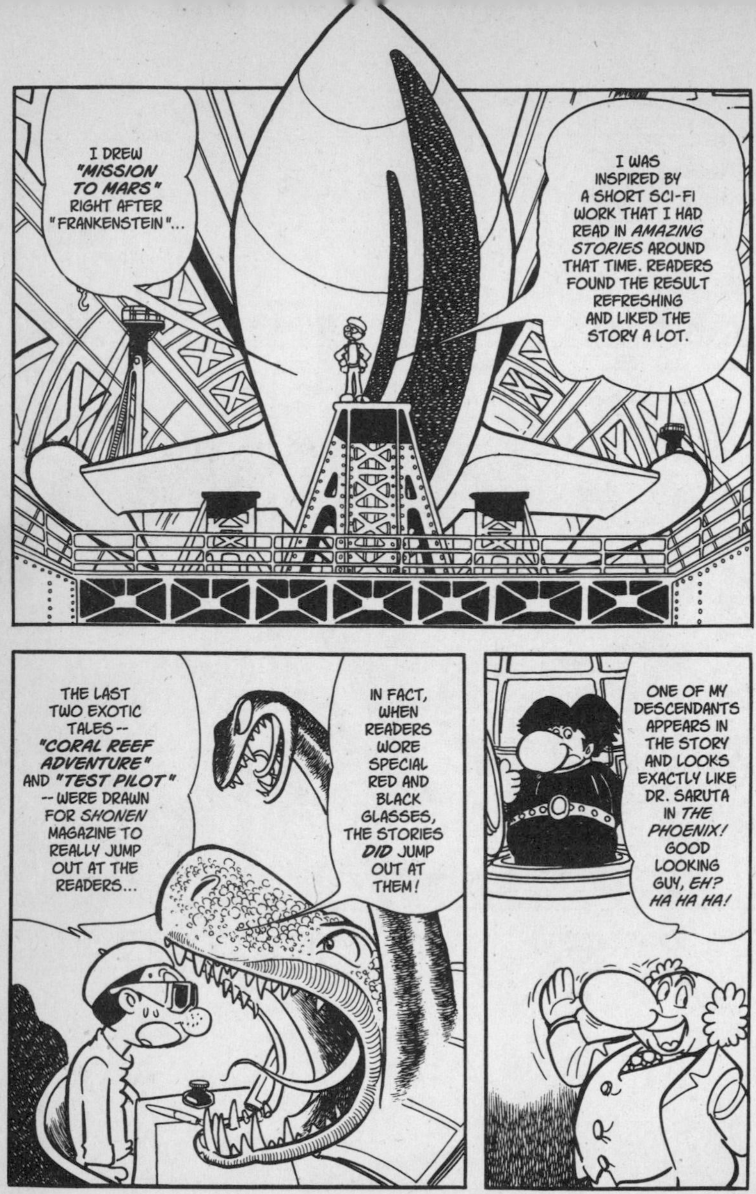
I DREW *"MISSION TO MARS"* RIGHT AFTER "FRANKENSTEIN"...
I WAS INSPIRED BY A SHORT SCI-FI WORK THAT I HAD READ IN *AMAZING STORIES* AROUND THAT TIME. READERS FOUND THE RESULT REFRESHING AND LIKED THE STORY A LOT.
THE LAST TWO EXOTIC TALES -- *"CORAL REEF ADVENTURE"* AND *"TEST PILOT"* -- WERE DRAWN FOR *SHONEN* MAGAZINE TO REALLY JUMP OUT AT THE READERS...
IN FACT, WHEN READERS WORE SPECIAL RED AND BLACK GLASSES, THE STORIES *DID* JUMP OUT AT THEM!
ONE OF MY DESCENDANTS APPEARS IN THE STORY AND LOOKS EXACTLY LIKE DR. SARUTA IN *THE PHOENIX!* GOOD LOOKING GUY, *EH? HA HA HA!*

ROBOT BOMBS

First serialized from December 1956 to
August 1957 in *Shonen* magazine.

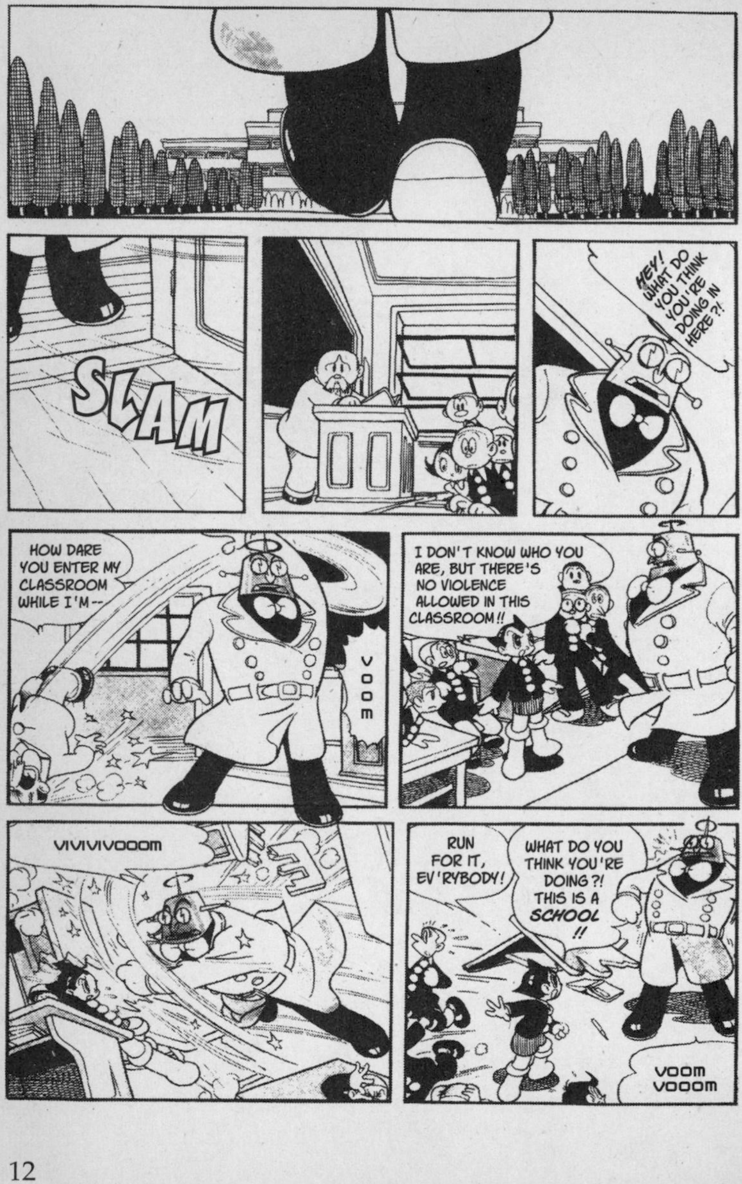
SLAM
HEY! WHAT DO YOU THINK YOU'RE DOING IN HERE?!
HOW DARE YOU ENTER MY CLASSROOM WHILE I'M --
VOOM
I DON'T KNOW WHO YOU ARE, BUT THERE'S NO VIOLENCE ALLOWED IN THIS CLASSROOM!!
VIVIVIVOOOM
RUN FOR IT, EV'RYBODY!
WHAT DO YOU THINK YOU'RE DOING?! THIS IS A SCHOOL!!
VOOM VOOOM

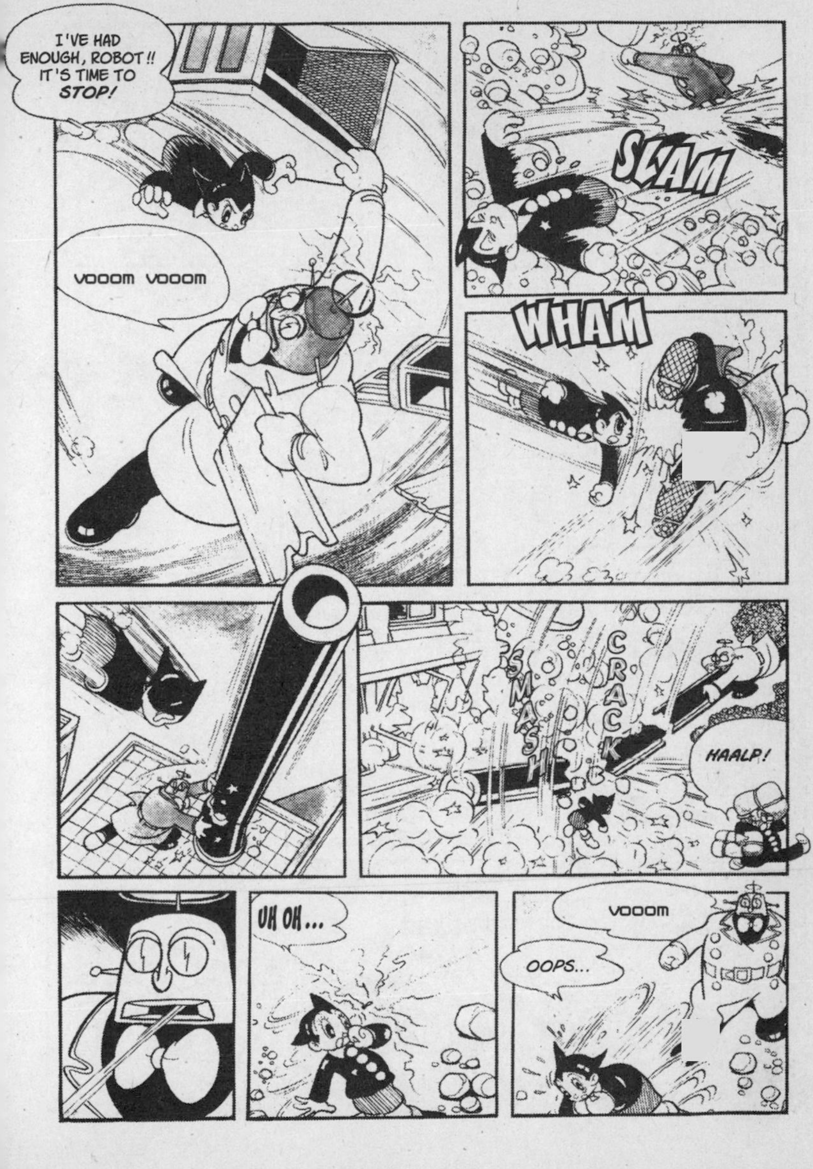
I'VE HAD ENOUGH, ROBOT!! IT'S TIME TO STOP!
VOOOM VOOOM
SLAM
WHAM
SMASH
CRACK
HAALP!
UH OH...
VOOOM
OOPS...

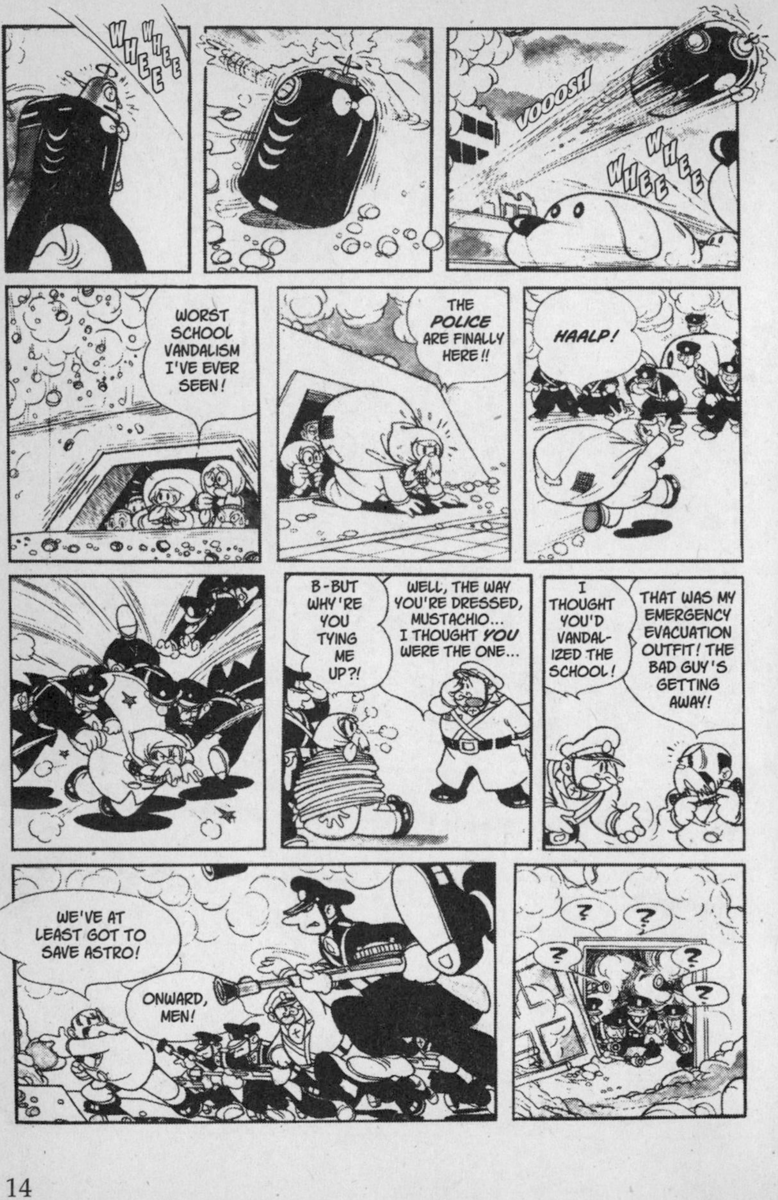
WHEEE
WHEEE
VOOOSH
WORST SCHOOL VANDALISM I'VE EVER SEEN!
THE *POLICE* ARE FINALLY HERE!!
HAALP!
B-BUT WHY'RE YOU TYING ME UP?!
WELL, THE WAY YOU'RE DRESSED, MUSTACHIO... I THOUGHT *YOU* WERE THE ONE...
I THOUGHT YOU'D VANDAL-IZED THE SCHOOL!
THAT WAS MY EMERGENCY EVACUATION OUTFIT! THE BAD GUY'S GETTING AWAY!
WE'VE AT LEAST GOT TO SAVE ASTRO!
ONWARD, MEN!
?
?
?
?
?

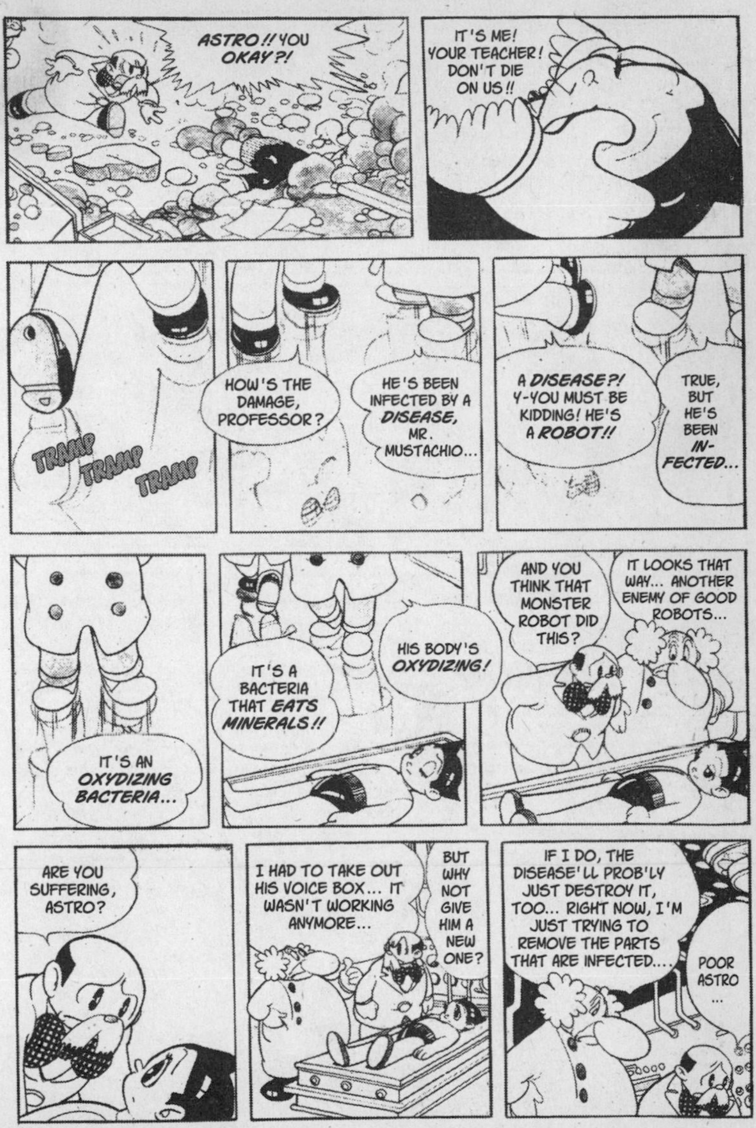
ASTRO!! YOU OKAY?!
IT'S ME! YOUR TEACHER! DON'T DIE ON US!!
TRAMP TRAMP TRAMP
HOW'S THE DAMAGE, PROFESSOR?
HE'S BEEN INFECTED BY A DISEASE, MR. MUSTACHIO...
A DISEASE?! Y-YOU MUST BE KIDDING! HE'S A ROBOT!!
TRUE, BUT HE'S BEEN INFECTED...
IT'S AN OXYDIZING BACTERIA...
HIS BODY'S OXYDIZING!
IT'S A BACTERIA THAT EATS MINERALS!!
AND YOU THINK THAT MONSTER ROBOT DID THIS?
IT LOOKS THAT WAY... ANOTHER ENEMY OF GOOD ROBOTS...
ARE YOU SUFFERING, ASTRO?
I HAD TO TAKE OUT HIS VOICE BOX... IT WASN'T WORKING ANYMORE...
BUT WHY NOT GIVE HIM A NEW ONE?
IF I DO, THE DISEASE'LL PROB'LY JUST DESTROY IT, TOO... RIGHT NOW, I'M JUST TRYING TO REMOVE THE PARTS THAT ARE INFECTED...
POOR ASTRO ...

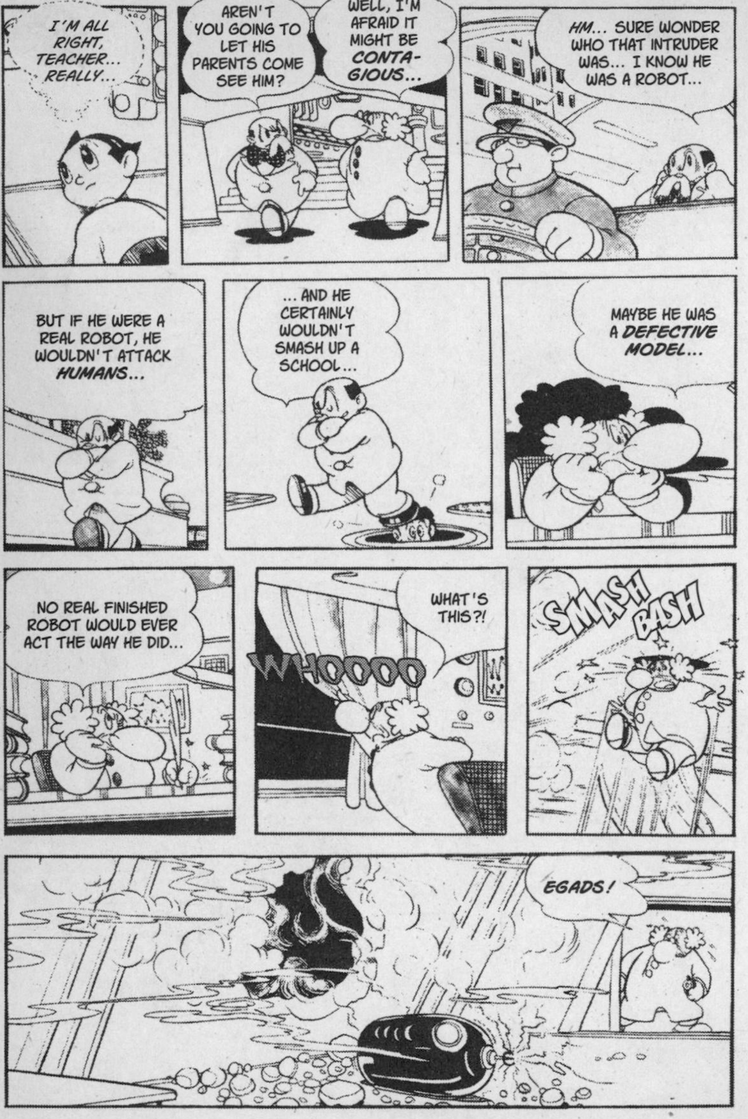
I'M ALL RIGHT, TEACHER... REALLY...
AREN'T YOU GOING TO LET HIS PARENTS COME SEE HIM?
WELL, I'M AFRAID IT MIGHT BE CONTAGIOUS...
HM... SURE WONDER WHO THAT INTRUDER WAS... I KNOW HE WAS A ROBOT...
BUT IF HE WERE A REAL ROBOT, HE WOULDN'T ATTACK HUMANS...
... AND HE CERTAINLY WOULDN'T SMASH UP A SCHOOL...
MAYBE HE WAS A DEFECTIVE MODEL...
NO REAL FINISHED ROBOT WOULD EVER ACT THE WAY HE DID...
WHAT'S THIS?!
WHOOOO
SMASH
BASH
EGADS!

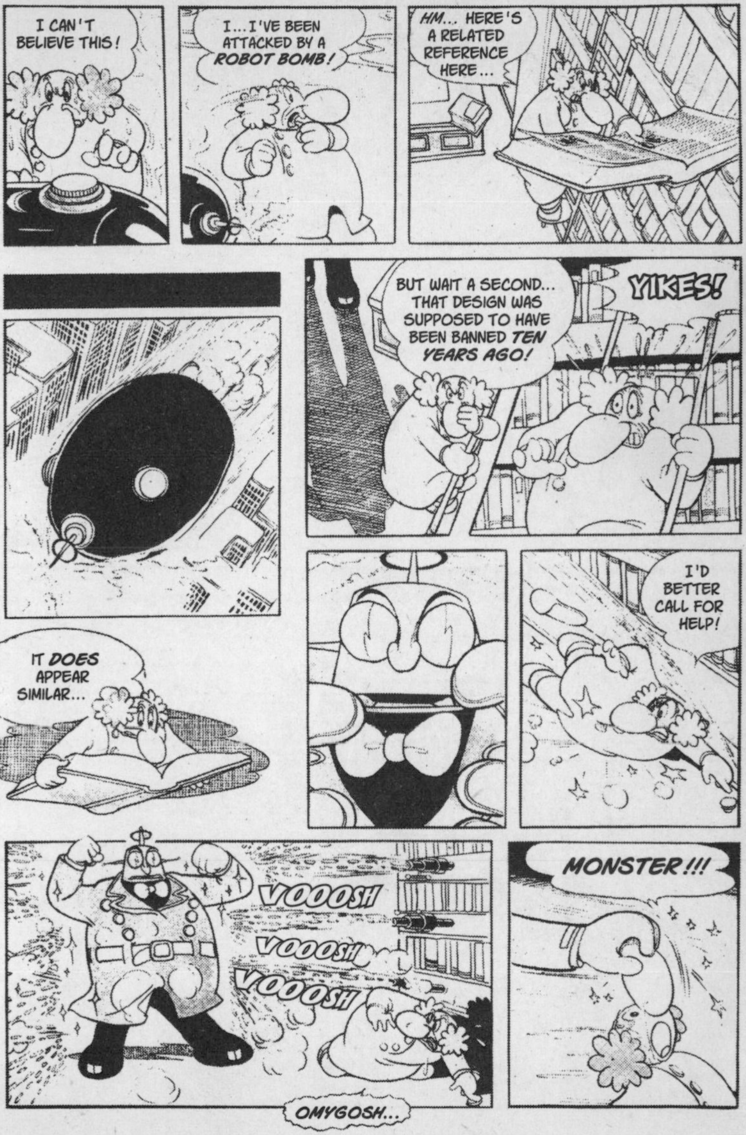
I CAN'T BELIEVE THIS!
I... I'VE BEEN ATTACKED BY A ROBOT BOMB!
HM... HERE'S A RELATED REFERENCE HERE...
BUT WAIT A SECOND... THAT DESIGN WAS SUPPOSED TO HAVE BEEN BANNED TEN YEARS AGO!
YIKES!
IT DOES APPEAR SIMILAR...
I'D BETTER CALL FOR HELP!
VOOOSH
VOOOSH
VOOOSH
OMYGOSH...
MONSTER!!!

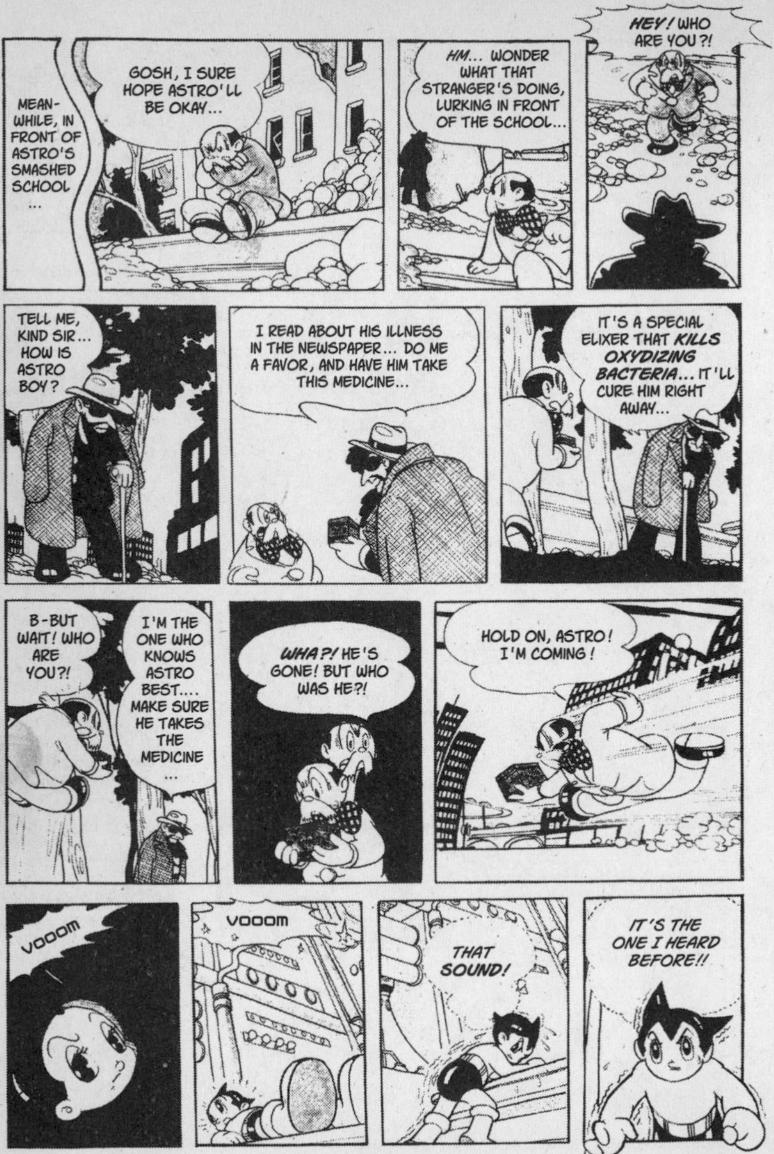
MEAN-WHILE, IN FRONT OF ASTRO'S SMASHED SCHOOL ...
GOSH, I SURE HOPE ASTRO'LL BE OKAY...
HM... WONDER WHAT THAT STRANGER'S DOING, LURKING IN FRONT OF THE SCHOOL...
HEY! WHO ARE YOU?!
TELL ME, KIND SIR... HOW IS ASTRO BOY?
I READ ABOUT HIS ILLNESS IN THE NEWSPAPER... DO ME A FAVOR, AND HAVE HIM TAKE THIS MEDICINE...
IT'S A SPECIAL ELIXER THAT KILLS OXYDIZING BACTERIA... IT'LL CURE HIM RIGHT AWAY...
B-BUT WAIT! WHO ARE YOU?!
I'M THE ONE WHO KNOWS ASTRO BEST.... MAKE SURE HE TAKES THE MEDICINE ...
WHA?! HE'S GONE! BUT WHO WAS HE?!
HOLD ON, ASTRO! I'M COMING!
VOOOM
VOOOM
THAT SOUND!
IT'S THE ONE I HEARD BEFORE!!

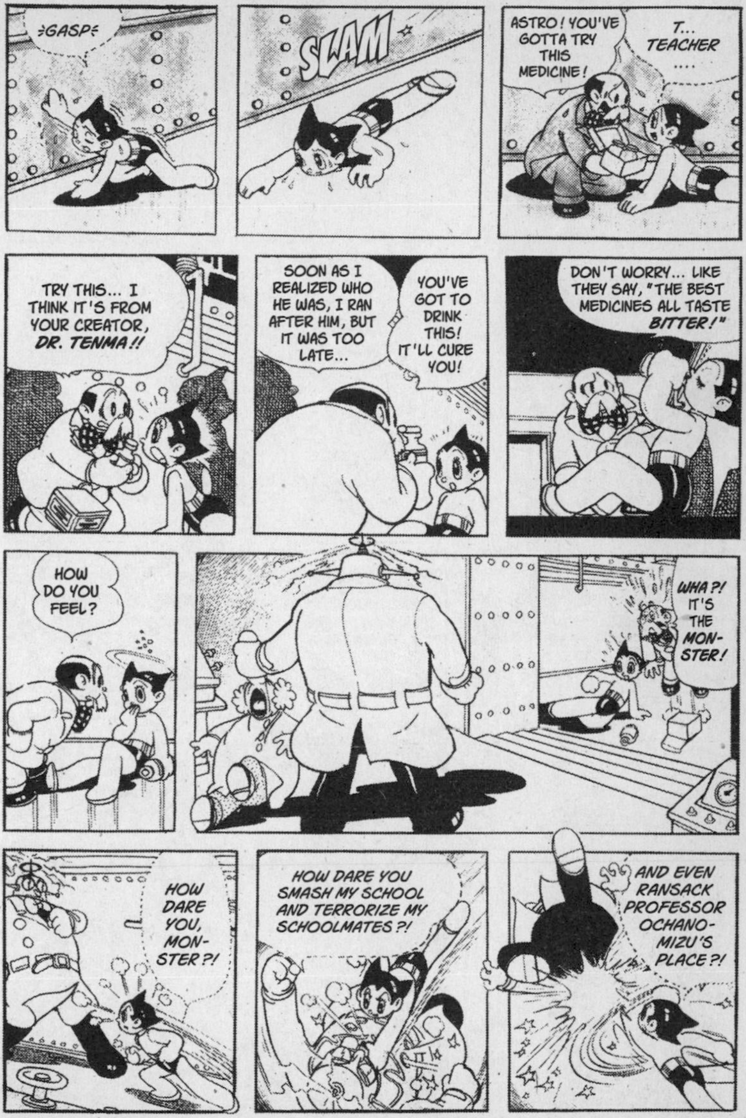
GASP
SLAM
ASTRO! YOU'VE GOTTA TRY THIS MEDICINE!
T... TEACHER ....
TRY THIS... I THINK IT'S FROM YOUR CREATOR, DR. TENMA!!
SOON AS I REALIZED WHO HE WAS, I RAN AFTER HIM, BUT IT WAS TOO LATE...
YOU'VE GOT TO DRINK THIS! IT'LL CURE YOU!
DON'T WORRY... LIKE THEY SAY, "THE BEST MEDICINES ALL TASTE BITTER!"
HOW DO YOU FEEL?
WHA?! IT'S THE MON-STER!
HOW DARE YOU, MON-STER?!
HOW DARE YOU SMASH MY SCHOOL AND TERRORIZE MY SCHOOLMATES?!
AND EVEN RANSACK PROFESSOR OCHANO-MIZU'S PLACE?!

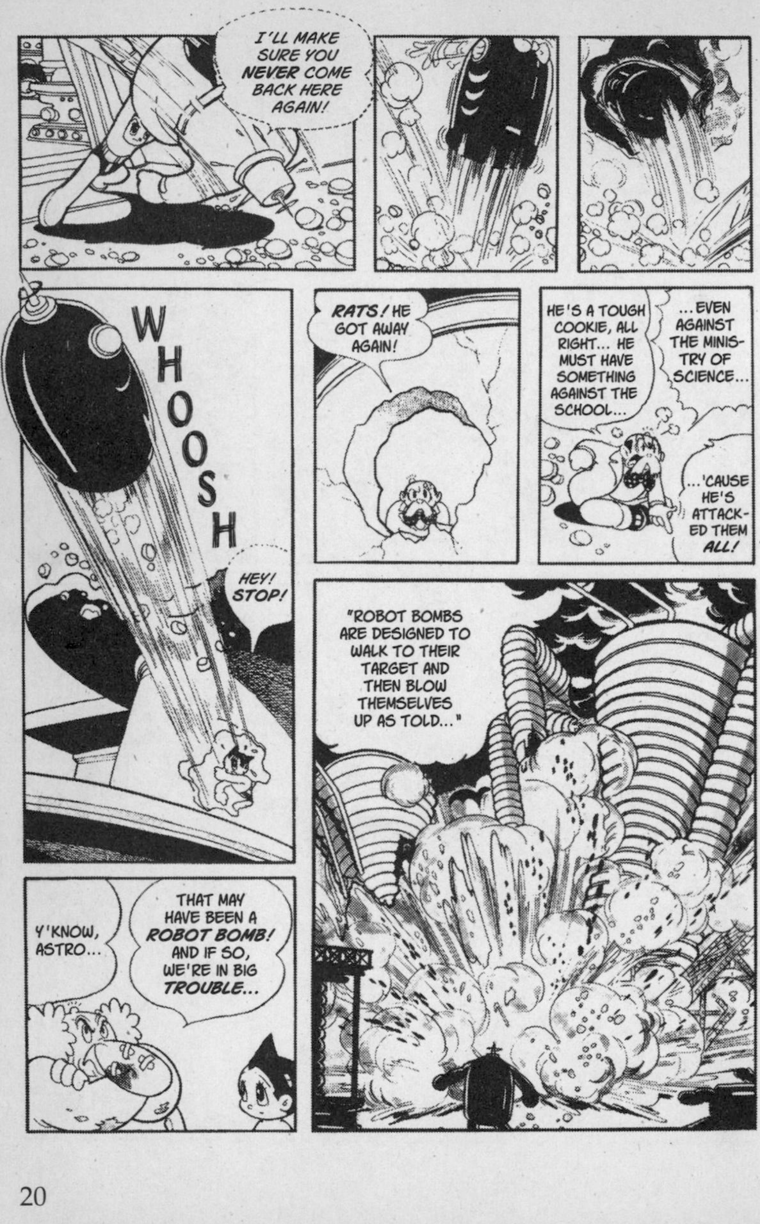
I'LL MAKE SURE YOU NEVER COME BACK HERE AGAIN!
WHOOSH
HEY! STOP!
RATS! HE GOT AWAY AGAIN!
HE'S A TOUGH COOKIE, ALL RIGHT... HE MUST HAVE SOMETHING AGAINST THE SCHOOL...
...EVEN AGAINST THE MINISTRY OF SCIENCE...
...'CAUSE HE'S ATTACKED THEM ALL!
Y'KNOW, ASTRO...
THAT MAY HAVE BEEN A ROBOT BOMB! AND IF SO, WE'RE IN BIG TROUBLE...
"ROBOT BOMBS ARE DESIGNED TO WALK TO THEIR TARGET AND THEN BLOW THEMSELVES UP AS TOLD..."

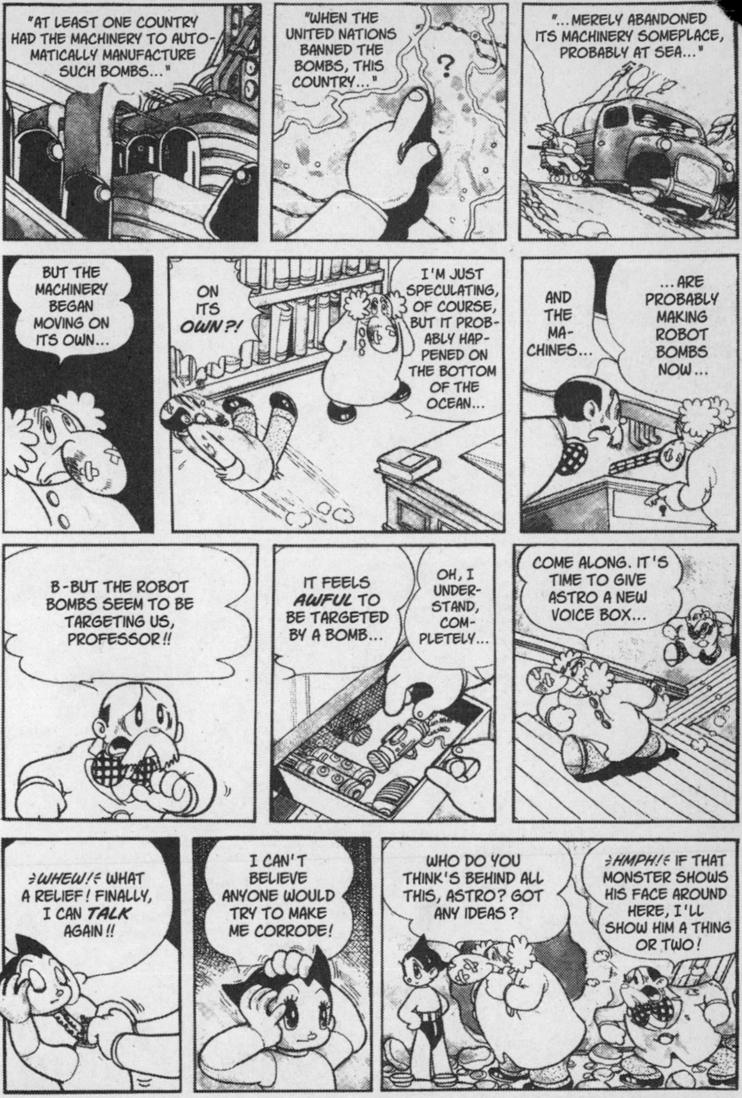
"AT LEAST ONE COUNTRY HAD THE MACHINERY TO AUTOMATICALLY MANUFACTURE SUCH BOMBS..."
"WHEN THE UNITED NATIONS BANNED THE BOMBS, THIS COUNTRY..."
?
"...MERELY ABANDONED ITS MACHINERY SOMEPLACE, PROBABLY AT SEA..."
BUT THE MACHINERY BEGAN MOVING ON ITS OWN...
ON ITS *OWN*?!
I'M JUST SPECULATING, OF COURSE, BUT IT PROBABLY HAPPENED ON THE BOTTOM OF THE OCEAN...
AND THE MACHINES...
...ARE PROBABLY MAKING ROBOT BOMBS NOW...
B-BUT THE ROBOT BOMBS SEEM TO BE TARGETING US, PROFESSOR!!
IT FEELS *AWFUL* TO BE TARGETED BY A BOMB...
OH, I UNDERSTAND, COMPLETELY...
COME ALONG. IT'S TIME TO GIVE ASTRO A NEW VOICE BOX...
WHEW! WHAT A RELIEF! FINALLY, I CAN *TALK* AGAIN!!
I CAN'T BELIEVE ANYONE WOULD TRY TO MAKE ME CORRODE!
WHO DO YOU THINK'S BEHIND ALL THIS, ASTRO? GOT ANY IDEAS?
HMPH! IF THAT MONSTER SHOWS HIS FACE AROUND HERE, I'LL SHOW HIM A THING OR TWO!

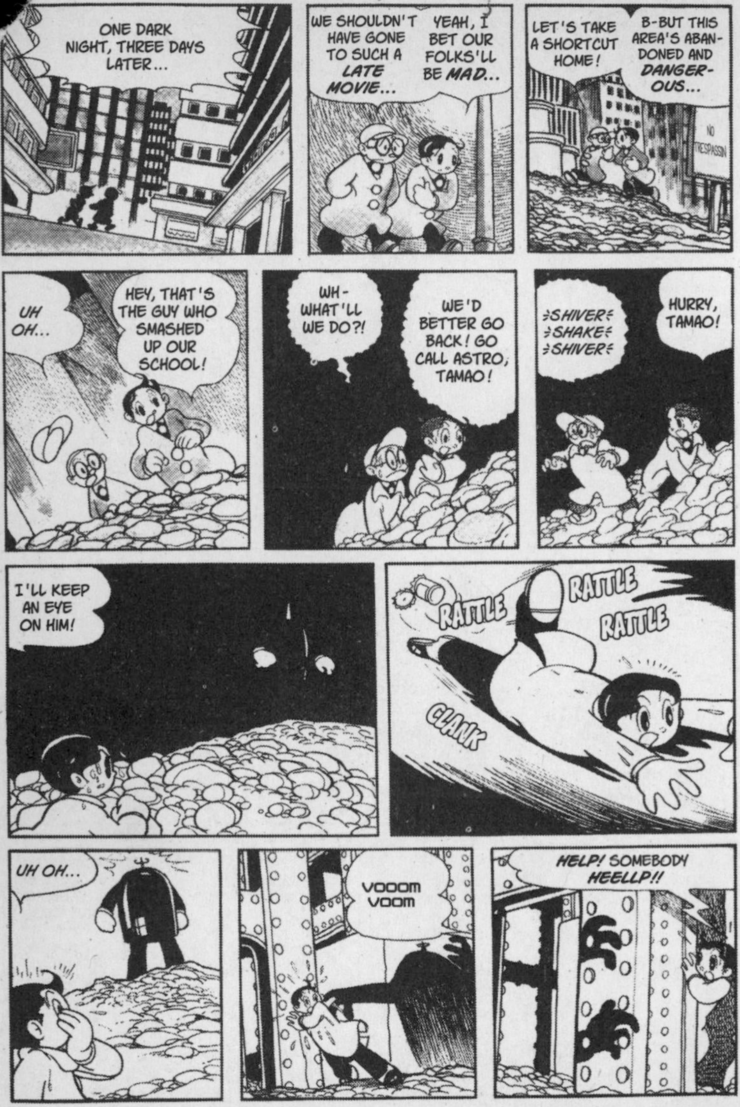

ONE DARK NIGHT, THREE DAYS LATER...
WE SHOULDN'T HAVE GONE TO SUCH A LATE MOVIE...
YEAH, I BET OUR FOLKS'LL BE MAD...
LET'S TAKE A SHORTCUT HOME!
B-BUT THIS AREA'S ABANDONED AND DANGEROUS...
NO TRESPASSIN
UH OH...
HEY, THAT'S THE GUY WHO SMASHED UP OUR SCHOOL!
WH-WHAT'LL WE DO?!
WE'D BETTER GO BACK! GO CALL ASTRO, TAMAO!
SHIVER SHAKE SHIVER
HURRY, TAMAO!
I'LL KEEP AN EYE ON HIM!
RATTLE
RATTLE
RATTLE
CLANK
UH OH...
VOOOM VOOM
HELP! SOMEBODY HEELLP!!

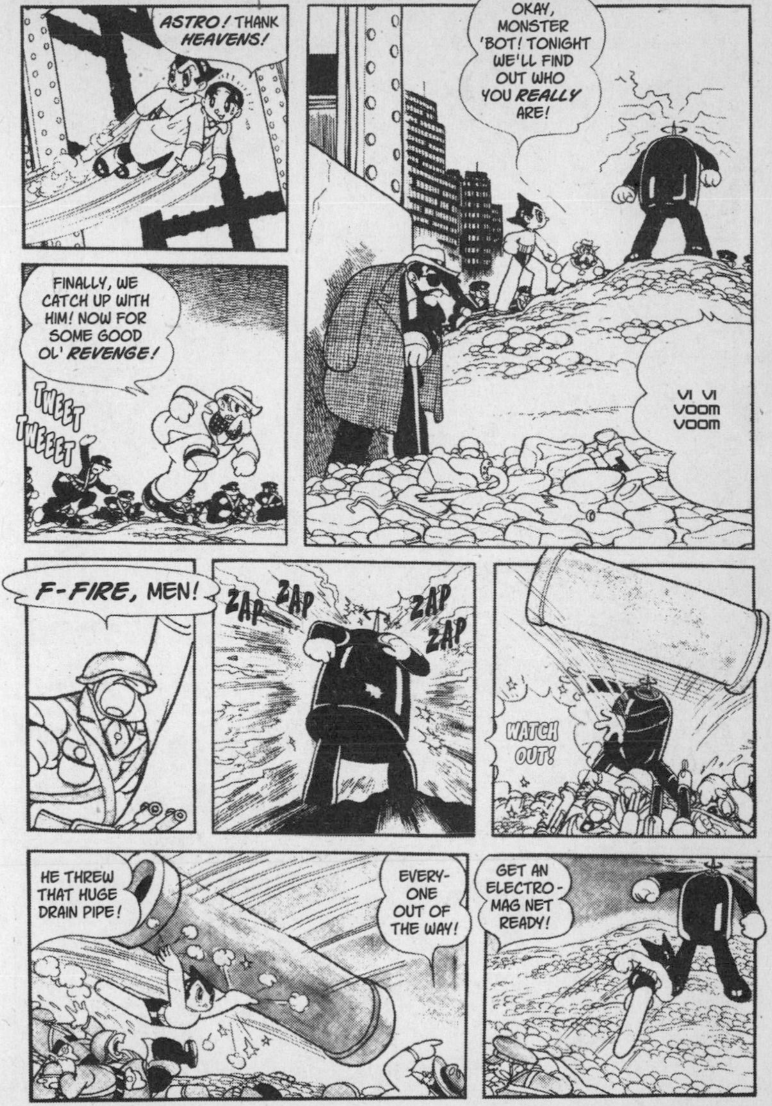

ASTRO! THANK HEAVENS!
FINALLY, WE CATCH UP WITH HIM! NOW FOR SOME GOOD OL' REVENGE!
TWEET TWEEET
OKAY, MONSTER 'BOT! TONIGHT WE'LL FIND OUT WHO YOU REALLY ARE!
VI VI VOOM VOOM
F-FIRE, MEN!
ZAP ZAP ZAP ZAP
WATCH OUT!
HE THREW THAT HUGE DRAIN PIPE!
EVERY-ONE OUT OF THE WAY!
GET AN ELECTRO-MAG NET READY!

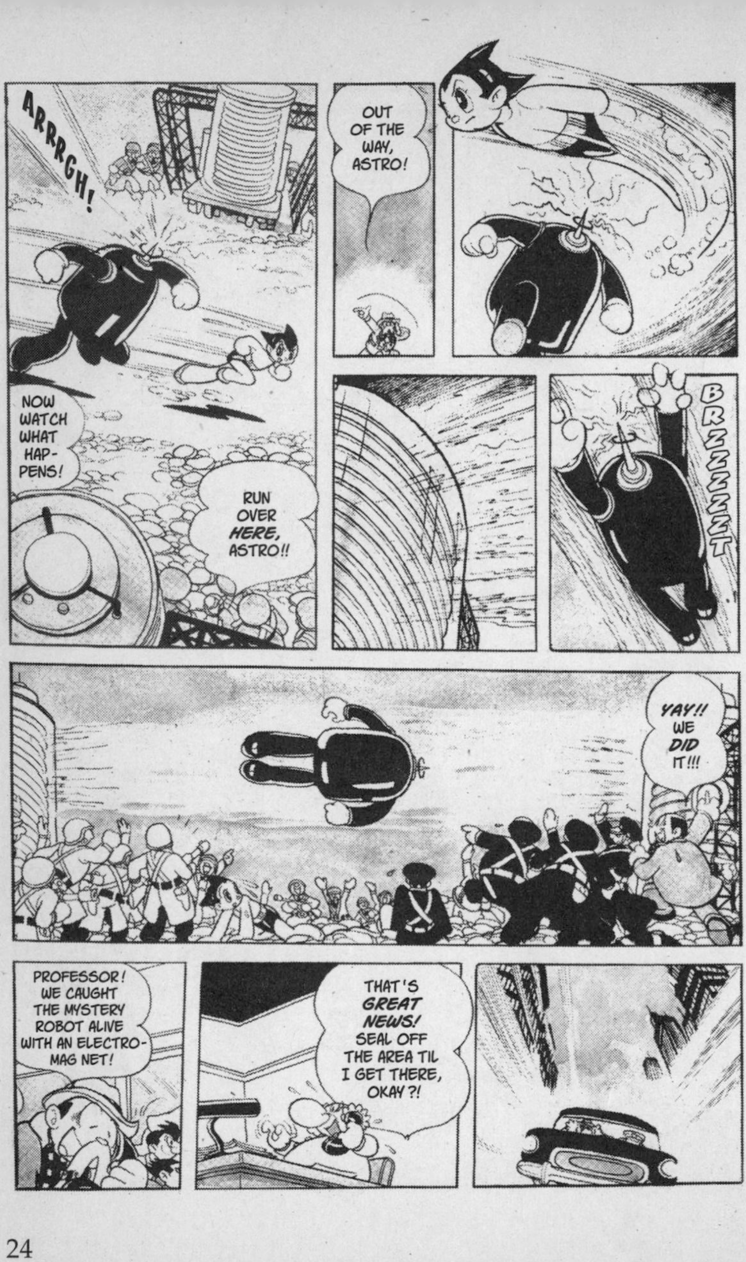
ARRRGH!
OUT OF THE WAY, ASTRO!
NOW WATCH WHAT HAP-PENS!
RUN OVER *HERE,* ASTRO!!
BRZZZZZT
YAY!! WE *DID* IT!!!
PROFESSOR! WE CAUGHT THE MYSTERY ROBOT ALIVE WITH AN ELECTRO-MAG NET!
THAT'S *GREAT NEWS!* SEAL OFF THE AREA TIL I GET THERE, OKAY?!

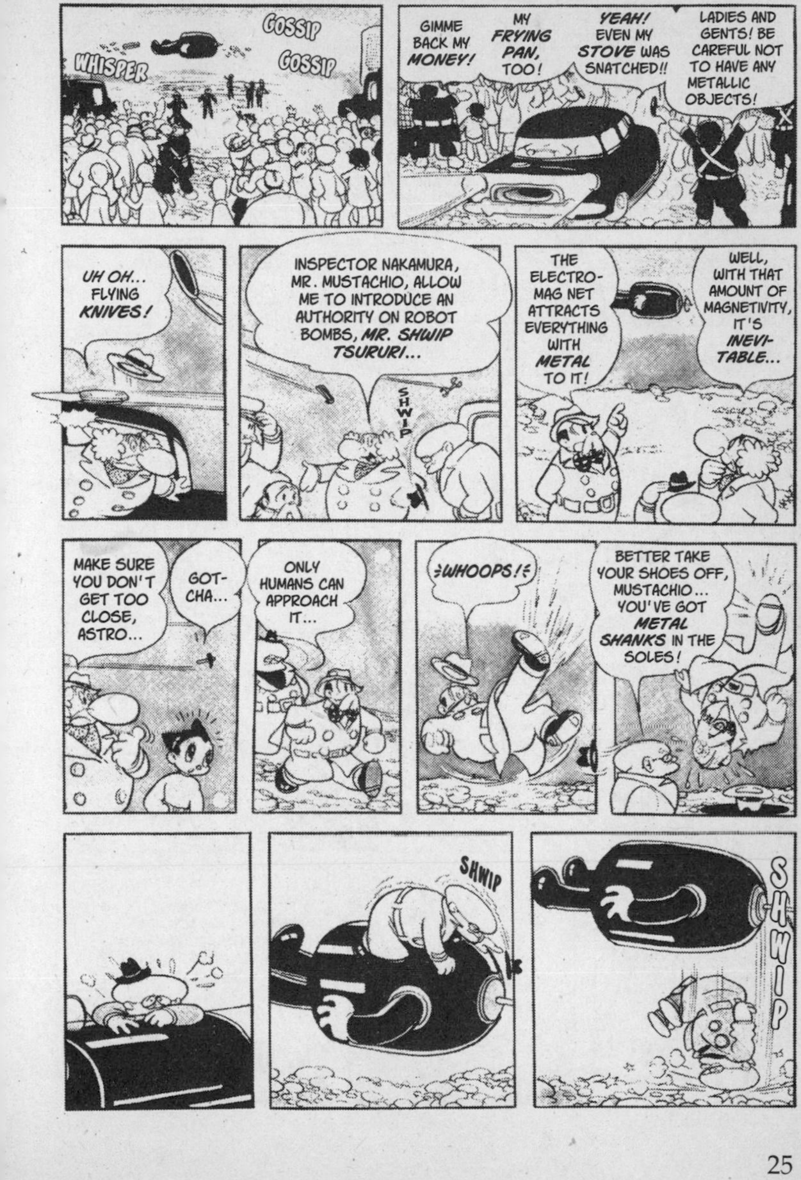
GOSSIP
WHISPER
GOSSIP
GIMME BACK MY MONEY!
MY FRYING PAN, TOO!
YEAH! EVEN MY STOVE WAS SNATCHED!!
LADIES AND GENTS! BE CAREFUL NOT TO HAVE ANY METALLIC OBJECTS!
UH OH... FLYING KNIVES!
INSPECTOR NAKAMURA, MR. MUSTACHIO, ALLOW ME TO INTRODUCE AN AUTHORITY ON ROBOT BOMBS, MR. SHWIP TSURURI...
SHWIP
THE ELECTRO-MAG NET ATTRACTS EVERYTHING WITH METAL TO IT!
WELL, WITH THAT AMOUNT OF MAGNETIVITY, IT'S INEVI-TABLE...
MAKE SURE YOU DON'T GET TOO CLOSE, ASTRO...
GOT-CHA...
ONLY HUMANS CAN APPROACH IT...
WHOOPS!
BETTER TAKE YOUR SHOES OFF, MUSTACHIO... YOU'VE GOT METAL SHANKS IN THE SOLES!
SHWIP
SHWIP

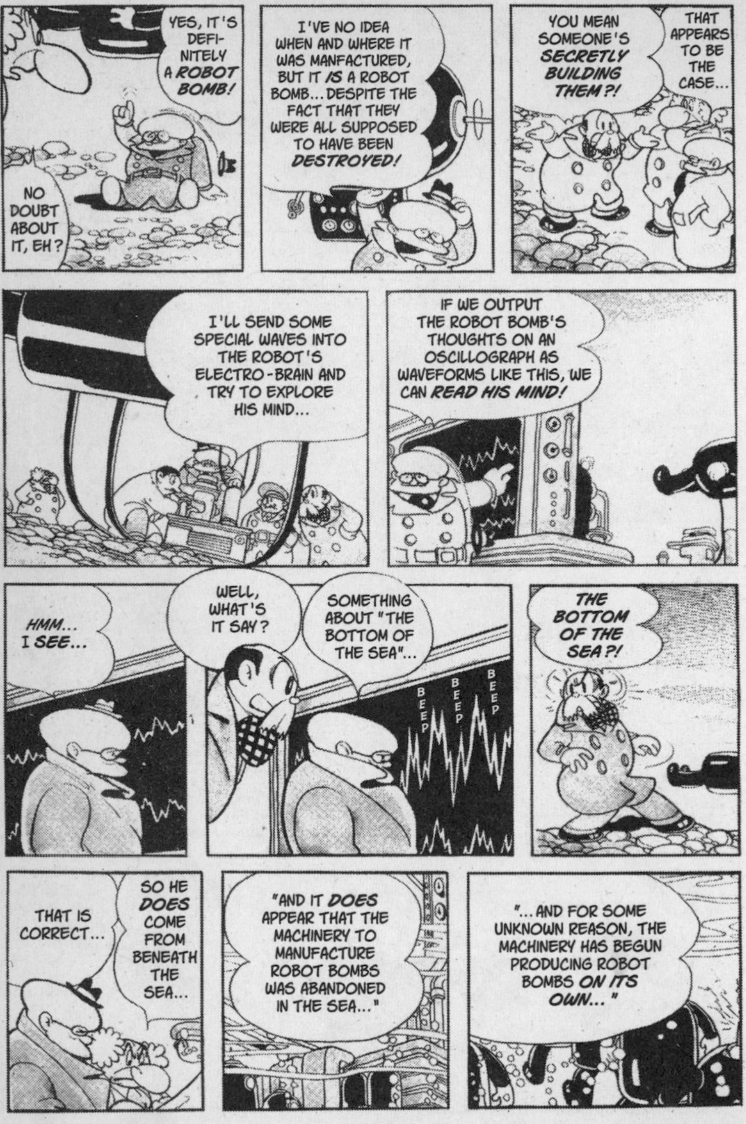
YES, IT'S DEFINITELY A ROBOT BOMB!
NO DOUBT ABOUT IT, EH?
I'VE NO IDEA WHEN AND WHERE IT WAS MANFACTURED, BUT IT IS A ROBOT BOMB... DESPITE THE FACT THAT THEY WERE ALL SUPPOSED TO HAVE BEEN DESTROYED!
YOU MEAN SOMEONE'S SECRETLY BUILDING THEM?!
THAT APPEARS TO BE THE CASE...
I'LL SEND SOME SPECIAL WAVES INTO THE ROBOT'S ELECTRO-BRAIN AND TRY TO EXPLORE HIS MIND...
IF WE OUTPUT THE ROBOT BOMB'S THOUGHTS ON AN OSCILLOGRAPH AS WAVEFORMS LIKE THIS, WE CAN READ HIS MIND!
HMM... I SEE...
WELL, WHAT'S IT SAY?
SOMETHING ABOUT "THE BOTTOM OF THE SEA"...
BEEP
BEEP
BEEP
THE BOTTOM OF THE SEA?!
THAT IS CORRECT...
SO HE DOES COME FROM BENEATH THE SEA...
"AND IT DOES APPEAR THAT THE MACHINERY TO MANUFACTURE ROBOT BOMBS WAS ABANDONED IN THE SEA..."
"...AND FOR SOME UNKNOWN REASON, THE MACHINERY HAS BEGUN PRODUCING ROBOT BOMBS ON ITS OWN..."

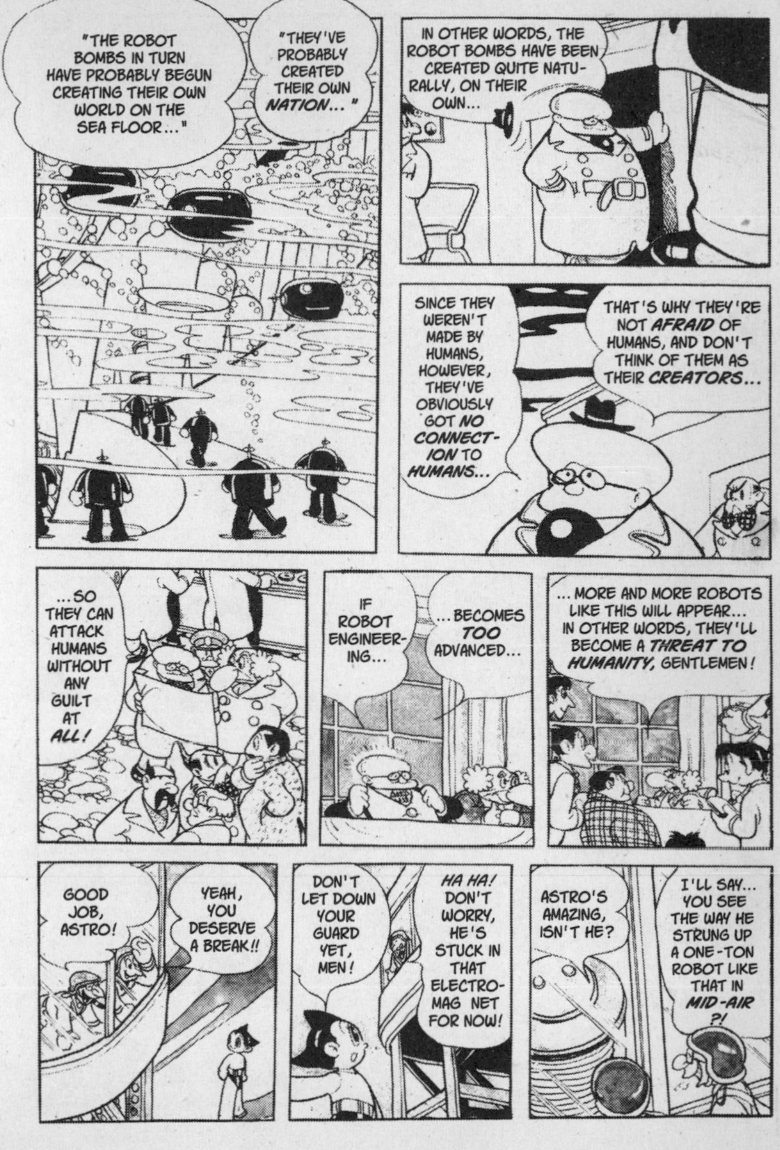
"THE ROBOT BOMBS IN TURN HAVE PROBABLY BEGUN CREATING THEIR OWN WORLD ON THE SEA FLOOR..."
"THEY'VE PROBABLY CREATED THEIR OWN NATION..."
IN OTHER WORDS, THE ROBOT BOMBS HAVE BEEN CREATED QUITE NATU-RALLY, ON THEIR OWN...
SINCE THEY WEREN'T MADE BY HUMANS, HOWEVER, THEY'VE OBVIOUSLY GOT NO CONNECT-ION TO HUMANS...
THAT'S WHY THEY'RE NOT AFRAID OF HUMANS, AND DON'T THINK OF THEM AS THEIR CREATORS...
...SO THEY CAN ATTACK HUMANS WITHOUT ANY GUILT AT ALL!
IF ROBOT ENGINEER-ING...
...BECOMES TOO ADVANCED...
...MORE AND MORE ROBOTS LIKE THIS WILL APPEAR... IN OTHER WORDS, THEY'LL BECOME A THREAT TO HUMANITY, GENTLEMEN!
GOOD JOB, ASTRO!
YEAH, YOU DESERVE A BREAK!!
DON'T LET DOWN YOUR GUARD YET, MEN!
HA HA! DON'T WORRY, HE'S STUCK IN THAT ELECTRO-MAG NET FOR NOW!
ASTRO'S AMAZING, ISN'T HE?
I'LL SAY... YOU SEE THE WAY HE STRUNG UP A ONE-TON ROBOT LIKE THAT IN MID-AIR ?!

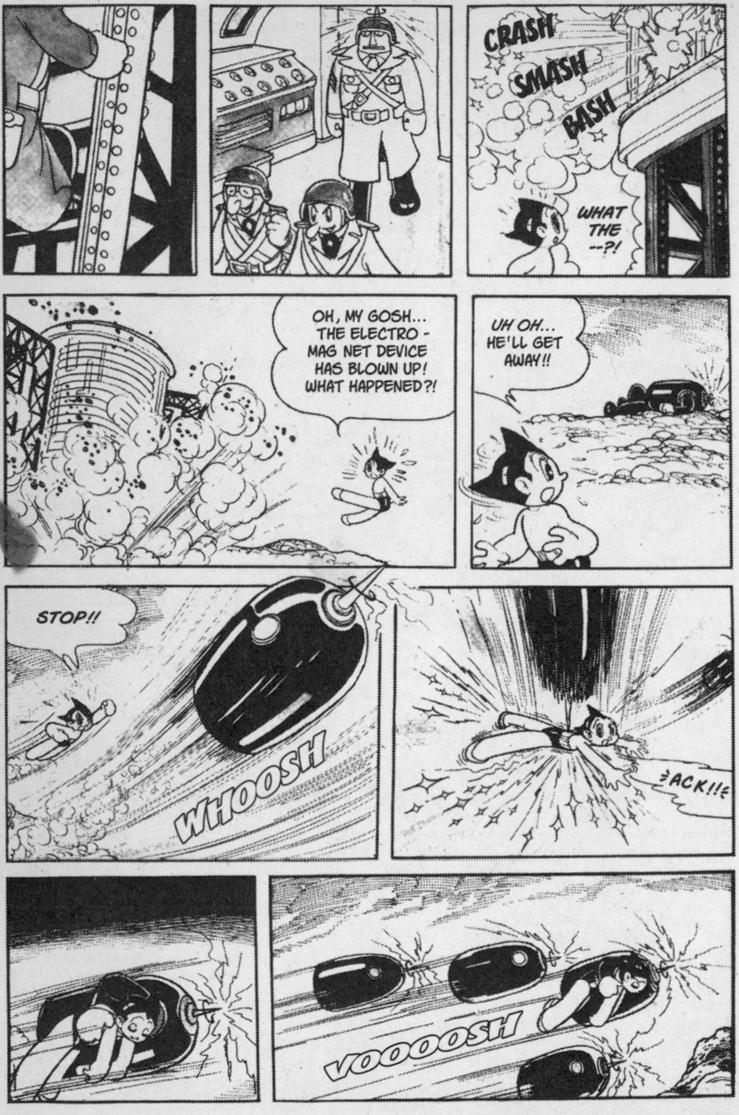
CRASH
SMASH
BASH
WHAT THE --?!
OH, MY GOSH... THE ELECTRO - MAG NET DEVICE HAS BLOWN UP! WHAT HAPPENED?!
UH OH... HE'LL GET AWAY!!
STOP!!
WHOOSH
ACK!!
VOOOOSH

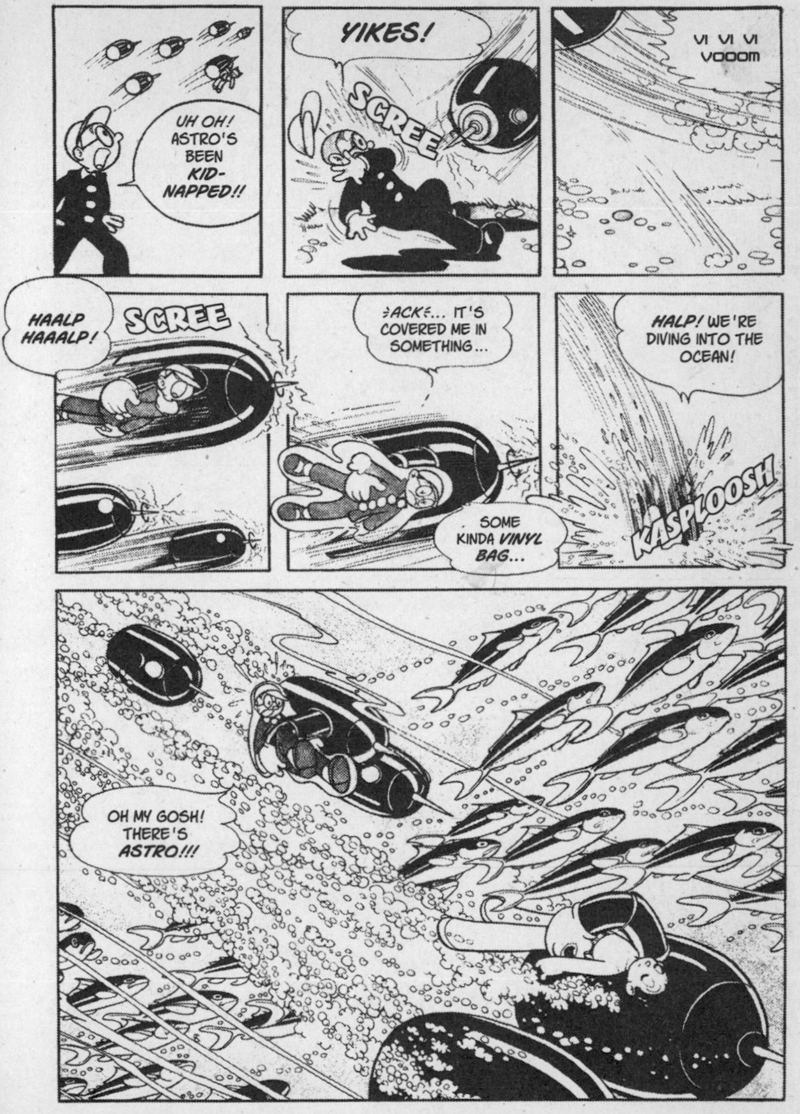
UH OH! ASTRO'S BEEN KID-NAPPED!!
YIKES!
SCREE
VI VI VI VOOOM
HAALP HAAALP!
SCREE
ACK... IT'S COVERED ME IN SOMETHING...
SOME KINDA VINYL BAG...
HALP! WE'RE DIVING INTO THE OCEAN!
KASPLOOSH
OH MY GOSH! THERE'S ASTRO!!!

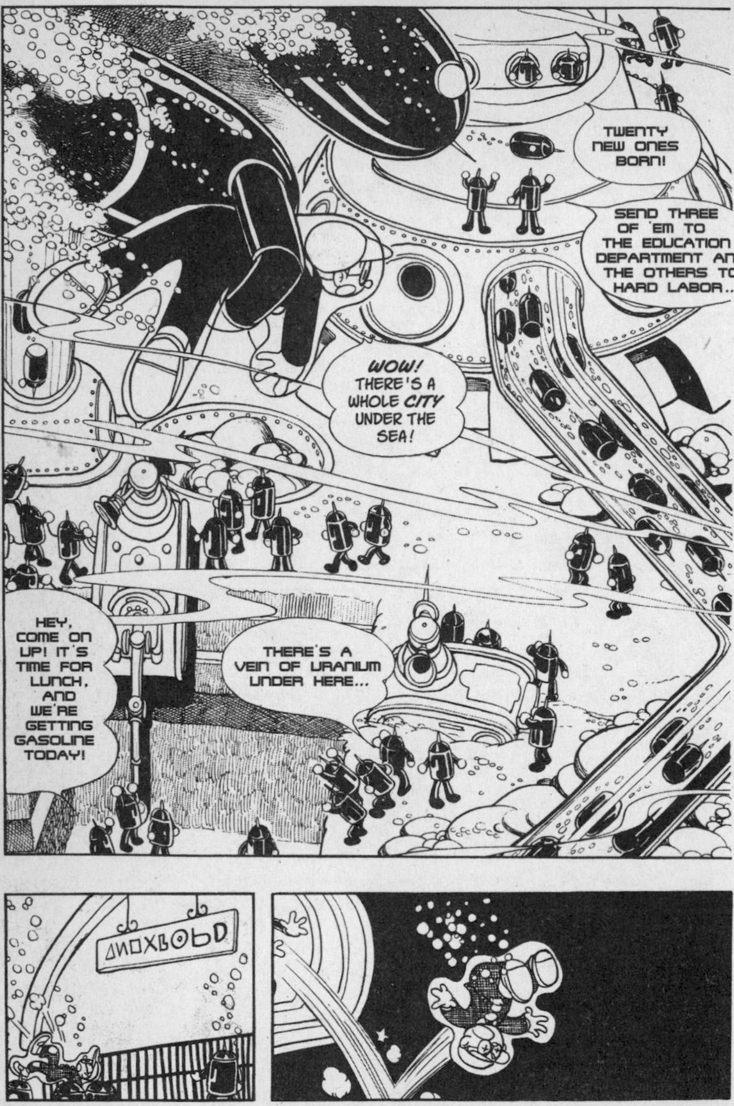
TWENTY NEW ONES BORN!
SEND THREE OF 'EM TO THE EDUCATION DEPARTMENT AND THE OTHERS TO HARD LABOR...
WOW! THERE'S A WHOLE CITY UNDER THE SEA!
HEY, COME ON UP! IT'S TIME FOR LUNCH, AND WE'RE GETTING GASOLINE TODAY!
THERE'S A VEIN OF URANIUM UNDER HERE...

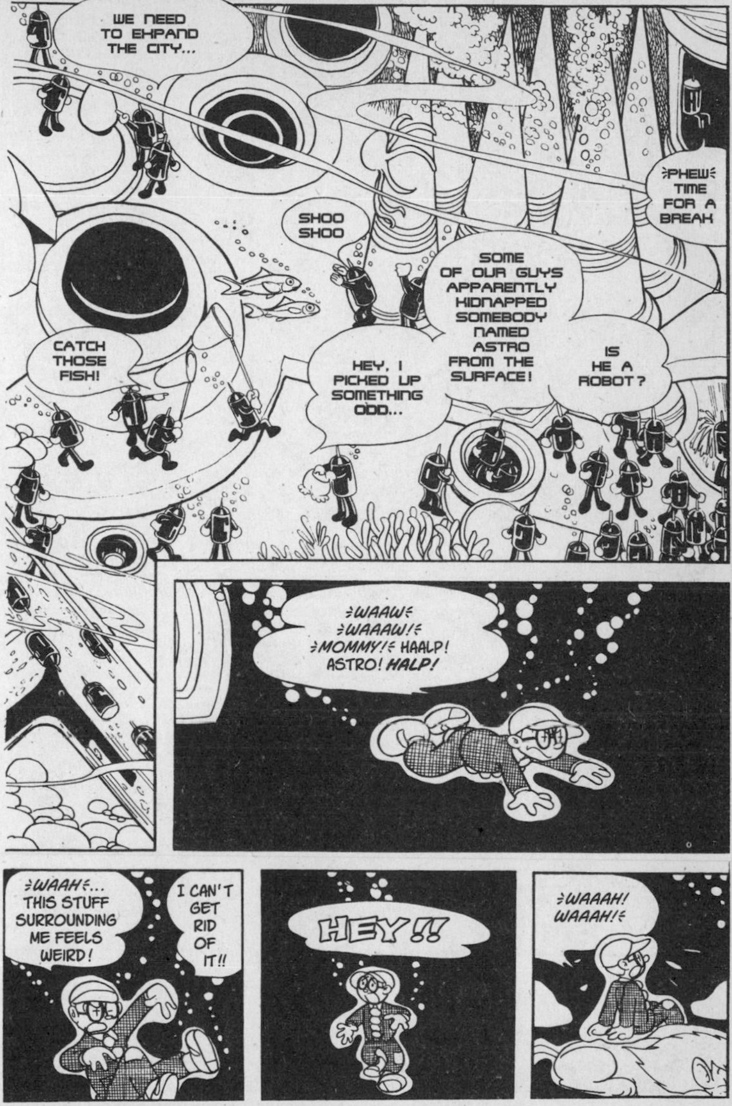
WE NEED TO EXPAND THE CITY...
PHEW TIME FOR A BREAK
SHOO SHOO
SOME OF OUR GUYS APPARENTLY KIDNAPPED SOMEBODY NAMED ASTRO FROM THE SURFACE!
CATCH THOSE FISH!
HEY, I PICKED UP SOMETHING ODD...
IS HE A ROBOT?
WAAW WAAAW! MOMMY! HAALP! ASTRO! HALP!
WAAH... THIS STUFF SURROUNDING ME FEELS WEIRD!
I CAN'T GET RID OF IT!!
HEY!!
WAAAH! WAAAH!

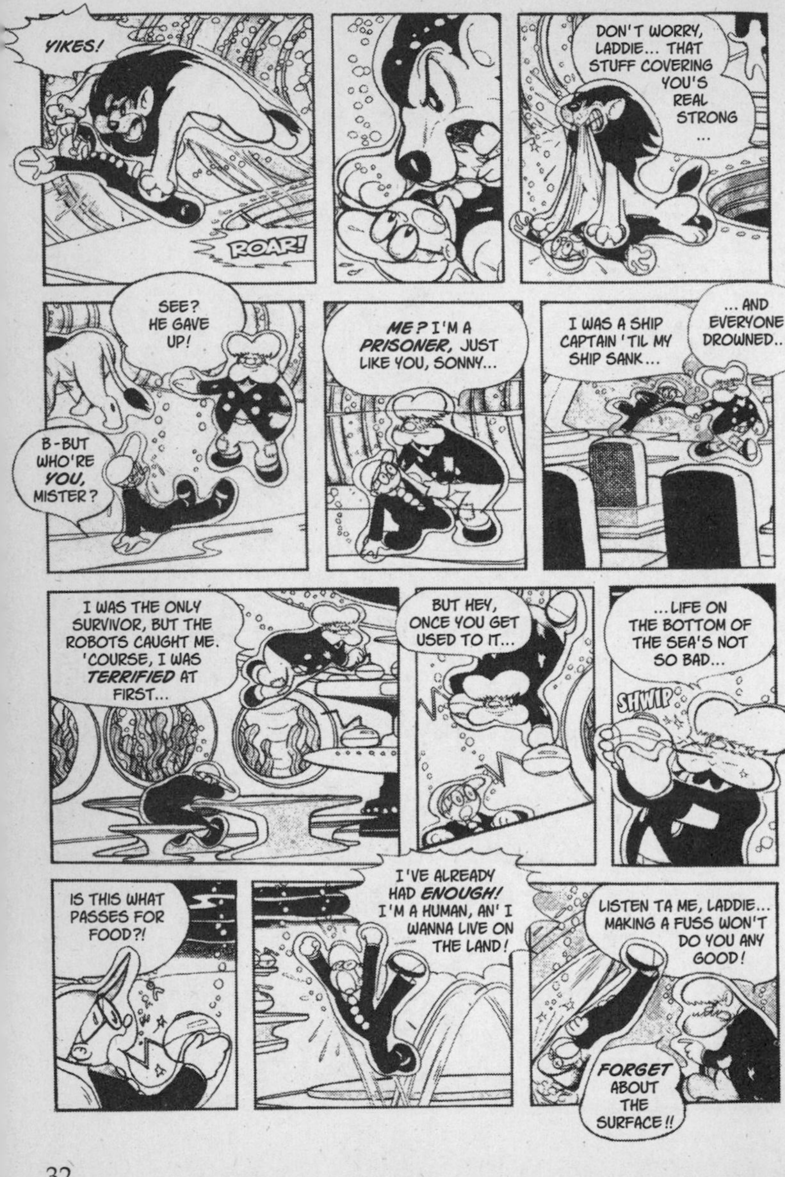
YIKES!
ROAR!
DON'T WORRY, LADDIE... THAT STUFF COVERING YOU'S REAL STRONG ...
SEE? HE GAVE UP!
B-BUT WHO'RE YOU, MISTER?
ME? I'M A PRISONER, JUST LIKE YOU, SONNY...
I WAS A SHIP CAPTAIN 'TIL MY SHIP SANK...
... AND EVERYONE DROWNED...
I WAS THE ONLY SURVIVOR, BUT THE ROBOTS CAUGHT ME. 'COURSE, I WAS TERRIFIED AT FIRST...
BUT HEY, ONCE YOU GET USED TO IT...
...LIFE ON THE BOTTOM OF THE SEA'S NOT SO BAD...
SHWIP
IS THIS WHAT PASSES FOR FOOD?!
I'VE ALREADY HAD ENOUGH! I'M A HUMAN, AN' I WANNA LIVE ON THE LAND!
LISTEN TA ME, LADDIE... MAKING A FUSS WON'T DO YOU ANY GOOD!
FORGET ABOUT THE SURFACE!!

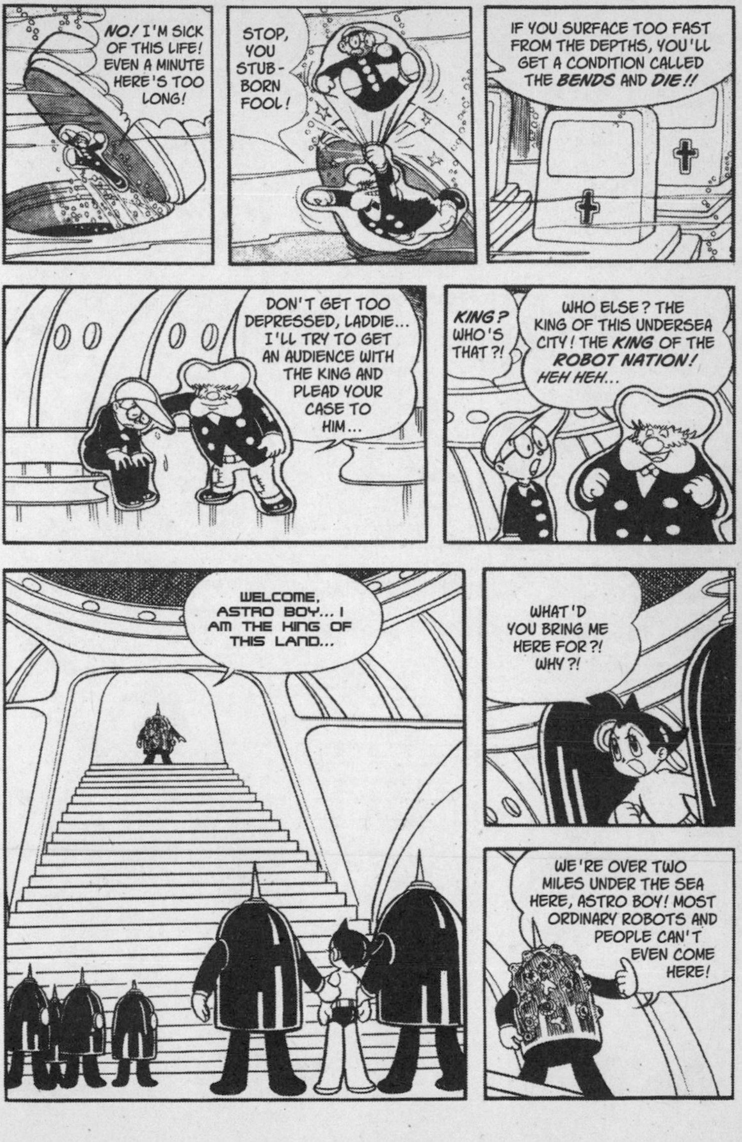
NO! I'M SICK OF THIS LIFE! EVEN A MINUTE HERE'S TOO LONG!
STOP, YOU STUBBORN FOOL!
IF YOU SURFACE TOO FAST FROM THE DEPTHS, YOU'LL GET A CONDITION CALLED THE BENDS AND DIE!!
DON'T GET TOO DEPRESSED, LADDIE... I'LL TRY TO GET AN AUDIENCE WITH THE KING AND PLEAD YOUR CASE TO HIM...
KING? WHO'S THAT?!
WHO ELSE? THE KING OF THIS UNDERSEA CITY! THE KING OF THE ROBOT NATION! HEH HEH...
WELCOME, ASTRO BOY... I AM THE KING OF THIS LAND...
WHAT'D YOU BRING ME HERE FOR?! WHY?!
WE'RE OVER TWO MILES UNDER THE SEA HERE, ASTRO BOY! MOST ORDINARY ROBOTS AND PEOPLE CAN'T EVEN COME HERE!

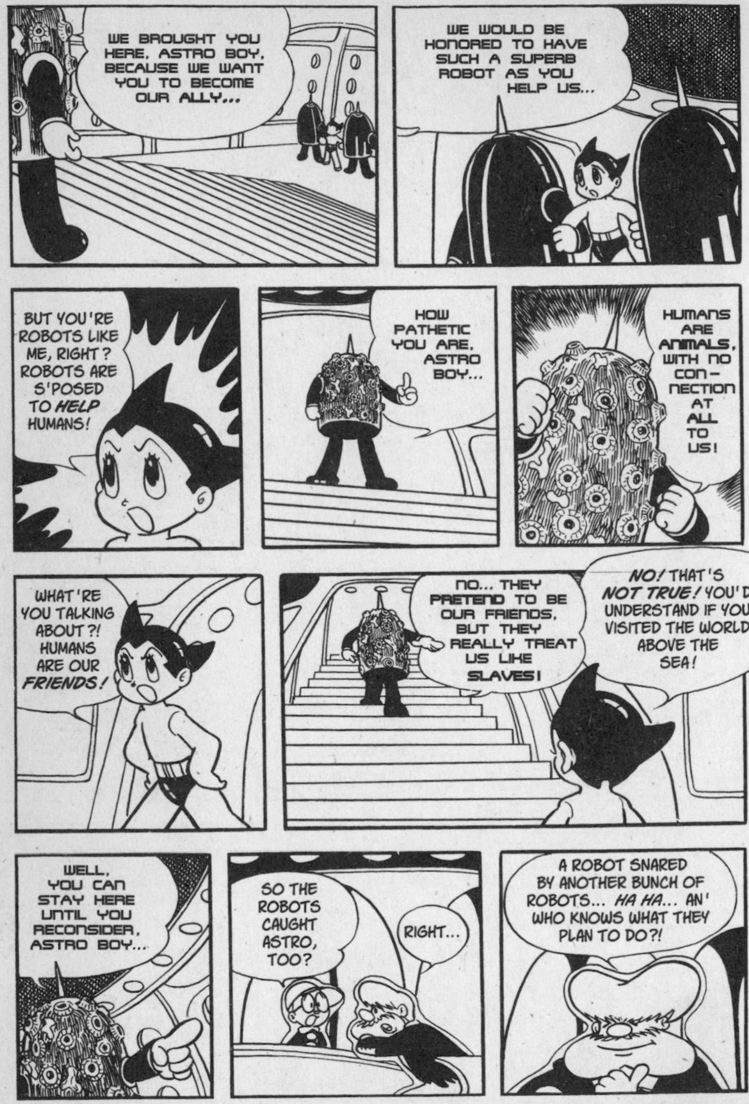
WE BROUGHT YOU HERE, ASTRO BOY, BECAUSE WE WANT YOU TO BECOME OUR ALLY...
WE WOULD BE HONORED TO HAVE SUCH A SUPERB ROBOT AS YOU HELP US...
BUT YOU'RE ROBOTS LIKE ME, RIGHT? ROBOTS ARE S'POSED TO HELP HUMANS!
HOW PATHETIC YOU ARE, ASTRO BOY...
HUMANS ARE ANIMALS, WITH NO CON-NECTION AT ALL TO US!
WHAT'RE YOU TALKING ABOUT?! HUMANS ARE OUR FRIENDS!
NO... THEY PRETEND TO BE OUR FRIENDS, BUT THEY REALLY TREAT US LIKE SLAVES!
NO! THAT'S NOT TRUE! YOU'D UNDERSTAND IF YOU VISITED THE WORLD ABOVE THE SEA!
WELL, YOU CAN STAY HERE UNTIL YOU RECONSIDER, ASTRO BOY...
SO THE ROBOTS CAUGHT ASTRO, TOO?
RIGHT...
A ROBOT SNARED BY ANOTHER BUNCH OF ROBOTS... HA HA... AN' WHO KNOWS WHAT THEY PLAN TO DO?!

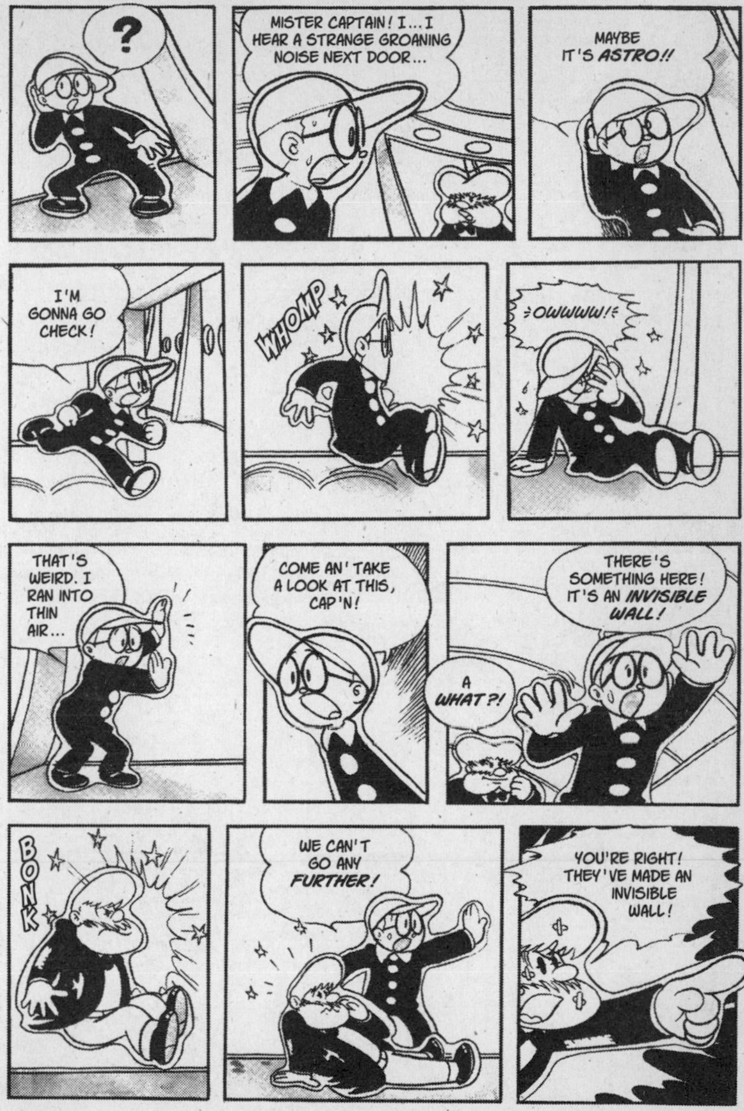
?
MISTER CAPTAIN! I... I HEAR A STRANGE GROANING NOISE NEXT DOOR...
MAYBE IT'S ASTRO!!
I'M GONNA GO CHECK!
WHOMP
OWWWW!
THAT'S WEIRD. I RAN INTO THIN AIR...
COME AN' TAKE A LOOK AT THIS, CAP'N!
THERE'S SOMETHING HERE! IT'S AN INVISIBLE WALL!
A WHAT?!
BONK
WE CAN'T GO ANY FURTHER!
YOU'RE RIGHT! THEY'VE MADE AN INVISIBLE WALL!

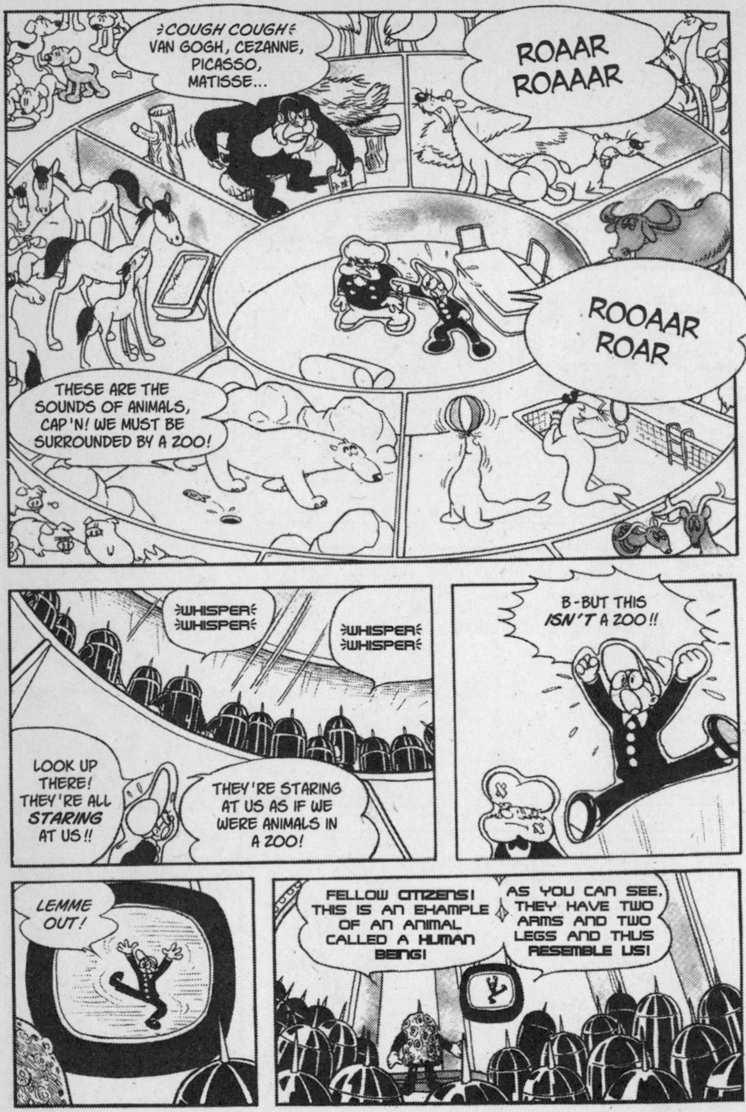

≥COUGH COUGH≤ VAN GOGH, CEZANNE, PICASSO, MATISSE...
ROAAR ROAAAR
ROOAAR ROAR
THESE ARE THE SOUNDS OF ANIMALS, CAP'N! WE MUST BE SURROUNDED BY A ZOO!
≥WHISPER≤ ≥WHISPER≤
≥WHISPER≤ ≥WHISPER≤
LOOK UP THERE! THEY'RE ALL STARING AT US!!
THEY'RE STARING AT US AS IF WE WERE ANIMALS IN A ZOO!
B-BUT THIS ISN'T A ZOO!!
LEMME OUT!
FELLOW CITIZENS! THIS IS AN EXAMPLE OF AN ANIMAL CALLED A HUMAN BEING!
AS YOU CAN SEE, THEY HAVE TWO ARMS AND TWO LEGS AND THUS RESEMBLE US!

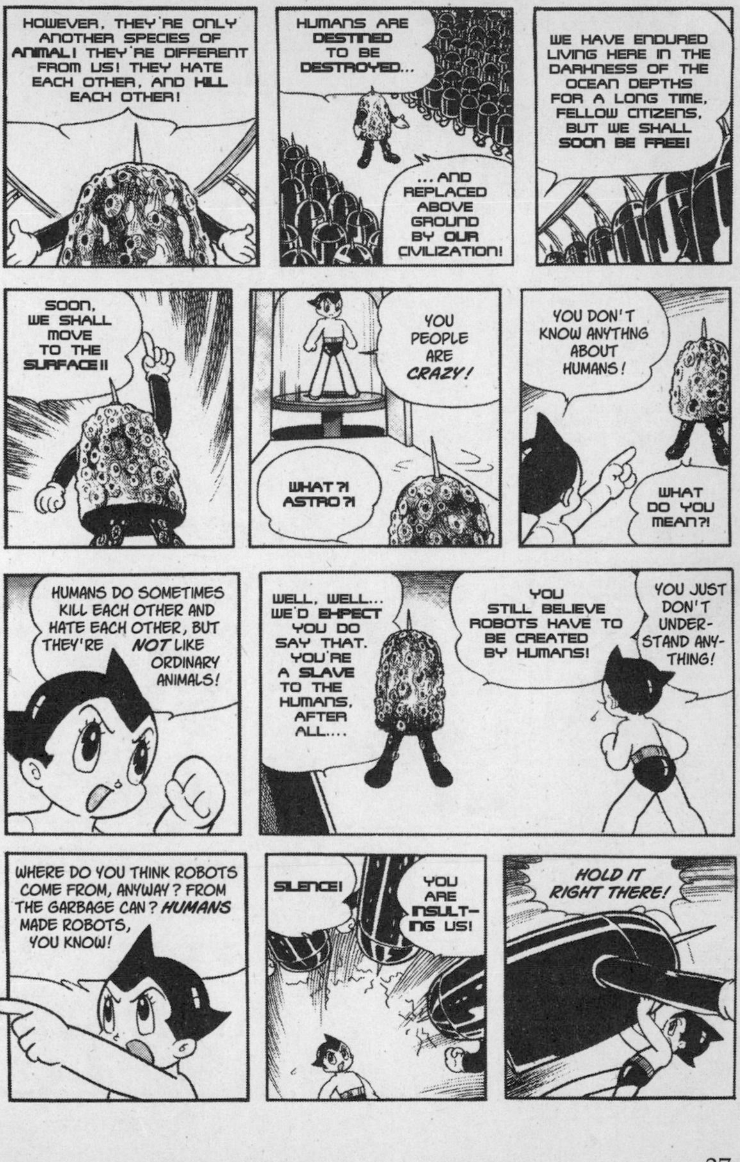
HOWEVER, THEY'RE ONLY ANOTHER SPECIES OF ANIMAL! THEY'RE DIFFERENT FROM US! THEY HATE EACH OTHER, AND KILL EACH OTHER!
HUMANS ARE DESTINED TO BE DESTROYED...
...AND REPLACED ABOVE GROUND BY OUR CIVILIZATION!
WE HAVE ENDURED LIVING HERE IN THE DARKNESS OF THE OCEAN DEPTHS FOR A LONG TIME, FELLOW CITIZENS, BUT WE SHALL SOON BE FREE!
SOON, WE SHALL MOVE TO THE SURFACE!!
YOU PEOPLE ARE CRAZY!
WHAT ?! ASTRO ?!
YOU DON'T KNOW ANYTHNG ABOUT HUMANS!
WHAT DO YOU MEAN?!
HUMANS DO SOMETIMES KILL EACH OTHER AND HATE EACH OTHER, BUT THEY'RE NOT LIKE ORDINARY ANIMALS!
WELL, WELL... WE'D EXPECT YOU DO SAY THAT. YOU'RE A SLAVE TO THE HUMANS, AFTER ALL....
YOU STILL BELIEVE ROBOTS HAVE TO BE CREATED BY HUMANS!
YOU JUST DON'T UNDER-STAND ANY-THING!
WHERE DO YOU THINK ROBOTS COME FROM, ANYWAY? FROM THE GARBAGE CAN? HUMANS MADE ROBOTS, YOU KNOW!
SILENCE!
YOU ARE INSULT-ING US!
HOLD IT RIGHT THERE!

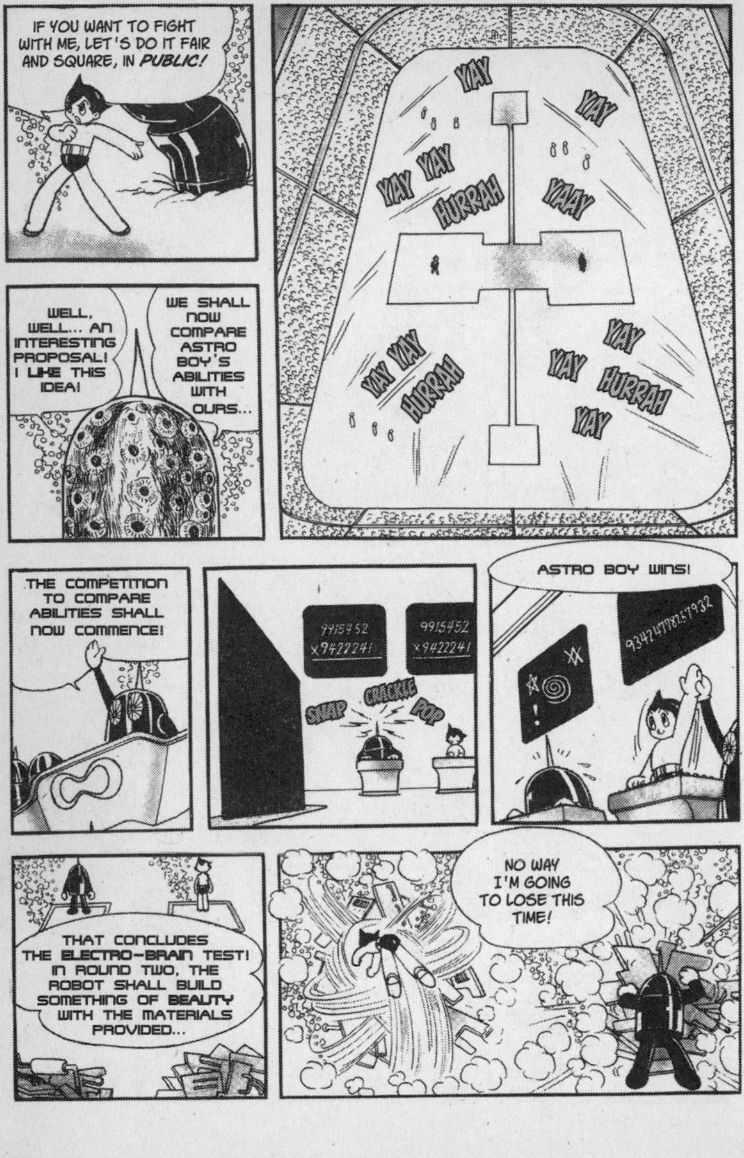
IF YOU WANT TO FIGHT WITH ME, LET'S DO IT FAIR AND SQUARE, IN *PUBLIC!*
WELL, WELL... AN INTERESTING PROPOSAL! I LIKE THIS IDEA!
WE SHALL NOW COMPARE ASTRO BOY'S ABILITIES WITH OURS...
YAY
YAY
YAY YAY
HURRAH
YAAY
YAY YAY
HURRAH
YAY
YAY
HURRAH
YAY
THE COMPETITION TO COMPARE ABILITIES SHALL NOW COMMENCE!
9915452
×9422241
9915452
×9422241
SNAP
CRACKLE
POP
ASTRO BOY WINS!
93424778257932
THAT CONCLUDES THE ELECTRO-BRAIN TEST! IN ROUND TWO, THE ROBOT SHALL BUILD SOMETHING OF BEAUTY WITH THE MATERIALS PROVIDED...
NO WAY I'M GOING TO LOSE THIS TIME!

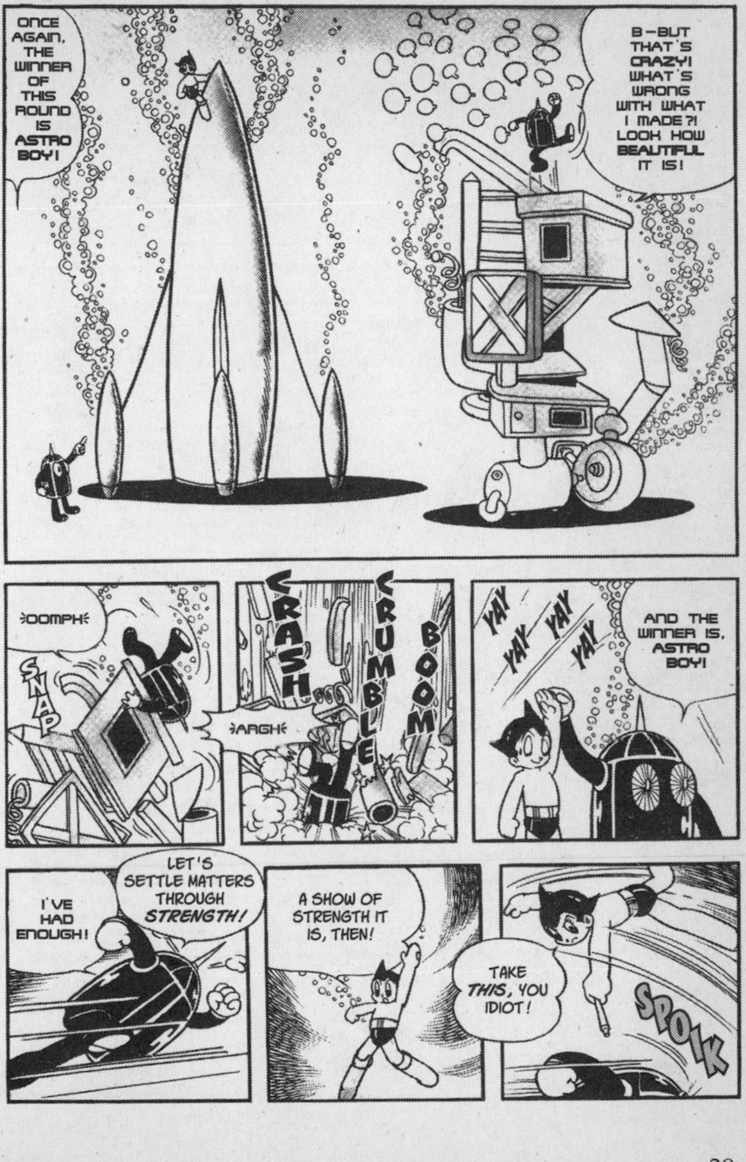
ONCE AGAIN, THE WINNER OF THIS ROUND IS ASTRO BOY!
B-BUT THAT'S CRAZY! WHAT'S WRONG WITH WHAT I MADE?! LOOK HOW BEAUTIFUL IT IS!
OOMPH
SNAP
CRASH
CRUMBLE
BOOM
ARGH
YAY
YAY
YAY
YAY
AND THE WINNER IS, ASTRO BOY!
I'VE HAD ENOUGH!
LET'S SETTLE MATTERS THROUGH *STRENGTH!*
A SHOW OF STRENGTH IT IS, THEN!
TAKE *THIS,* YOU IDIOT!
SPOIK

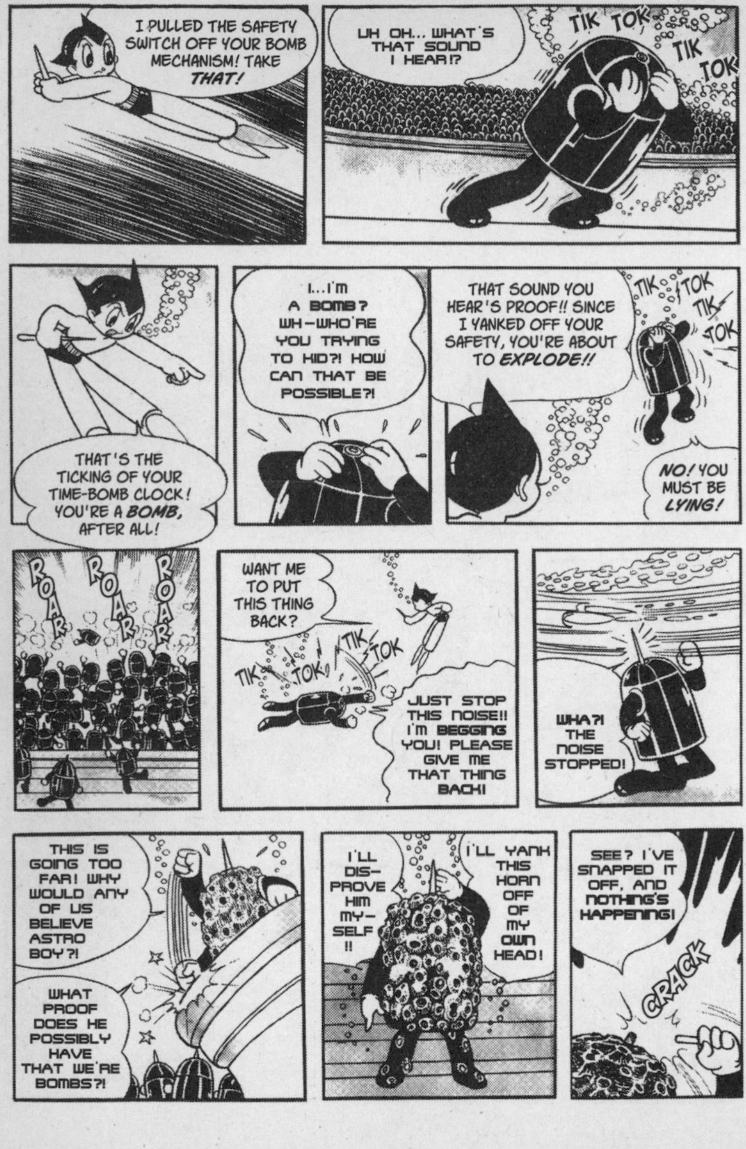
I PULLED THE SAFETY SWITCH OFF YOUR BOMB MECHANISM! TAKE THAT!
UH OH... WHAT'S THAT SOUND I HEAR!?
TIK TOK TIK TOK
THAT'S THE TICKING OF YOUR TIME-BOMB CLOCK! YOU'RE A BOMB, AFTER ALL!
I...I'M A BOMB? WH-WHO'RE YOU TRYING TO KID?! HOW CAN THAT BE POSSIBLE?!
THAT SOUND YOU HEAR'S PROOF!! SINCE I YANKED OFF YOUR SAFETY, YOU'RE ABOUT TO EXPLODE!!
TIK TOK TIK TOK
NO! YOU MUST BE LYING!
ROAR ROAR ROAR
WANT ME TO PUT THIS THING BACK?
TIK TOK TIK TOK
JUST STOP THIS NOISE!! I'M BEGGING YOU! PLEASE GIVE ME THAT THING BACK!
WHA?! THE NOISE STOPPED!
THIS IS GOING TOO FAR! WHY WOULD ANY OF US BELIEVE ASTRO BOY?!
WHAT PROOF DOES HE POSSIBLY HAVE THAT WE'RE BOMBS?!
I'LL DIS-PROVE HIM MY-SELF !!
I'LL YANK THIS HORN OFF OF MY OWN HEAD!
SEE? I'VE SNAPPED IT OFF, AND NOTHING'S HAPPENING!
CRACK

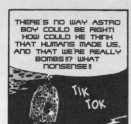

THERE'S NO WAY ASTRO BOY COULD BE RIGHT! HOW COULD HE THINK THAT HUMANS MADE US, AND THAT WE'RE REALLY BOMBS!? WHAT NONSENSE!!

TIK TOK

I HAVE A SENSE OF HONOR...

TIK TOK

IT FINALLY HAPPENED! HE BLEW HIMSELF UP!

KABABOOOM

OH, MY GOSH... HIS HIGHNESS...!

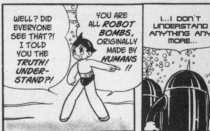

WELL? DID EVERYONE SEE THAT?! I TOLD YOU THE *TRUTH!* UNDER- STAND?!

YOU ARE ALL *ROBOT BOMBS,* ORIGINALLY MADE BY *HUMANS* !!

I...I DON'T UNDERSTAND ANYTHING ANY MORE...

IF YOU WANT TO LEARN MORE, GO TO THE SURFACE, AND MEET PROFESSOR OCHANOMIZU! YOU'RE ALL HIGHLY DANGEROUS, SO YOU NEED TO HAVE HUMANS TAKE APART YOUR TRIGGER MECHANISMS!

WHAT DO *YOU* WANT NOW?

I HAVE SOME- THING TO REPORT...

41

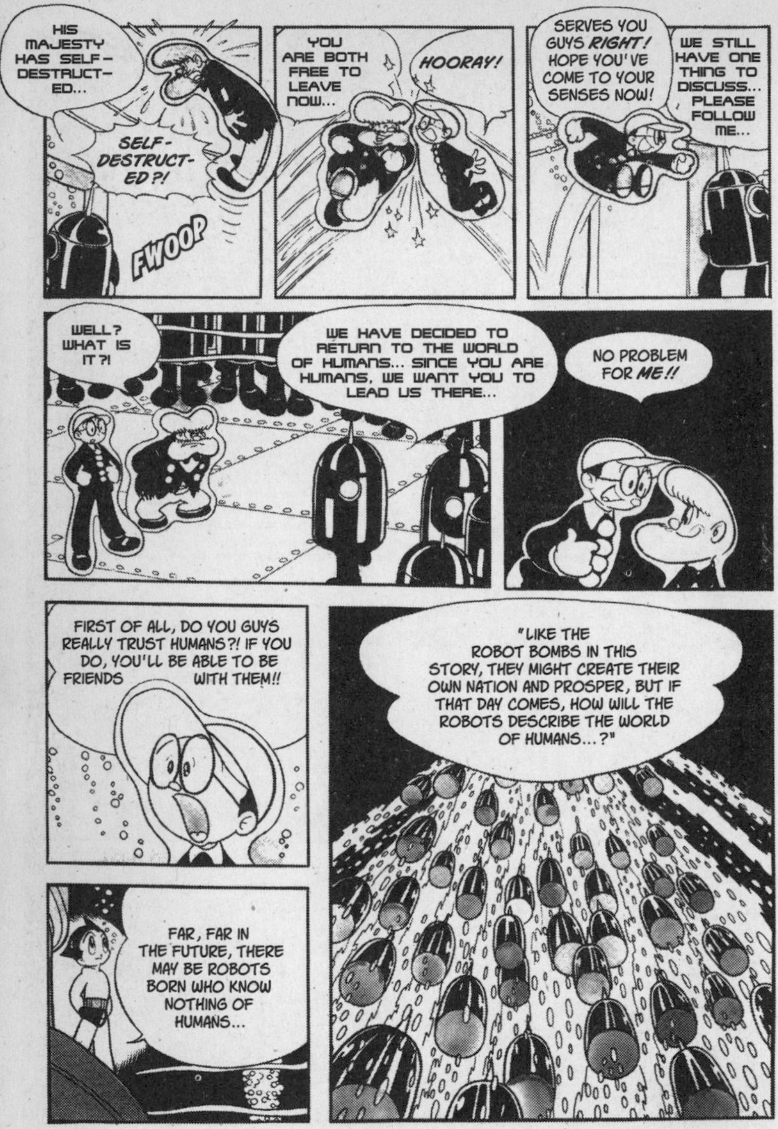
HIS MAJESTY HAS SELF-DESTRUCTED...
SELF-DESTRUCTED?!
FWOOP
YOU ARE BOTH FREE TO LEAVE NOW...
HOORAY!
SERVES YOU GUYS RIGHT! HOPE YOU'VE COME TO YOUR SENSES NOW!
WE STILL HAVE ONE THING TO DISCUSS... PLEASE FOLLOW ME...
WELL? WHAT IS IT?!
WE HAVE DECIDED TO RETURN TO THE WORLD OF HUMANS... SINCE YOU ARE HUMANS, WE WANT YOU TO LEAD US THERE...
NO PROBLEM FOR ME!!
FIRST OF ALL, DO YOU GUYS REALLY TRUST HUMANS?! IF YOU DO, YOU'LL BE ABLE TO BE FRIENDS WITH THEM!!
FAR, FAR IN THE FUTURE, THERE MAY BE ROBOTS BORN WHO KNOW NOTHING OF HUMANS...
"LIKE THE ROBOT BOMBS IN THIS STORY, THEY MIGHT CREATE THEIR OWN NATION AND PROSPER, BUT IF THAT DAY COMES, HOW WILL THE ROBOTS DESCRIBE THE WORLD OF HUMANS...?"

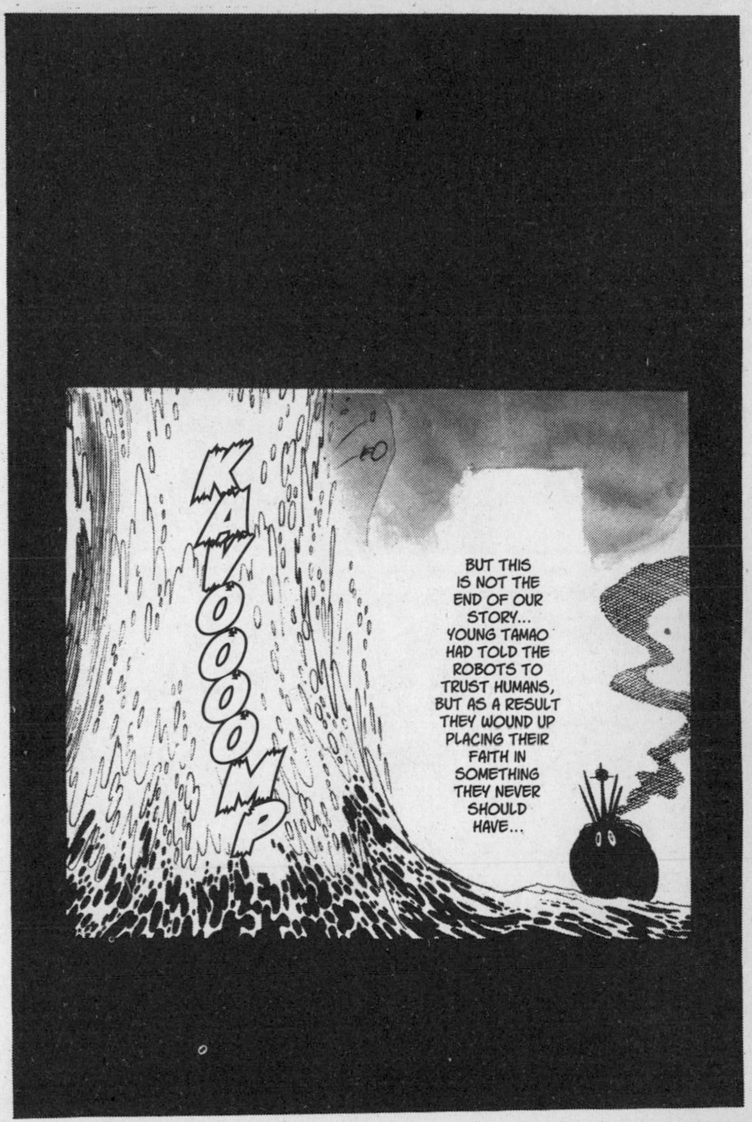
KAVOOOOMP
BUT THIS IS NOT THE END OF OUR STORY... YOUNG TAMAO HAD TOLD THE ROBOTS TO TRUST HUMANS, BUT AS A RESULT THEY WOUND UP PLACING THEIR FAITH IN SOMETHING THEY NEVER SHOULD HAVE...

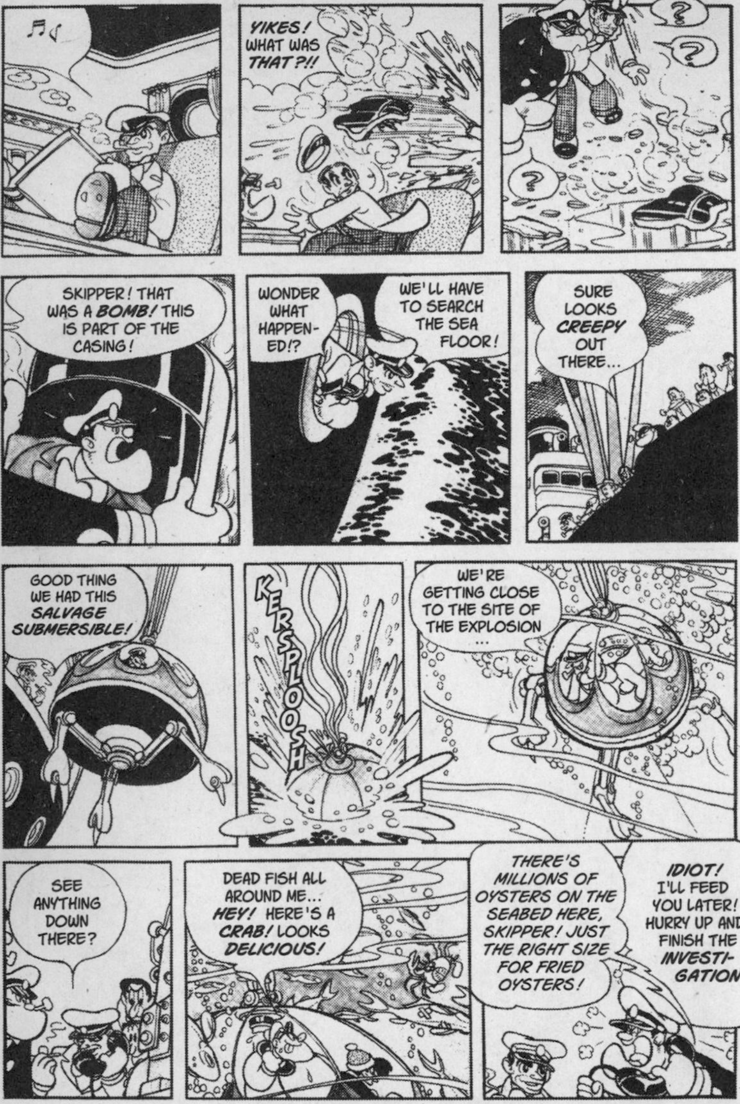
YIKES! WHAT WAS THAT?!!
SKIPPER! THAT WAS A BOMB! THIS IS PART OF THE CASING!
WONDER WHAT HAPPENED!?
WE'LL HAVE TO SEARCH THE SEA FLOOR!
SURE LOOKS CREEPY OUT THERE...
GOOD THING WE HAD THIS SALVAGE SUBMERSIBLE!
KERSPLOOSH
WE'RE GETTING CLOSE TO THE SITE OF THE EXPLOSION ...
SEE ANYTHING DOWN THERE?
DEAD FISH ALL AROUND ME... HEY! HERE'S A CRAB! LOOKS DELICIOUS!
THERE'S MILLIONS OF OYSTERS ON THE SEABED HERE, SKIPPER! JUST THE RIGHT SIZE FOR FRIED OYSTERS!
IDIOT! I'LL FEED YOU LATER! HURRY UP AND FINISH THE INVESTIGATION!

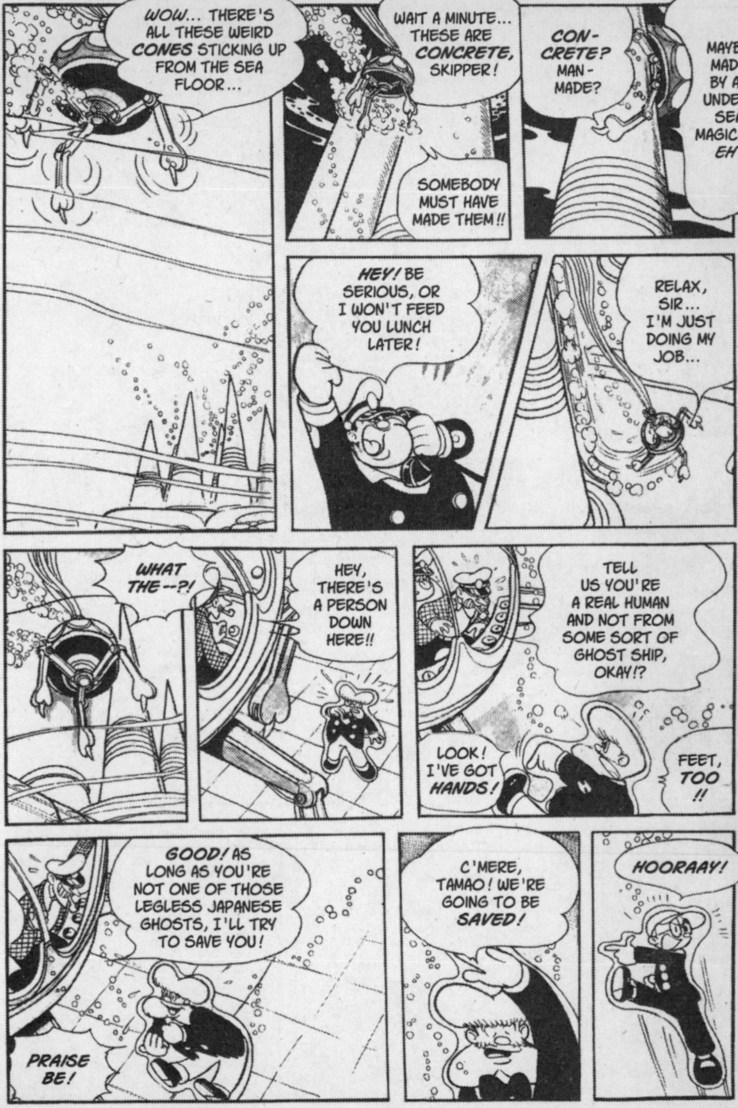
WOW... THERE'S ALL THESE WEIRD CONES STICKING UP FROM THE SEA FLOOR...
WAIT A MINUTE... THESE ARE CONCRETE, SKIPPER!
SOMEBODY MUST HAVE MADE THEM!!
CON-CRETE? MAN-MADE?
MAYBE MADE BY AN UNDER-SEA MAGICIAN, EH?
HEY! BE SERIOUS, OR I WON'T FEED YOU LUNCH LATER!
RELAX, SIR... I'M JUST DOING MY JOB...
WHAT THE--?!
HEY, THERE'S A PERSON DOWN HERE!!
TELL US YOU'RE A REAL HUMAN AND NOT FROM SOME SORT OF GHOST SHIP, OKAY!?
LOOK! I'VE GOT HANDS!
FEET, TOO!!
GOOD! AS LONG AS YOU'RE NOT ONE OF THOSE LEGLESS JAPANESE GHOSTS, I'LL TRY TO SAVE YOU!
PRAISE BE!
C'MERE, TAMAO! WE'RE GOING TO BE SAVED!
HOORAAY!

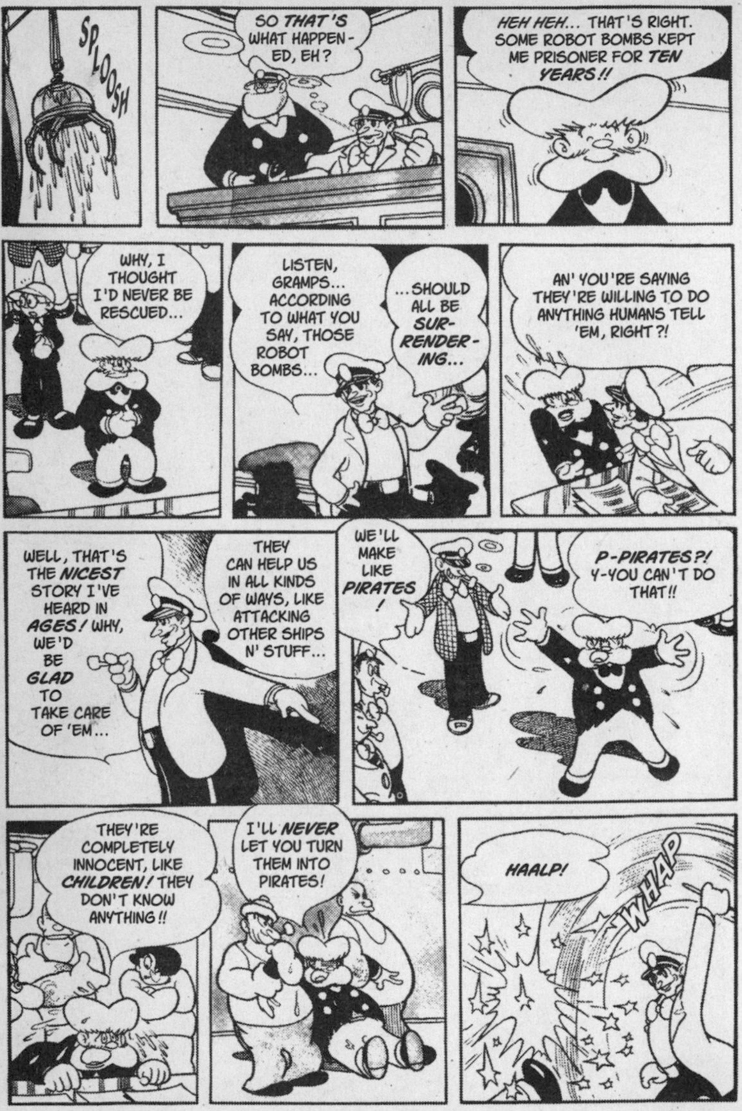
SPLOOSH
SO THAT'S WHAT HAPPEN-ED, EH?
HEH HEH... THAT'S RIGHT. SOME ROBOT BOMBS KEPT ME PRISONER FOR TEN YEARS!!
WHY, I THOUGHT I'D NEVER BE RESCUED...
LISTEN, GRAMPS... ACCORDING TO WHAT YOU SAY, THOSE ROBOT BOMBS...
...SHOULD ALL BE SUR-RENDER-ING...
AN' YOU'RE SAYING THEY'RE WILLING TO DO ANYTHING HUMANS TELL 'EM, RIGHT?!
WELL, THAT'S THE NICEST STORY I'VE HEARD IN AGES! WHY, WE'D BE GLAD TO TAKE CARE OF 'EM...
THEY CAN HELP US IN ALL KINDS OF WAYS, LIKE ATTACKING OTHER SHIPS N' STUFF...
WE'LL MAKE LIKE PIRATES!
P-PIRATES?! Y-YOU CAN'T DO THAT!!
THEY'RE COMPLETELY INNOCENT, LIKE CHILDREN! THEY DON'T KNOW ANYTHING!!
I'LL NEVER LET YOU TURN THEM INTO PIRATES!
HAALP!
WHAP

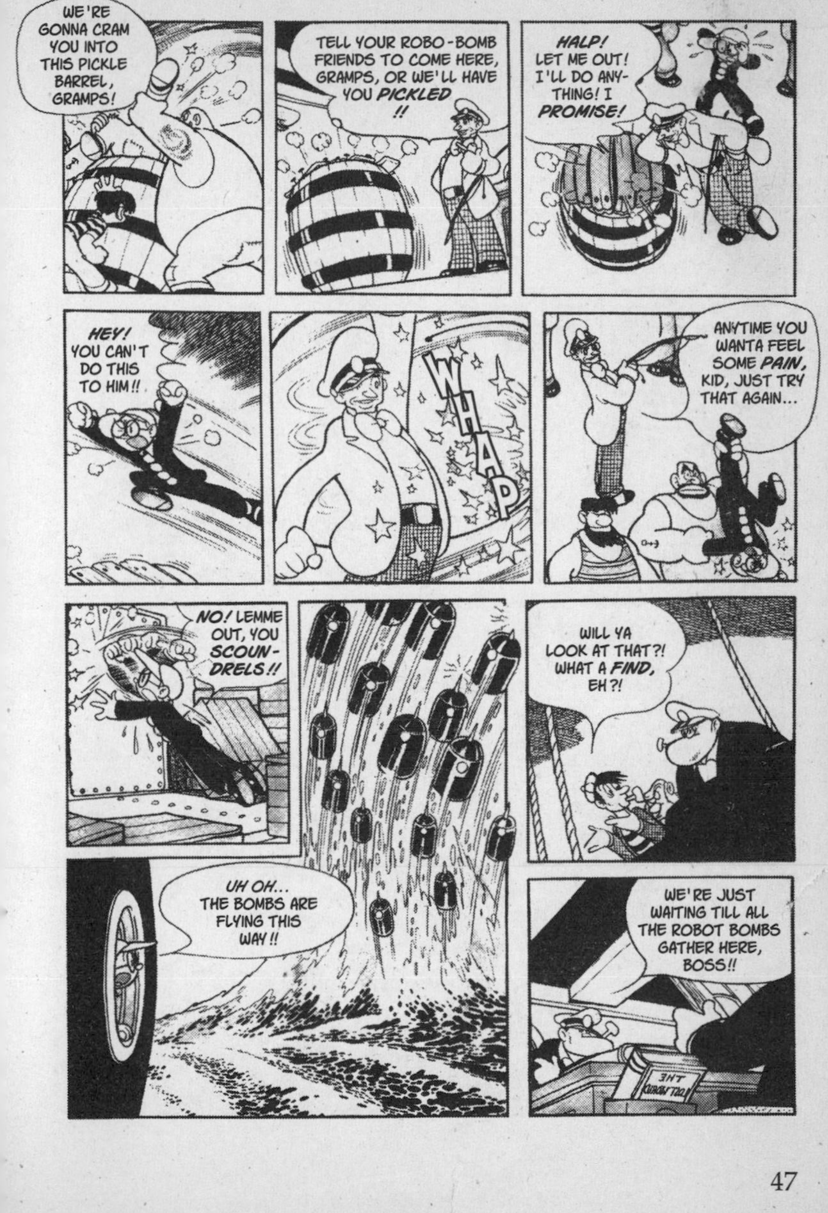
WE'RE GONNA CRAM YOU INTO THIS PICKLE BARREL, GRAMPS!
TELL YOUR ROBO-BOMB FRIENDS TO COME HERE, GRAMPS, OR WE'LL HAVE YOU PICKLED !!
HALP! LET ME OUT! I'LL DO ANYTHING! I PROMISE!
HEY! YOU CAN'T DO THIS TO HIM!!
WHAP
ANYTIME YOU WANTA FEEL SOME PAIN, KID, JUST TRY THAT AGAIN...
NO! LEMME OUT, YOU SCOUNDRELS!!
UH OH... THE BOMBS ARE FLYING THIS WAY!!
WILL YA LOOK AT THAT?! WHAT A FIND, EH?!
WE'RE JUST WAITING TILL ALL THE ROBOT BOMBS GATHER HERE, BOSS!!

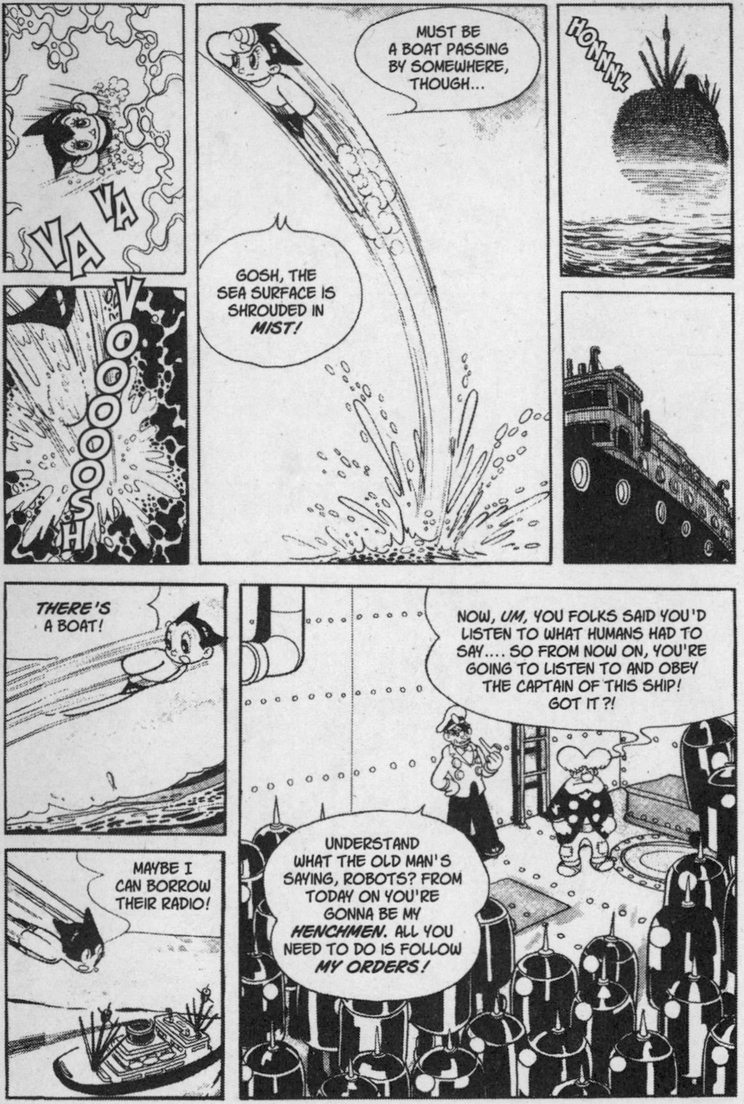
VA VA
VOOOOOOSH
MUST BE A BOAT PASSING BY SOMEWHERE, THOUGH...
GOSH, THE SEA SURFACE IS SHROUDED IN MIST!
HONNNK
THERE'S A BOAT!
MAYBE I CAN BORROW THEIR RADIO!
NOW, UM, YOU FOLKS SAID YOU'D LISTEN TO WHAT HUMANS HAD TO SAY.... SO FROM NOW ON, YOU'RE GOING TO LISTEN TO AND OBEY THE CAPTAIN OF THIS SHIP! GOT IT?!
UNDERSTAND WHAT THE OLD MAN'S SAYING, ROBOTS? FROM TODAY ON YOU'RE GONNA BE MY HENCHMEN. ALL YOU NEED TO DO IS FOLLOW MY ORDERS!

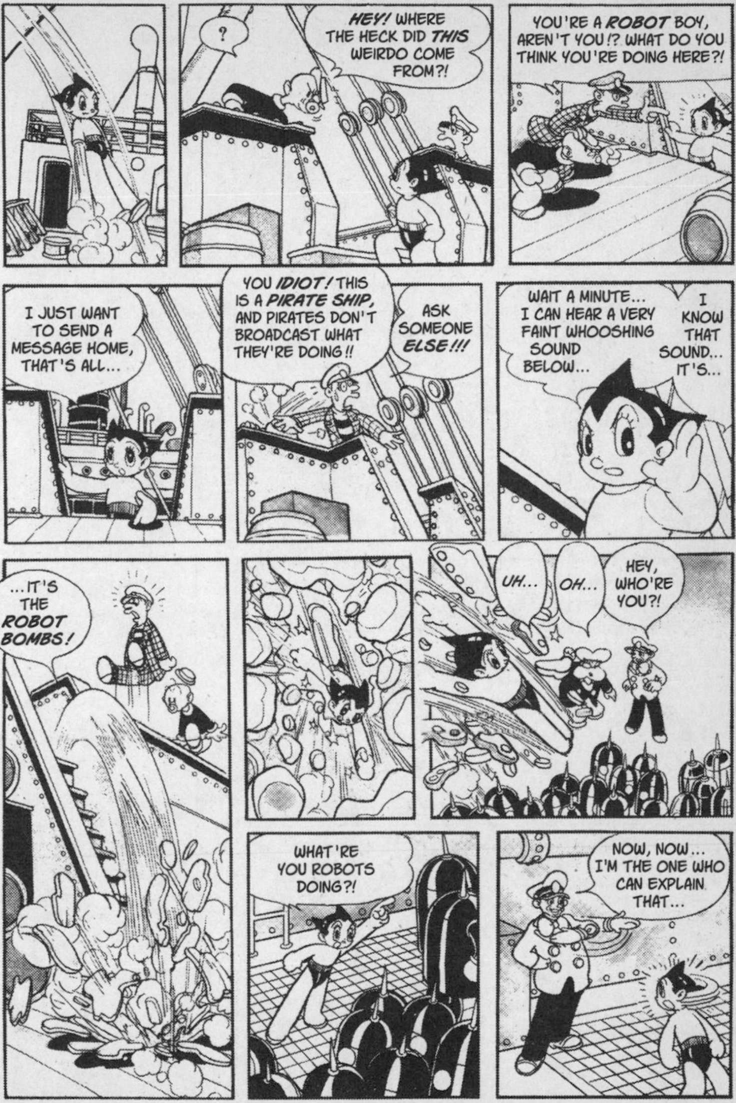
?
HEY! WHERE THE HECK DID THIS WEIRDO COME FROM?!
YOU'RE A ROBOT BOY, AREN'T YOU!? WHAT DO YOU THINK YOU'RE DOING HERE?!
I JUST WANT TO SEND A MESSAGE HOME, THAT'S ALL...
YOU IDIOT! THIS IS A PIRATE SHIP, AND PIRATES DON'T BROADCAST WHAT THEY'RE DOING!!
ASK SOMEONE ELSE!!!
WAIT A MINUTE... I CAN HEAR A VERY FAINT WHOOSHING SOUND BELOW...
I KNOW THAT SOUND... IT'S...
...IT'S THE ROBOT BOMBS!
UH...
OH...
HEY, WHO'RE YOU?!
WHAT'RE YOU ROBOTS DOING?!
NOW, NOW... I'M THE ONE WHO CAN EXPLAIN THAT...

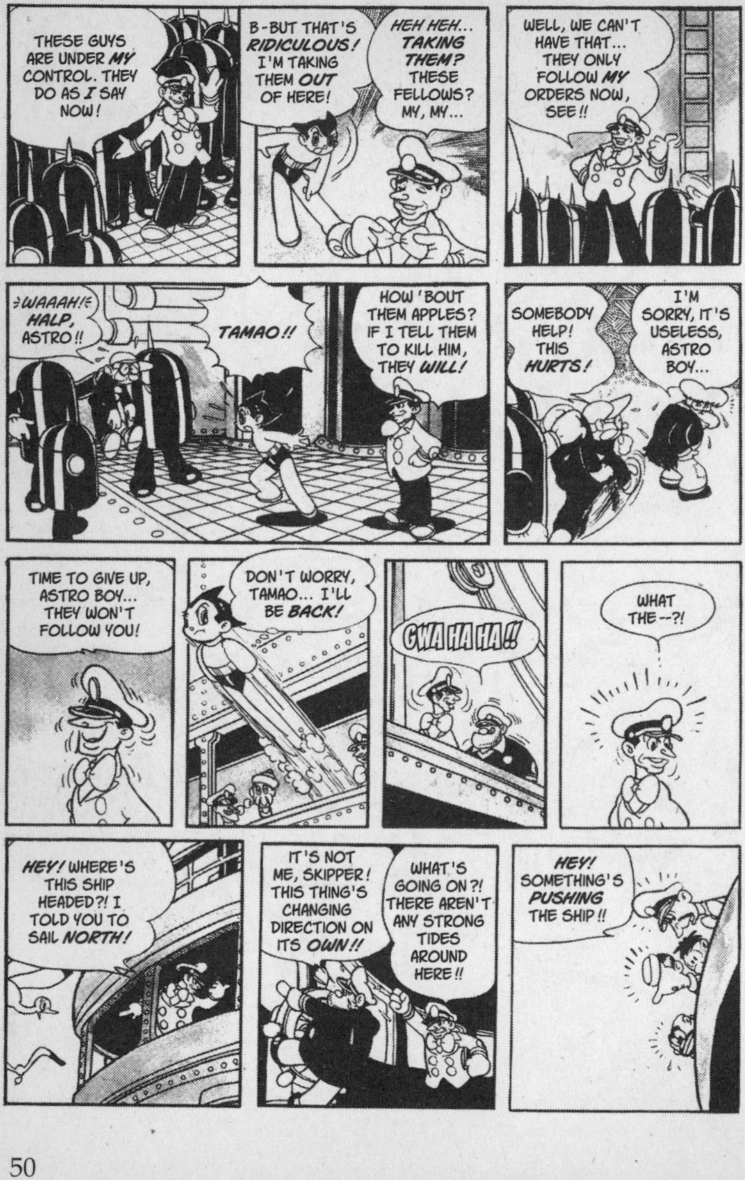
THESE GUYS ARE UNDER MY CONTROL. THEY DO AS I SAY NOW!
B-BUT THAT'S RIDICULOUS! I'M TAKING THEM OUT OF HERE!
HEH HEH... TAKING THEM? THESE FELLOWS? MY, MY...
WELL, WE CAN'T HAVE THAT... THEY ONLY FOLLOW MY ORDERS NOW, SEE!!
WAAAH!! HALP, ASTRO!!
TAMAO!!
HOW 'BOUT THEM APPLES? IF I TELL THEM TO KILL HIM, THEY WILL!
SOMEBODY HELP! THIS HURTS!
I'M SORRY, IT'S USELESS, ASTRO BOY...
TIME TO GIVE UP, ASTRO BOY... THEY WON'T FOLLOW YOU!
DON'T WORRY, TAMAO... I'LL BE BACK!
GWA HA HA!!
WHAT THE--?!
HEY! WHERE'S THIS SHIP HEADED?! I TOLD YOU TO SAIL NORTH!
IT'S NOT ME, SKIPPER! THIS THING'S CHANGING DIRECTION ON ITS OWN!!
WHAT'S GOING ON?! THERE AREN'T ANY STRONG TIDES AROUND HERE!!
HEY! SOMETHING'S PUSHING THE SHIP!!

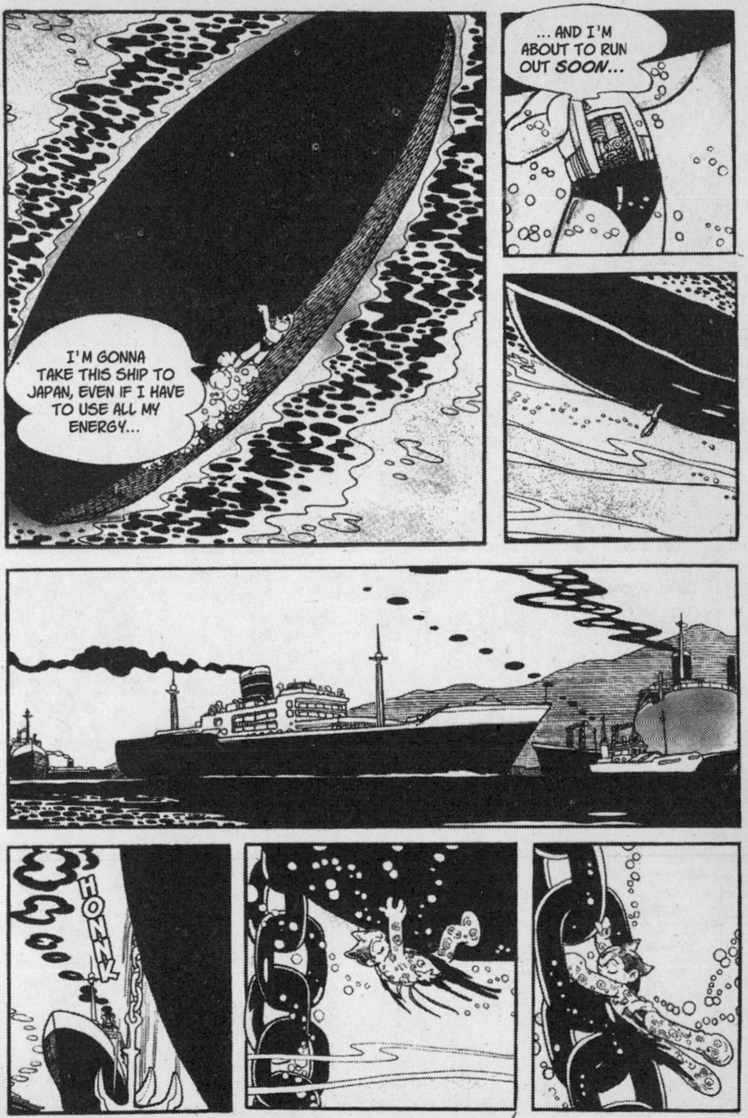
I'M GONNA TAKE THIS SHIP TO JAPAN, EVEN IF I HAVE TO USE ALL MY ENERGY...
... AND I'M ABOUT TO RUN OUT *SOON*...
HONNK

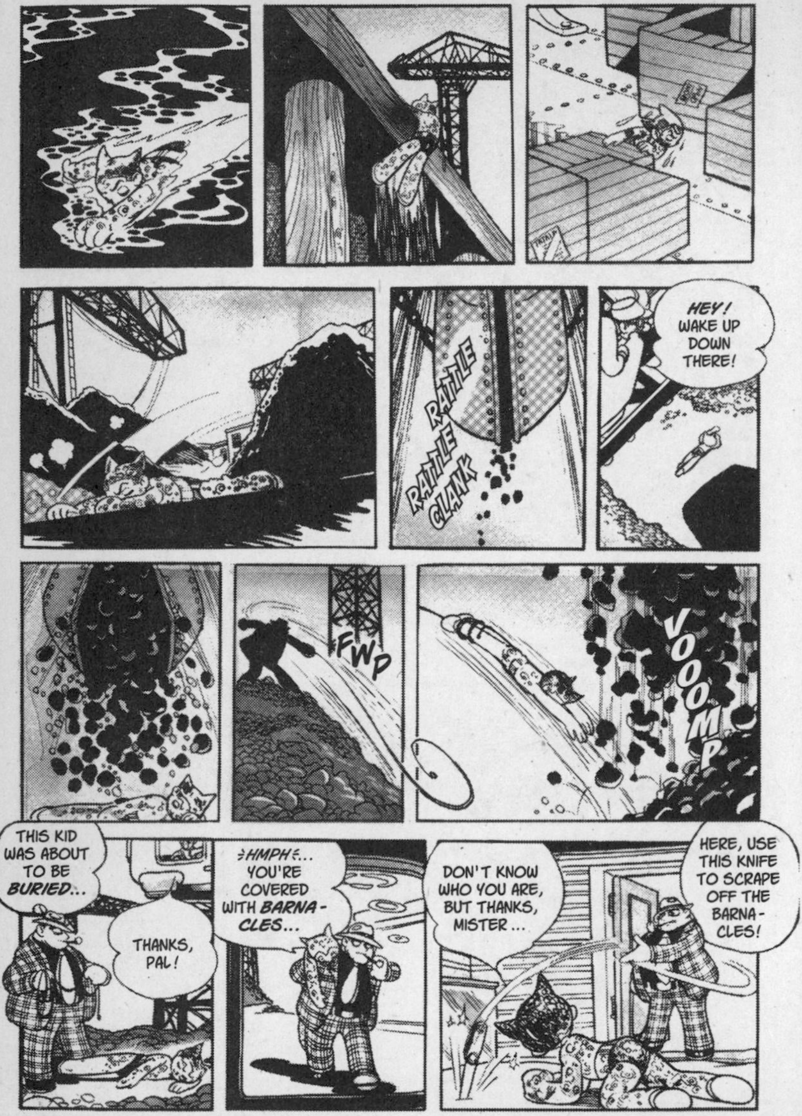
RATTLE
RATTLE
CLANK
HEY! WAKE UP DOWN THERE!
FWP
VOOOOMP
THIS KID WAS ABOUT TO BE BURIED...
THANKS, PAL!
HMPH... YOU'RE COVERED WITH BARNA-CLES...
DON'T KNOW WHO YOU ARE, BUT THANKS, MISTER...
HERE, USE THIS KNIFE TO SCRAPE OFF THE BARNA-CLES!

YOU'RE A *ROBOT*, AREN'T YOU... BUT WHAT'RE YOU DOING ON THIS ISLAND?

I HITCHED A RIDE ON A PIRATE SHIP...

PIRATES, HUH? ⨳HMPH⨳... AND WAS THIS THE LEADER?

THAT'S HIM... ALONG WITH THIS GUY, TOO...

⨳HMPH⨳... I GO BY THE NAME OF *BOONE MARUKUBI*, OTHERWISE KNOWN AS *"THICK-NECK"*...

... THE GUY IN THE PHOTO'S *MASON*, AND IN THE OLD DAYS I WAS HIS RIGHT-HAND MAN...

THE MAN'S GOT A HEART OF STONE... HE'S AS CRUEL AS THEY COME...

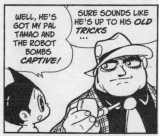

WELL, HE'S GOT MY PAL TAMAO AND THE ROBOT BOMBS *CAPTIVE!*

SURE SOUNDS LIKE HE'S UP TO HIS *OLD TRICKS* ...

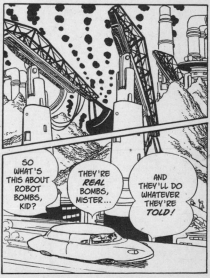

TELL YA WHAT... I'LL GO HAVE A WORD WITH HIM FOR YOU...

CLIMB IN...

SO WHAT'S THIS ABOUT ROBOT BOMBS, KID?

THEY'RE *REAL* BOMBS, MISTER...

AND THEY'LL DO WHATEVER THEY'RE *TOLD!*

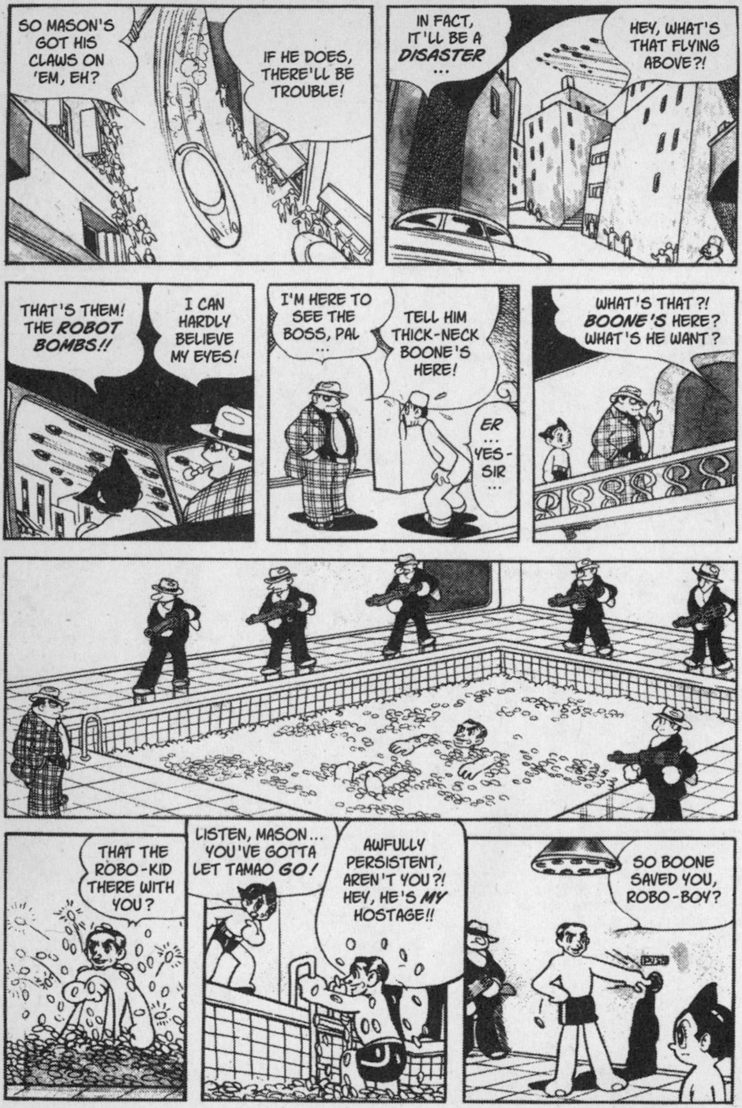
SO MASON'S GOT HIS CLAWS ON 'EM, EH?
IF HE DOES, THERE'LL BE TROUBLE!
IN FACT, IT'LL BE A DISASTER ...
HEY, WHAT'S THAT FLYING ABOVE?!
THAT'S THEM! THE ROBOT BOMBS!!
I CAN HARDLY BELIEVE MY EYES!
I'M HERE TO SEE THE BOSS, PAL ...
TELL HIM THICK-NECK BOONE'S HERE!
ER ... YES-SIR ...
WHAT'S THAT?! BOONE'S HERE? WHAT'S HE WANT?
THAT THE ROBO-KID THERE WITH YOU?
LISTEN, MASON... YOU'VE GOTTA LET TAMAO GO!
AWFULLY PERSISTENT, AREN'T YOU?! HEY, HE'S MY HOSTAGE!!
SO BOONE SAVED YOU, ROBO-BOY?

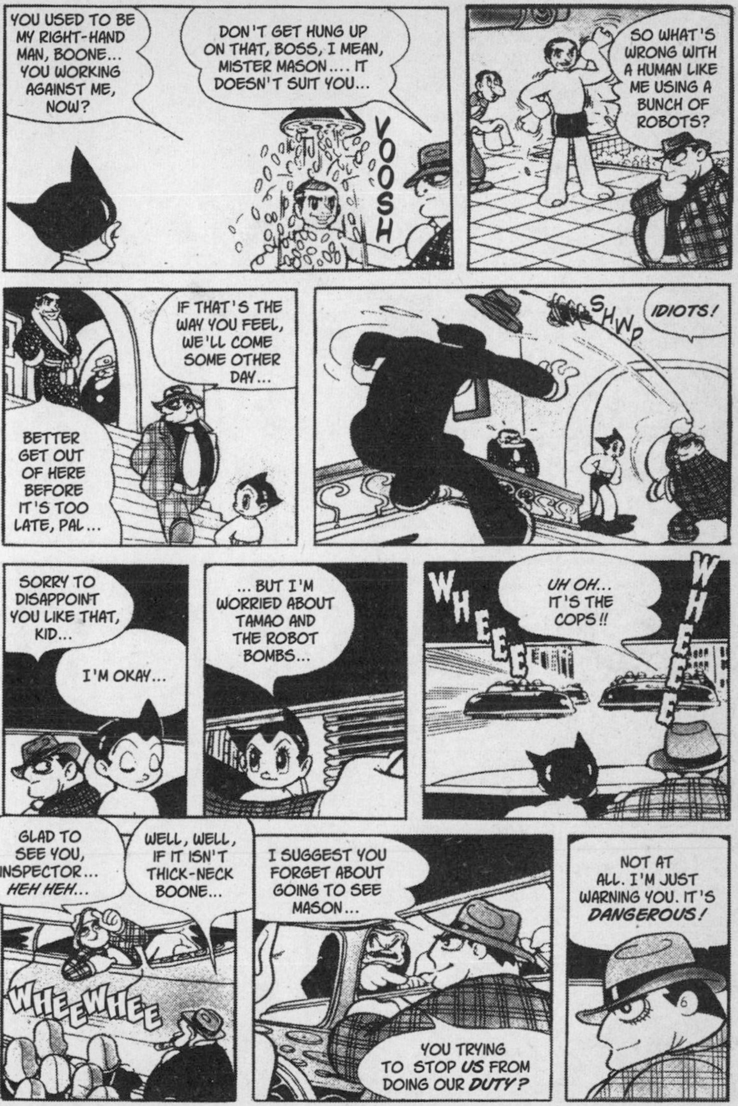
YOU USED TO BE MY RIGHT-HAND MAN, BOONE... YOU WORKING AGAINST ME, NOW?
DON'T GET HUNG UP ON THAT, BOSS, I MEAN, MISTER MASON.... IT DOESN'T SUIT YOU...
VOOSH
SO WHAT'S WRONG WITH A HUMAN LIKE ME USING A BUNCH OF ROBOTS?
IF THAT'S THE WAY YOU FEEL, WE'LL COME SOME OTHER DAY...
BETTER GET OUT OF HERE BEFORE IT'S TOO LATE, PAL...
SHWP
IDIOTS!
SORRY TO DISAPPOINT YOU LIKE THAT, KID...
I'M OKAY...
... BUT I'M WORRIED ABOUT TAMAO AND THE ROBOT BOMBS...
WHEEE
UH OH... IT'S THE COPS!!
WHEEE
GLAD TO SEE YOU, INSPECTOR... *HEH HEH*...
WELL, WELL, IF IT ISN'T THICK-NECK BOONE...
WHEEWHEE
I SUGGEST YOU FORGET ABOUT GOING TO SEE MASON...
YOU TRYING TO STOP *US* FROM DOING OUR *DUTY*?
NOT AT ALL. I'M JUST WARNING YOU. IT'S *DANGEROUS*!

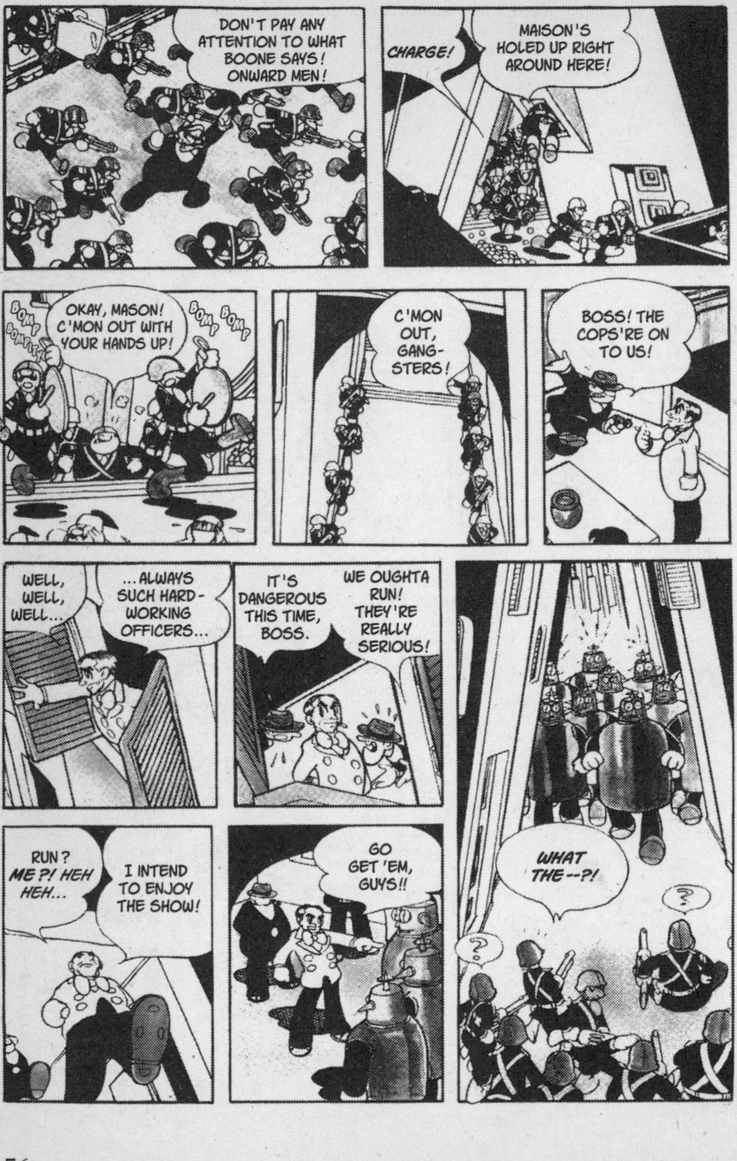
DON'T PAY ANY ATTENTION TO WHAT BOONE SAYS! ONWARD MEN!
CHARGE!
MAISON'S HOLED UP RIGHT AROUND HERE!
BOMP BOMPITTY
OKAY, MASON! C'MON OUT WITH YOUR HANDS UP!
BOMP BOMP
C'MON OUT, GANG-STERS!
BOSS! THE COPS'RE ON TO US!
WELL, WELL, WELL...
...ALWAYS SUCH HARD-WORKING OFFICERS...
IT'S DANGEROUS THIS TIME, BOSS.
WE OUGHTA RUN! THEY'RE REALLY SERIOUS!
RUN? ME?! HEH HEH...
I INTEND TO ENJOY THE SHOW!
GO GET 'EM, GUYS!!
WHAT THE--?!
?
?

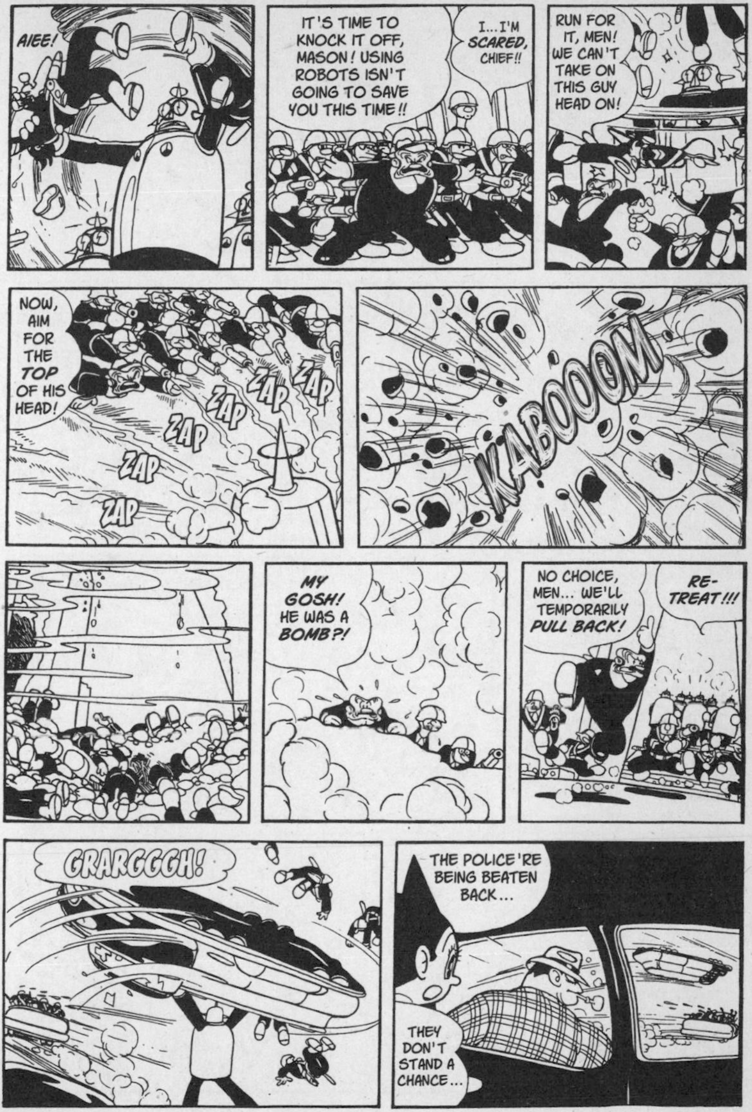
AIEE!
IT'S TIME TO KNOCK IT OFF, MASON! USING ROBOTS ISN'T GOING TO SAVE YOU THIS TIME!!
I...I'M SCARED, CHIEF!!
RUN FOR IT, MEN! WE CAN'T TAKE ON THIS GUY HEAD ON!
NOW, AIM FOR THE TOP OF HIS HEAD!
ZAP ZAP ZAP ZAP ZAP ZAP ZAP
KABOOOM
MY GOSH! HE WAS A BOMB?!
NO CHOICE, MEN... WE'LL TEMPORARILY PULL BACK!
RE-TREAT!!!
GRARGGGH!
THE POLICE'RE BEING BEATEN BACK...
THEY DON'T STAND A CHANCE...

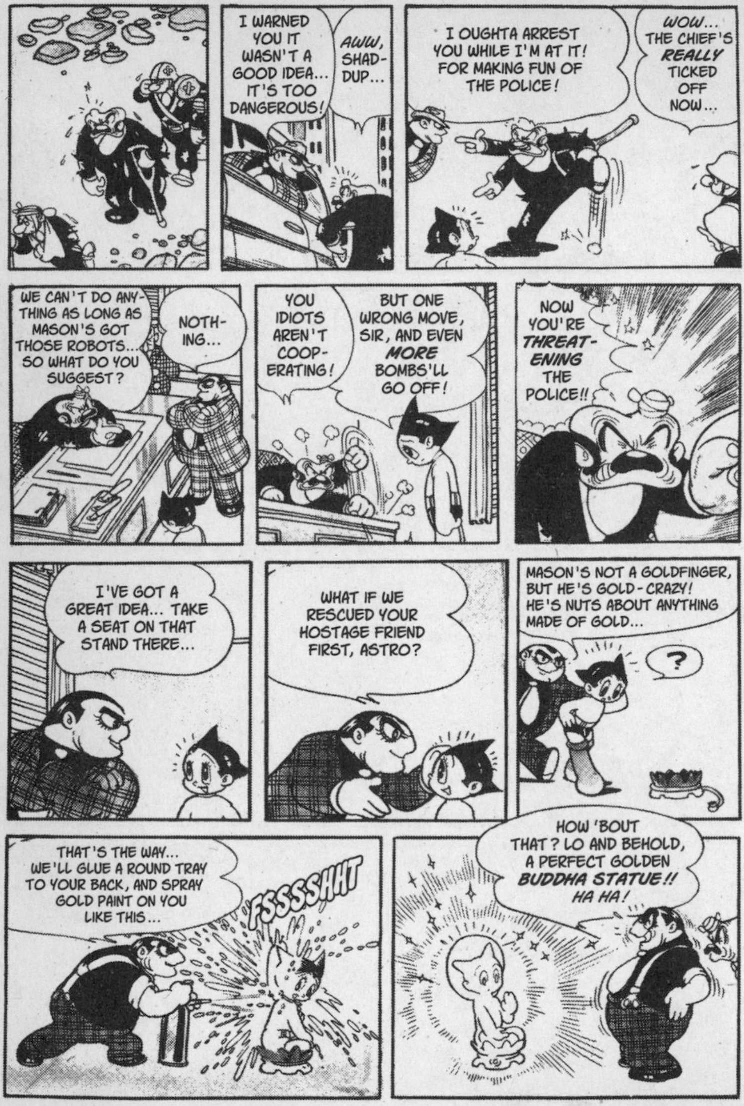
I WARNED YOU IT WASN'T A GOOD IDEA... IT'S TOO DANGEROUS!
AWW, SHADDUP...
I OUGHTA ARREST YOU WHILE I'M AT IT! FOR MAKING FUN OF THE POLICE!
WOW... THE CHIEF'S REALLY TICKED OFF NOW...
WE CAN'T DO ANYTHING AS LONG AS MASON'S GOT THOSE ROBOTS... SO WHAT DO YOU SUGGEST?
NOTHING...
YOU IDIOTS AREN'T COOPERATING!
BUT ONE WRONG MOVE, SIR, AND EVEN MORE BOMBS'LL GO OFF!
NOW YOU'RE THREATENING THE POLICE!!
I'VE GOT A GREAT IDEA... TAKE A SEAT ON THAT STAND THERE...
WHAT IF WE RESCUED YOUR HOSTAGE FRIEND FIRST, ASTRO?
MASON'S NOT A GOLDFINGER, BUT HE'S GOLD-CRAZY! HE'S NUTS ABOUT ANYTHING MADE OF GOLD...
?
THAT'S THE WAY... WE'LL GLUE A ROUND TRAY TO YOUR BACK, AND SPRAY GOLD PAINT ON YOU LIKE THIS...
FSSSSHHT
HOW 'BOUT THAT? LO AND BEHOLD, A PERFECT GOLDEN BUDDHA STATUE!! HA HA!

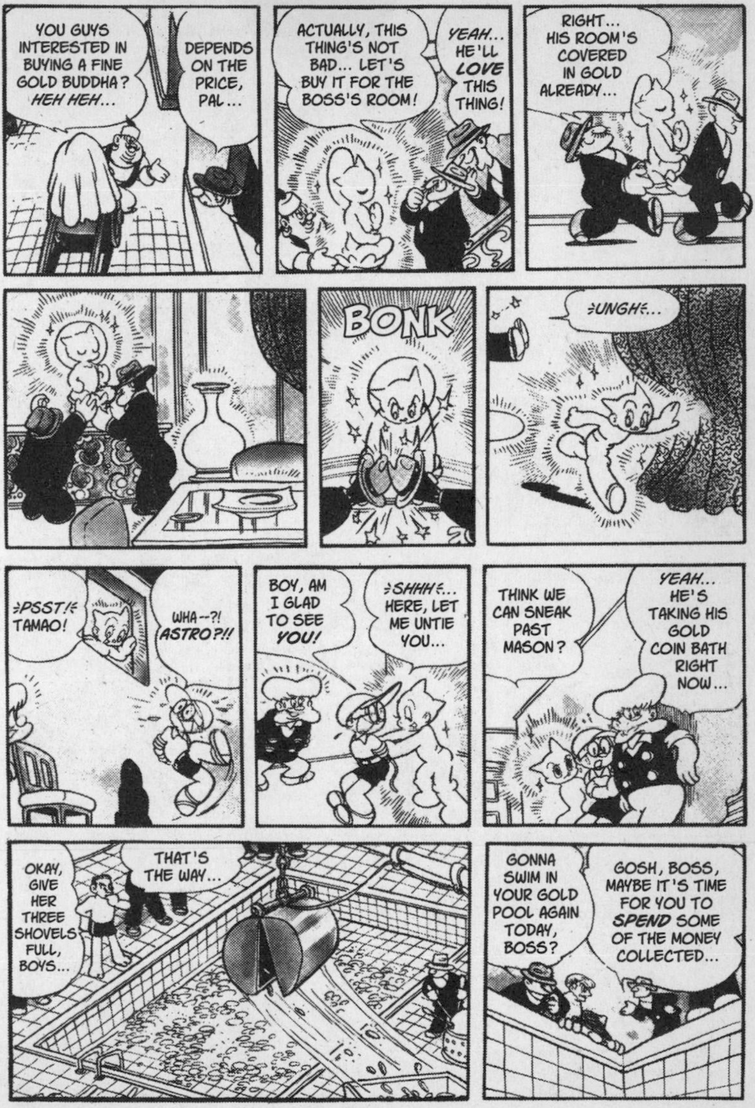
YOU GUYS INTERESTED IN BUYING A FINE GOLD BUDDHA? HEH HEH...
DEPENDS ON THE PRICE, PAL...
ACTUALLY, THIS THING'S NOT BAD... LET'S BUY IT FOR THE BOSS'S ROOM!
YEAH... HE'LL LOVE THIS THING!
RIGHT... HIS ROOM'S COVERED IN GOLD ALREADY...
BONK
UNGH...
PSST! TAMAO!
WHA--?! ASTRO?!!
BOY, AM I GLAD TO SEE YOU!
SHHH... HERE, LET ME UNTIE YOU...
THINK WE CAN SNEAK PAST MASON?
YEAH... HE'S TAKING HIS GOLD COIN BATH RIGHT NOW...
OKAY, GIVE HER THREE SHOVELS FULL, BOYS...
THAT'S THE WAY...
GONNA SWIM IN YOUR GOLD POOL AGAIN TODAY, BOSS?
GOSH, BOSS, MAYBE IT'S TIME FOR YOU TO SPEND SOME OF THE MONEY COLLECTED...

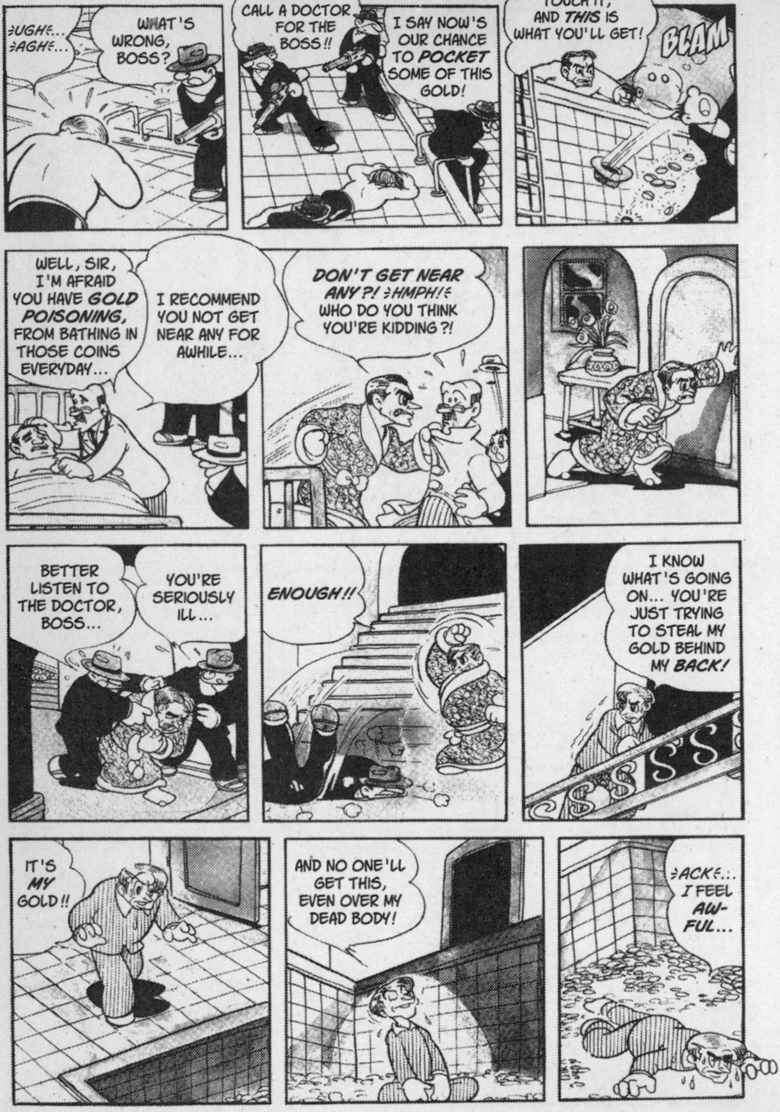

≑UGH≑... ≑AGH≑...
WHAT'S WRONG, BOSS?
SOMEBODY CALL A DOCTOR FOR THE BOSS!!
I SAY NOW'S OUR CHANCE TO POCKET SOME OF THIS GOLD!
TOUCH IT, AND THIS IS WHAT YOU'LL GET!
BLAM
WELL, SIR, I'M AFRAID YOU HAVE GOLD POISONING, FROM BATHING IN THOSE COINS EVERYDAY...
I RECOMMEND YOU NOT GET NEAR ANY FOR AWHILE...
DON'T GET NEAR ANY?! ≑HMPH!≑ WHO DO YOU THINK YOU'RE KIDDING?!
BETTER LISTEN TO THE DOCTOR, BOSS...
YOU'RE SERIOUSLY ILL...
ENOUGH!!
I KNOW WHAT'S GOING ON... YOU'RE JUST TRYING TO STEAL MY GOLD BEHIND MY BACK!
IT'S MY GOLD!!
AND NO ONE'LL GET THIS, EVEN OVER MY DEAD BODY!
≑ACK≑... I FEEL AW-FUL...

BOSS PROB'LY DOESN'T HAVE LONG FOR THIS WORLD, GUYS...

THE PEARLY GATES ARE ABOUT TO OPEN, *EH...?*

NO MATTER HOW TOUGH HE IS, IT'LL TAKE MORE THAN ROBOT BOMBS TO WIN OUT OVER AN ILLNESS...

SO WHAT HAPPENS TO ALL THE *LOOT* WHEN THE BOSS CROAKS?

WE DIVVY IT UP AMONG *OURSELVES,* THAT'S WHAT! HA HA!

WHY THOSE *TRAITORS!*

OKAY, ROBOTS... SOME OF MY MEN ARE UPSTAIRS PLOTTING TO GET MY LOOT... I WANT YOU TO SEND 'EM ALL TO THE GREAT BEYOND! UNDERSTAND?!

AND IF ASTRO BOY SHOWS UP HERE, BLOW THE WHOLE BUILDING UP, OKAY?

I WANT THE REST OF YOU TO STUFF YOUR CHEST HATCHES WITH MY GOLD COINS!

MAKE SURE YOU FLY OUT OF HERE BEFORE ASTRO BOY ARRIVES!

HEAD FOR MANILA! GOT IT?

IF I CAN JUST GET RID OF ASTRO BOY, EVERYTHING ELSE'LL BE A CINCH...

OKAY... *MONEY BAGS,* GO FOR IT!

HEH HEH... I'LL TEACH MY ENEMIES NOT TO UNDERESTIMATE ME!

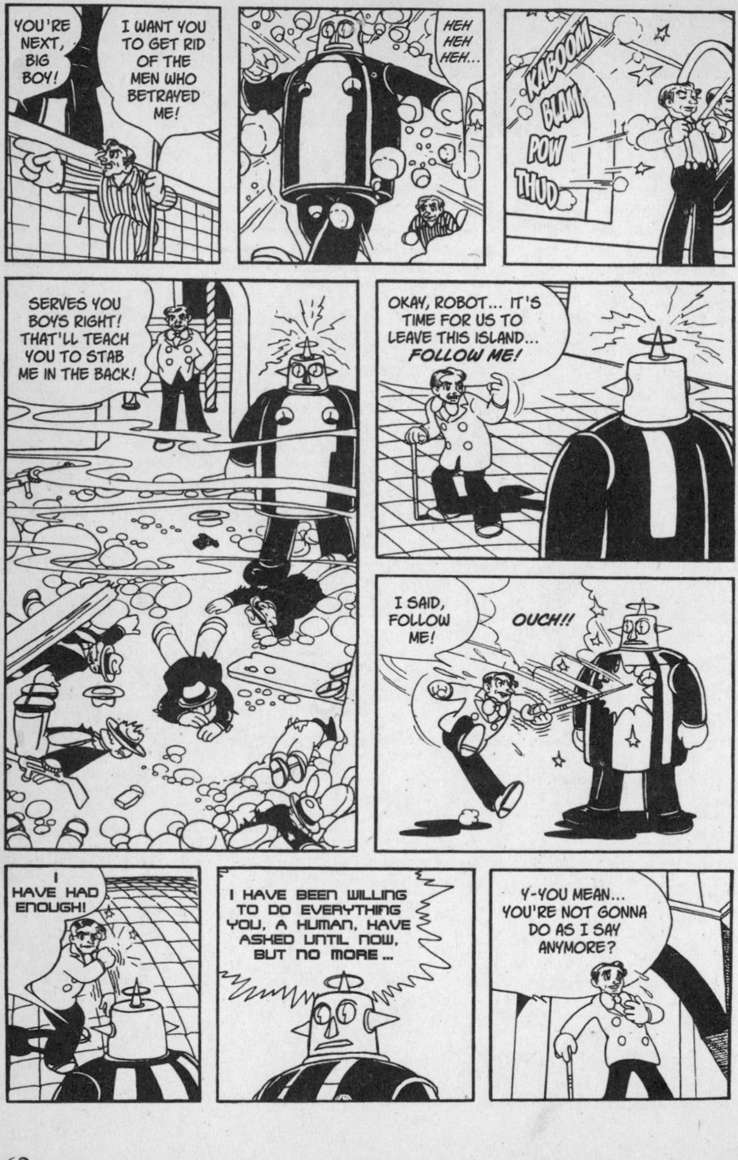
YOU'RE NEXT, BIG BOY!
I WANT YOU TO GET RID OF THE MEN WHO BETRAYED ME!
HEH HEH HEH...
KABOOM
BLAM
POW
THUD
SERVES YOU BOYS RIGHT! THAT'LL TEACH YOU TO STAB ME IN THE BACK!
OKAY, ROBOT... IT'S TIME FOR US TO LEAVE THIS ISLAND... FOLLOW ME!
I SAID, FOLLOW ME!
OUCH!!
I HAVE HAD ENOUGH!
I HAVE BEEN WILLING TO DO EVERYTHING YOU, A HUMAN, HAVE ASKED UNTIL NOW, BUT NO MORE...
Y-YOU MEAN... YOU'RE NOT GONNA DO AS I SAY ANYMORE?

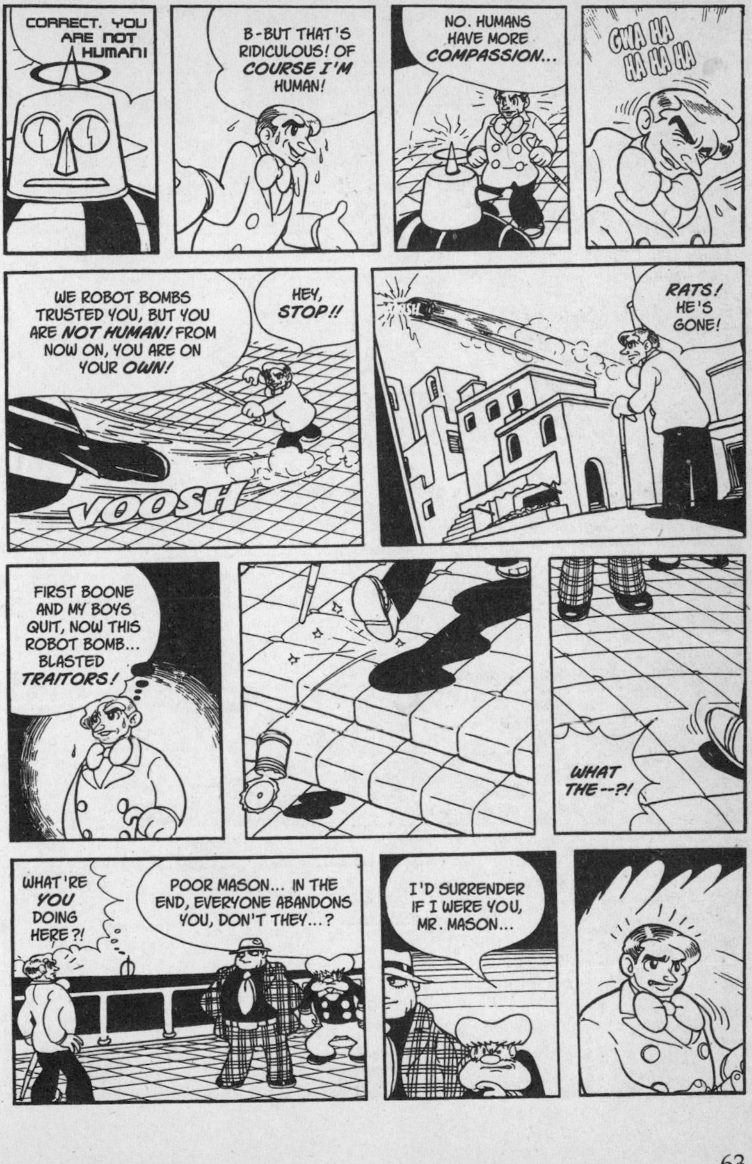
CORRECT. YOU ARE NOT HUMAN!
B-BUT THAT'S RIDICULOUS! OF COURSE I'M HUMAN!
NO. HUMANS HAVE MORE COMPASSION...
GWA HA HA HA HA
WE ROBOT BOMBS TRUSTED YOU, BUT YOU ARE NOT HUMAN! FROM NOW ON, YOU ARE ON YOUR OWN!
HEY, STOP!!
VOOSH
RATS! HE'S GONE!
FIRST BOONE AND MY BOYS QUIT, NOW THIS ROBOT BOMB... BLASTED TRAITORS!
WHAT THE--?!
WHAT'RE YOU DOING HERE?!
POOR MASON... IN THE END, EVERYONE ABANDONS YOU, DON'T THEY...?
I'D SURRENDER IF I WERE YOU, MR. MASON...

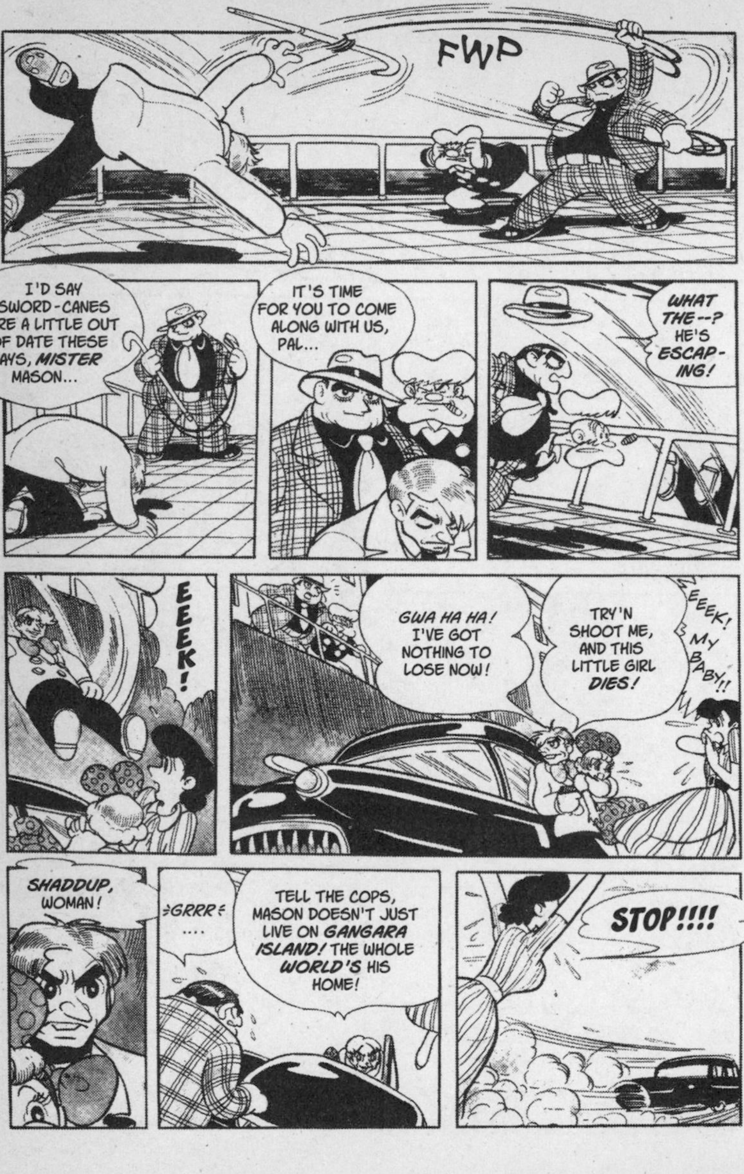
FWP
I'D SAY SWORD-CANES ARE A LITTLE OUT OF DATE THESE DAYS, MISTER MASON...
IT'S TIME FOR YOU TO COME ALONG WITH US, PAL...
WHAT THE--? HE'S ESCAPING!
EEEEK!
GWA HA HA! I'VE GOT NOTHING TO LOSE NOW!
TRY'N SHOOT ME, AND THIS LITTLE GIRL DIES!
EEEK! MY BABY!!
SHADDUP, WOMAN!
GRRR ....
TELL THE COPS, MASON DOESN'T JUST LIVE ON GANGARA ISLAND! THE WHOLE WORLD'S HIS HOME!
STOP!!!!

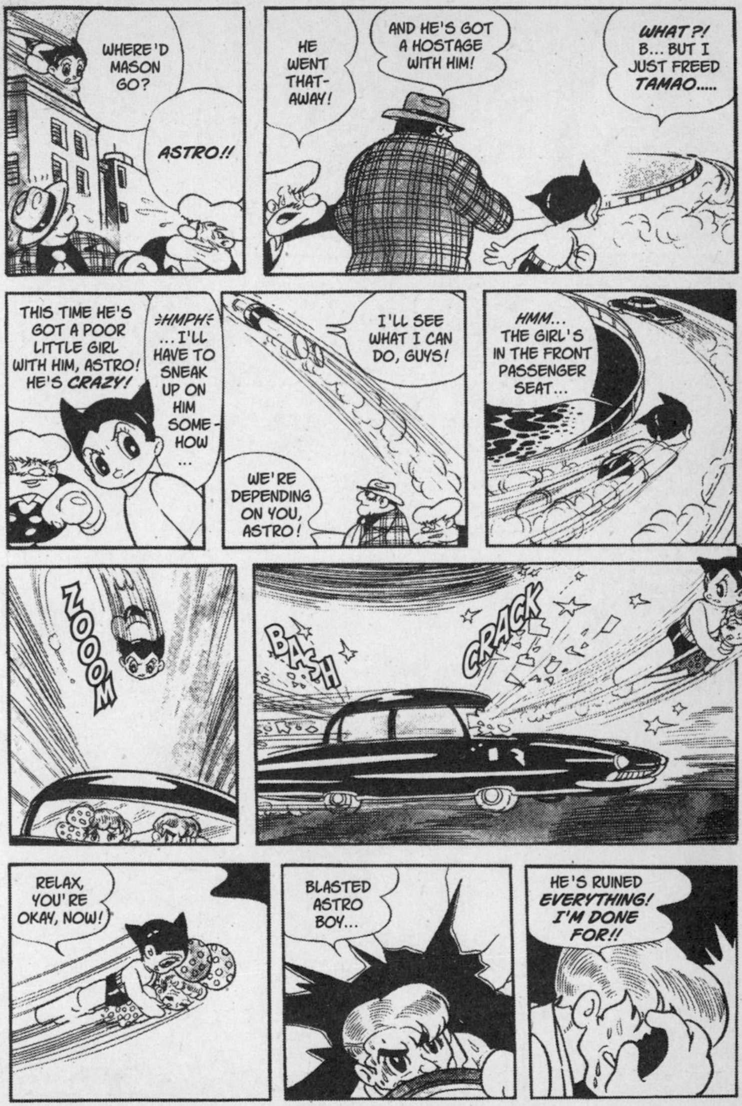
WHERE'D MASON GO?
ASTRO!!
HE WENT THAT-AWAY!
AND HE'S GOT A HOSTAGE WITH HIM!
WHAT?! B... BUT I JUST FREED TAMAO.....
THIS TIME HE'S GOT A POOR LITTLE GIRL WITH HIM, ASTRO! HE'S CRAZY!
HMPH ...I'LL HAVE TO SNEAK UP ON HIM SOME-HOW ...
I'LL SEE WHAT I CAN DO, GUYS!
WE'RE DEPENDING ON YOU, ASTRO!
HMM... THE GIRL'S IN THE FRONT PASSENGER SEAT...
ZOOOOM
BASH
CRACK
RELAX, YOU'RE OKAY, NOW!
BLASTED ASTRO BOY...
HE'S RUINED EVERYTHING! I'M DONE FOR!!

ARGH...

UH OH...

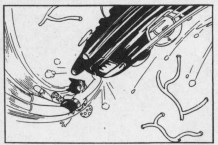

YOU OKAY, MR. MASON?

WH... WHY'D YOU TRY TO RESCUE ME?

'CUZ ROBOTS'RE DESIGNED TO HELP PEOPLE, THAT'S WHY!

EVEN BAD GUYS LIKE ME?

ASTRO BOY...YOU BEAT ME FAIR AND SQUARE....BUT TELL ME ONE THING...

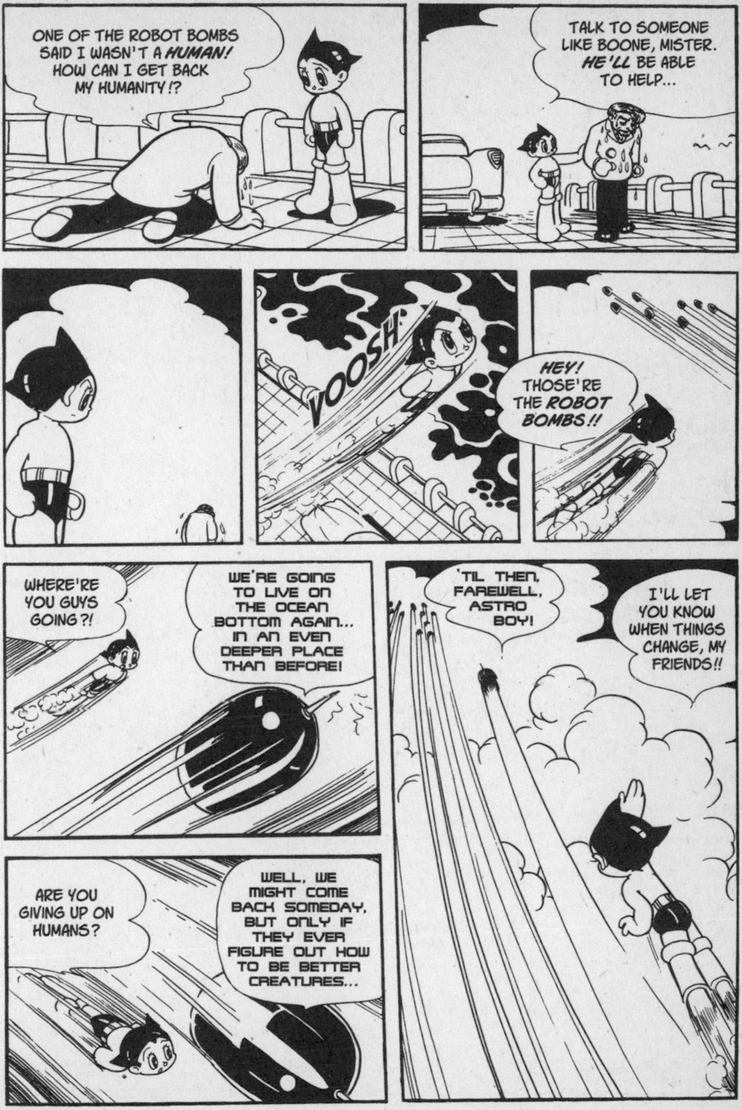
ONE OF THE ROBOT BOMBS SAID I WASN'T A *HUMAN!* HOW CAN I GET BACK MY HUMANITY !?
TALK TO SOMEONE LIKE BOONE, MISTER. *HE'LL* BE ABLE TO HELP...
VOOSH
HEY! THOSE'RE THE *ROBOT BOMBS!!*
WHERE'RE YOU GUYS GOING ?!
WE'RE GOING TO LIVE ON THE OCEAN BOTTOM AGAIN... IN AN EVEN DEEPER PLACE THAN BEFORE!
ARE YOU GIVING UP ON HUMANS?
WELL, WE MIGHT COME BACK SOMEDAY, BUT ONLY IF THEY EVER FIGURE OUT HOW TO BE BETTER CREATURES...
'TIL THEN, FAREWELL, ASTRO BOY!
I'LL LET YOU KNOW WHEN THINGS CHANGE, MY FRIENDS!!

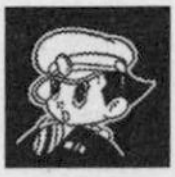

MISSION TO MARS

First serialized from December 1953 to May 1954 in *Shonen* magazine.

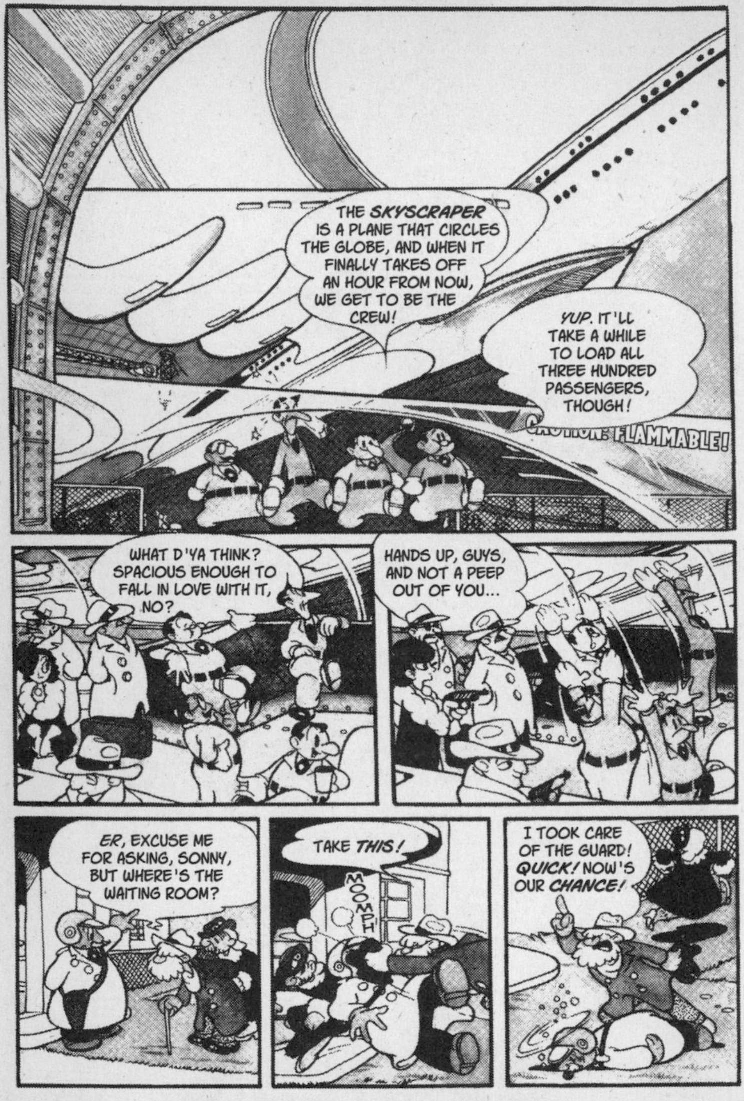
THE *SKYSCRAPER* IS A PLANE THAT CIRCLES THE GLOBE, AND WHEN IT FINALLY TAKES OFF AN HOUR FROM NOW, WE GET TO BE THE CREW!
YUP. IT'LL TAKE A WHILE TO LOAD ALL THREE HUNDRED PASSENGERS, THOUGH!
FLAMMABLE!
WHAT D'YA THINK? SPACIOUS ENOUGH TO FALL IN LOVE WITH IT, NO?
HANDS UP, GUYS, AND NOT A PEEP OUT OF YOU...
ER, EXCUSE ME FOR ASKING, SONNY, BUT WHERE'S THE WAITING ROOM?
TAKE ***THIS!***
MOOMPH
I TOOK CARE OF THE GUARD! ***QUICK!*** NOW'S OUR ***CHANCE!***

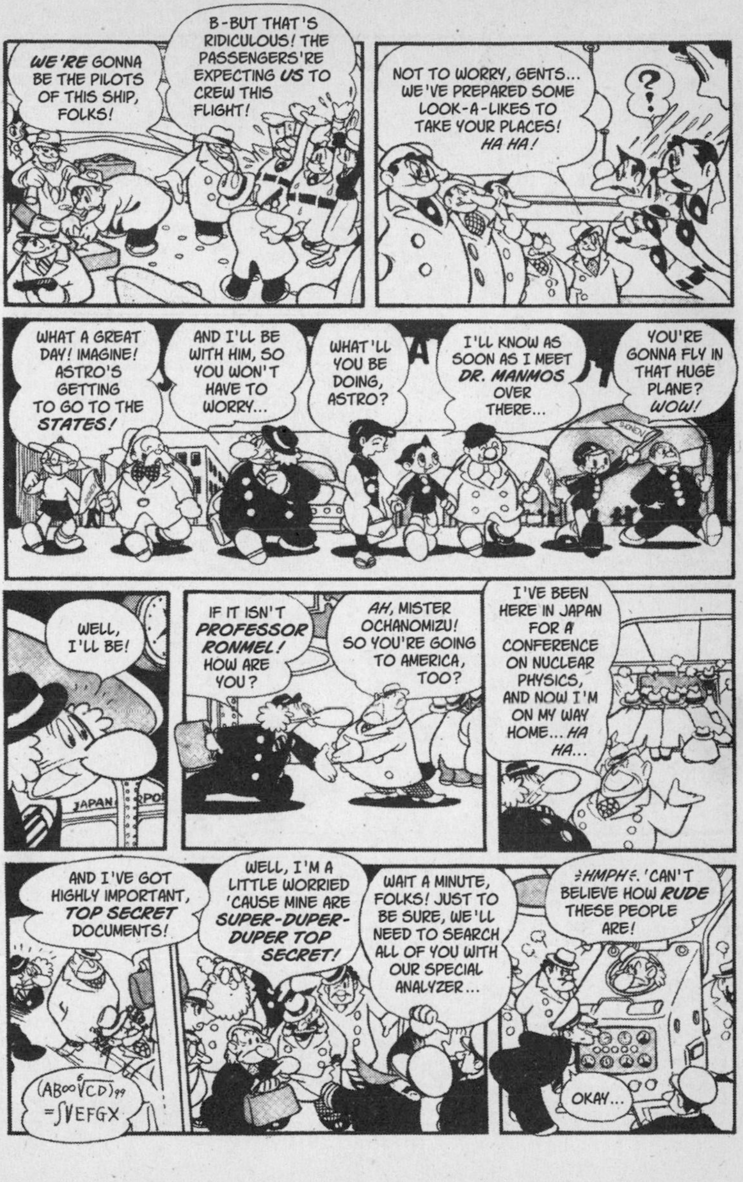
WE'RE GONNA BE THE PILOTS OF THIS SHIP, FOLKS!
B-BUT THAT'S RIDICULOUS! THE PASSENGERS'RE EXPECTING US TO CREW THIS FLIGHT!
NOT TO WORRY, GENTS... WE'VE PREPARED SOME LOOK-A-LIKES TO TAKE YOUR PLACES! HA HA!
?!
WHAT A GREAT DAY! IMAGINE! ASTRO'S GETTING TO GO TO THE STATES!
AND I'LL BE WITH HIM, SO YOU WON'T HAVE TO WORRY...
WHAT'LL YOU BE DOING, ASTRO?
I'LL KNOW AS SOON AS I MEET DR. MANMOS OVER THERE...
YOU'RE GONNA FLY IN THAT HUGE PLANE? WOW!
WELL, I'LL BE!
IF IT ISN'T PROFESSOR RONMEL! HOW ARE YOU?
AH, MISTER OCHANOMIZU! SO YOU'RE GOING TO AMERICA, TOO?
I'VE BEEN HERE IN JAPAN FOR A CONFERENCE ON NUCLEAR PHYSICS, AND NOW I'M ON MY WAY HOME... HA HA...
AND I'VE GOT HIGHLY IMPORTANT, TOP SECRET DOCUMENTS!
(AB∞⁶√CD)99 =∫√EFGX
WELL, I'M A LITTLE WORRIED 'CAUSE MINE ARE SUPER-DUPER-DUPER TOP SECRET!
WAIT A MINUTE, FOLKS! JUST TO BE SURE, WE'LL NEED TO SEARCH ALL OF YOU WITH OUR SPECIAL ANALYZER...
≠HMPH≠. 'CAN'T BELIEVE HOW RUDE THESE PEOPLE ARE!
OKAY...

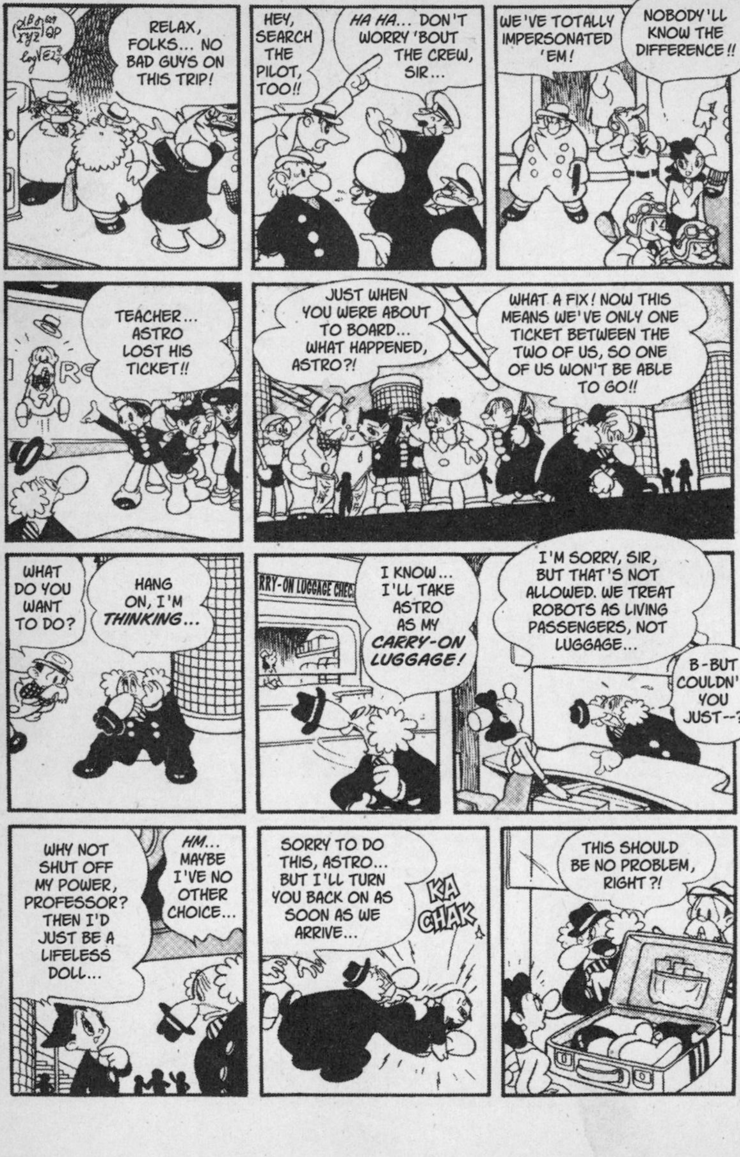
RELAX, FOLKS... NO BAD GUYS ON THIS TRIP!
HEY, SEARCH THE PILOT, TOO!!
HA HA... DON'T WORRY 'BOUT THE CREW, SIR...
WE'VE TOTALLY IMPERSONATED 'EM!
NOBODY'LL KNOW THE DIFFERENCE!!
TEACHER... ASTRO LOST HIS TICKET!!
JUST WHEN YOU WERE ABOUT TO BOARD... WHAT HAPPENED, ASTRO?!
WHAT A FIX! NOW THIS MEANS WE'VE ONLY ONE TICKET BETWEEN THE TWO OF US, SO ONE OF US WON'T BE ABLE TO GO!!
WHAT DO YOU WANT TO DO?
HANG ON, I'M *THINKING*...
I KNOW... I'LL TAKE ASTRO AS MY *CARRY-ON LUGGAGE!*
I'M SORRY, SIR, BUT THAT'S NOT ALLOWED. WE TREAT ROBOTS AS LIVING PASSENGERS, NOT LUGGAGE...
B-BUT COULDN'T YOU JUST--?
WHY NOT SHUT OFF MY POWER, PROFESSOR? THEN I'D JUST BE A LIFELESS DOLL...
HM... MAYBE I'VE NO OTHER CHOICE...
SORRY TO DO THIS, ASTRO... BUT I'LL TURN YOU BACK ON AS SOON AS WE ARRIVE...
KA CHAK
THIS SHOULD BE NO PROBLEM, RIGHT?!

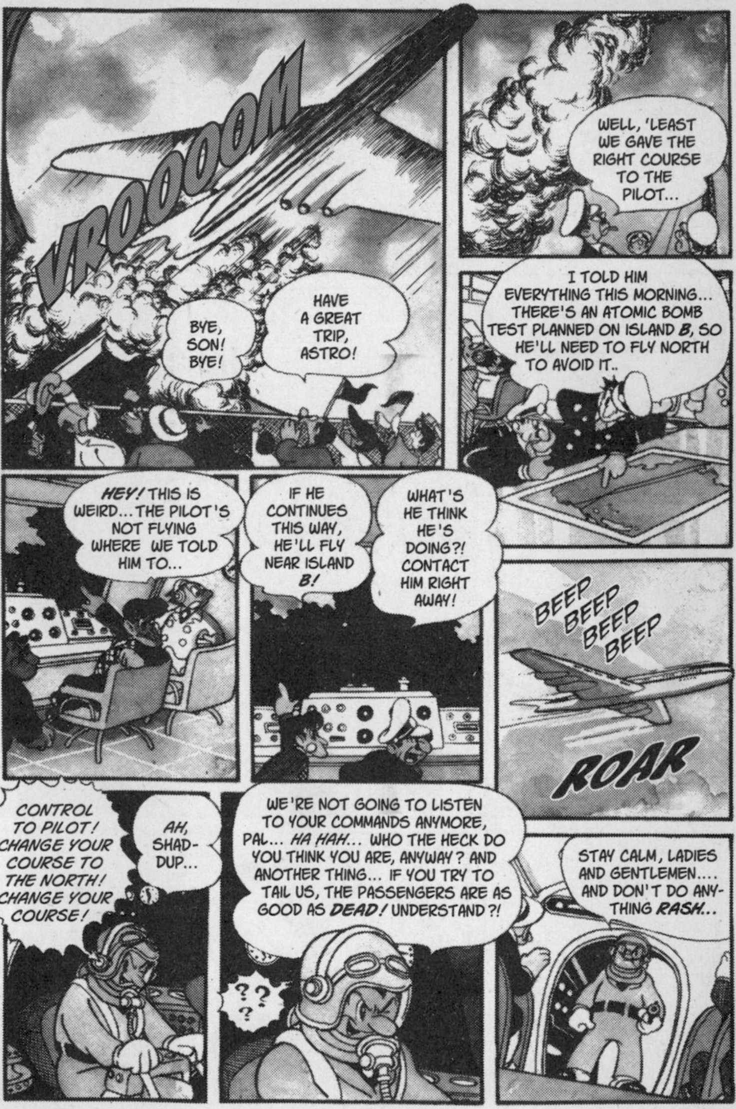
VROOOOOM
BYE, SON! BYE!
HAVE A GREAT TRIP, ASTRO!
WELL, 'LEAST WE GAVE THE RIGHT COURSE TO THE PILOT...
I TOLD HIM EVERYTHING THIS MORNING... THERE'S AN ATOMIC BOMB TEST PLANNED ON ISLAND B, SO HE'LL NEED TO FLY NORTH TO AVOID IT..
HEY! THIS IS WEIRD... THE PILOT'S NOT FLYING WHERE WE TOLD HIM TO...
IF HE CONTINUES THIS WAY, HE'LL FLY NEAR ISLAND B!
WHAT'S HE THINK HE'S DOING?! CONTACT HIM RIGHT AWAY!
BEEP BEEP BEEP BEEP
ROAR
CONTROL TO PILOT! CHANGE YOUR COURSE TO THE NORTH! CHANGE YOUR COURSE!
AH, SHAD-DUP...
WE'RE NOT GOING TO LISTEN TO YOUR COMMANDS ANYMORE, PAL... HA HAH... WHO THE HECK DO YOU THINK YOU ARE, ANYWAY? AND ANOTHER THING... IF YOU TRY TO TAIL US, THE PASSENGERS ARE AS GOOD AS DEAD! UNDERSTAND?!
???
STAY CALM, LADIES AND GENTLEMEN.... AND DON'T DO ANY-THING RASH...

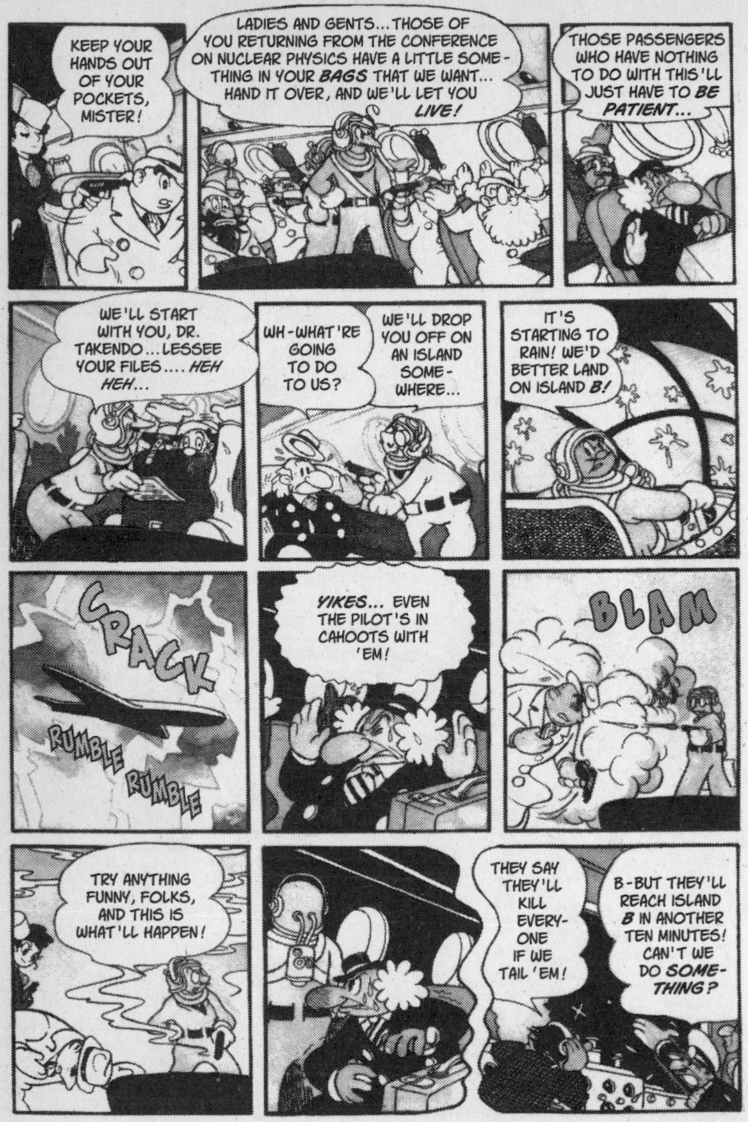
KEEP YOUR HANDS OUT OF YOUR POCKETS, MISTER!
LADIES AND GENTS... THOSE OF YOU RETURNING FROM THE CONFERENCE ON NUCLEAR PHYSICS HAVE A LITTLE SOMETHING IN YOUR BAGS THAT WE WANT... HAND IT OVER, AND WE'LL LET YOU LIVE!
THOSE PASSENGERS WHO HAVE NOTHING TO DO WITH THIS'LL JUST HAVE TO BE PATIENT...
WE'LL START WITH YOU, DR. TAKENDO... LESSEE YOUR FILES.... HEH HEH...
WH-WHAT'RE GOING TO DO TO US?
WE'LL DROP YOU OFF ON AN ISLAND SOMEWHERE...
IT'S STARTING TO RAIN! WE'D BETTER LAND ON ISLAND B!
CRACK
RUMBLE RUMBLE
YIKES... EVEN THE PILOT'S IN CAHOOTS WITH 'EM!
BLAM
TRY ANYTHING FUNNY, FOLKS, AND THIS IS WHAT'LL HAPPEN!
THEY SAY THEY'LL KILL EVERYONE IF WE TAIL 'EM!
B-BUT THEY'LL REACH ISLAND B IN ANOTHER TEN MINUTES! CAN'T WE DO SOMETHING?

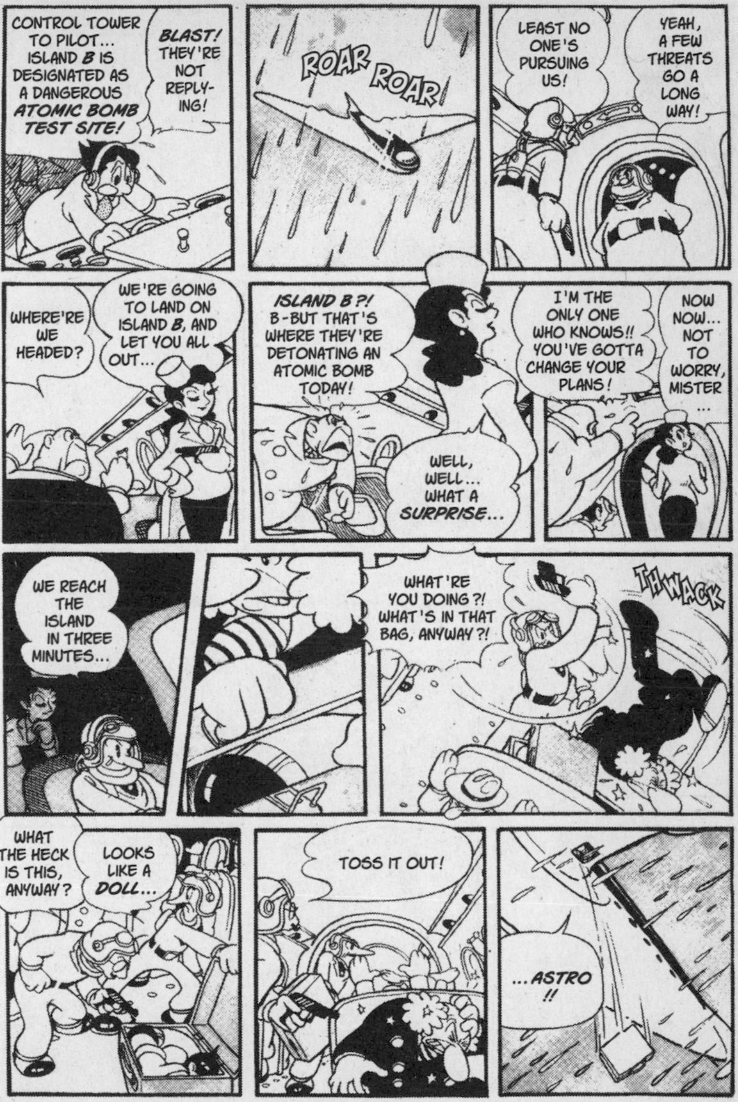

CONTROL TOWER TO PILOT… ISLAND B IS DESIGNATED AS A DANGEROUS ATOMIC BOMB TEST SITE!
BLAST! THEY'RE NOT REPLYING!
ROAR ROAR
LEAST NO ONE'S PURSUING US!
YEAH, A FEW THREATS GO A LONG WAY!
WHERE'RE WE HEADED?
WE'RE GOING TO LAND ON ISLAND B, AND LET YOU ALL OUT…
ISLAND B?! B-BUT THAT'S WHERE THEY'RE DETONATING AN ATOMIC BOMB TODAY!
WELL, WELL… WHAT A SURPRISE…
I'M THE ONLY ONE WHO KNOWS!! YOU'VE GOTTA CHANGE YOUR PLANS!
NOW NOW… NOT TO WORRY, MISTER…
WE REACH THE ISLAND IN THREE MINUTES…
WHAT'RE YOU DOING?! WHAT'S IN THAT BAG, ANYWAY?!
THWACK
WHAT THE HECK IS THIS, ANYWAY?
LOOKS LIKE A DOLL…
TOSS IT OUT!
…ASTRO !!

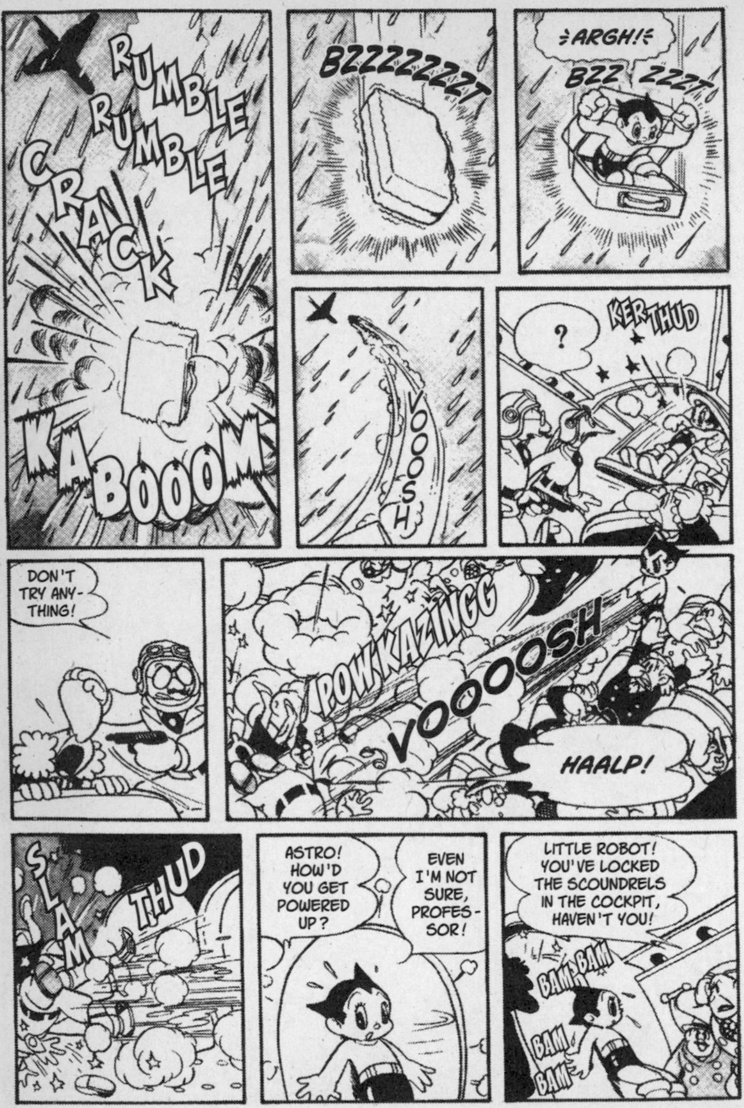
RUMBLE
RUMBLE
CRACK
KABOOOM
BZZZZZZZZT
ARGH!
BZZ ZZZT
VOOOOSH
?
KERTHUD
DON'T TRY ANY-THING!
POWKAZINGG
VOOOOOSH
HAALP!
SLAM
THUD
ASTRO! HOW'D YOU GET POWERED UP?
EVEN I'M NOT SURE, PROFES-SOR!
LITTLE ROBOT! YOU'VE LOCKED THE SCOUNDRELS IN THE COCKPIT, HAVEN'T YOU!
BAM BAM
BAM
BAM

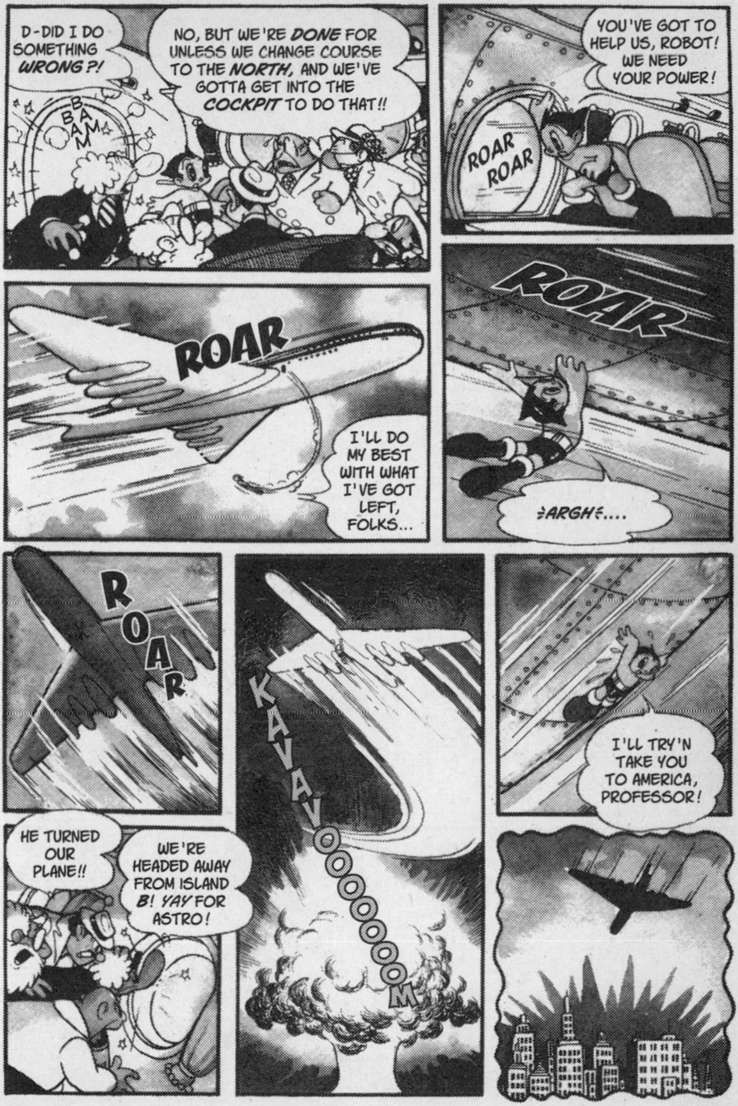
D-DID I DO SOMETHING *WRONG?!*
BAMM
NO, BUT WE'RE *DONE* FOR UNLESS WE CHANGE COURSE TO THE *NORTH,* AND WE'VE GOTTA GET INTO THE *COCKPIT* TO DO THAT!!
YOU'VE GOT TO HELP US, ROBOT! WE NEED YOUR POWER!
ROAR ROAR
ROAR
I'LL DO MY BEST WITH WHAT I'VE GOT LEFT, FOLKS...
ROAR
ARGH....
ROAR
KAVAVOOOOOOOOM
I'LL TRY'N TAKE YOU TO AMERICA, PROFESSOR!
HE TURNED OUR PLANE!!
WE'RE HEADED AWAY FROM ISLAND *B*! *YAY* FOR ASTRO!

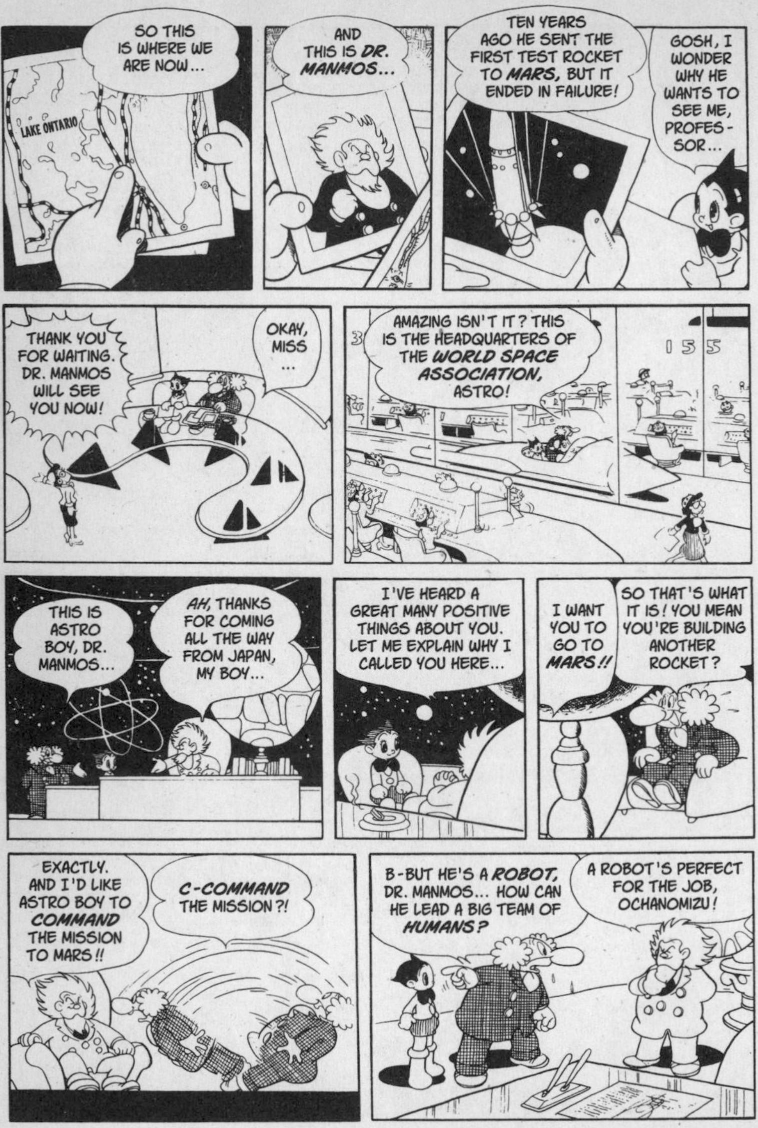
LAKE ONTARIO
SO THIS IS WHERE WE ARE NOW...
AND THIS IS DR. MANMOS...
TEN YEARS AGO HE SENT THE FIRST TEST ROCKET TO MARS, BUT IT ENDED IN FAILURE!
GOSH, I WONDER WHY HE WANTS TO SEE ME, PROFES-SOR...
THANK YOU FOR WAITING. DR. MANMOS WILL SEE YOU NOW!
OKAY, MISS ...
AMAZING ISN'T IT? THIS IS THE HEADQUARTERS OF THE WORLD SPACE ASSOCIATION, ASTRO!
THIS IS ASTRO BOY, DR. MANMOS...
AH, THANKS FOR COMING ALL THE WAY FROM JAPAN, MY BOY...
I'VE HEARD A GREAT MANY POSITIVE THINGS ABOUT YOU. LET ME EXPLAIN WHY I CALLED YOU HERE...
I WANT YOU TO GO TO MARS!!
SO THAT'S WHAT IT IS! YOU MEAN YOU'RE BUILDING ANOTHER ROCKET?
EXACTLY. AND I'D LIKE ASTRO BOY TO COMMAND THE MISSION TO MARS!!
C-COMMAND THE MISSION?!
B-BUT HE'S A ROBOT, DR. MANMOS... HOW CAN HE LEAD A BIG TEAM OF HUMANS?
A ROBOT'S PERFECT FOR THE JOB, OCHANOMIZU!

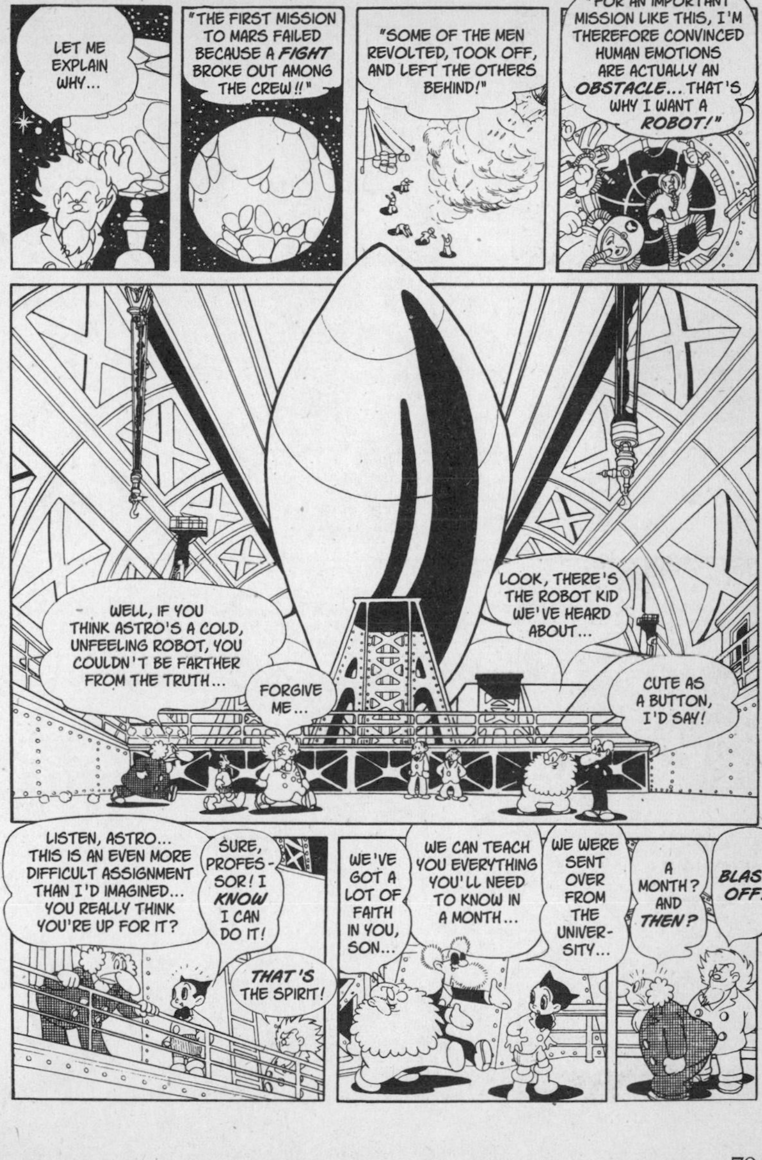
LET ME EXPLAIN WHY...
"THE FIRST MISSION TO MARS FAILED BECAUSE A FIGHT BROKE OUT AMONG THE CREW!!"
"SOME OF THE MEN REVOLTED, TOOK OFF, AND LEFT THE OTHERS BEHIND!"
"FOR AN IMPORTANT MISSION LIKE THIS, I'M THEREFORE CONVINCED HUMAN EMOTIONS ARE ACTUALLY AN OBSTACLE... THAT'S WHY I WANT A ROBOT!"
WELL, IF YOU THINK ASTRO'S A COLD, UNFEELING ROBOT, YOU COULDN'T BE FARTHER FROM THE TRUTH...
FORGIVE ME...
LOOK, THERE'S THE ROBOT KID WE'VE HEARD ABOUT...
CUTE AS A BUTTON, I'D SAY!
LISTEN, ASTRO... THIS IS AN EVEN MORE DIFFICULT ASSIGNMENT THAN I'D IMAGINED... YOU REALLY THINK YOU'RE UP FOR IT?
SURE, PROFES-SOR! I KNOW I CAN DO IT!
THAT'S THE SPIRIT!
WE'VE GOT A LOT OF FAITH IN YOU, SON...
WE CAN TEACH YOU EVERYTHING YOU'LL NEED TO KNOW IN A MONTH...
WE WERE SENT OVER FROM THE UNIVER-SITY...
A MONTH? AND THEN?
BLAST OFF!

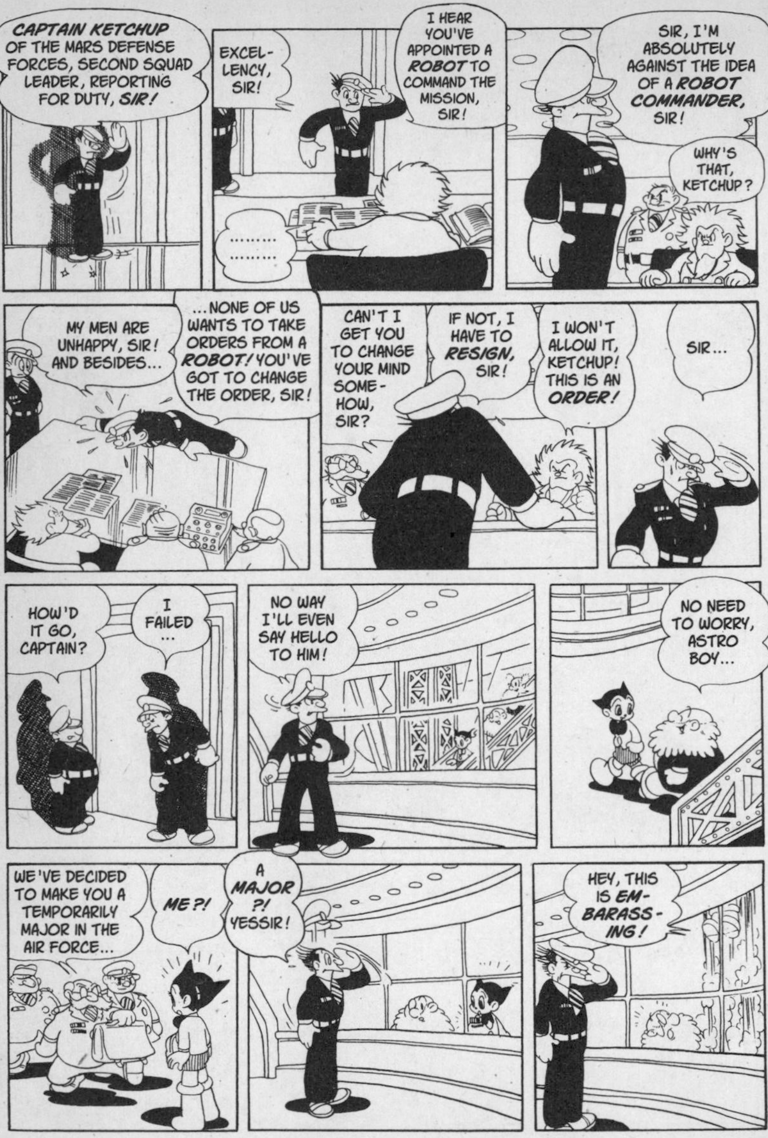
CAPTAIN KETCHUP OF THE MARS DEFENSE FORCES, SECOND SQUAD LEADER, REPORTING FOR DUTY, SIR!
EXCEL-LENCY, SIR!
I HEAR YOU'VE APPOINTED A ROBOT TO COMMAND THE MISSION, SIR!
....
....
SIR, I'M ABSOLUTELY AGAINST THE IDEA OF A ROBOT COMMANDER, SIR!
WHY'S THAT, KETCHUP?
MY MEN ARE UNHAPPY, SIR! AND BESIDES...
...NONE OF US WANTS TO TAKE ORDERS FROM A ROBOT! YOU'VE GOT TO CHANGE THE ORDER, SIR!
CAN'T I GET YOU TO CHANGE YOUR MIND SOME-HOW, SIR?
IF NOT, I HAVE TO RESIGN, SIR!
I WON'T ALLOW IT, KETCHUP! THIS IS AN ORDER!
SIR...
HOW'D IT GO, CAPTAIN?
I FAILED ...
NO WAY I'LL EVEN SAY HELLO TO HIM!
NO NEED TO WORRY, ASTRO BOY...
WE'VE DECIDED TO MAKE YOU A TEMPORARILY MAJOR IN THE AIR FORCE...
ME?!
A MAJOR ?! YESSIR!
...!
HEY, THIS IS EM-BARASS-ING!

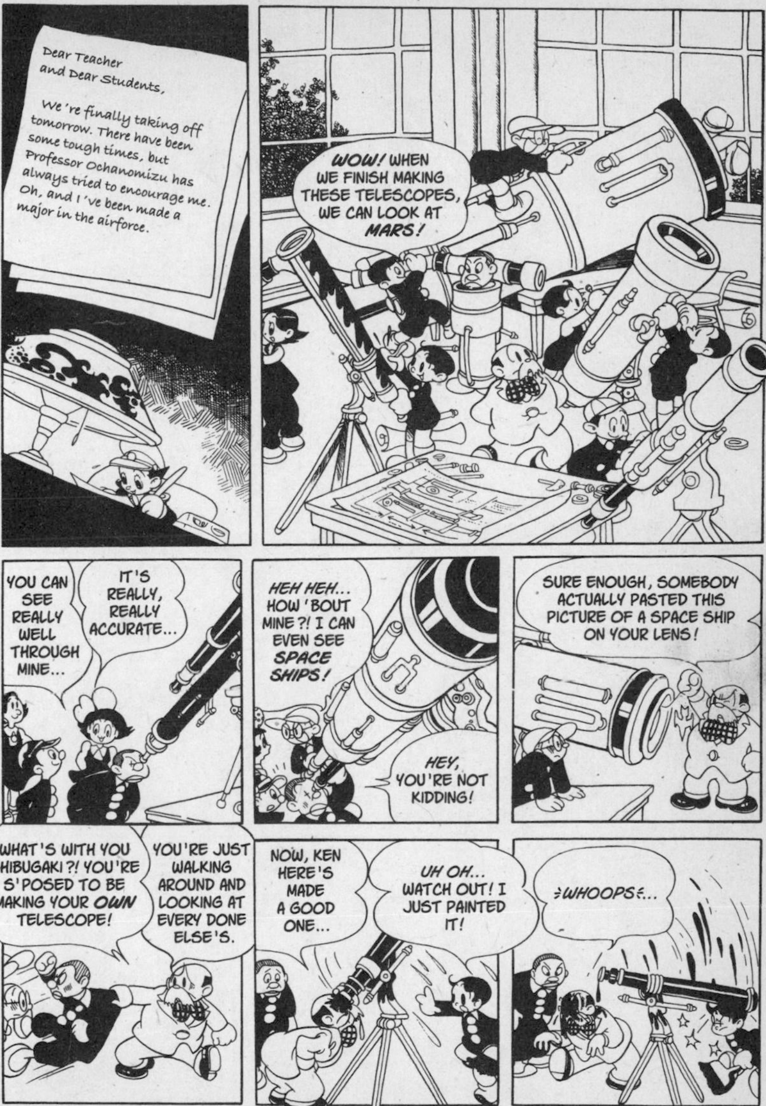
Dear Teacher
and Dear Students,
We're finally taking off tomorrow. There have been some tough times, but Professor Ochanomizu has always tried to encourage me. Oh, and I've been made a major in the airforce.
WOW! WHEN WE FINISH MAKING THESE TELESCOPES, WE CAN LOOK AT MARS!
YOU CAN SEE REALLY WELL THROUGH MINE...
IT'S REALLY, REALLY ACCURATE...
HEH HEH... HOW 'BOUT MINE?! I CAN EVEN SEE SPACE SHIPS!
HEY, YOU'RE NOT KIDDING!
SURE ENOUGH, SOMEBODY ACTUALLY PASTED THIS PICTURE OF A SPACE SHIP ON YOUR LENS!
WHAT'S WITH YOU SHIBUGAKI?! YOU'RE S'POSED TO BE MAKING YOUR OWN TELESCOPE!
YOU'RE JUST WALKING AROUND AND LOOKING AT EVERY DONE ELSE'S.
NOW, KEN HERE'S MADE A GOOD ONE...
UH OH... WATCH OUT! I JUST PAINTED IT!
WHOOPS...

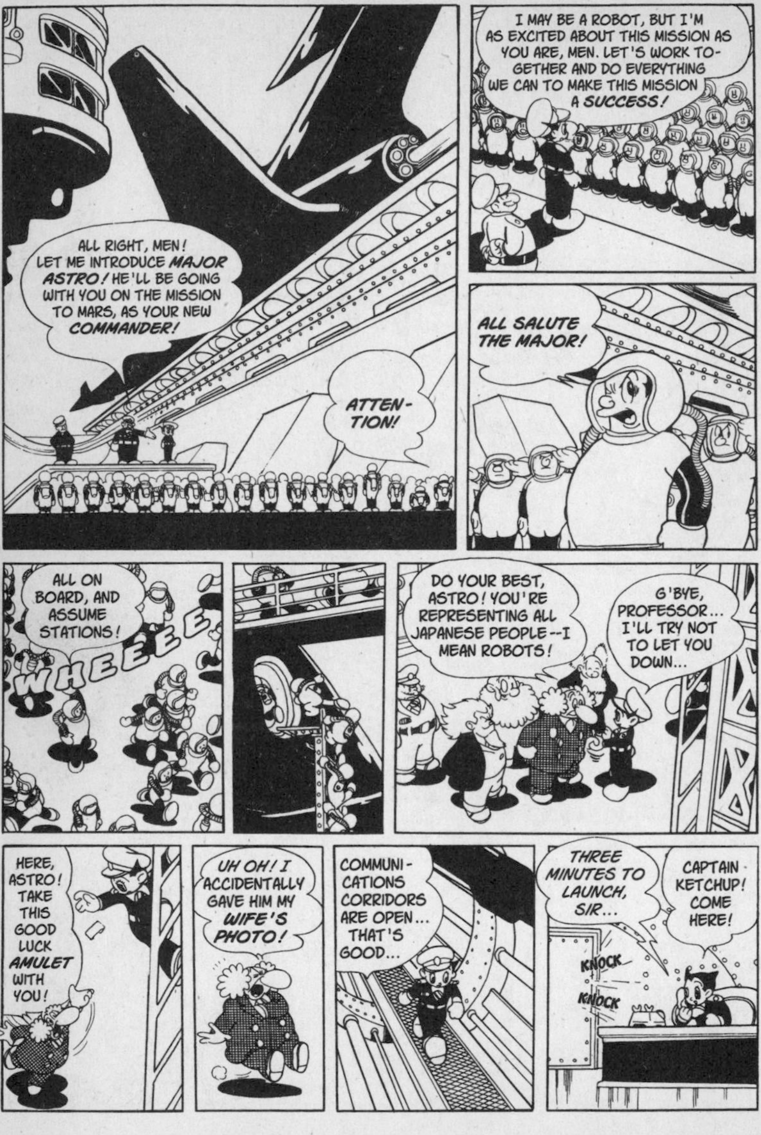
ALL RIGHT, MEN! LET ME INTRODUCE MAJOR ASTRO! HE'LL BE GOING WITH YOU ON THE MISSION TO MARS, AS YOUR NEW COMMANDER!
ATTEN-TION!
I MAY BE A ROBOT, BUT I'M AS EXCITED ABOUT THIS MISSION AS YOU ARE, MEN. LET'S WORK TO-GETHER AND DO EVERYTHING WE CAN TO MAKE THIS MISSION A SUCCESS!
ALL SALUTE THE MAJOR!
ALL ON BOARD, AND ASSUME STATIONS!
WHEEEE
DO YOUR BEST, ASTRO! YOU'RE REPRESENTING ALL JAPANESE PEOPLE--I MEAN ROBOTS!
G'BYE, PROFESSOR... I'LL TRY NOT TO LET YOU DOWN...
HERE, ASTRO! TAKE THIS GOOD LUCK AMULET WITH YOU!
UH OH! I ACCIDENTALLY GAVE HIM MY WIFE'S PHOTO!
COMMUNI-CATIONS CORRIDORS ARE OPEN... THAT'S GOOD...
THREE MINUTES TO LAUNCH, SIR...
KNOCK
KNOCK
CAPTAIN KETCHUP! COME HERE!

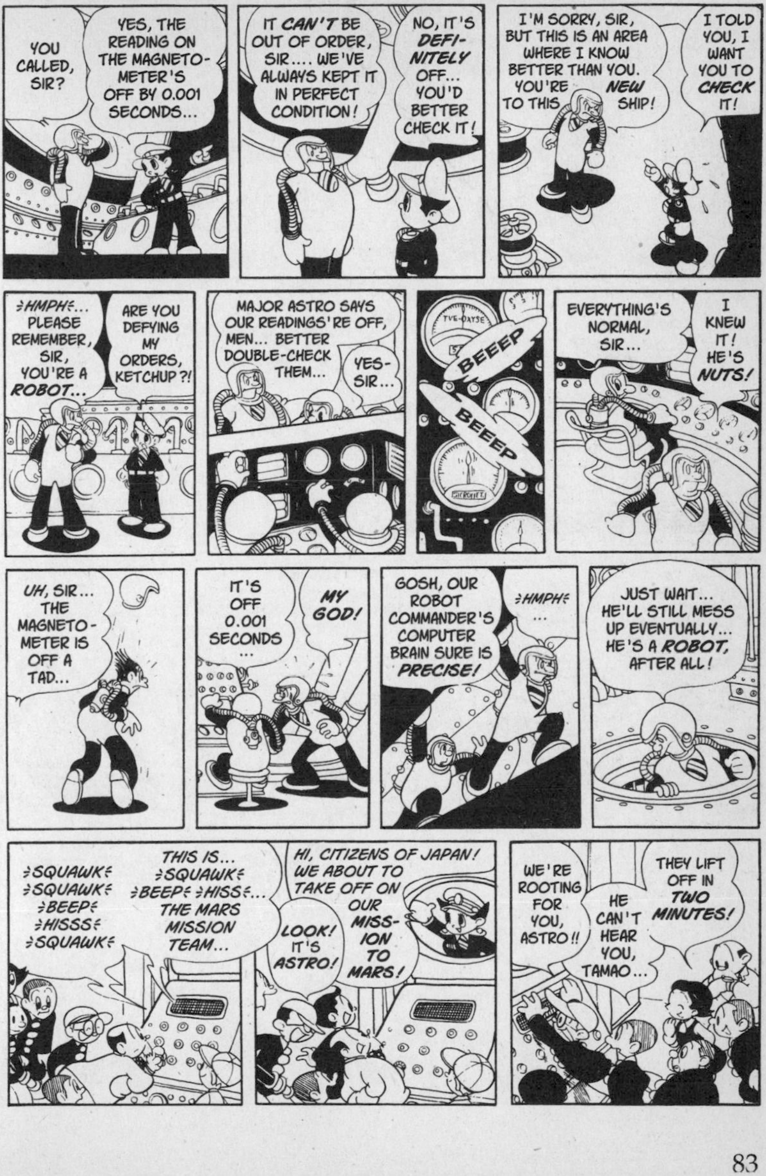
YOU CALLED, SIR?
YES, THE READING ON THE MAGNETO-METER'S OFF BY 0.001 SECONDS...
IT CAN'T BE OUT OF ORDER, SIR.... WE'VE ALWAYS KEPT IT IN PERFECT CONDITION!
NO, IT'S DEFI-NITELY OFF... YOU'D BETTER CHECK IT!
I'M SORRY, SIR, BUT THIS IS AN AREA WHERE I KNOW BETTER THAN YOU. YOU'RE NEW TO THIS SHIP!
I TOLD YOU, I WANT YOU TO CHECK IT!
HMPH... PLEASE REMEMBER, SIR, YOU'RE A ROBOT...
ARE YOU DEFYING MY ORDERS, KETCHUP?!
MAJOR ASTRO SAYS OUR READINGS'RE OFF, MEN... BETTER DOUBLE-CHECK THEM...
YES-SIR...
BEEEP
BEEEP
EVERYTHING'S NORMAL, SIR...
I KNEW IT! HE'S NUTS!
UH, SIR... THE MAGNETO-METER IS OFF A TAD...
IT'S OFF 0.001 SECONDS ...
MY GOD!
GOSH, OUR ROBOT COMMANDER'S COMPUTER BRAIN SURE IS PRECISE!
HMPH ...
JUST WAIT... HE'LL STILL MESS UP EVENTUALLY... HE'S A ROBOT, AFTER ALL!
SQUAWK SQUAWK BEEP HISSS SQUAWK
THIS IS... SQUAWK BEEP HISS... THE MARS MISSION TEAM...
HI, CITIZENS OF JAPAN! WE ABOUT TO TAKE OFF ON OUR MISS-ION TO MARS!
LOOK! IT'S ASTRO!
WE'RE ROOTING FOR YOU, ASTRO!!
HE CAN'T HEAR YOU, TAMAO...
THEY LIFT OFF IN TWO MINUTES!

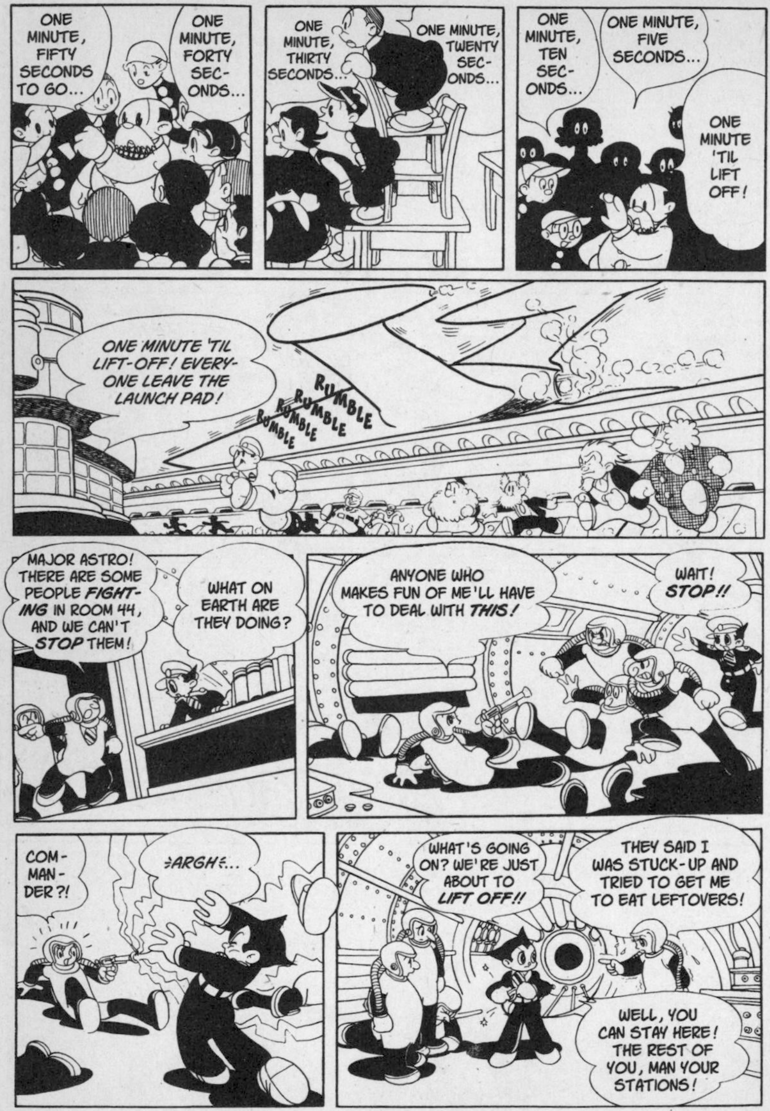
ONE MINUTE, FIFTY SECONDS TO GO...
ONE MINUTE, FORTY SEC-ONDS...
ONE MINUTE, THIRTY SECONDS...
ONE MINUTE, TWENTY SEC-ONDS...
ONE MINUTE, TEN SEC-ONDS...
ONE MINUTE, FIVE SECONDS...
ONE MINUTE 'TIL LIFT OFF!
ONE MINUTE 'TIL LIFT-OFF! EVERY-ONE LEAVE THE LAUNCH PAD!
RUMBLE RUMBLE RUMBLE RUMBLE
MAJOR ASTRO! THERE ARE SOME PEOPLE FIGHT-ING IN ROOM 44, AND WE CAN'T STOP THEM!
WHAT ON EARTH ARE THEY DOING?
ANYONE WHO MAKES FUN OF ME'LL HAVE TO DEAL WITH THIS!
WAIT! STOP!!
COM-MAN-DER?!
ARGH...
WHAT'S GOING ON? WE'RE JUST ABOUT TO LIFT OFF!!
THEY SAID I WAS STUCK-UP AND TRIED TO GET ME TO EAT LEFTOVERS!
WELL, YOU CAN STAY HERE! THE REST OF YOU, MAN YOUR STATIONS!

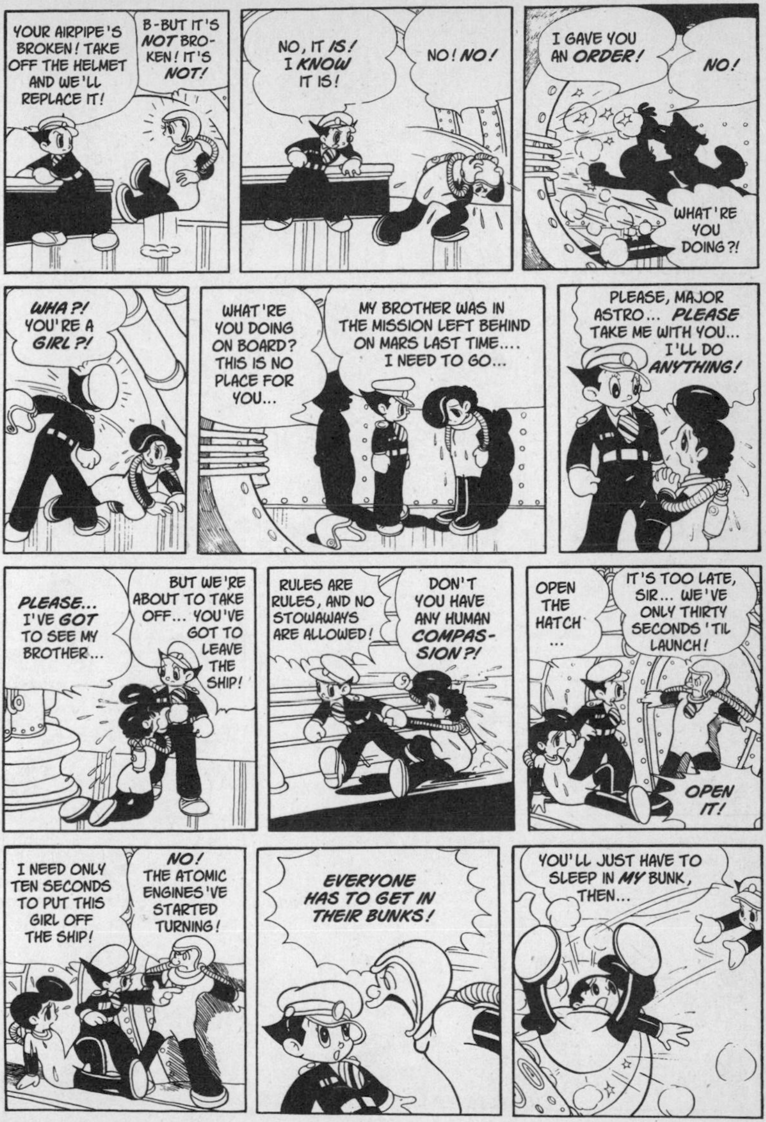
YOUR AIRPIPE'S BROKEN! TAKE OFF THE HELMET AND WE'LL REPLACE IT!
B-BUT IT'S NOT BRO-KEN! IT'S NOT!
NO, IT IS! I KNOW IT IS!
NO! NO!
I GAVE YOU AN ORDER!
NO!
WHAT'RE YOU DOING?!
WHA?! YOU'RE A GIRL?!
WHAT'RE YOU DOING ON BOARD? THIS IS NO PLACE FOR YOU...
MY BROTHER WAS IN THE MISSION LEFT BEHIND ON MARS LAST TIME.... I NEED TO GO...
PLEASE, MAJOR ASTRO... PLEASE TAKE ME WITH YOU... I'LL DO ANYTHING!
PLEASE... I'VE GOT TO SEE MY BROTHER...
BUT WE'RE ABOUT TO TAKE OFF... YOU'VE GOT TO LEAVE THE SHIP!
RULES ARE RULES, AND NO STOWAWAYS ARE ALLOWED!
DON'T YOU HAVE ANY HUMAN COMPAS-SION?!
OPEN THE HATCH ...
IT'S TOO LATE, SIR... WE'VE ONLY THIRTY SECONDS 'TIL LAUNCH!
OPEN IT!
I NEED ONLY TEN SECONDS TO PUT THIS GIRL OFF THE SHIP!
NO! THE ATOMIC ENGINES'VE STARTED TURNING!
EVERYONE HAS TO GET IN THEIR BUNKS!
YOU'LL JUST HAVE TO SLEEP IN MY BUNK, THEN...

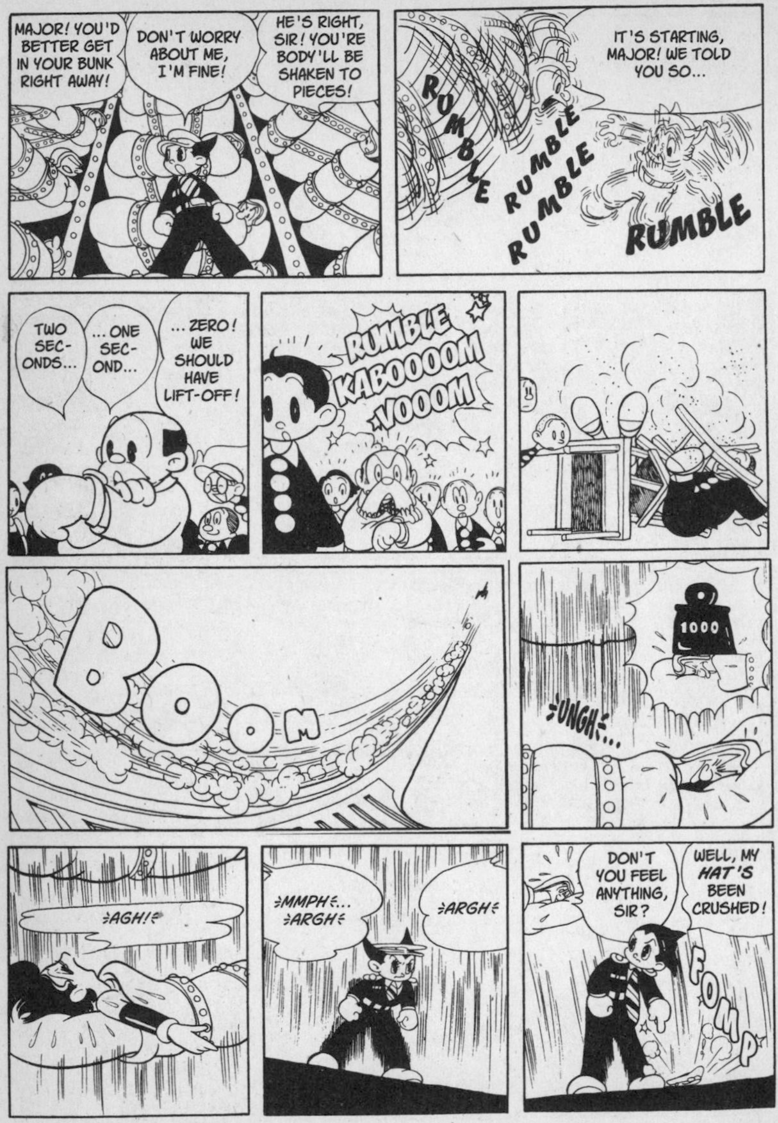
MAJOR! YOU'D BETTER GET IN YOUR BUNK RIGHT AWAY!
DON'T WORRY ABOUT ME, I'M FINE!
HE'S RIGHT, SIR! YOU'RE BODY'LL BE SHAKEN TO PIECES!
IT'S STARTING, MAJOR! WE TOLD YOU SO...
RUMBLE
RUMBLE
RUMBLE
RUMBLE
TWO SEC-ONDS...
... ONE SEC-OND...
... ZERO! WE SHOULD HAVE LIFT-OFF!
RUMBLE
KABOOOOM
VOOOM
BOOOM
1000
UNGH...
AGH!
MMPH...
ARGH
ARGH
DON'T YOU FEEL ANYTHING, SIR?
WELL, MY *HAT'S* BEEN CRUSHED!
FOMP

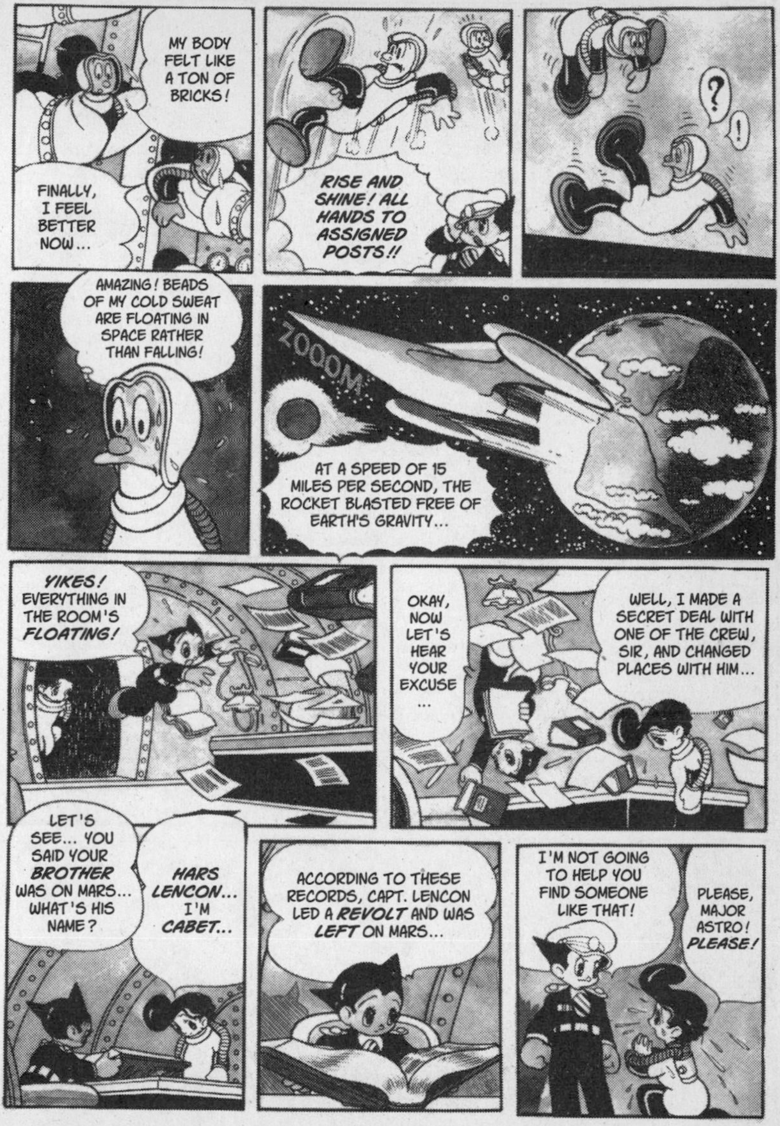
MY BODY FELT LIKE A TON OF BRICKS!
FINALLY, I FEEL BETTER NOW...
RISE AND SHINE! ALL HANDS TO ASSIGNED POSTS!!
?
!
AMAZING! BEADS OF MY COLD SWEAT ARE FLOATING IN SPACE RATHER THAN FALLING!
ZOOOM
AT A SPEED OF 15 MILES PER SECOND, THE ROCKET BLASTED FREE OF EARTH'S GRAVITY...
YIKES! EVERYTHING IN THE ROOM'S FLOATING!
OKAY, NOW LET'S HEAR YOUR EXCUSE ...
WELL, I MADE A SECRET DEAL WITH ONE OF THE CREW, SIR, AND CHANGED PLACES WITH HIM...
LET'S SEE... YOU SAID YOUR BROTHER WAS ON MARS... WHAT'S HIS NAME?
HARS LENCON... I'M CABET...
ACCORDING TO THESE RECORDS, CAPT. LENCON LED A REVOLT AND WAS LEFT ON MARS...
I'M NOT GOING TO HELP YOU FIND SOMEONE LIKE THAT!
PLEASE, MAJOR ASTRO! PLEASE!

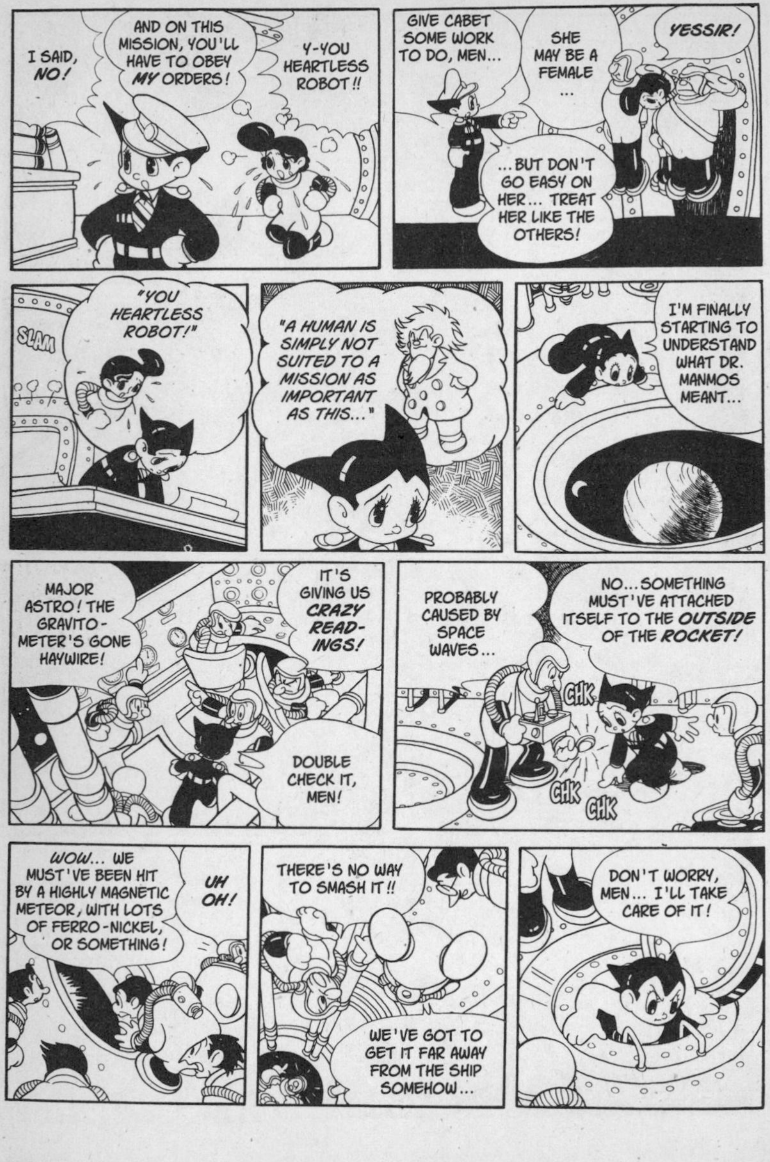
I SAID, NO!
AND ON THIS MISSION, YOU'LL HAVE TO OBEY MY ORDERS!
Y-YOU HEARTLESS ROBOT!!
GIVE CABET SOME WORK TO DO, MEN...
SHE MAY BE A FEMALE ...
...BUT DON'T GO EASY ON HER... TREAT HER LIKE THE OTHERS!
YESSIR!
SLAM
"YOU HEARTLESS ROBOT!"
"A HUMAN IS SIMPLY NOT SUITED TO A MISSION AS IMPORTANT AS THIS..."
I'M FINALLY STARTING TO UNDERSTAND WHAT DR. MANMOS MEANT...
MAJOR ASTRO! THE GRAVITO-METER'S GONE HAYWIRE!
IT'S GIVING US CRAZY READ-INGS!
DOUBLE CHECK IT, MEN!
PROBABLY CAUSED BY SPACE WAVES...
NO... SOMETHING MUST'VE ATTACHED ITSELF TO THE OUTSIDE OF THE ROCKET!
CHK
CHK
CHK
WOW... WE MUST'VE BEEN HIT BY A HIGHLY MAGNETIC METEOR, WITH LOTS OF FERRO-NICKEL, OR SOMETHING!
UH OH!
THERE'S NO WAY TO SMASH IT!!
WE'VE GOT TO GET IT FAR AWAY FROM THE SHIP SOMEHOW...
DON'T WORRY, MEN... I'LL TAKE CARE OF IT!

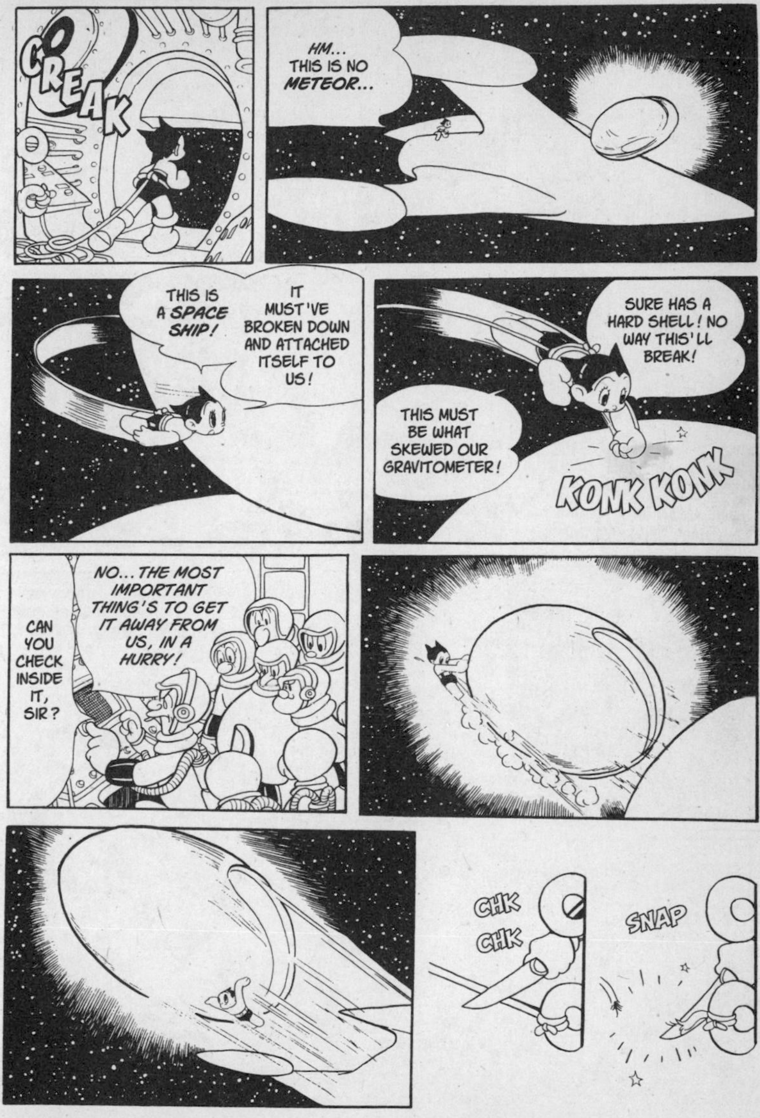
CREAK
HM... THIS IS NO METEOR...
THIS IS A SPACE SHIP!
IT MUST'VE BROKEN DOWN AND ATTACHED ITSELF TO US!
SURE HAS A HARD SHELL! NO WAY THIS'LL BREAK!
THIS MUST BE WHAT SKEWED OUR GRAVITOMETER!
KONK KONK
CAN YOU CHECK INSIDE IT, SIR?
NO... THE MOST IMPORTANT THING'S TO GET IT AWAY FROM US, IN A HURRY!
CHK CHK
SNAP

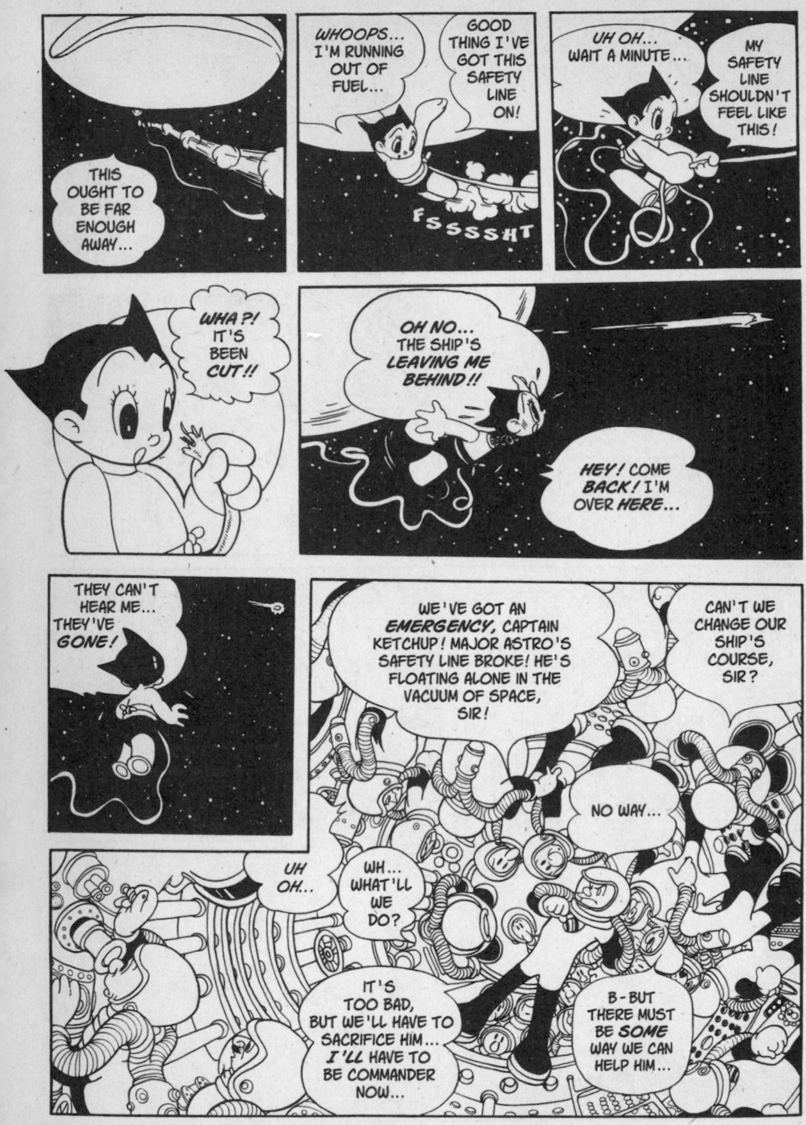
THIS OUGHT TO BE FAR ENOUGH AWAY...
WHOOPS... I'M RUNNING OUT OF FUEL...
GOOD THING I'VE GOT THIS SAFETY LINE ON!
FSSSSHT
UH OH... WAIT A MINUTE...
MY SAFETY LINE SHOULDN'T FEEL LIKE THIS!
WHA?! IT'S BEEN CUT!!
OH NO... THE SHIP'S LEAVING ME BEHIND!!
HEY! COME BACK! I'M OVER HERE...
THEY CAN'T HEAR ME... THEY'VE GONE!
WE'VE GOT AN EMERGENCY, CAPTAIN KETCHUP! MAJOR ASTRO'S SAFETY LINE BROKE! HE'S FLOATING ALONE IN THE VACUUM OF SPACE, SIR!
CAN'T WE CHANGE OUR SHIP'S COURSE, SIR?
NO WAY...
UH OH...
WH... WHAT'LL WE DO?
IT'S TOO BAD, BUT WE'LL HAVE TO SACRIFICE HIM... I'LL HAVE TO BE COMMANDER NOW...
B-BUT THERE MUST BE SOME WAY WE CAN HELP HIM...

GOSH, I...I MIGHT BE STUCK FLOATING HERE FOREVER!

WAIT A MINUTE... I'VE STILL GOT THIS SPACE SHIP HERE...

IF I CAN GET INSIDE IT, MAYBE I CAN DO SOMETHING...

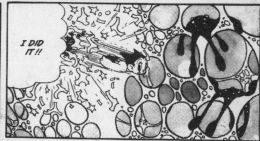

I DID IT!!

WH... WHAT IS THIS THING?

THIS IS NO EARTH SPACE SHIP...

IT MUST BE A SHIP USED BY *ALIENS!!*

91

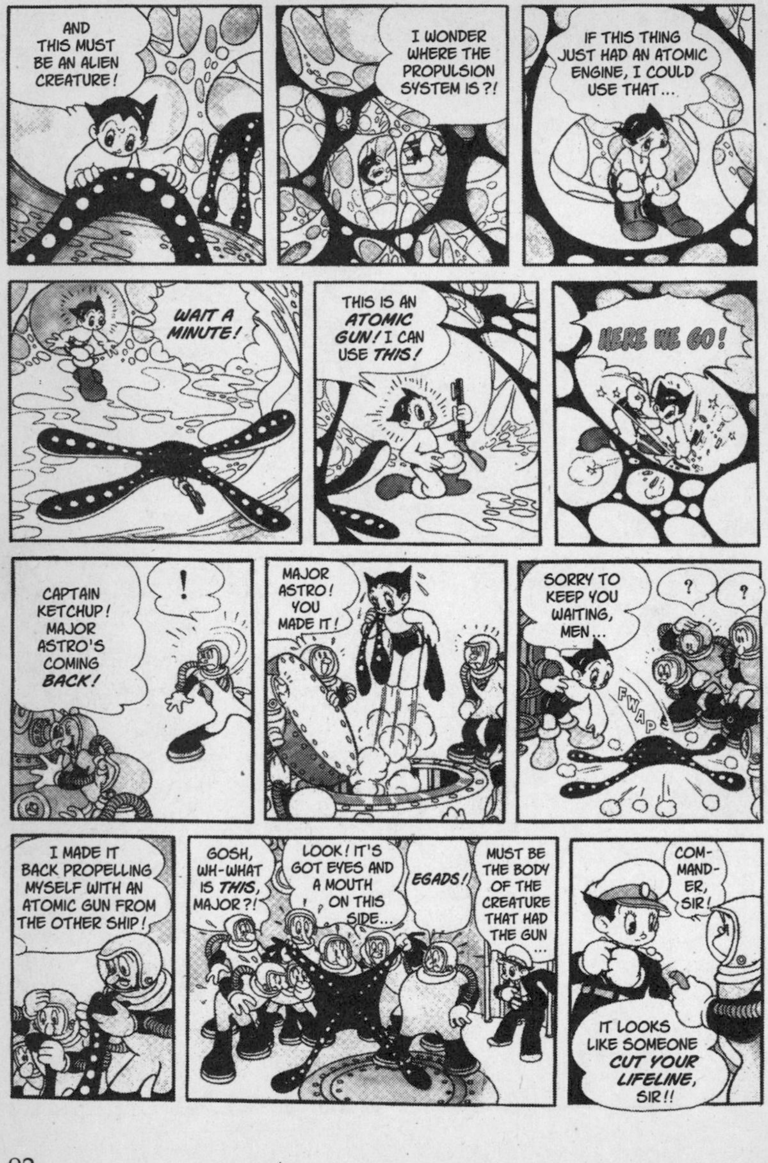
AND THIS MUST BE AN ALIEN CREATURE!
I WONDER WHERE THE PROPULSION SYSTEM IS?!
IF THIS THING JUST HAD AN ATOMIC ENGINE, I COULD USE THAT...
WAIT A MINUTE!
THIS IS AN ATOMIC GUN! I CAN USE THIS!
HERE WE GO!
CAPTAIN KETCHUP! MAJOR ASTRO'S COMING BACK!
!
MAJOR ASTRO! YOU MADE IT!
SORRY TO KEEP YOU WAITING, MEN...
?
?
FWAP
I MADE IT BACK PROPELLING MYSELF WITH AN ATOMIC GUN FROM THE OTHER SHIP!
GOSH, WH-WHAT IS THIS, MAJOR?!
LOOK! IT'S GOT EYES AND A MOUTH ON THIS SIDE...
EGADS!
MUST BE THE BODY OF THE CREATURE THAT HAD THE GUN...
COM-MANDER, SIR!
IT LOOKS LIKE SOMEONE CUT YOUR LIFELINE, SIR!!

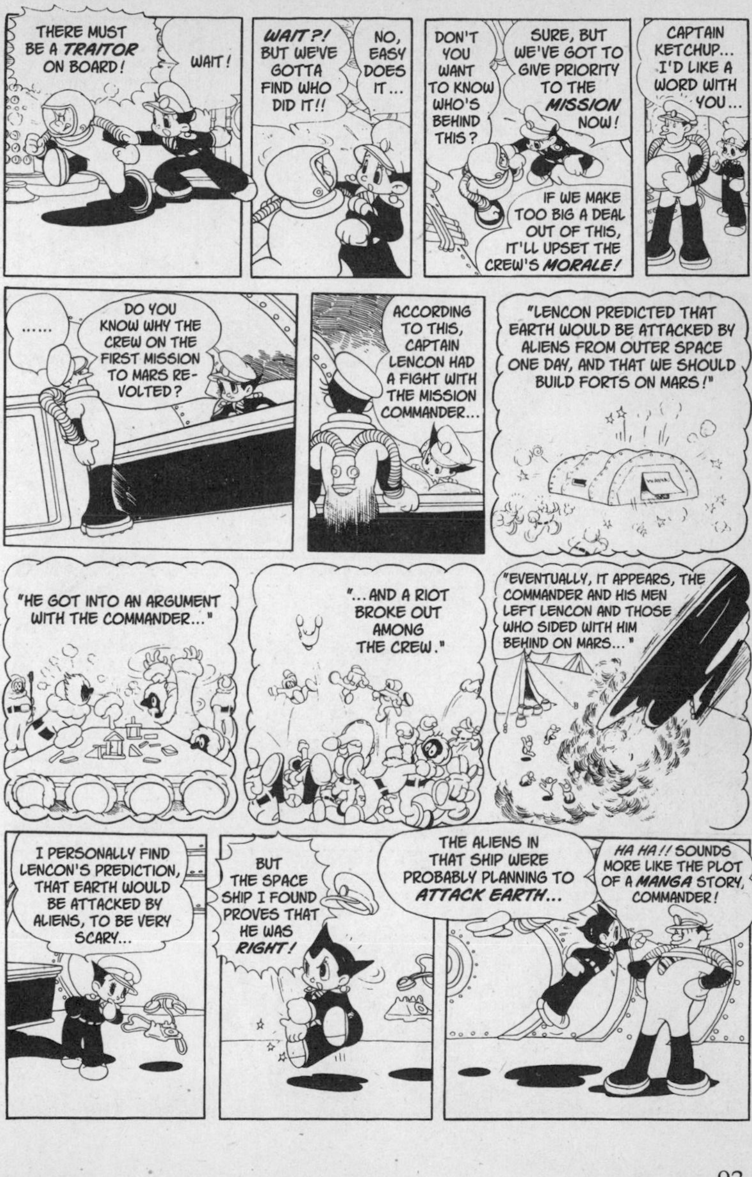

THERE MUST BE A TRAITOR ON BOARD!
WAIT!
WAIT?! BUT WE'VE GOTTA FIND WHO DID IT!!
NO, EASY DOES IT...
DON'T YOU WANT TO KNOW WHO'S BEHIND THIS?
SURE, BUT WE'VE GOT TO GIVE PRIORITY TO THE MISSION NOW!
IF WE MAKE TOO BIG A DEAL OUT OF THIS, IT'LL UPSET THE CREW'S MORALE!
CAPTAIN KETCHUP... I'D LIKE A WORD WITH YOU...
......
DO YOU KNOW WHY THE CREW ON THE FIRST MISSION TO MARS RE-VOLTED?
ACCORDING TO THIS, CAPTAIN LENCON HAD A FIGHT WITH THE MISSION COMMANDER...
"LENCON PREDICTED THAT EARTH WOULD BE ATTACKED BY ALIENS FROM OUTER SPACE ONE DAY, AND THAT WE SHOULD BUILD FORTS ON MARS!"
"HE GOT INTO AN ARGUMENT WITH THE COMMANDER..."
"...AND A RIOT BROKE OUT AMONG THE CREW."
"EVENTUALLY, IT APPEARS, THE COMMANDER AND HIS MEN LEFT LENCON AND THOSE WHO SIDED WITH HIM BEHIND ON MARS..."
I PERSONALLY FIND LENCON'S PREDICTION, THAT EARTH WOULD BE ATTACKED BY ALIENS, TO BE VERY SCARY...
BUT THE SPACE SHIP I FOUND PROVES THAT HE WAS RIGHT!
THE ALIENS IN THAT SHIP WERE PROBABLY PLANNING TO ATTACK EARTH...
HA HA!! SOUNDS MORE LIKE THE PLOT OF A MANGA STORY, COMMANDER!

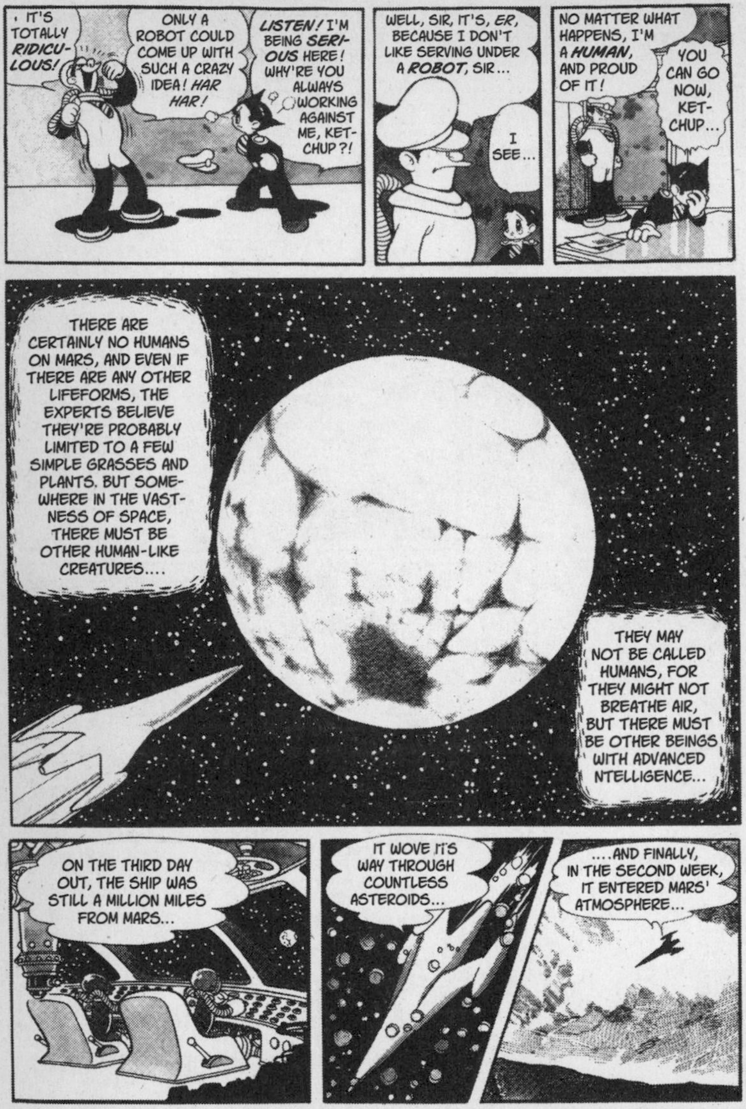
IT'S TOTALLY RIDICULOUS!
ONLY A ROBOT COULD COME UP WITH SUCH A CRAZY IDEA! HAR HAR!
LISTEN! I'M BEING SERIOUS HERE! WHY'RE YOU ALWAYS WORKING AGAINST ME, KETCHUP?!
WELL, SIR, IT'S, ER, BECAUSE I DON'T LIKE SERVING UNDER A ROBOT, SIR...
I SEE...
NO MATTER WHAT HAPPENS, I'M A HUMAN, AND PROUD OF IT!
YOU CAN GO NOW, KETCHUP...
THERE ARE CERTAINLY NO HUMANS ON MARS, AND EVEN IF THERE ARE ANY OTHER LIFEFORMS, THE EXPERTS BELIEVE THEY'RE PROBABLY LIMITED TO A FEW SIMPLE GRASSES AND PLANTS. BUT SOMEWHERE IN THE VASTNESS OF SPACE, THERE MUST BE OTHER HUMAN-LIKE CREATURES....
THEY MAY NOT BE CALLED HUMANS, FOR THEY MIGHT NOT BREATHE AIR, BUT THERE MUST BE OTHER BEINGS WITH ADVANCED NTELLIGENCE...
ON THE THIRD DAY OUT, THE SHIP WAS STILL A MILLION MILES FROM MARS...
IT WOVE IT'S WAY THROUGH COUNTLESS ASTEROIDS...
....AND FINALLY, IN THE SECOND WEEK, IT ENTERED MARS' ATMOSPHERE...

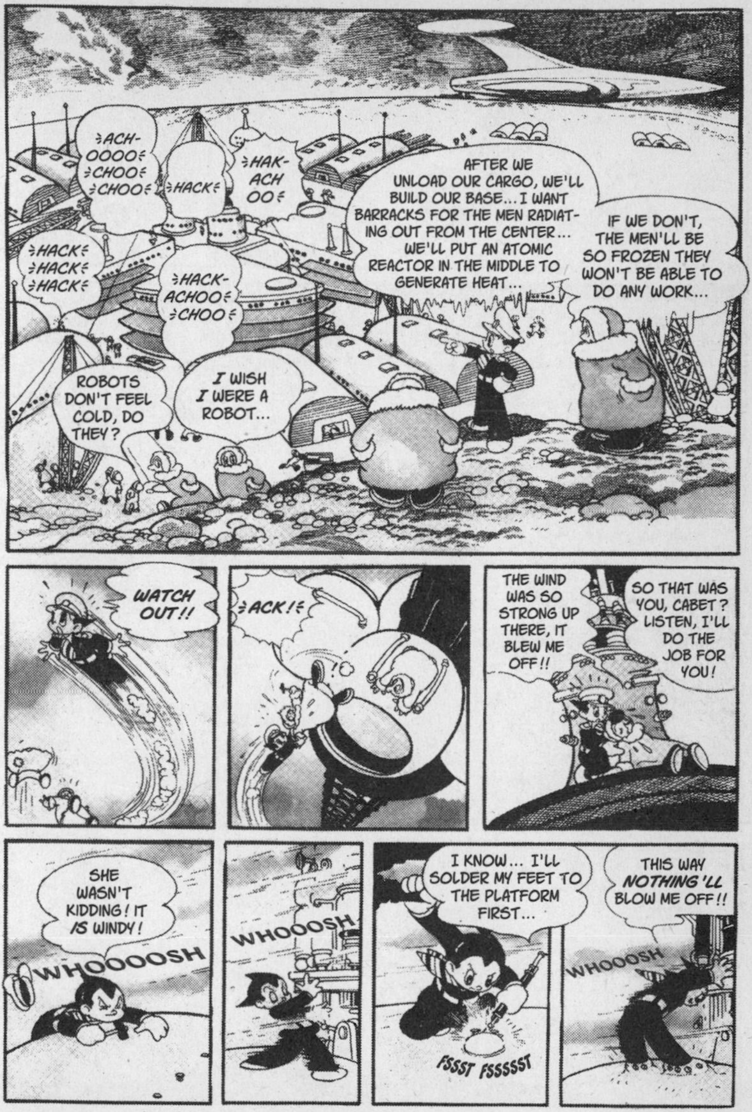
ACH-OOOO CHOO CHOO
HACK
HAK-ACH OO
HACK HACK HACK
HACK-ACHOO CHOO
AFTER WE UNLOAD OUR CARGO, WE'LL BUILD OUR BASE... I WANT BARRACKS FOR THE MEN RADIATING OUT FROM THE CENTER... WE'LL PUT AN ATOMIC REACTOR IN THE MIDDLE TO GENERATE HEAT...
IF WE DON'T, THE MEN'LL BE SO FROZEN THEY WON'T BE ABLE TO DO ANY WORK...
ROBOTS DON'T FEEL COLD, DO THEY?
I WISH I WERE A ROBOT...
WATCH OUT!!
ACK!
THE WIND WAS SO STRONG UP THERE, IT BLEW ME OFF!!
SO THAT WAS YOU, CABET? LISTEN, I'LL DO THE JOB FOR YOU!
SHE WASN'T KIDDING! IT IS WINDY!
WHOOOOOSH
WHOOOSH
I KNOW... I'LL SOLDER MY FEET TO THE PLATFORM FIRST...
FSSST FSSSSST
THIS WAY NOTHING'LL BLOW ME OFF!!
WHOOOSH

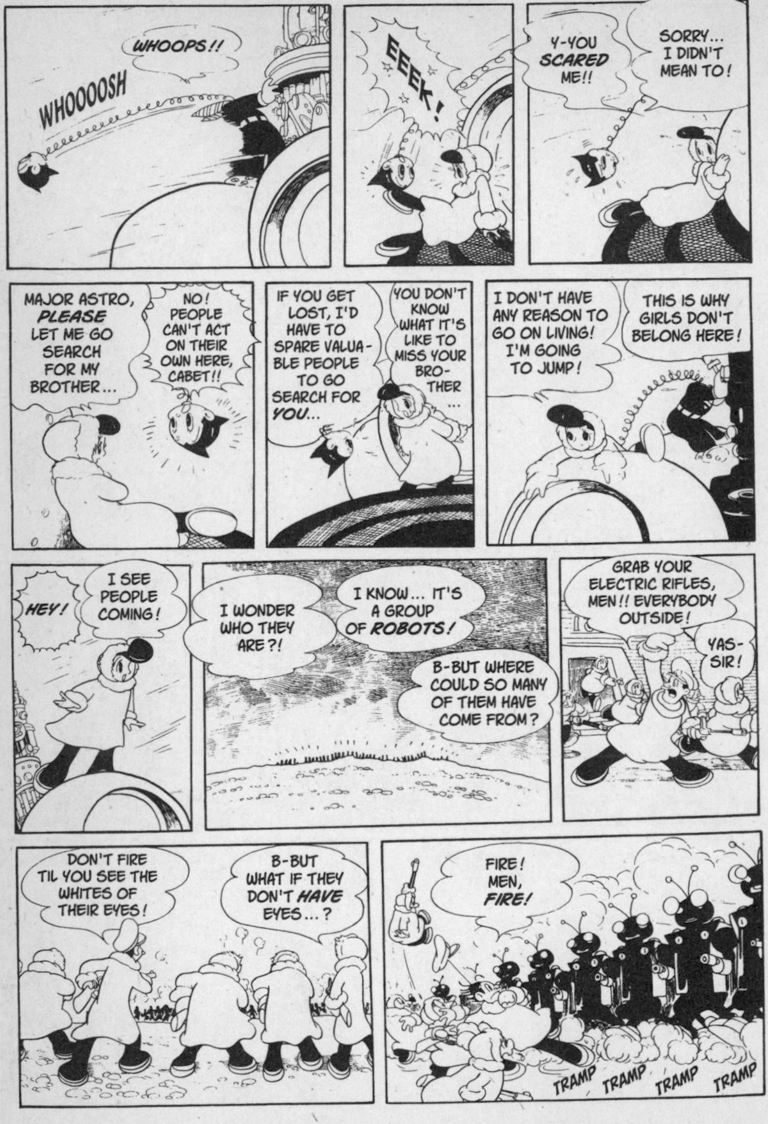

WHOOOOSH
WHOOPS!!
EEEK!
Y-YOU SCARED ME!!
SORRY... I DIDN'T MEAN TO!
MAJOR ASTRO, PLEASE LET ME GO SEARCH FOR MY BROTHER...
NO! PEOPLE CAN'T ACT ON THEIR OWN HERE, CABET!!
IF YOU GET LOST, I'D HAVE TO SPARE VALUA-BLE PEOPLE TO GO SEARCH FOR YOU...
YOU DON'T KNOW WHAT IT'S LIKE TO MISS YOUR BRO-THER ...
I DON'T HAVE ANY REASON TO GO ON LIVING! I'M GOING TO JUMP!
THIS IS WHY GIRLS DON'T BELONG HERE!
HEY!
I SEE PEOPLE COMING!
I WONDER WHO THEY ARE?!
I KNOW... IT'S A GROUP OF ROBOTS!
B-BUT WHERE COULD SO MANY OF THEM HAVE COME FROM?
GRAB YOUR ELECTRIC RIFLES, MEN!! EVERYBODY OUTSIDE!
YAS-SIR!
DON'T FIRE TIL YOU SEE THE WHITES OF THEIR EYES!
B-BUT WHAT IF THEY DON'T HAVE EYES...?
FIRE! MEN, FIRE!
TRAMP TRAMP TRAMP TRAMP

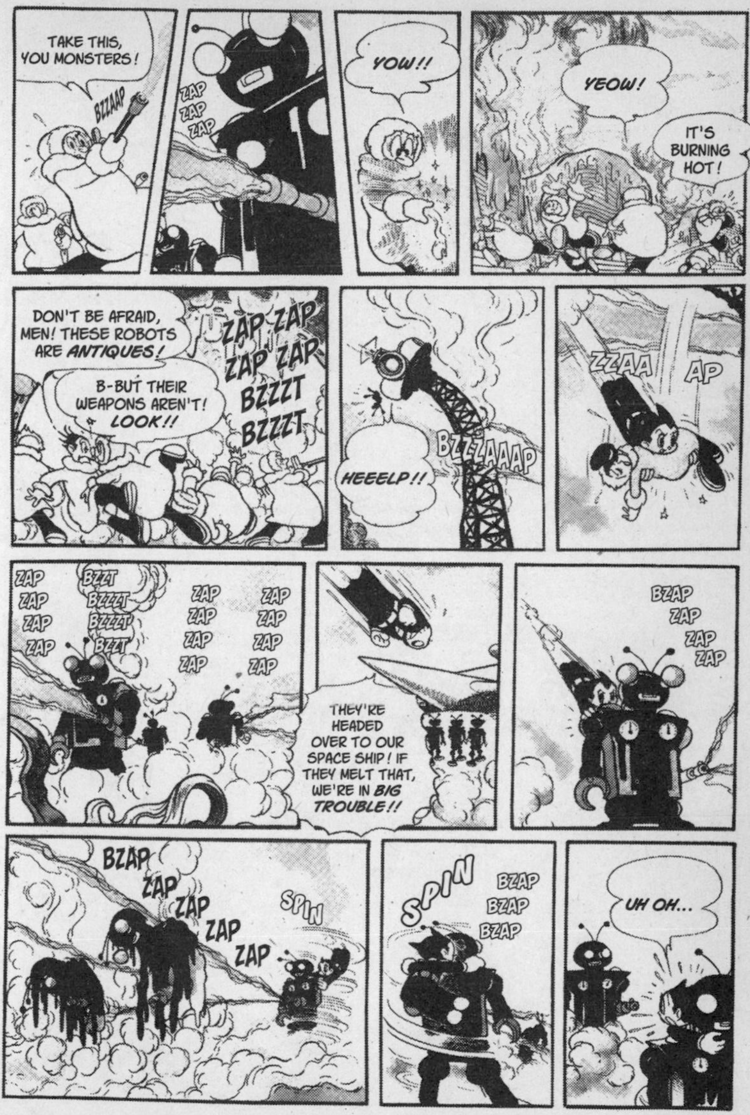
TAKE THIS, YOU MONSTERS!
BZZAAP
ZAP ZAP ZAP
YOW!!
YEOW!
IT'S BURNING HOT!
DON'T BE AFRAID, MEN! THESE ROBOTS ARE *ANTIQUES!*
B-BUT THEIR WEAPONS AREN'T! *LOOK!!*
ZAP ZAP ZAP ZAP BZZZT BZZZT
HEEELP!!
BZZZAAAP
ZZAAA AP
ZAP ZAP ZAP ZAP
BZZT BZZZT BZZZT BZZT
ZAP ZAP ZAP ZAP
ZAP ZAP ZAP ZAP
THEY'RE HEADED OVER TO OUR SPACE SHIP! IF THEY MELT THAT, WE'RE IN *BIG TROUBLE!!*
BZAP ZAP ZAP ZAP
BZAP ZAP ZAP ZAP ZAP
SPIN
SPIN
BZAP BZAP BZAP
UH OH...

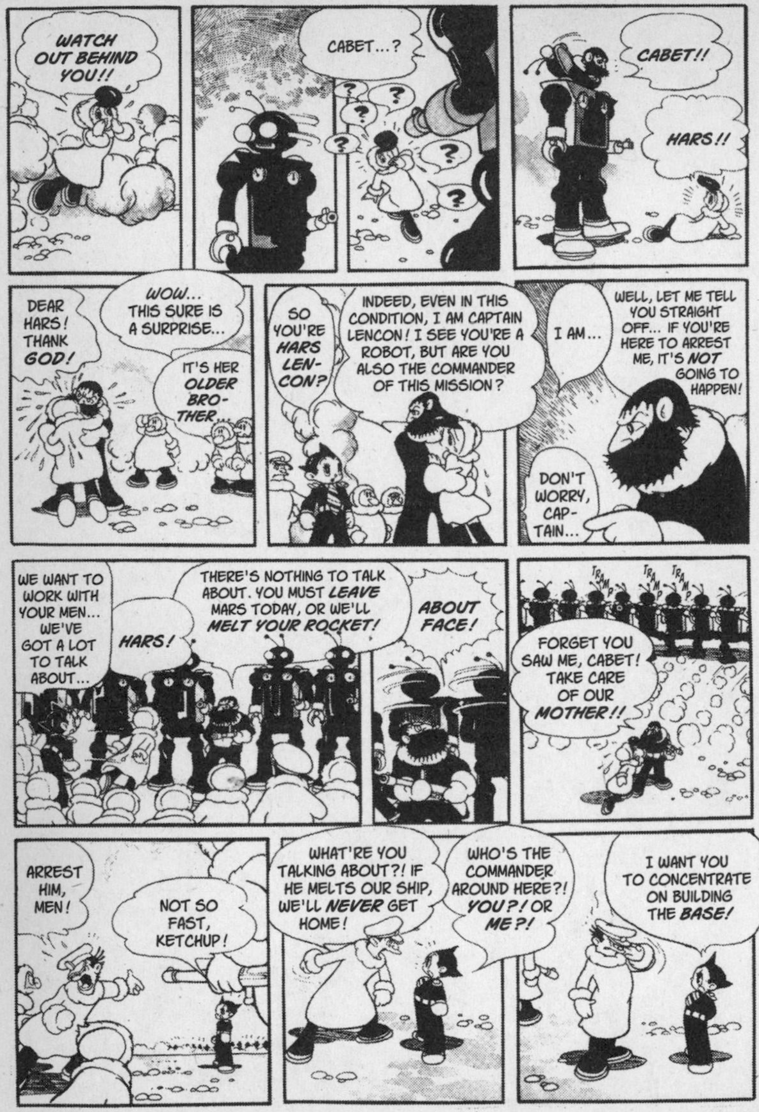
WATCH OUT BEHIND YOU!!
CABET...?
CABET!!
HARS!!
DEAR HARS! THANK GOD!
WOW... THIS SURE IS A SURPRISE...
IT'S HER OLDER BROTHER...
SO YOU'RE HARS LENCON?
INDEED, EVEN IN THIS CONDITION, I AM CAPTAIN LENCON! I SEE YOU'RE A ROBOT, BUT ARE YOU ALSO THE COMMANDER OF THIS MISSION?
I AM...
WELL, LET ME TELL YOU STRAIGHT OFF... IF YOU'RE HERE TO ARREST ME, IT'S NOT GOING TO HAPPEN!
DON'T WORRY, CAPTAIN...
WE WANT TO WORK WITH YOUR MEN... WE'VE GOT A LOT TO TALK ABOUT...
HARS!
THERE'S NOTHING TO TALK ABOUT. YOU MUST LEAVE MARS TODAY, OR WE'LL MELT YOUR ROCKET!
ABOUT FACE!
TRAMP TRAMP TRAMP
FORGET YOU SAW ME, CABET! TAKE CARE OF OUR MOTHER!!
ARREST HIM, MEN!
NOT SO FAST, KETCHUP!
WHAT'RE YOU TALKING ABOUT?! IF HE MELTS OUR SHIP, WE'LL NEVER GET HOME!
WHO'S THE COMMANDER AROUND HERE?! YOU?! OR ME?!
I WANT YOU TO CONCENTRATE ON BUILDING THE BASE!

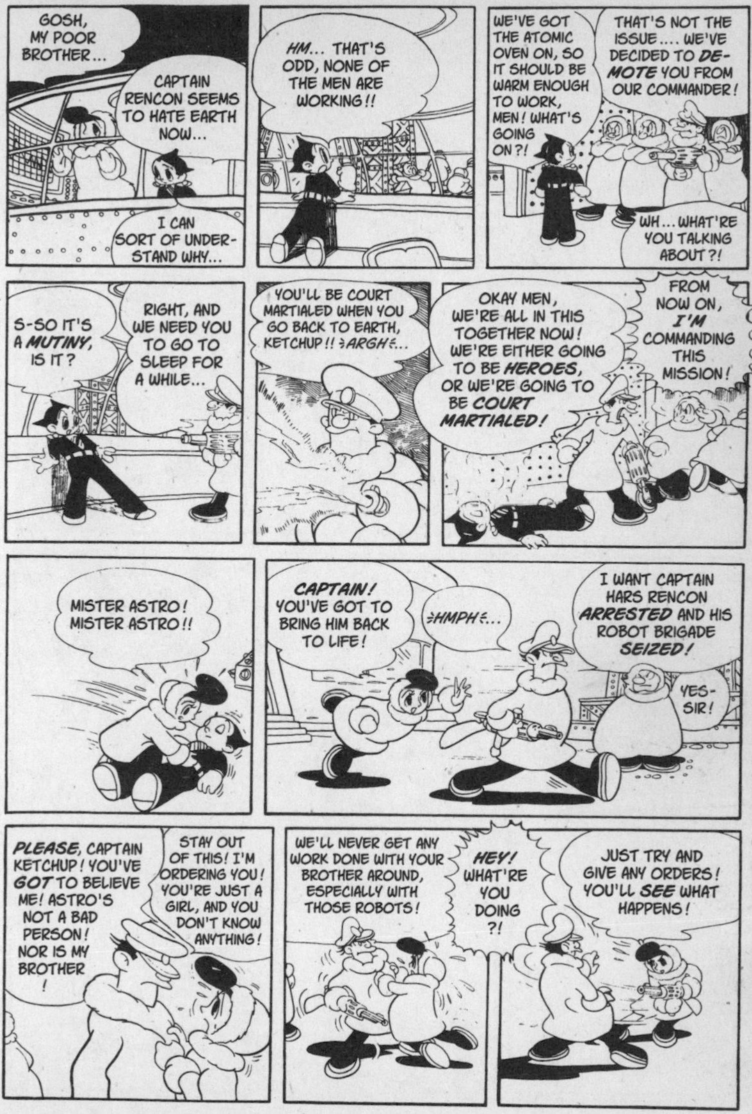
GOSH, MY POOR BROTHER...
CAPTAIN RENCON SEEMS TO HATE EARTH NOW...
I CAN SORT OF UNDER-STAND WHY...
HM... THAT'S ODD, NONE OF THE MEN ARE WORKING!!
WE'VE GOT THE ATOMIC OVEN ON, SO IT SHOULD BE WARM ENOUGH TO WORK, MEN! WHAT'S GOING ON?!
THAT'S NOT THE ISSUE.... WE'VE DECIDED TO DE-MOTE YOU FROM OUR COMMANDER!
WH... WHAT'RE YOU TALKING ABOUT?!
S-SO IT'S A MUTINY, IS IT?
RIGHT, AND WE NEED YOU TO GO TO SLEEP FOR A WHILE...
YOU'LL BE COURT MARTIALED WHEN YOU GO BACK TO EARTH, KETCHUP!! ARGH...
OKAY MEN, WE'RE ALL IN THIS TOGETHER NOW! WE'RE EITHER GOING TO BE HEROES, OR WE'RE GOING TO BE COURT MARTIALED!
FROM NOW ON, I'M COMMANDING THIS MISSION!
MISTER ASTRO! MISTER ASTRO!!
CAPTAIN! YOU'VE GOT TO BRING HIM BACK TO LIFE!
HMPH...
I WANT CAPTAIN HARS RENCON ARRESTED AND HIS ROBOT BRIGADE SEIZED!
YES-SIR!
PLEASE, CAPTAIN KETCHUP! YOU'VE GOT TO BELIEVE ME! ASTRO'S NOT A BAD PERSON! NOR IS MY BROTHER!
STAY OUT OF THIS! I'M ORDERING YOU! YOU'RE JUST A GIRL, AND YOU DON'T KNOW ANYTHING!
WE'LL NEVER GET ANY WORK DONE WITH YOUR BROTHER AROUND, ESPECIALLY WITH THOSE ROBOTS!
HEY! WHAT'RE YOU DOING?!
JUST TRY AND GIVE ANY ORDERS! YOU'LL SEE WHAT HAPPENS!

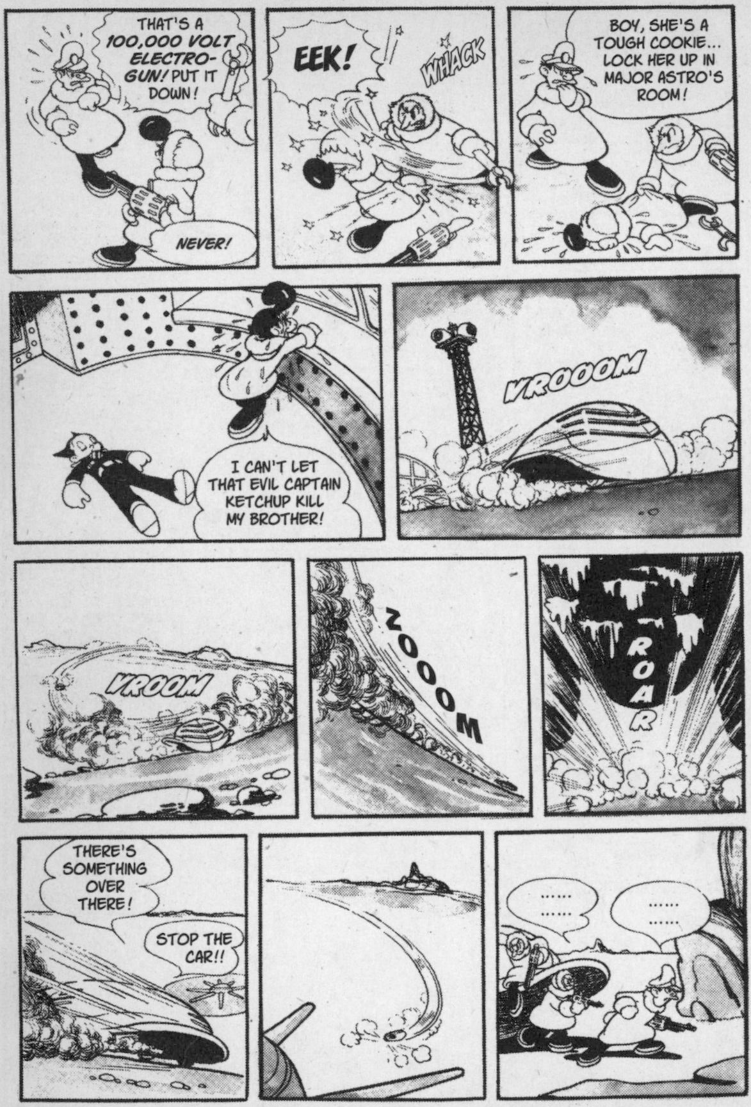
THAT'S A 100,000 VOLT ELECTRO-GUN! PUT IT DOWN!
NEVER!
EEK!
WHACK
BOY, SHE'S A TOUGH COOKIE... LOCK HER UP IN MAJOR ASTRO'S ROOM!
I CAN'T LET THAT EVIL CAPTAIN KETCHUP KILL MY BROTHER!
VROOOM
VROOM
ZOOOOM
ROAR
THERE'S SOMETHING OVER THERE!
STOP THE CAR!!
....
....

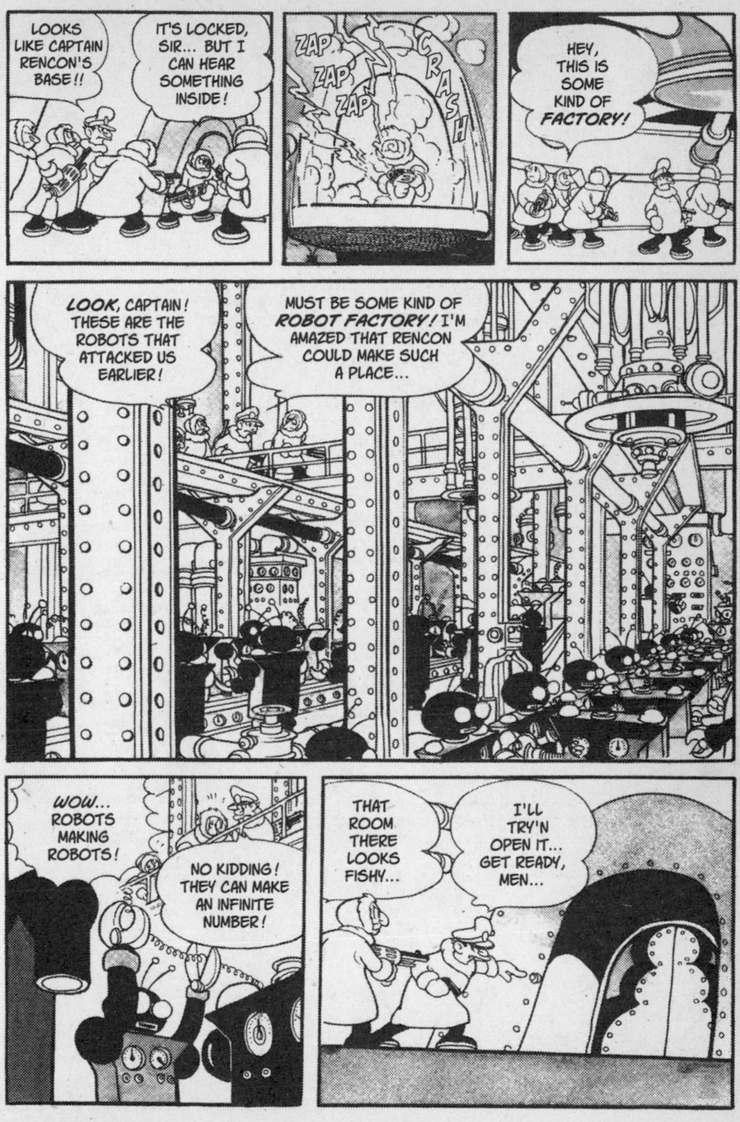
LOOKS LIKE CAPTAIN RENCON'S BASE!!
IT'S LOCKED, SIR... BUT I CAN HEAR SOMETHING INSIDE!
ZAP
ZAP
ZAP
CRASH
HEY, THIS IS SOME KIND OF FACTORY!
LOOK, CAPTAIN! THESE ARE THE ROBOTS THAT ATTACKED US EARLIER!
MUST BE SOME KIND OF ROBOT FACTORY! I'M AMAZED THAT RENCON COULD MAKE SUCH A PLACE...
WOW... ROBOTS MAKING ROBOTS!
NO KIDDING! THEY CAN MAKE AN INFINITE NUMBER!
THAT ROOM THERE LOOKS FISHY...
I'LL TRY'N OPEN IT... GET READY, MEN...

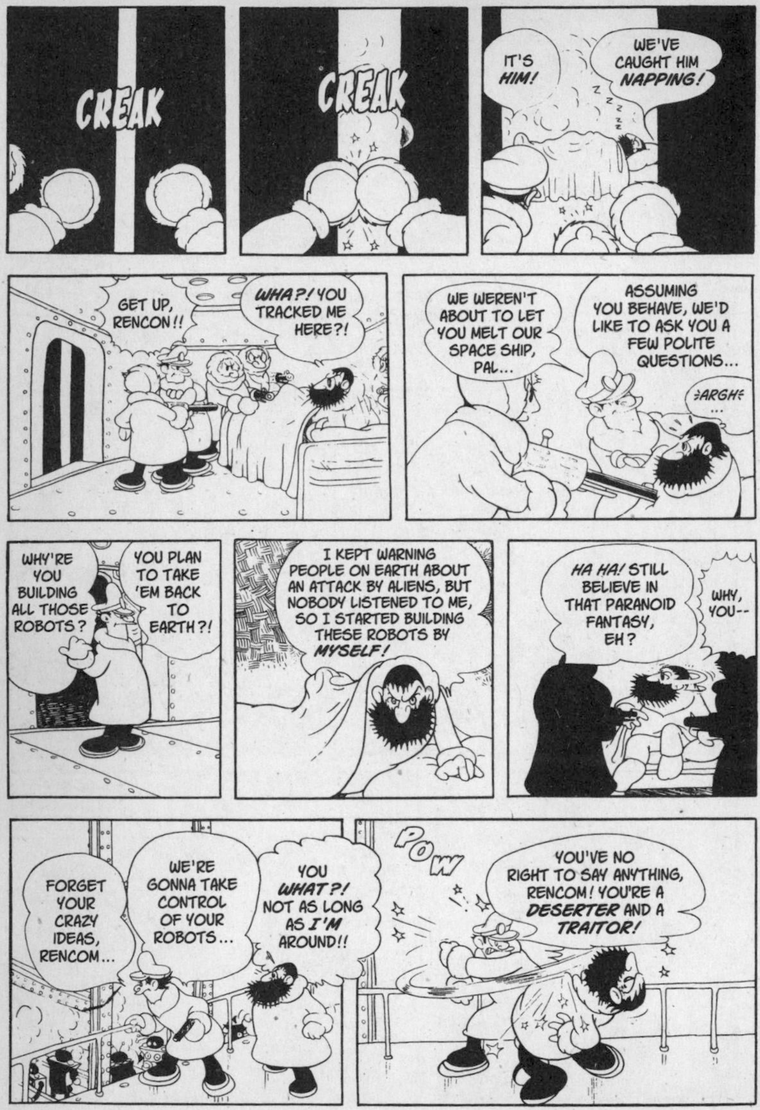
CREAK
CREAK
IT'S HIM!
WE'VE CAUGHT HIM NAPPING!
Z Z Z Z
GET UP, RENCON!!
WHA?! YOU TRACKED ME HERE?!
WE WEREN'T ABOUT TO LET YOU MELT OUR SPACE SHIP, PAL...
ASSUMING YOU BEHAVE, WE'D LIKE TO ASK YOU A FEW POLITE QUESTIONS...
ARGH...
WHY'RE YOU BUILDING ALL THOSE ROBOTS?
YOU PLAN TO TAKE 'EM BACK TO EARTH?!
I KEPT WARNING PEOPLE ON EARTH ABOUT AN ATTACK BY ALIENS, BUT NOBODY LISTENED TO ME, SO I STARTED BUILDING THESE ROBOTS BY MYSELF!
HA HA! STILL BELIEVE IN THAT PARANOID FANTASY, EH?
WHY, YOU--
FORGET YOUR CRAZY IDEAS, RENCOM...
WE'RE GONNA TAKE CONTROL OF YOUR ROBOTS...
YOU WHAT?! NOT AS LONG AS I'M AROUND!!
POW
YOU'VE NO RIGHT TO SAY ANYTHING, RENCOM! YOU'RE A DESERTER AND A TRAITOR!

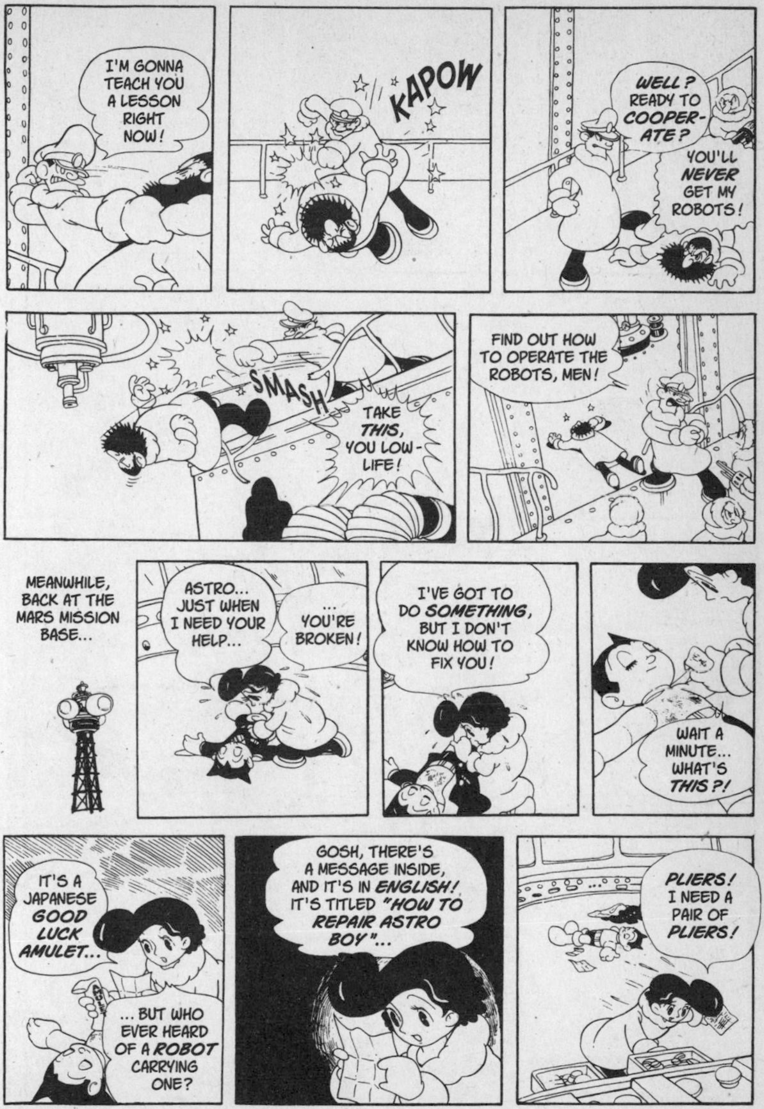

I'M GONNA TEACH YOU A LESSON RIGHT NOW!
KAPOW
WELL? READY TO COOPER-ATE?
YOU'LL NEVER GET MY ROBOTS!
SMASH
TAKE THIS, YOU LOW-LIFE!
FIND OUT HOW TO OPERATE THE ROBOTS, MEN!
MEANWHILE, BACK AT THE MARS MISSION BASE...
ASTRO... JUST WHEN I NEED YOUR HELP...
... YOU'RE BROKEN!
I'VE GOT TO DO SOMETHING, BUT I DON'T KNOW HOW TO FIX YOU!
WAIT A MINUTE... WHAT'S THIS?!
IT'S A JAPANESE GOOD LUCK AMULET...
... BUT WHO EVER HEARD OF A ROBOT CARRYING ONE?
GOSH, THERE'S A MESSAGE INSIDE, AND IT'S IN ENGLISH! IT'S TITLED "HOW TO REPAIR ASTRO BOY"...
PLIERS! I NEED A PAIR OF PLIERS!

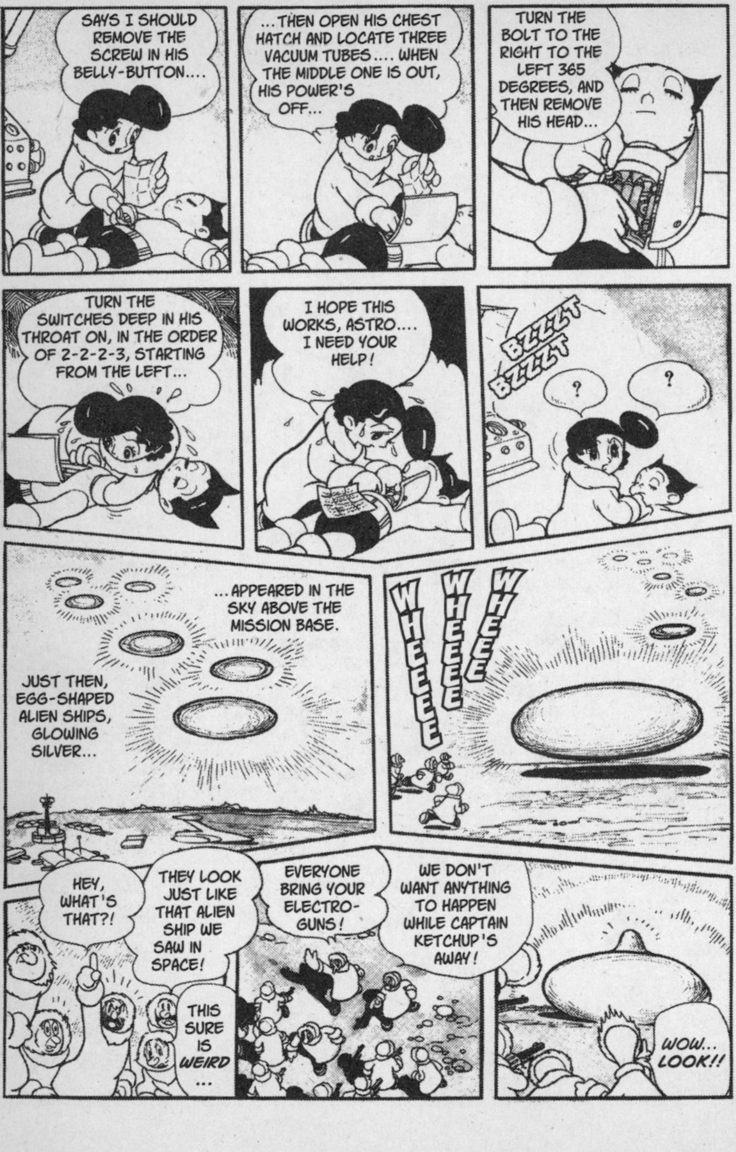
SAYS I SHOULD REMOVE THE SCREW IN HIS BELLY-BUTTON....
...THEN OPEN HIS CHEST HATCH AND LOCATE THREE VACUUM TUBES.... WHEN THE MIDDLE ONE IS OUT, HIS POWER'S OFF...
TURN THE BOLT TO THE RIGHT TO THE LEFT 365 DEGREES, AND THEN REMOVE HIS HEAD...
TURN THE SWITCHES DEEP IN HIS THROAT ON, IN THE ORDER OF 2-2-2-3, STARTING FROM THE LEFT...
I HOPE THIS WORKS, ASTRO.... I NEED YOUR HELP!
BZZZZT
BZZZZT
?
?
JUST THEN, EGG-SHAPED ALIEN SHIPS, GLOWING SILVER...
...APPEARED IN THE SKY ABOVE THE MISSION BASE.
WHEEEE
WHEEEE
WHEEEE
HEY, WHAT'S THAT?!
THEY LOOK JUST LIKE THAT ALIEN SHIP WE SAW IN SPACE!
THIS SURE IS *WEIRD* ...
EVERYONE BRING YOUR ELECTRO-GUNS!
WE DON'T WANT ANYTHING TO HAPPEN WHILE CAPTAIN KETCHUP'S AWAY!
WOW... LOOK!!

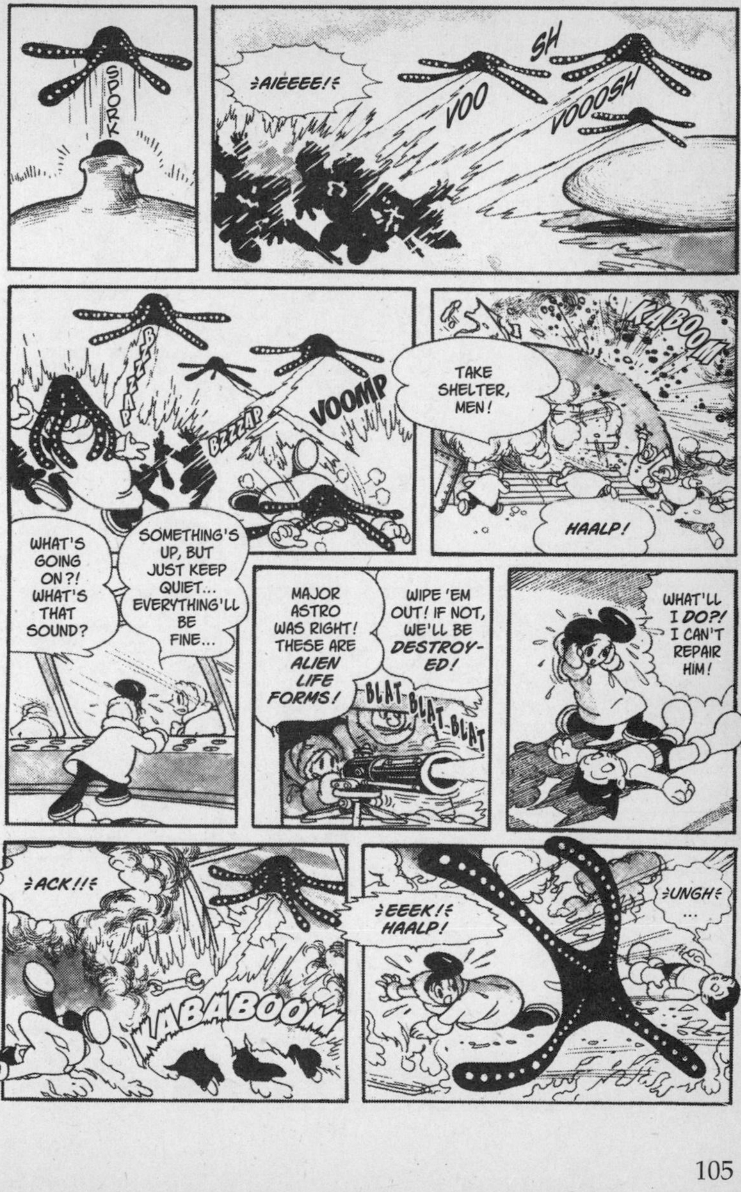
SPORK
AIEEEE!
SH
VOO
VOOOSH
BZZZAP
VOOMP
TAKE SHELTER, MEN!
KABOOM
HAALP!
WHAT'S GOING ON?! WHAT'S THAT SOUND?
SOMETHING'S UP, BUT JUST KEEP QUIET... EVERYTHING'LL BE FINE...
MAJOR ASTRO WAS RIGHT! THESE ARE ALIEN LIFE FORMS!
WIPE 'EM OUT! IF NOT, WE'LL BE DESTROY-ED!
BLAT BLAT BLAT BLAT
WHAT'LL I DO?! I CAN'T REPAIR HIM!
ACK!!
KABABOOM
EEEK! HAALP!
UNGH ...

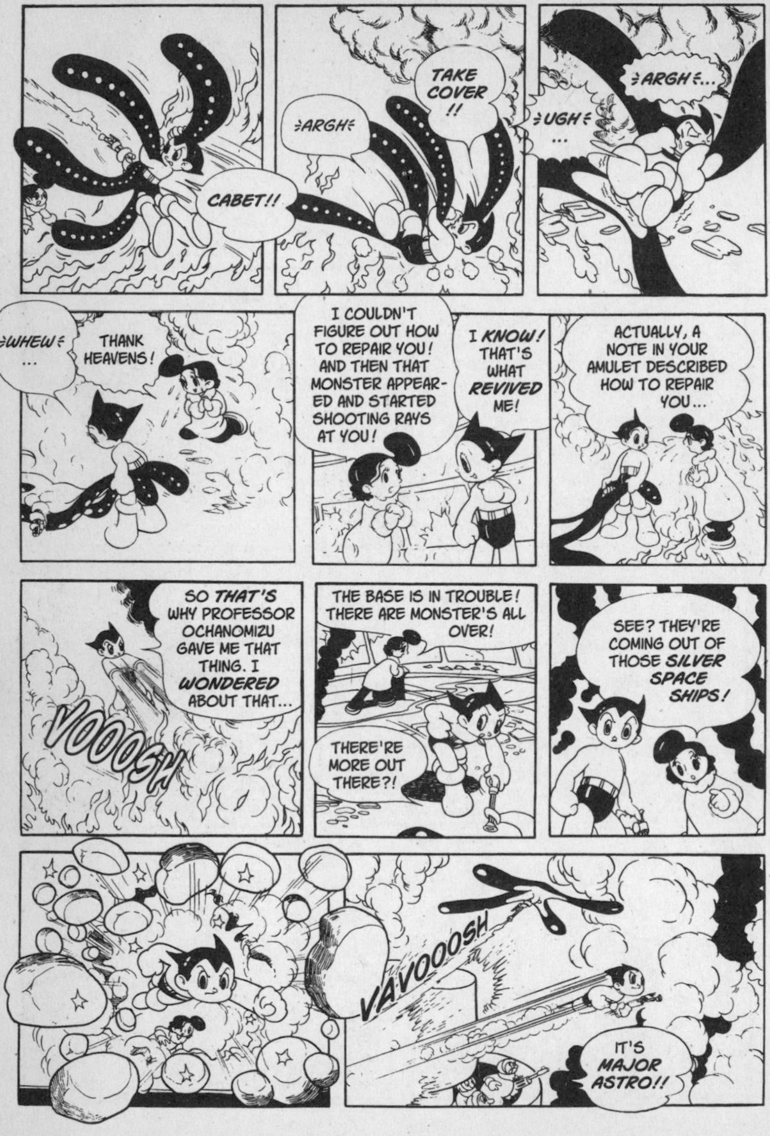
CABET!!
ARGH
TAKE COVER !!
UGH ...
ARGH ...
WHEW ...
THANK HEAVENS!
I COULDN'T FIGURE OUT HOW TO REPAIR YOU! AND THEN THAT MONSTER APPEARED AND STARTED SHOOTING RAYS AT YOU!
I KNOW! THAT'S WHAT REVIVED ME!
ACTUALLY, A NOTE IN YOUR AMULET DESCRIBED HOW TO REPAIR YOU...
SO THAT'S WHY PROFESSOR OCHANOMIZU GAVE ME THAT THING. I WONDERED ABOUT THAT...
VOOOSH
THE BASE IS IN TROUBLE! THERE ARE MONSTER'S ALL OVER!
THERE'RE MORE OUT THERE?!
SEE? THEY'RE COMING OUT OF THOSE SILVER SPACE SHIPS!
VAVOOOSH
IT'S MAJOR ASTRO!!

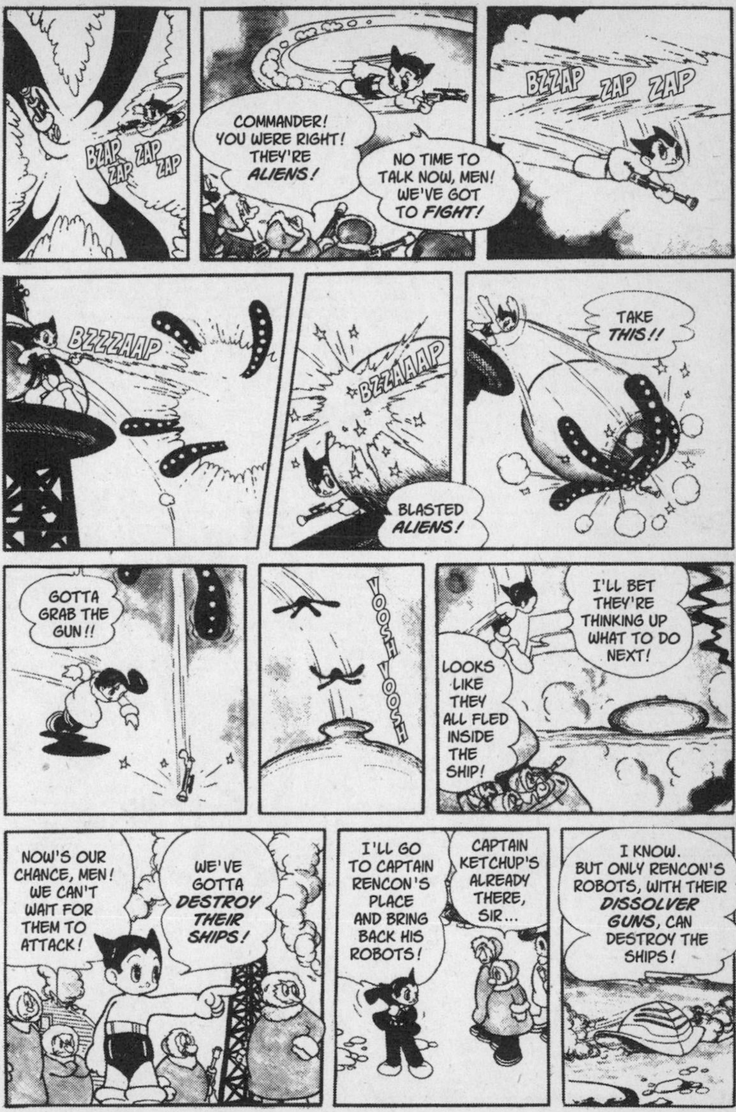

BZAP
ZAP
ZAP
ZAP
COMMANDER! YOU WERE RIGHT! THEY'RE *ALIENS!*
NO TIME TO TALK NOW, MEN! WE'VE GOT TO *FIGHT!*
BZZAP
ZAP
ZAP
BZZZAAP
BZZAAAP
BLASTED *ALIENS!*
TAKE *THIS!!*
GOTTA GRAB THE GUN!!
VOOSH
VOOSH
I'LL BET THEY'RE THINKING UP WHAT TO DO NEXT!
LOOKS LIKE THEY ALL FLED INSIDE THE SHIP!
NOW'S OUR CHANCE, MEN! WE CAN'T WAIT FOR THEM TO ATTACK!
WE'VE GOTTA *DESTROY THEIR SHIPS!*
I'LL GO TO CAPTAIN RENCON'S PLACE AND BRING BACK HIS ROBOTS!
CAPTAIN KETCHUP'S ALREADY THERE, SIR...
I KNOW. BUT ONLY RENCON'S ROBOTS, WITH THEIR *DISSOLVER GUNS*, CAN DESTROY THE SHIPS!

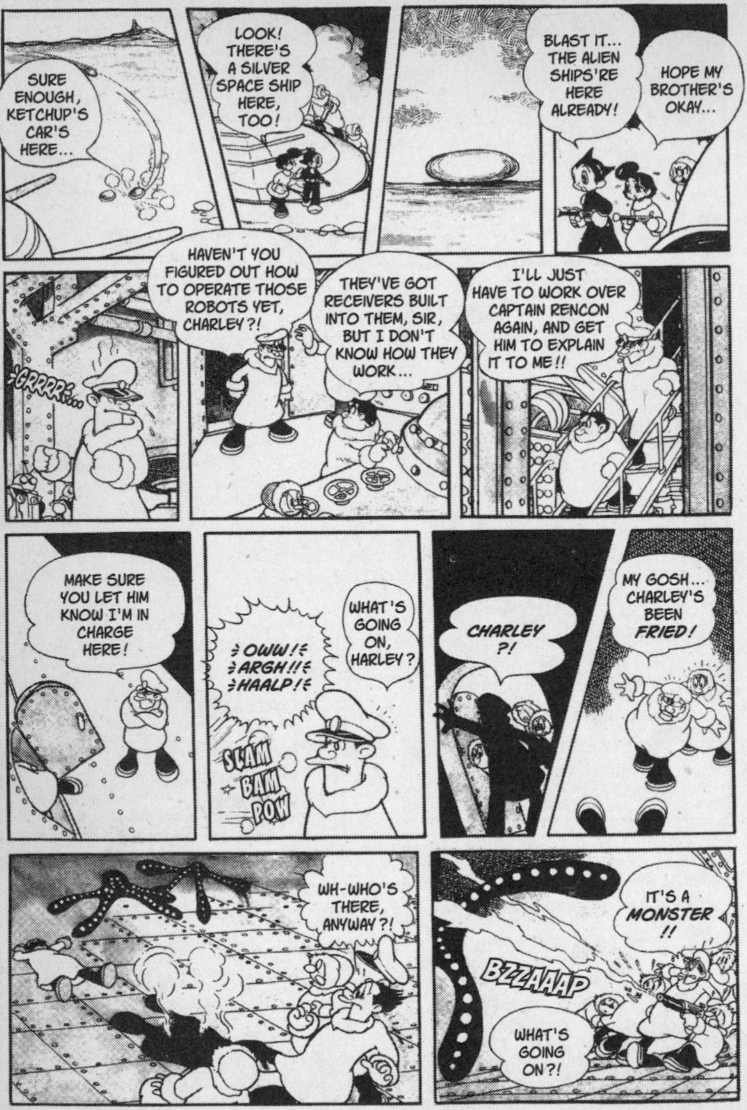
SURE ENOUGH, KETCHUP'S CAR'S HERE...
LOOK! THERE'S A SILVER SPACE SHIP HERE, TOO!
BLAST IT... THE ALIEN SHIPS'RE HERE ALREADY!
HOPE MY BROTHER'S OKAY...
GRRRR...
HAVEN'T YOU FIGURED OUT HOW TO OPERATE THOSE ROBOTS YET, CHARLEY?!
THEY'VE GOT RECEIVERS BUILT INTO THEM, SIR, BUT I DON'T KNOW HOW THEY WORK...
I'LL JUST HAVE TO WORK OVER CAPTAIN RENCON AGAIN, AND GET HIM TO EXPLAIN IT TO ME!!
MAKE SURE YOU LET HIM KNOW I'M IN CHARGE HERE!
OWW! ARGH!! HAALP!
WHAT'S GOING ON, HARLEY?
SLAM BAM POW
CHARLEY?!
MY GOSH... CHARLEY'S BEEN FRIED!
WH-WHO'S THERE, ANYWAY?!
IT'S A MONSTER!!
BZZAAAP
WHAT'S GOING ON?!

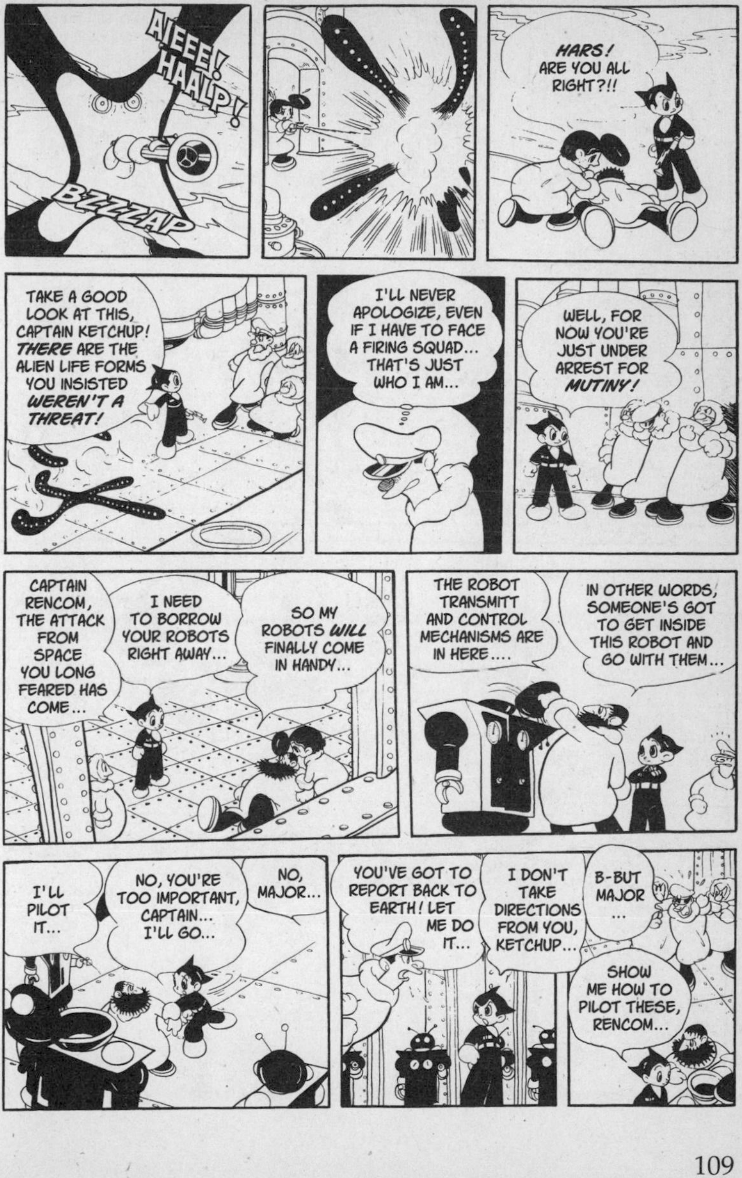
AIEEE! HAALP!
BZZZAP
HARS! ARE YOU ALL RIGHT?!!
TAKE A GOOD LOOK AT THIS, CAPTAIN KETCHUP! THERE ARE THE ALIEN LIFE FORMS YOU INSISTED WEREN'T A THREAT!
I'LL NEVER APOLOGIZE, EVEN IF I HAVE TO FACE A FIRING SQUAD... THAT'S JUST WHO I AM...
WELL, FOR NOW YOU'RE JUST UNDER ARREST FOR MUTINY!
CAPTAIN RENCOM, THE ATTACK FROM SPACE YOU LONG FEARED HAS COME...
I NEED TO BORROW YOUR ROBOTS RIGHT AWAY...
SO MY ROBOTS WILL FINALLY COME IN HANDY...
THE ROBOT TRANSMITT AND CONTROL MECHANISMS ARE IN HERE....
IN OTHER WORDS, SOMEONE'S GOT TO GET INSIDE THIS ROBOT AND GO WITH THEM...
I'LL PILOT IT...
NO, YOU'RE TOO IMPORTANT, CAPTAIN... I'LL GO...
NO, MAJOR...
YOU'VE GOT TO REPORT BACK TO EARTH! LET ME DO IT...
I DON'T TAKE DIRECTIONS FROM YOU, KETCHUP...
B-BUT MAJOR ...
SHOW ME HOW TO PILOT THESE, RENCOM...

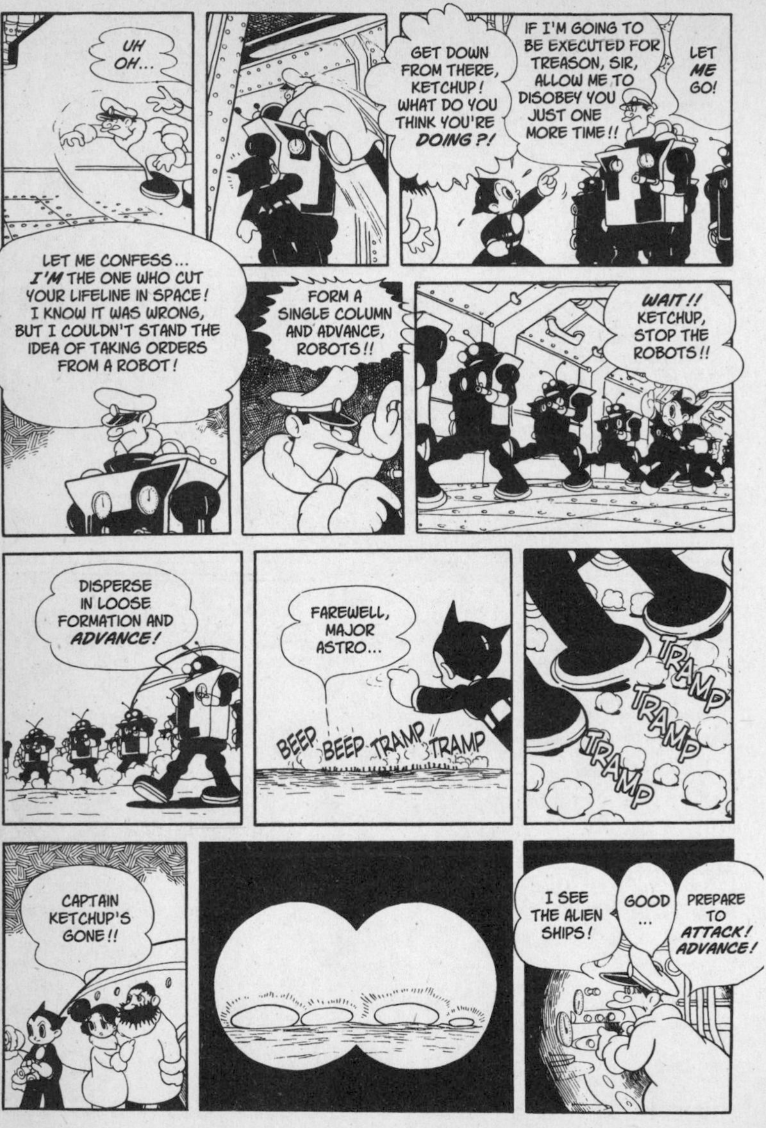

UH OH...
GET DOWN FROM THERE, KETCHUP! WHAT DO YOU THINK YOU'RE *DOING?!*
IF I'M GOING TO BE EXECUTED FOR TREASON, SIR, ALLOW ME TO DISOBEY YOU JUST ONE MORE TIME!!
LET *ME* GO!
LET ME CONFESS... *I'M* THE ONE WHO CUT YOUR LIFELINE IN SPACE! I KNOW IT WAS WRONG, BUT I COULDN'T STAND THE IDEA OF TAKING ORDERS FROM A ROBOT!
FORM A SINGLE COLUMN AND ADVANCE, ROBOTS!!
WAIT!! KETCHUP, STOP THE ROBOTS!!
DISPERSE IN LOOSE FORMATION AND *ADVANCE!*
FAREWELL, MAJOR ASTRO...
BEEP BEEP TRAMP TRAMP
TRAMP TRAMP TRAMP
CAPTAIN KETCHUP'S GONE!!
I SEE THE ALIEN SHIPS!
GOOD...
PREPARE TO *ATTACK! ADVANCE!*

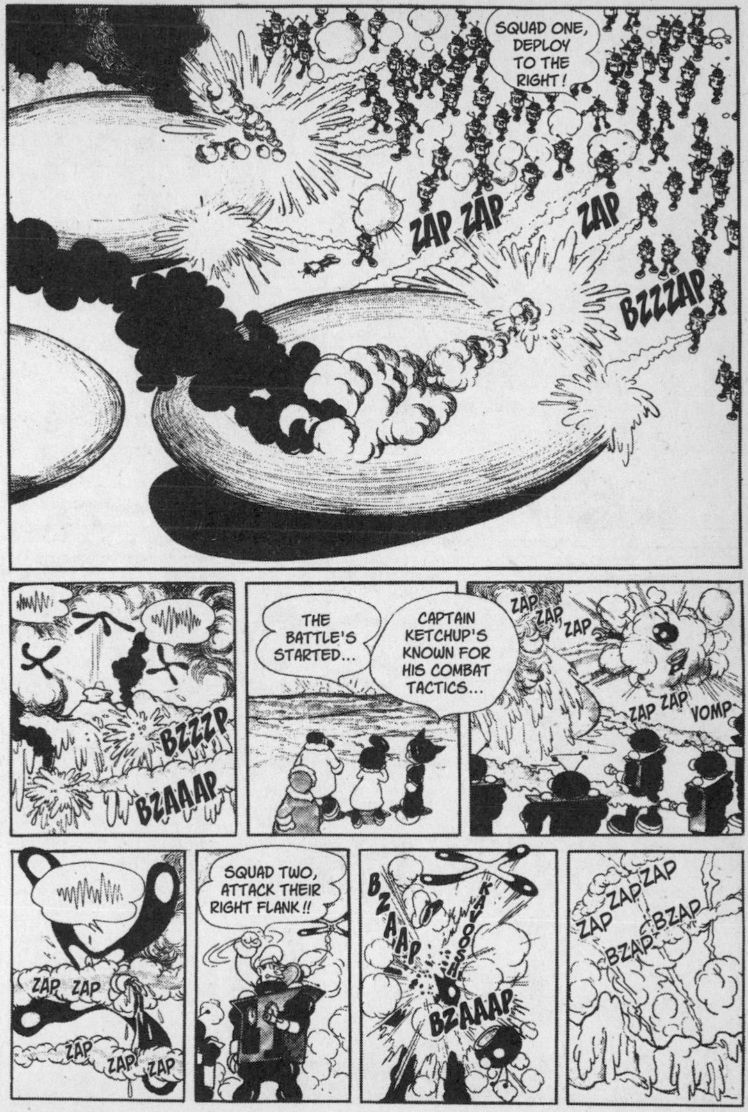
SQUAD ONE, DEPLOY TO THE RIGHT!
ZAP ZAP
ZAP
BZZZAP
BZZZP
BZAAAP
THE BATTLE'S STARTED...
CAPTAIN KETCHUP'S KNOWN FOR HIS COMBAT TACTICS...
ZAP
ZAP
ZAP
ZAP ZAP
VOMP
ZAP ZAP
ZAP
ZAP
ZAP
SQUAD TWO, ATTACK THEIR RIGHT FLANK!!
BZAAP
KAVOOSH
BZAAAP
ZAP ZAP ZAP
ZAP
BZAP BZAP

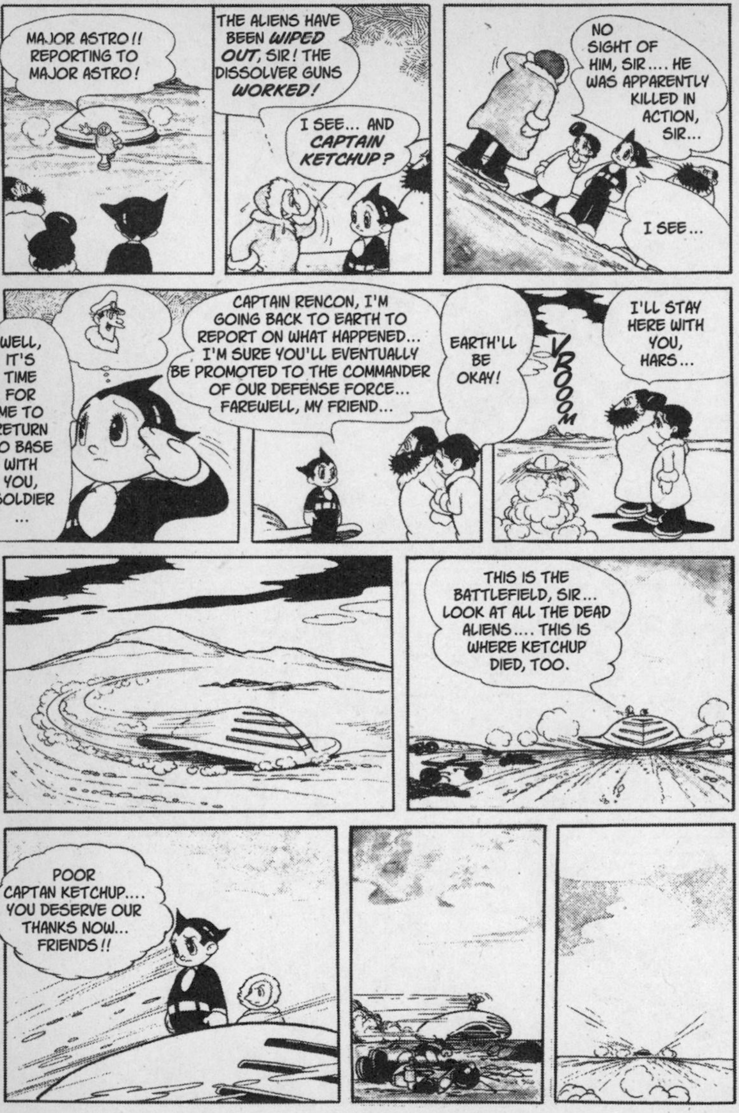
MAJOR ASTRO!! REPORTING TO MAJOR ASTRO!
THE ALIENS HAVE BEEN WIPED OUT, SIR! THE DISSOLVER GUNS WORKED!
I SEE... AND CAPTAIN KETCHUP?
NO SIGHT OF HIM, SIR.... HE WAS APPARENTLY KILLED IN ACTION, SIR...
I SEE...
WELL, IT'S TIME FOR ME TO RETURN TO BASE WITH YOU, SOLDIER ...
CAPTAIN RENCON, I'M GOING BACK TO EARTH TO REPORT ON WHAT HAPPENED... I'M SURE YOU'LL EVENTUALLY BE PROMOTED TO THE COMMANDER OF OUR DEFENSE FORCE... FAREWELL, MY FRIEND...
EARTH'LL BE OKAY!
VROOOOM
I'LL STAY HERE WITH YOU, HARS...
THIS IS THE BATTLEFIELD, SIR... LOOK AT ALL THE DEAD ALIENS.... THIS IS WHERE KETCHUP DIED, TOO.
POOR CAPTAN KETCHUP.... YOU DESERVE OUR THANKS NOW... FRIENDS!!

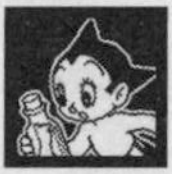

SEA SERPENT ISLAND

First appeared in the August 1953 supplement of *Shonen* magazine.

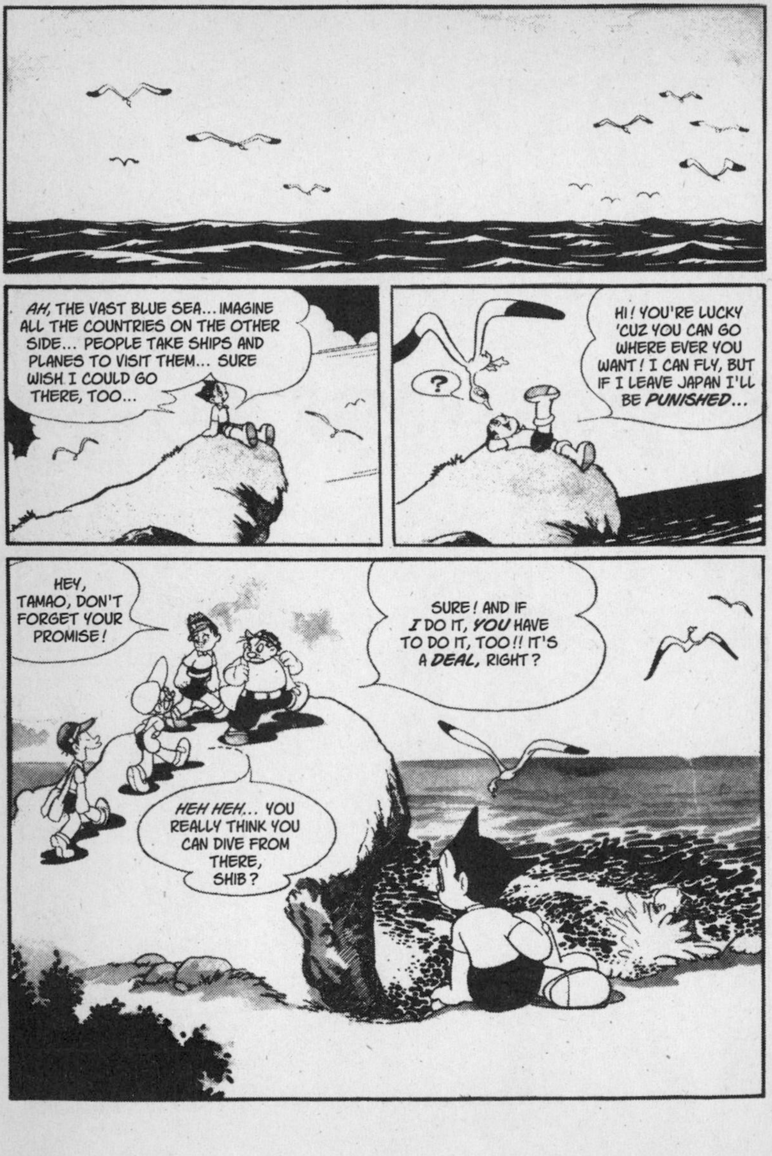
AH, THE VAST BLUE SEA... IMAGINE ALL THE COUNTRIES ON THE OTHER SIDE... PEOPLE TAKE SHIPS AND PLANES TO VISIT THEM... SURE WISH I COULD GO THERE, TOO...
?
HI! YOU'RE LUCKY 'CUZ YOU CAN GO WHERE EVER YOU WANT! I CAN FLY, BUT IF I LEAVE JAPAN I'LL BE PUNISHED...
HEY, TAMAO, DON'T FORGET YOUR PROMISE!
SURE! AND IF I DO IT, YOU HAVE TO DO IT, TOO!! IT'S A DEAL, RIGHT?
HEH HEH... YOU REALLY THINK YOU CAN DIVE FROM THERE, SHIB?

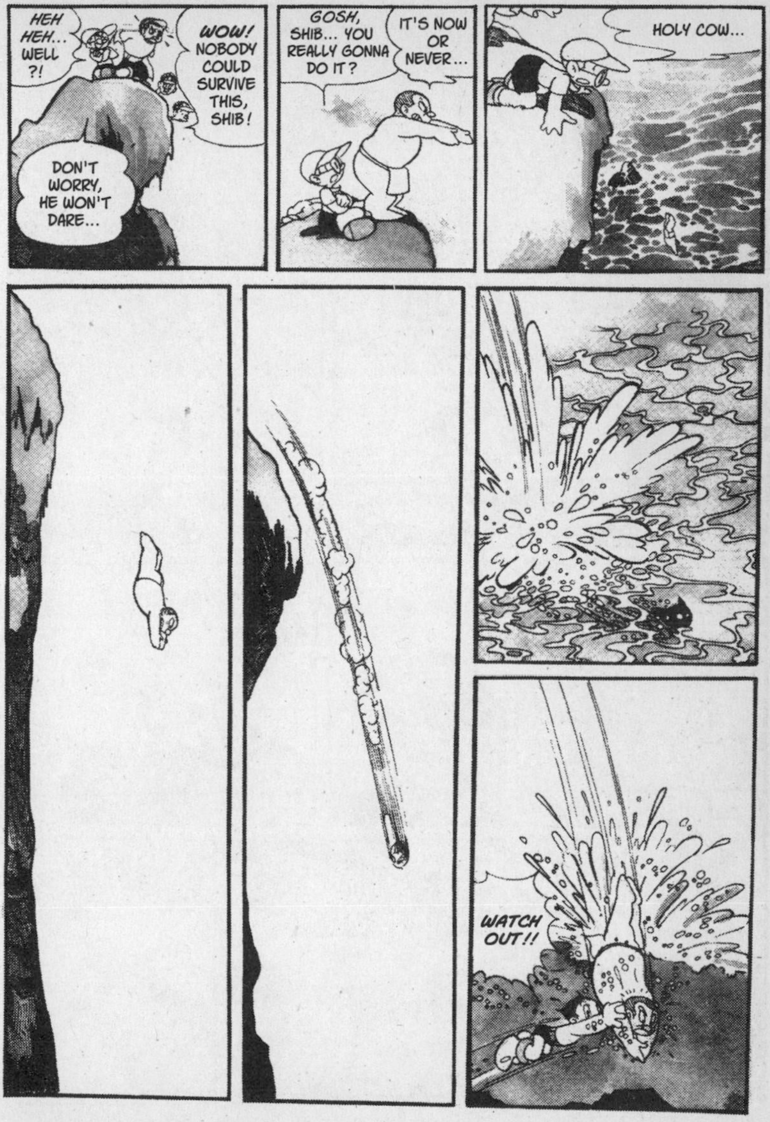
HEH HEH... WELL ?!
WOW! NOBODY COULD SURVIVE THIS, SHIB!
DON'T WORRY, HE WON'T DARE...
GOSH, SHIB... YOU REALLY GONNA DO IT?
IT'S NOW OR NEVER...
HOLY COW...
WATCH OUT!!

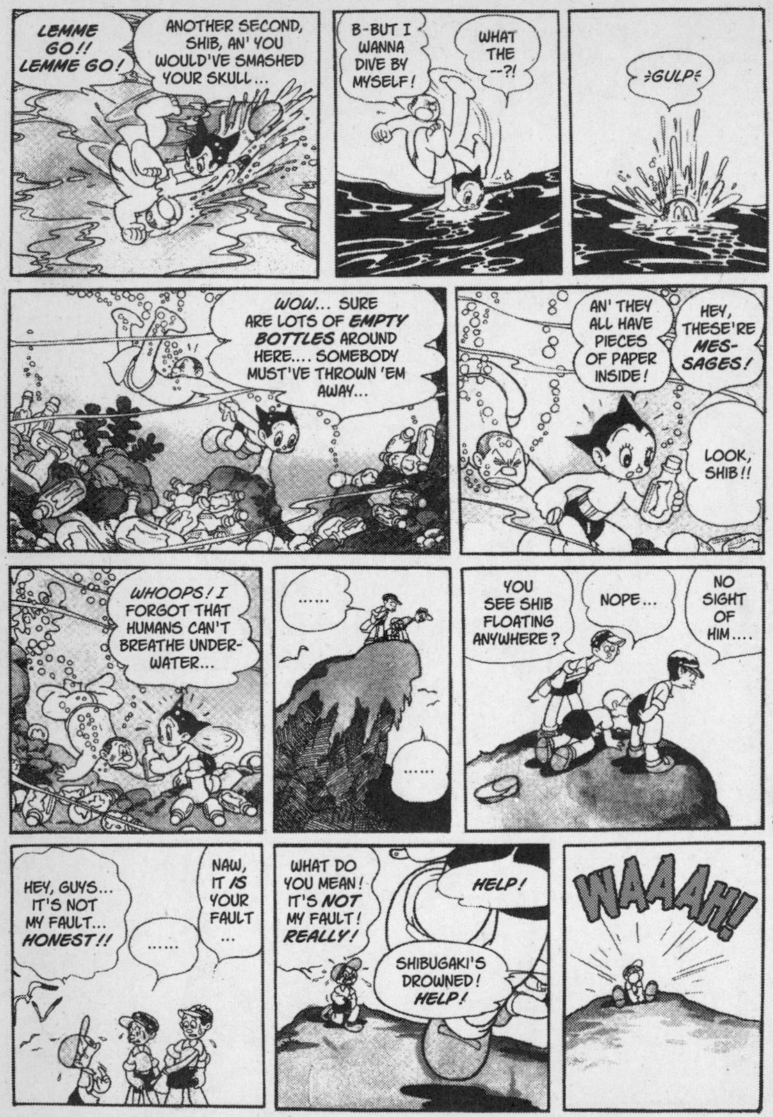
LEMME GO!! LEMME GO!
ANOTHER SECOND, SHIB, AN' YOU WOULD'VE SMASHED YOUR SKULL...
B-BUT I WANNA DIVE BY MYSELF!
WHAT THE --?!
GULP
WOW... SURE ARE LOTS OF EMPTY BOTTLES AROUND HERE.... SOMEBODY MUST'VE THROWN 'EM AWAY...
AN' THEY ALL HAVE PIECES OF PAPER INSIDE!
HEY, THESE'RE MES-SAGES!
LOOK, SHIB!!
WHOOPS! I FORGOT THAT HUMANS CAN'T BREATHE UNDER-WATER...
......
......
YOU SEE SHIB FLOATING ANYWHERE?
NOPE...
NO SIGHT OF HIM....
HEY, GUYS... IT'S NOT MY FAULT... HONEST!!
......
NAW, IT IS YOUR FAULT...
WHAT DO YOU MEAN! IT'S NOT MY FAULT! REALLY!
HELP!
SHIBUGAKI'S DROWNED! HELP!
WAAAH!

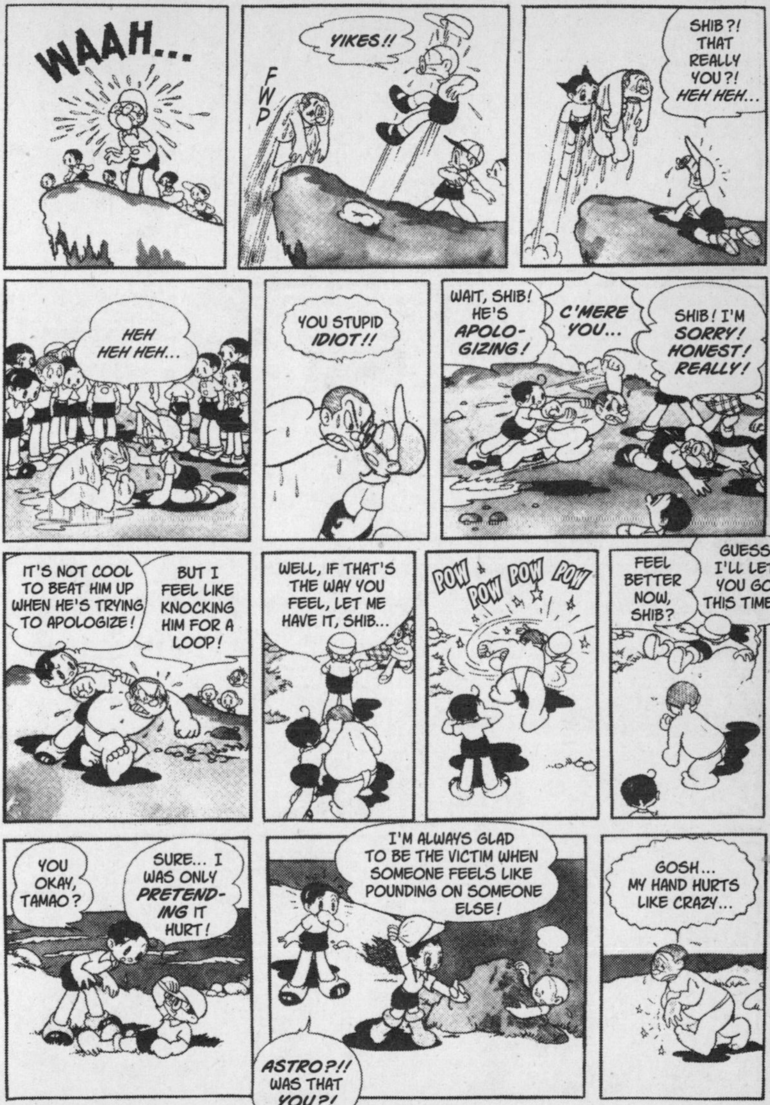
WAAH...
YIKES!!
FWP
SHIB?! THAT REALLY YOU?! HEH HEH...
HEH HEH HEH...
YOU STUPID IDIOT!!
WAIT, SHIB! HE'S APOLOGIZING!
C'MERE YOU...
SHIB! I'M SORRY! HONEST! REALLY!
IT'S NOT COOL TO BEAT HIM UP WHEN HE'S TRYING TO APOLOGIZE!
BUT I FEEL LIKE KNOCKING HIM FOR A LOOP!
WELL, IF THAT'S THE WAY YOU FEEL, LET ME HAVE IT, SHIB...
POW POW POW POW
FEEL BETTER NOW, SHIB?
GUESS I'LL LET YOU GO THIS TIME...
YOU OKAY, TAMAO?
SURE... I WAS ONLY PRETENDING IT HURT!
I'M ALWAYS GLAD TO BE THE VICTIM WHEN SOMEONE FEELS LIKE POUNDING ON SOMEONE ELSE!
ASTRO?!! WAS THAT YOU?!
GOSH... MY HAND HURTS LIKE CRAZY...

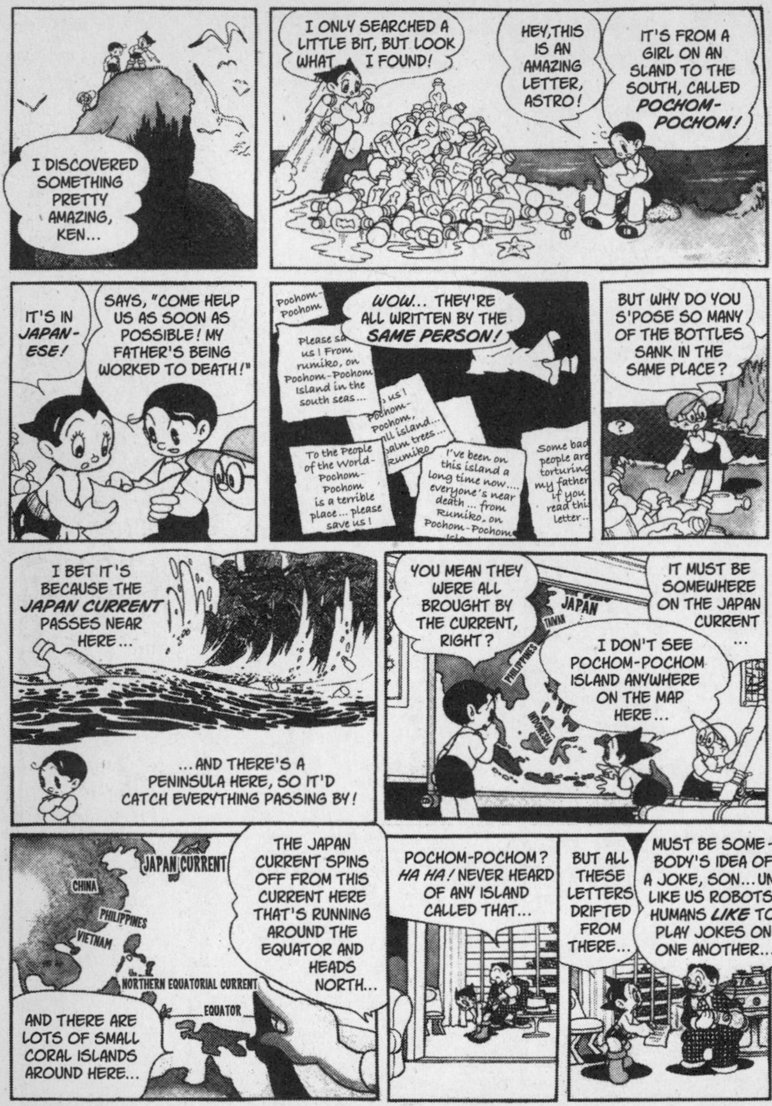
I DISCOVERED SOMETHING PRETTY AMAZING, KEN...
I ONLY SEARCHED A LITTLE BIT, BUT LOOK WHAT I FOUND!
HEY,THIS IS AN AMAZING LETTER, ASTRO!
IT'S FROM A GIRL ON AN SLAND TO THE SOUTH, CALLED POCHOM-POCHOM!
IT'S IN JAPANESE!
SAYS, "COME HELP US AS SOON AS POSSIBLE! MY FATHER'S BEING WORKED TO DEATH!"
Pochom-Pochom
WOW... THEY'RE ALL WRITTEN BY THE SAME PERSON!
Please sa us! From rumiko, on Pochom-Pochom Island in the south seas...
us! Pochom-Pochom, ll island... alm trees... Rumiko
To the People of the World- Pochom-Pochom is a terrible place... please save us!
I've been on this island a long time now.... everyone's near death ... from Rumiko, on Pochom-Pochom
Some bad people are torturing my father if you read thi letter...
BUT WHY DO YOU S'POSE SO MANY OF THE BOTTLES SANK IN THE SAME PLACE?
I BET IT'S BECAUSE THE JAPAN CURRENT PASSES NEAR HERE...
...AND THERE'S A PENINSULA HERE, SO IT'D CATCH EVERYTHING PASSING BY!
YOU MEAN THEY WERE ALL BROUGHT BY THE CURRENT, RIGHT?
IT MUST BE SOMEWHERE ON THE JAPAN CURRENT...
JAPAN
TAIWAN
PHILIPPINES
INDONESIA
I DON'T SEE POCHOM-POCHOM ISLAND ANYWHERE ON THE MAP HERE...
JAPAN CURRENT
CHINA
PHILIPPINES
VIETNAM
NORTHERN EQUATORIAL CURRENT
EQUATOR
THE JAPAN CURRENT SPINS OFF FROM THIS CURRENT HERE THAT'S RUNNING AROUND THE EQUATOR AND HEADS NORTH...
AND THERE ARE LOTS OF SMALL CORAL ISLANDS AROUND HERE...
POCHOM-POCHOM? HA HA! NEVER HEARD OF ANY ISLAND CALLED THAT...
BUT ALL THESE LETTERS DRIFTED FROM THERE...
MUST BE SOME-BODY'S IDEA OF A JOKE, SON... UN-LIKE US ROBOTS, HUMANS LIKE TO PLAY JOKES ON ONE ANOTHER...

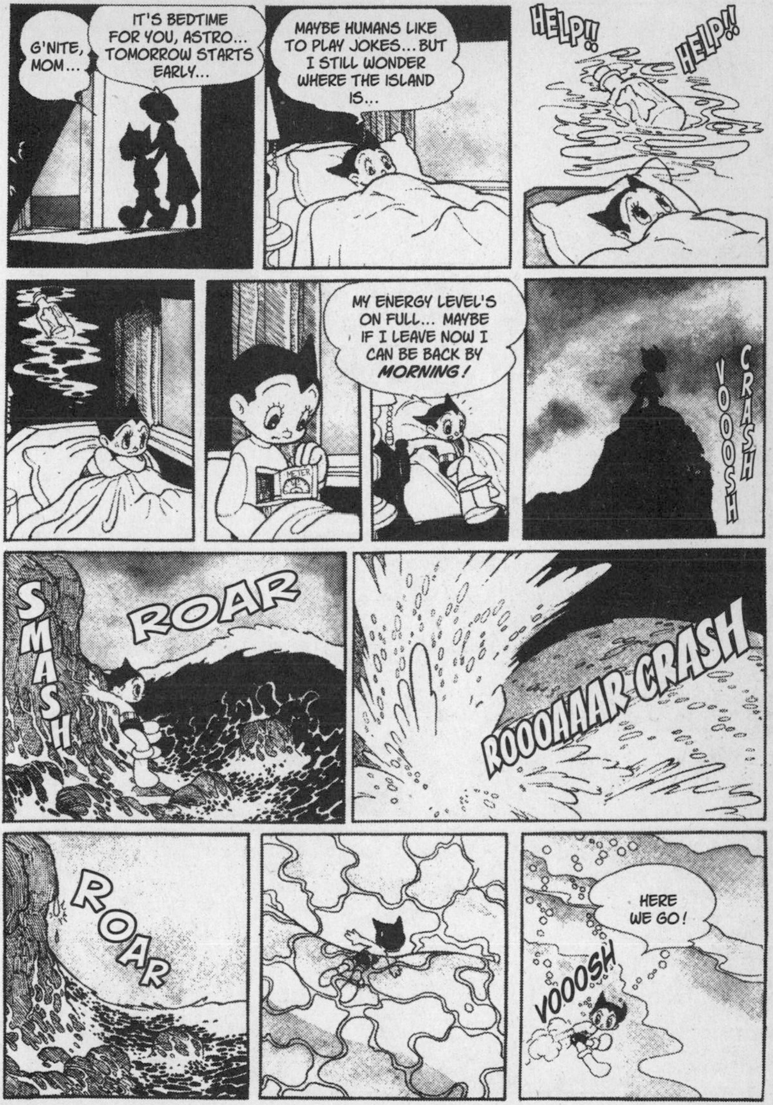

G'NITE, MOM...
IT'S BEDTIME FOR YOU, ASTRO... TOMORROW STARTS EARLY...
MAYBE HUMANS LIKE TO PLAY JOKES... BUT I STILL WONDER WHERE THE ISLAND IS...
HELP!!
HELP!!
MY ENERGY LEVEL'S ON FULL... MAYBE IF I LEAVE NOW I CAN BE BACK BY MORNING!
METER
VOOOSH
CRASH
SMASH
ROAR
ROOOAAAR CRASH
ROAR
HERE WE GO!
VOOOSH

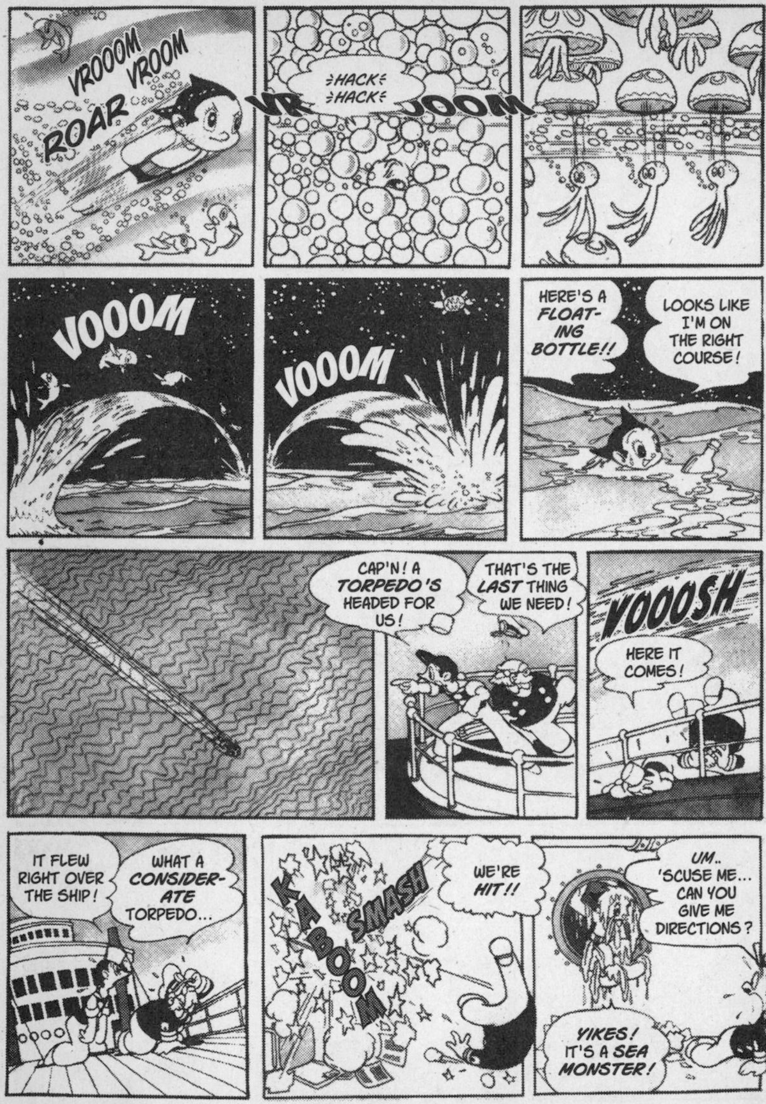
VROOOM
VROOM
ROAR
HACK
HACK
VR
JOOM
VOOOM
VOOOM
HERE'S A FLOATING BOTTLE!!
LOOKS LIKE I'M ON THE RIGHT COURSE!
CAP'N! A TORPEDO'S HEADED FOR US!
THAT'S THE LAST THING WE NEED!
VOOOSH
HERE IT COMES!
IT FLEW RIGHT OVER THE SHIP!
WHAT A CONSIDERATE TORPEDO...
KABOOOM
SMASH
WE'RE HIT!!
UM.. 'SCUSE ME... CAN YOU GIVE ME DIRECTIONS?
YIKES! IT'S A SEA MONSTER!

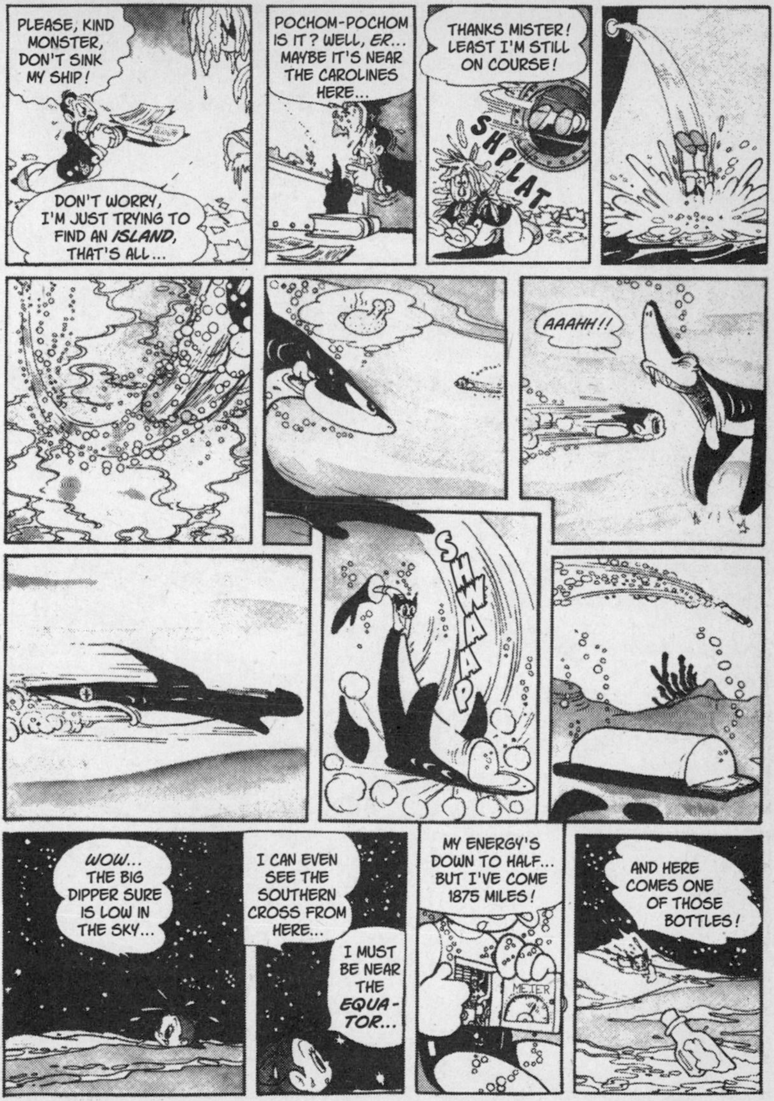
PLEASE, KIND MONSTER, DON'T SINK MY SHIP!
DON'T WORRY, I'M JUST TRYING TO FIND AN ISLAND, THAT'S ALL...
POCHOM-POCHOM IS IT? WELL, ER... MAYBE IT'S NEAR THE CAROLINES HERE...
THANKS MISTER! LEAST I'M STILL ON COURSE!
SHPLAT
AAAHH!!
SHWAAP
WOW... THE BIG DIPPER SURE IS LOW IN THE SKY...
I CAN EVEN SEE THE SOUTHERN CROSS FROM HERE...
I MUST BE NEAR THE EQUATOR...
MY ENERGY'S DOWN TO HALF... BUT I'VE COME 1875 MILES!
METER
AND HERE COMES ONE OF THOSE BOTTLES!

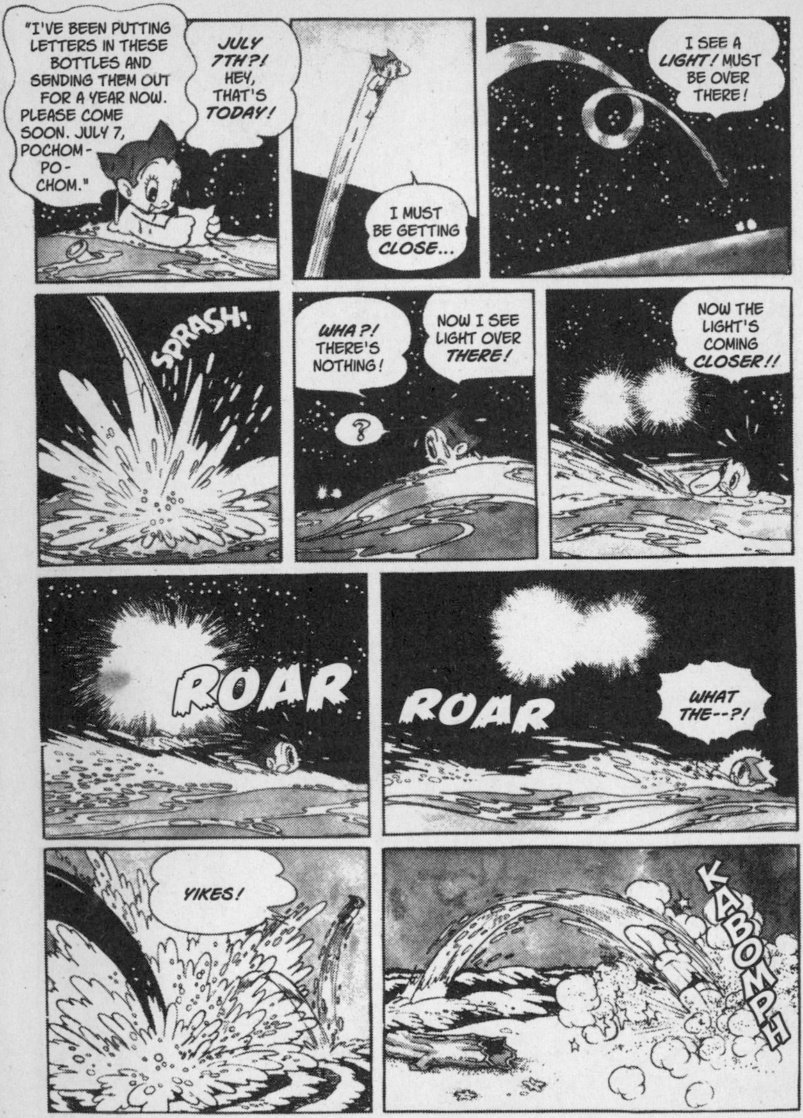
"I'VE BEEN PUTTING LETTERS IN THESE BOTTLES AND SENDING THEM OUT FOR A YEAR NOW. PLEASE COME SOON. JULY 7, POCHOMPOCHOM."
JULY 7TH?! HEY, THAT'S TODAY!
I MUST BE GETTING CLOSE...
I SEE A LIGHT! MUST BE OVER THERE!
SPRASH
WHA?! THERE'S NOTHING!
NOW I SEE LIGHT OVER THERE!
?
NOW THE LIGHT'S COMING CLOSER!!
ROAR
ROAR
WHAT THE--?!
YIKES!
KABOMPH

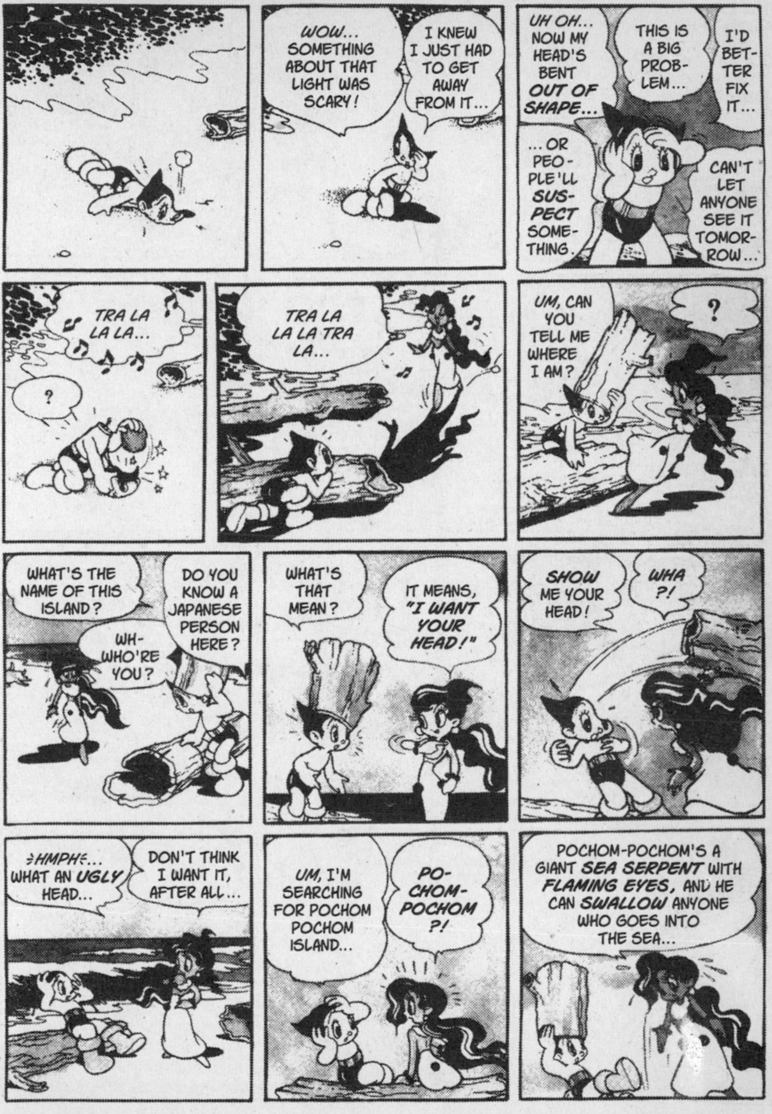
WOW... SOMETHING ABOUT THAT LIGHT WAS SCARY!
I KNEW I JUST HAD TO GET AWAY FROM IT...
UH OH... NOW MY HEAD'S BENT OUT OF SHAPE...
THIS IS A BIG PROBLEM...
I'D BETTER FIX IT...
...OR PEOPLE'LL SUSPECT SOMETHING.
CAN'T LET ANYONE SEE IT TOMORROW...
TRA LA LA LA...
?
TRA LA LA LA TRA LA...
UM, CAN YOU TELL ME WHERE I AM?
?
WHAT'S THE NAME OF THIS ISLAND?
DO YOU KNOW A JAPANESE PERSON HERE?
WH-WHO'RE YOU?
WHAT'S THAT MEAN?
IT MEANS, "I WANT YOUR HEAD!"
SHOW ME YOUR HEAD!
WHA?!
HMPH... WHAT AN UGLY HEAD...
DON'T THINK I WANT IT, AFTER ALL...
UM, I'M SEARCHING FOR POCHOM POCHOM ISLAND...
POCHOM-POCHOM?!
POCHOM-POCHOM'S A GIANT SEA SERPENT WITH FLAMING EYES, AND HE CAN SWALLOW ANYONE WHO GOES INTO THE SEA...

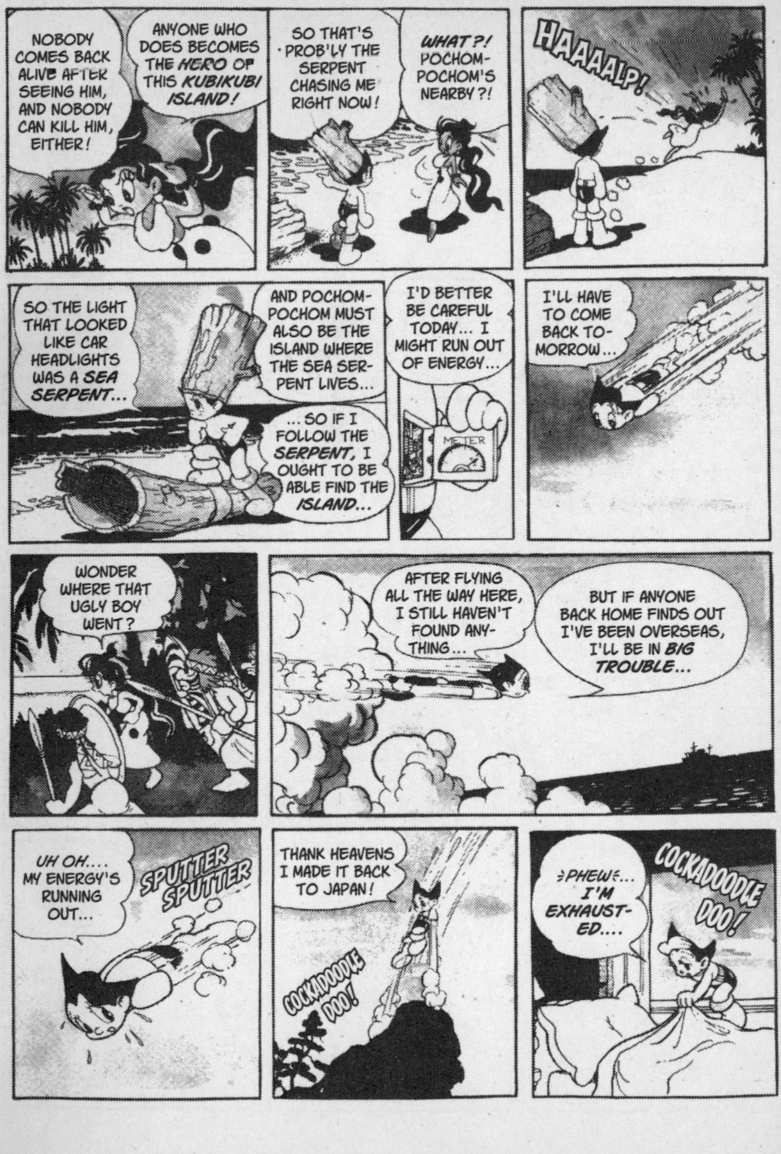
NOBODY COMES BACK ALIVE AFTER SEEING HIM, AND NOBODY CAN KILL HIM, EITHER!
ANYONE WHO DOES BECOMES THE *HERO* OF THIS *KUBIKUBI ISLAND!*
SO THAT'S PROB'LY THE SERPENT CHASING ME RIGHT NOW!
WHAT?! POCHOM-POCHOM'S NEARBY?!
HAAAAALP!
SO THE LIGHT THAT LOOKED LIKE CAR HEADLIGHTS WAS A *SEA SERPENT...*
AND POCHOM-POCHOM MUST ALSO BE THE ISLAND WHERE THE SEA SER-PENT LIVES...
...SO IF I FOLLOW THE *SERPENT,* I OUGHT TO BE ABLE FIND THE *ISLAND...*
I'D BETTER BE CAREFUL TODAY... I MIGHT RUN OUT OF ENERGY...
METER
I'LL HAVE TO COME BACK TO-MORROW...
WONDER WHERE THAT UGLY BOY WENT?
AFTER FLYING ALL THE WAY HERE, I STILL HAVEN'T FOUND ANY-THING...
BUT IF ANYONE BACK HOME FINDS OUT I'VE BEEN OVERSEAS, I'LL BE IN *BIG TROUBLE...*
UH OH.... MY ENERGY'S RUNNING OUT...
SPUTTER SPUTTER
THANK HEAVENS I MADE IT BACK TO JAPAN!
COCKADOODLE DOO!
PHEW... *I'M EXHAUST-ED....*
COCKADOODLE DOO!

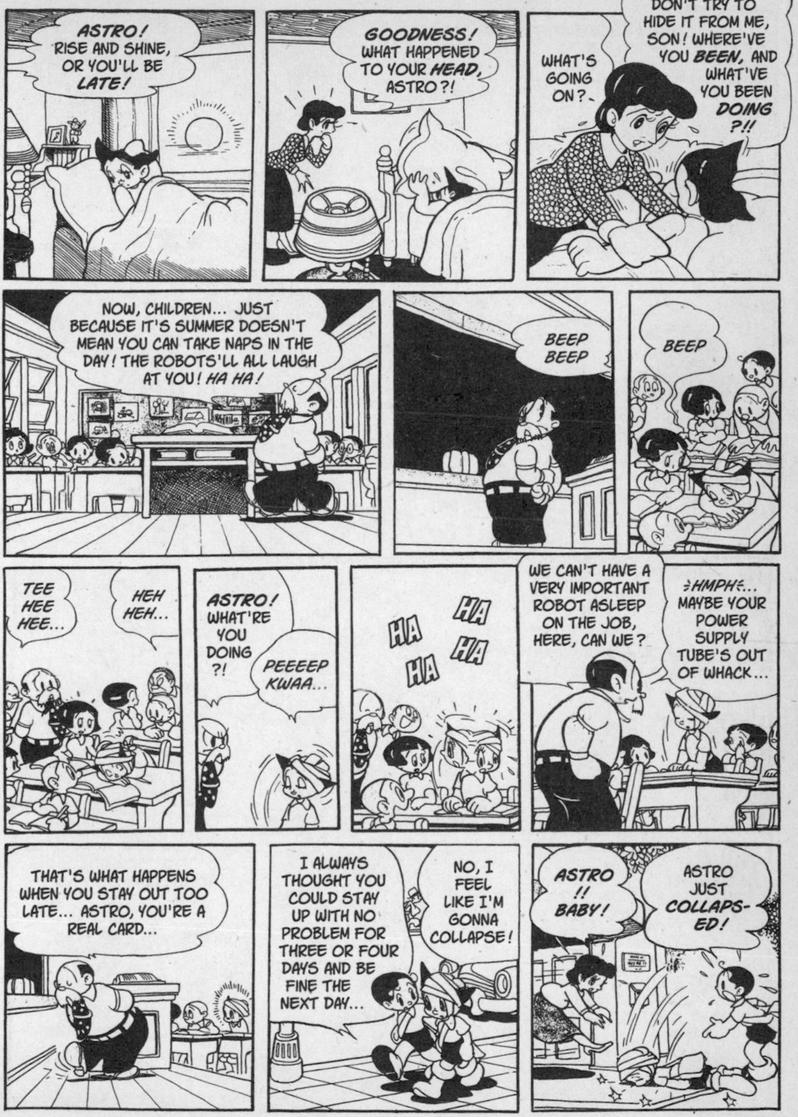
ASTRO! RISE AND SHINE, OR YOU'LL BE LATE!
GOODNESS! WHAT HAPPENED TO YOUR HEAD, ASTRO?!
WHAT'S GOING ON?
DON'T TRY TO HIDE IT FROM ME, SON! WHERE'VE YOU BEEN, AND WHAT'VE YOU BEEN DOING?!!
NOW, CHILDREN... JUST BECAUSE IT'S SUMMER DOESN'T MEAN YOU CAN TAKE NAPS IN THE DAY! THE ROBOTS'LL ALL LAUGH AT YOU! HA HA!
BEEP BEEP
BEEP
TEE HEE HEE...
HEH HEH...
ASTRO! WHAT'RE YOU DOING?!
PEEEEP KWAA...
HA HA HA HA
WE CAN'T HAVE A VERY IMPORTANT ROBOT ASLEEP ON THE JOB, HERE, CAN WE?
HMPH... MAYBE YOUR POWER SUPPLY TUBE'S OUT OF WHACK...
THAT'S WHAT HAPPENS WHEN YOU STAY OUT TOO LATE... ASTRO, YOU'RE A REAL CARD...
I ALWAYS THOUGHT YOU COULD STAY UP WITH NO PROBLEM FOR THREE OR FOUR DAYS AND BE FINE THE NEXT DAY...
NO, I FEEL LIKE I'M GONNA COLLAPSE!
ASTRO!! BABY!
ASTRO JUST COLLAPSED!

DON'T WORRY, ASTRO... YOU'RE JUST RUNNING OUT OF ENERGY, THAT'S ALL... ANOTHER REFILL, AND YOU'LL FEEL *FINE*!

WHAT A *RELIEF!*

HMM... I FILLED YOU UP *LAST NIGHT*, TOO, THOUGH...

HERE'S A NEW HEAD FOR YOU, ASTRO...

THANKS, MOM...

THAT'S THE LAST ONE, SO DON'T SMASH IT, OKAY?

ASTRO'S FINALLY ASLEEP... WONDER WHAT ON EARTH HE WAS DOING?

HE DOES THINGS LIKE THIS EVERY ONCE IN AWHILE! WE'D BETTER KEEP OUR EYES ON HIM...

VROOOM

2 HOURS LATER...

THERE'S SO MUCH FOG IT'S HARD TO SEE TONIGHT...

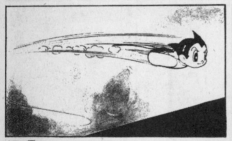
I'LL SET MY HEARING TO 1000X... MAYBE I CAN PICK UP SOMETHING...

RUMBLE RUMBLE

ROAR ROAR ROAR

HEY... THAT SOUNDS LIKE A SHIP'S EMERGENCY SIREN!

HONK WHOOO HONNK

126

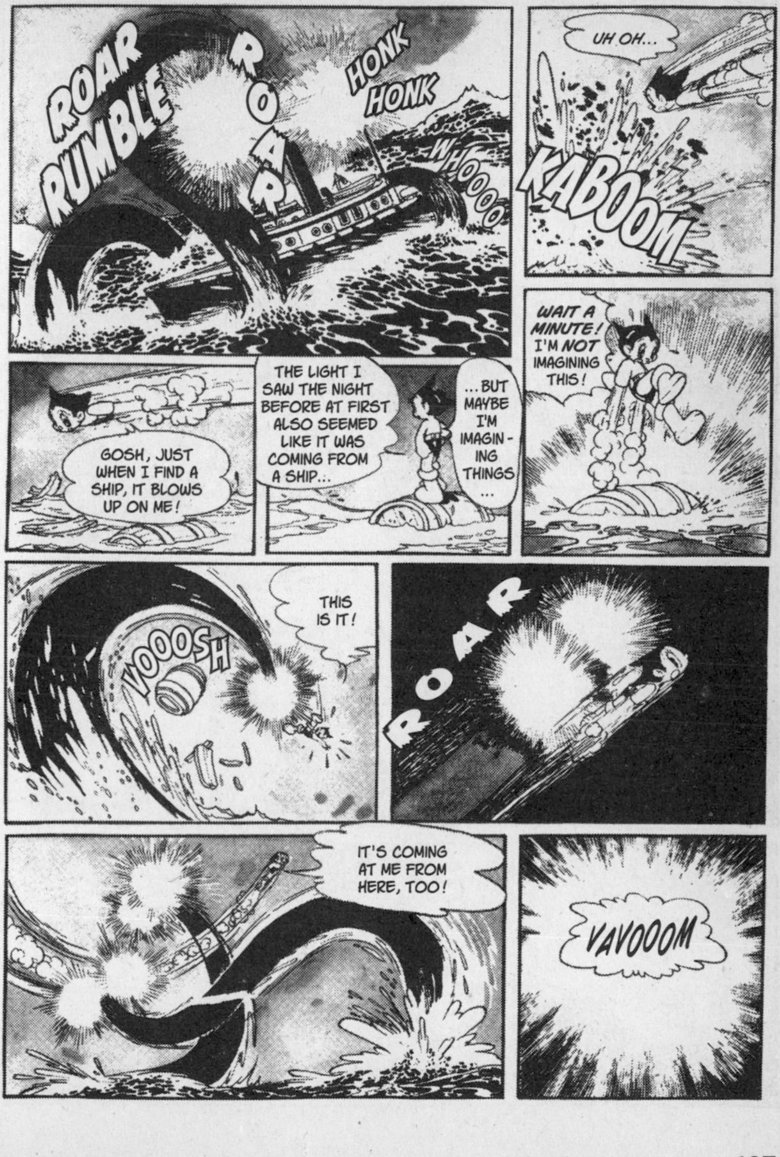
ROAR
RUMBLE
ROAR
HONK
HONK
WHOOOO
UH OH...
KABOOM
GOSH, JUST WHEN I FIND A SHIP, IT BLOWS UP ON ME!
THE LIGHT I SAW THE NIGHT BEFORE AT FIRST ALSO SEEMED LIKE IT WAS COMING FROM A SHIP...
...BUT MAYBE I'M IMAGIN-ING THINGS...
WAIT A MINUTE! I'M NOT IMAGINING THIS!
THIS IS IT!
VOOOSH
ROAR
IT'S COMING AT ME FROM HERE, TOO!
VAVOOOM

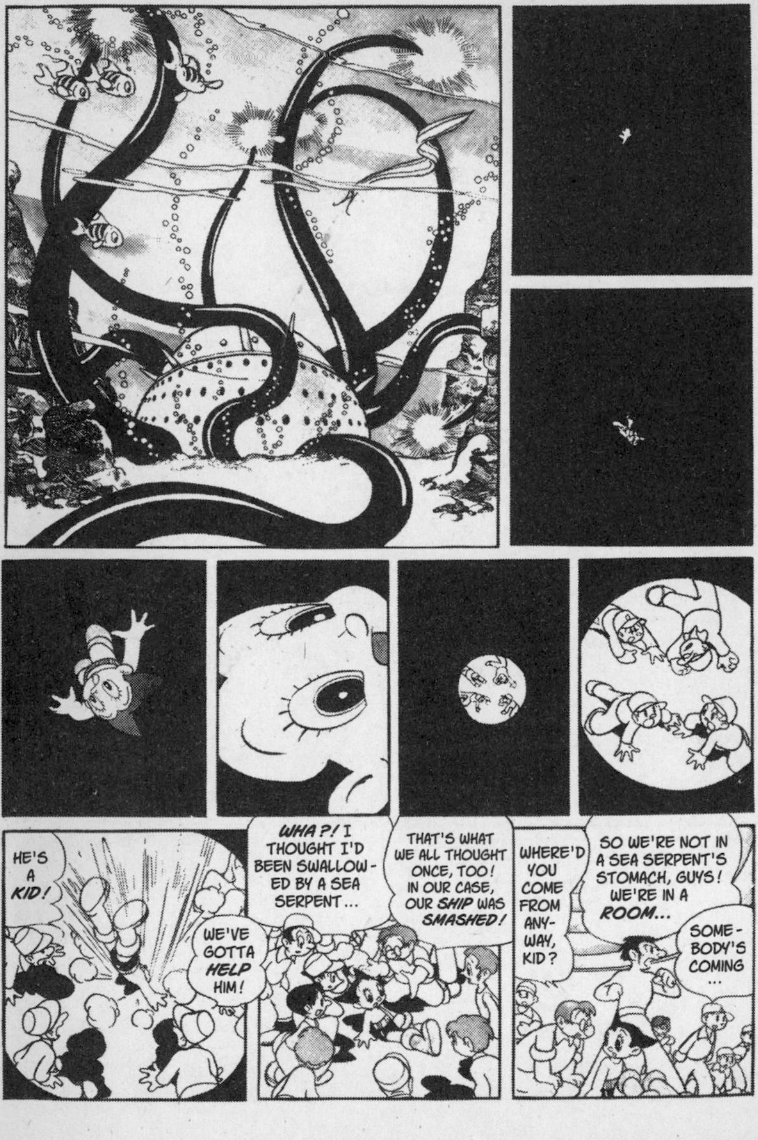
HE'S A KID!
WE'VE GOTTA HELP HIM!
WHA?! I THOUGHT I'D BEEN SWALLOW-ED BY A SEA SERPENT...
THAT'S WHAT WE ALL THOUGHT ONCE, TOO! IN OUR CASE, OUR SHIP WAS SMASHED!
WHERE'D YOU COME FROM ANY-WAY, KID?
SO WE'RE NOT IN A SEA SERPENT'S STOMACH, GUYS! WE'RE IN A ROOM...
SOME-BODY'S COMING...

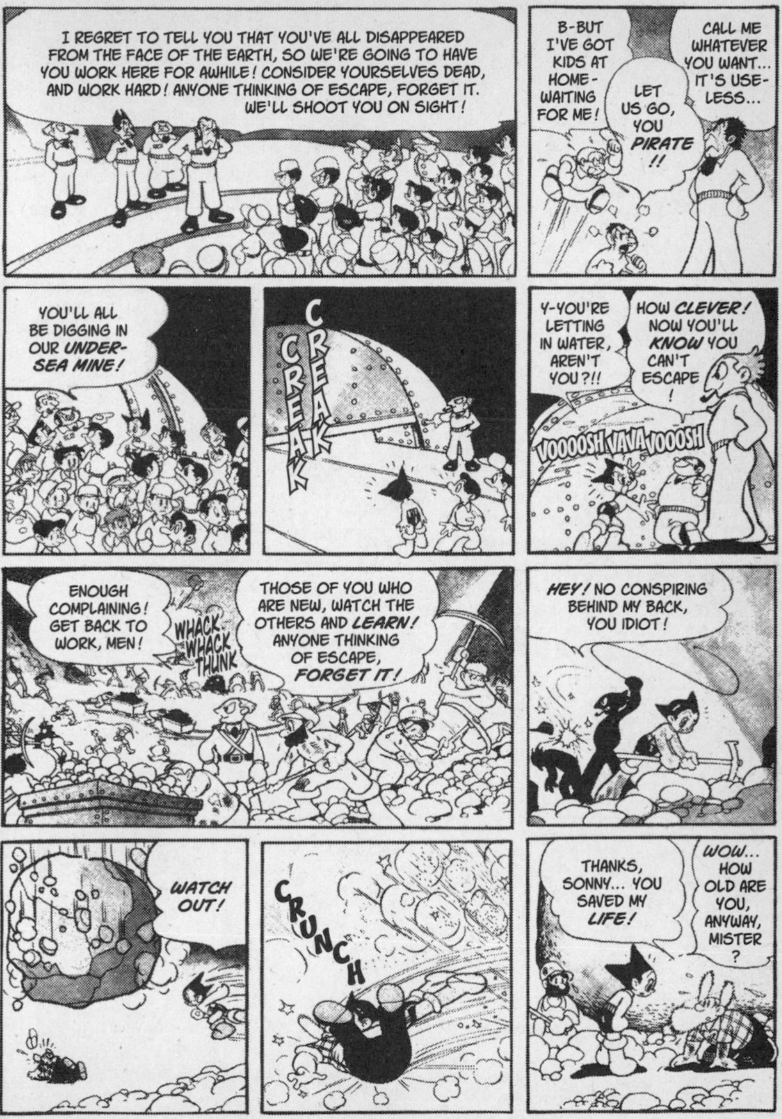
I REGRET TO TELL YOU THAT YOU'VE ALL DISAPPEARED FROM THE FACE OF THE EARTH, SO WE'RE GOING TO HAVE YOU WORK HERE FOR AWHILE! CONSIDER YOURSELVES DEAD, AND WORK HARD! ANYONE THINKING OF ESCAPE, FORGET IT. WE'LL SHOOT YOU ON SIGHT!
B-BUT I'VE GOT KIDS AT HOME-WAITING FOR ME!
LET US GO, YOU PIRATE !!
CALL ME WHATEVER YOU WANT... IT'S USE-LESS...
YOU'LL ALL BE DIGGING IN OUR UNDER-SEA MINE!
CREAK CREAK
Y-YOU'RE LETTING IN WATER, AREN'T YOU?!!
HOW CLEVER! NOW YOU'LL KNOW YOU CAN'T ESCAPE!
VOOOOSH VAVA VOOOSH
ENOUGH COMPLAINING! GET BACK TO WORK, MEN!
WHACK WHACK THUNK
THOSE OF YOU WHO ARE NEW, WATCH THE OTHERS AND LEARN! ANYONE THINKING OF ESCAPE, FORGET IT!
HEY! NO CONSPIRING BEHIND MY BACK, YOU IDIOT!
WATCH OUT!
CRUNCH
THANKS, SONNY... YOU SAVED MY LIFE!
WOW... HOW OLD ARE YOU, ANYWAY, MISTER?

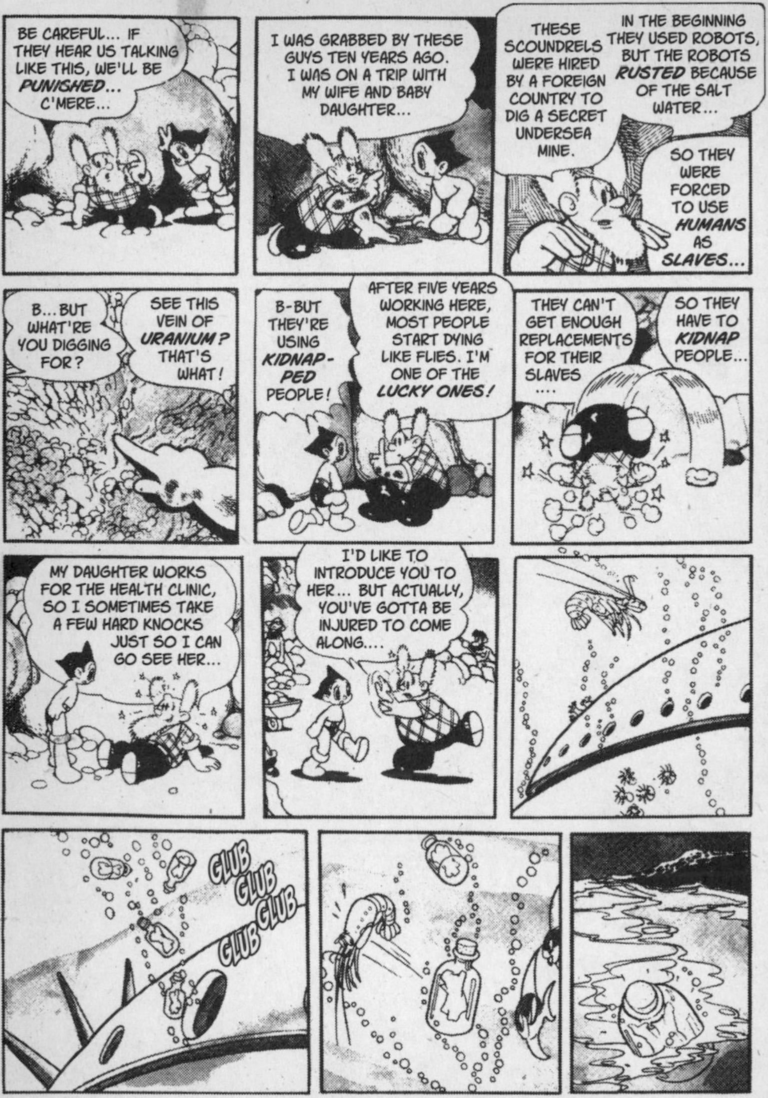
BE CAREFUL... IF THEY HEAR US TALKING LIKE THIS, WE'LL BE PUNISHED... C'MERE...
I WAS GRABBED BY THESE GUYS TEN YEARS AGO. I WAS ON A TRIP WITH MY WIFE AND BABY DAUGHTER...
THESE SCOUNDRELS WERE HIRED BY A FOREIGN COUNTRY TO DIG A SECRET UNDERSEA MINE.
IN THE BEGINNING THEY USED ROBOTS, BUT THE ROBOTS RUSTED BECAUSE OF THE SALT WATER...
SO THEY WERE FORCED TO USE HUMANS AS SLAVES...
B... BUT WHAT'RE YOU DIGGING FOR?
SEE THIS VEIN OF URANIUM? THAT'S WHAT!
B-BUT THEY'RE USING KIDNAP-PED PEOPLE!
AFTER FIVE YEARS WORKING HERE, MOST PEOPLE START DYING LIKE FLIES. I'M ONE OF THE LUCKY ONES!
THEY CAN'T GET ENOUGH REPLACEMENTS FOR THEIR SLAVES ....
SO THEY HAVE TO KIDNAP PEOPLE...
MY DAUGHTER WORKS FOR THE HEALTH CLINIC, SO I SOMETIMES TAKE A FEW HARD KNOCKS JUST SO I CAN GO SEE HER...
I'D LIKE TO INTRODUCE YOU TO HER... BUT ACTUALLY, YOU'VE GOTTA BE INJURED TO COME ALONG....
GLUB GLUB GLUB GLUB

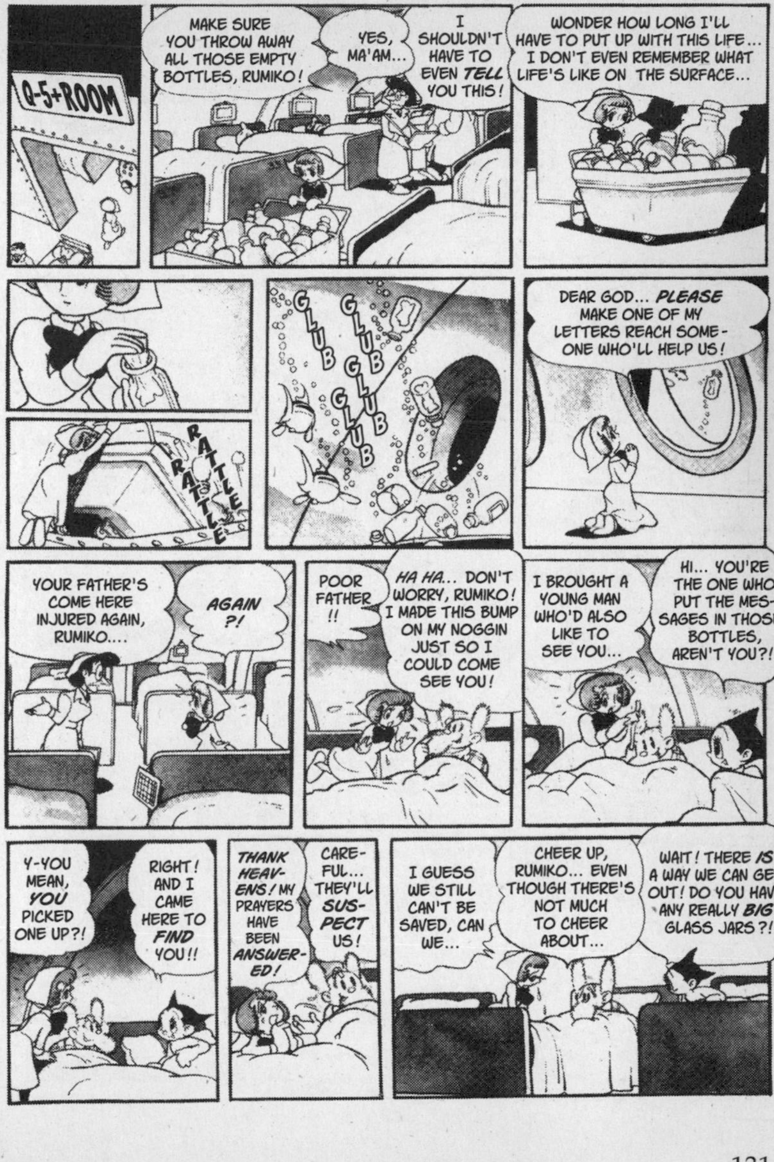
Q-5+ROOM
MAKE SURE YOU THROW AWAY ALL THOSE EMPTY BOTTLES, RUMIKO!
YES, MA'AM...
I SHOULDN'T HAVE TO EVEN TELL YOU THIS!
WONDER HOW LONG I'LL HAVE TO PUT UP WITH THIS LIFE... I DON'T EVEN REMEMBER WHAT LIFE'S LIKE ON THE SURFACE...
RATTLE RATTLE
GLUB GLUB GLUB GLUB
DEAR GOD... PLEASE MAKE ONE OF MY LETTERS REACH SOME-ONE WHO'LL HELP US!
YOUR FATHER'S COME HERE INJURED AGAIN, RUMIKO....
AGAIN ?!
POOR FATHER !!
HA HA... DON'T WORRY, RUMIKO! I MADE THIS BUMP ON MY NOGGIN JUST SO I COULD COME SEE YOU!
I BROUGHT A YOUNG MAN WHO'D ALSO LIKE TO SEE YOU...
HI... YOU'RE THE ONE WHO PUT THE MES-SAGES IN THOSE BOTTLES, AREN'T YOU?!
Y-YOU MEAN, YOU PICKED ONE UP?!
RIGHT! AND I CAME HERE TO FIND YOU!!
THANK HEAV-ENS! MY PRAYERS HAVE BEEN ANSWER-ED!
CARE-FUL... THEY'LL SUS-PECT US!
I GUESS WE STILL CAN'T BE SAVED, CAN WE...
CHEER UP, RUMIKO... EVEN THOUGH THERE'S NOT MUCH TO CHEER ABOUT...
WAIT! THERE IS A WAY WE CAN GET OUT! DO YOU HAVE ANY REALLY BIG GLASS JARS?!

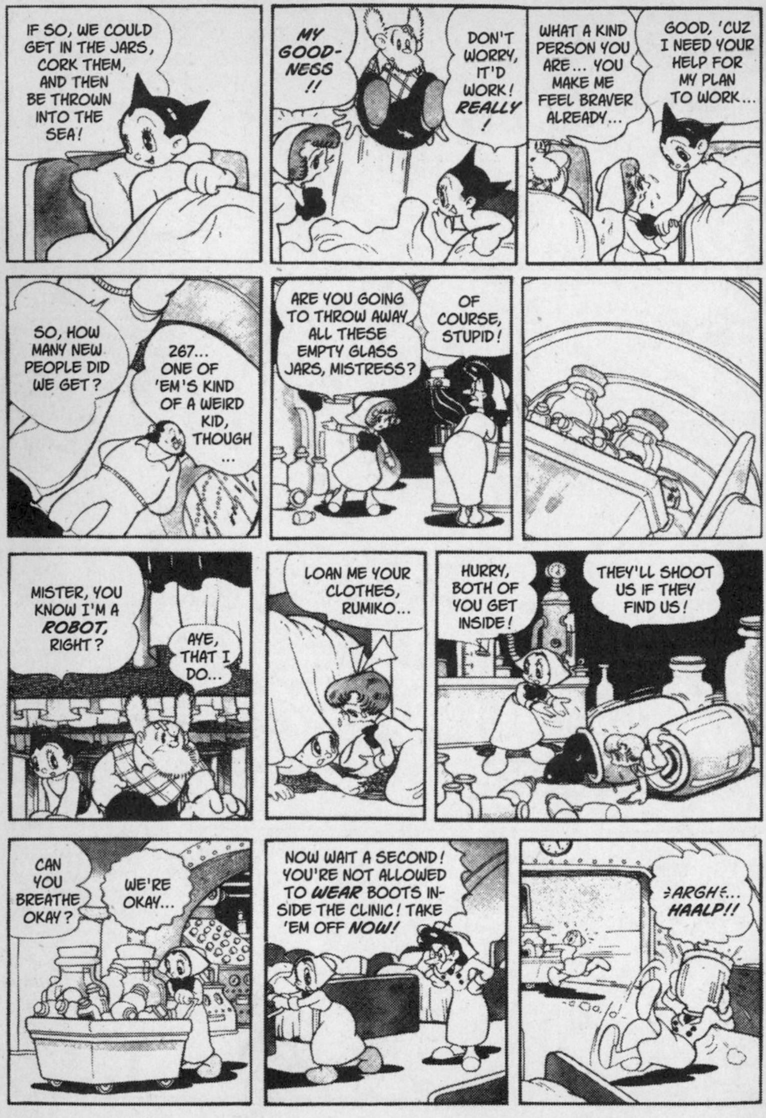
IF SO, WE COULD GET IN THE JARS, CORK THEM, AND THEN BE THROWN INTO THE SEA!
MY GOODNESS!!
DON'T WORRY, IT'D WORK! REALLY!
WHAT A KIND PERSON YOU ARE... YOU MAKE ME FEEL BRAVER ALREADY...
GOOD, 'CUZ I NEED YOUR HELP FOR MY PLAN TO WORK...
SO, HOW MANY NEW PEOPLE DID WE GET?
267... ONE OF 'EM'S KIND OF A WEIRD KID, THOUGH...
ARE YOU GOING TO THROW AWAY ALL THESE EMPTY GLASS JARS, MISTRESS?
OF COURSE, STUPID!
MISTER, YOU KNOW I'M A ROBOT, RIGHT?
AYE, THAT I DO...
LOAN ME YOUR CLOTHES, RUMIKO...
HURRY, BOTH OF YOU GET INSIDE!
THEY'LL SHOOT US IF THEY FIND US!
CAN YOU BREATHE OKAY?
WE'RE OKAY...
NOW WAIT A SECOND! YOU'RE NOT ALLOWED TO WEAR BOOTS INSIDE THE CLINIC! TAKE 'EM OFF NOW!
ARGH... HAALP!!

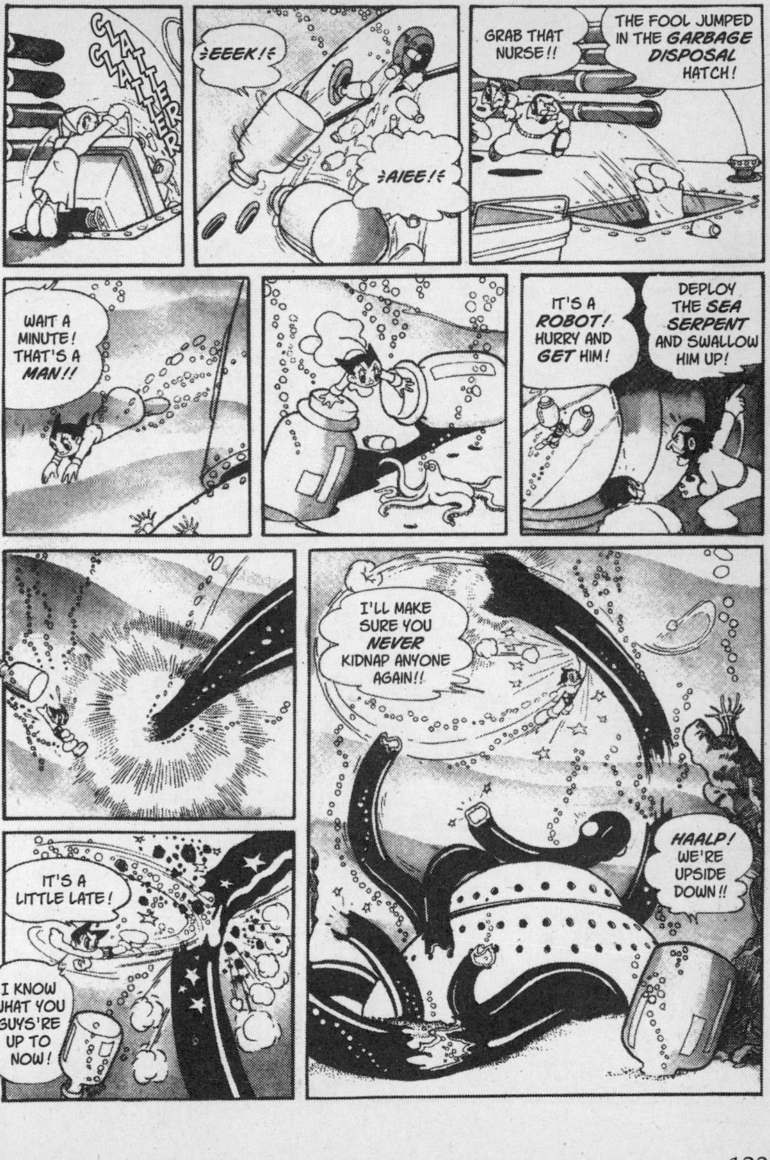
CLATTER CLATTER
EEEK!
AIEE!
GRAB THAT NURSE!!
THE FOOL JUMPED IN THE GARBAGE DISPOSAL HATCH!
WAIT A MINUTE! THAT'S A MAN!!
IT'S A ROBOT! HURRY AND GET HIM!
DEPLOY THE SEA SERPENT AND SWALLOW HIM UP!
I'LL MAKE SURE YOU NEVER KIDNAP ANYONE AGAIN!!
HAALP! WE'RE UPSIDE DOWN!!
IT'S A LITTLE LATE!
I KNOW WHAT YOU GUYS'RE UP TO NOW!

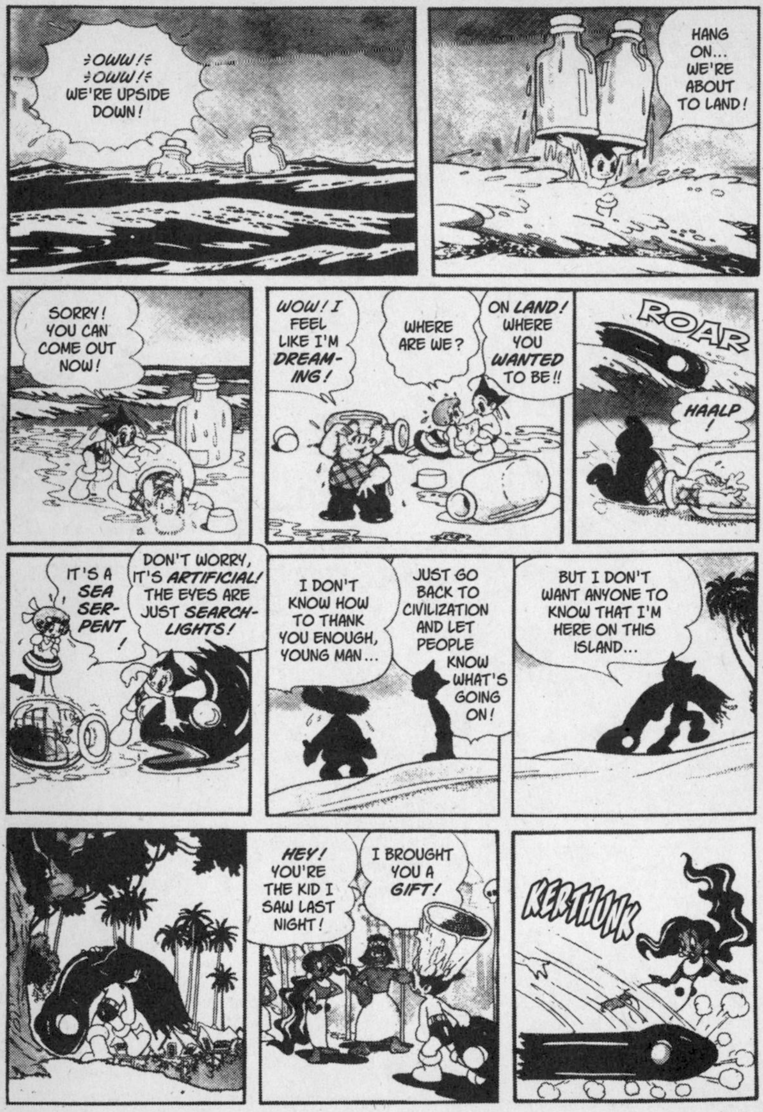
OWW! OWW! WE'RE UPSIDE DOWN!
HANG ON... WE'RE ABOUT TO LAND!
SORRY! YOU CAN COME OUT NOW!
WOW! I FEEL LIKE I'M DREAMING!
WHERE ARE WE?
ON LAND! WHERE YOU WANTED TO BE!!
ROAR
HAALP!
IT'S A SEA SERPENT!
DON'T WORRY, IT'S ARTIFICIAL! THE EYES ARE JUST SEARCHLIGHTS!
I DON'T KNOW HOW TO THANK YOU ENOUGH, YOUNG MAN...
JUST GO BACK TO CIVILIZATION AND LET PEOPLE KNOW WHAT'S GOING ON!
BUT I DON'T WANT ANYONE TO KNOW THAT I'M HERE ON THIS ISLAND...
HEY! YOU'RE THE KID I SAW LAST NIGHT!
I BROUGHT YOU A GIFT!
KERTHUNK

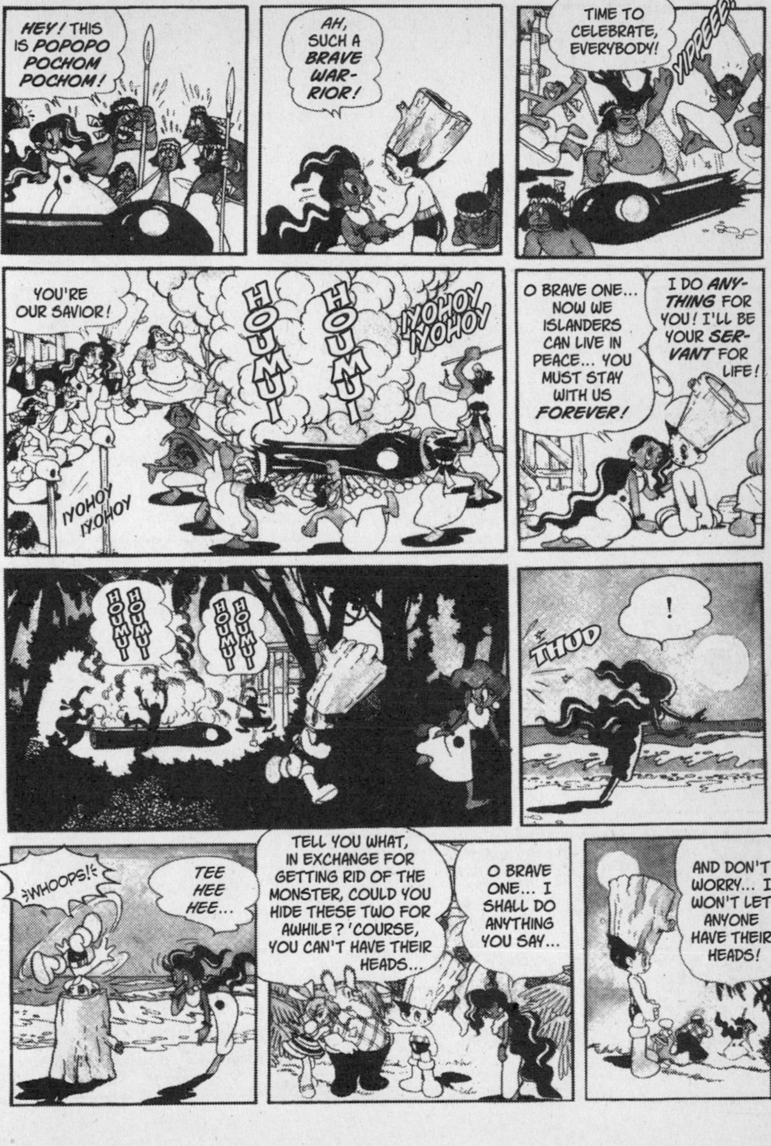
HEY! THIS IS POPOPO POCHOM POCHOM!
AH, SUCH A BRAVE WARRIOR!
TIME TO CELEBRATE, EVERYBODY!
YIPPEEE!
YOU'RE OUR SAVIOR!
HOUMUI
HOUMUI
IYOHOY IYOHOY
IYOHOY IYOHOY
O BRAVE ONE... NOW WE ISLANDERS CAN LIVE IN PEACE... YOU MUST STAY WITH US FOREVER!
I DO ANYTHING FOR YOU! I'LL BE YOUR SERVANT FOR LIFE!
HOUMUI HOUMUI
HOUMUI HOUMUI
!
THUD
WHOOPS!
TEE HEE HEE...
TELL YOU WHAT, IN EXCHANGE FOR GETTING RID OF THE MONSTER, COULD YOU HIDE THESE TWO FOR AWHILE? 'COURSE, YOU CAN'T HAVE THEIR HEADS...
O BRAVE ONE... I SHALL DO ANYTHING YOU SAY...
AND DON'T WORRY... I WON'T LET ANYONE HAVE THEIR HEADS!

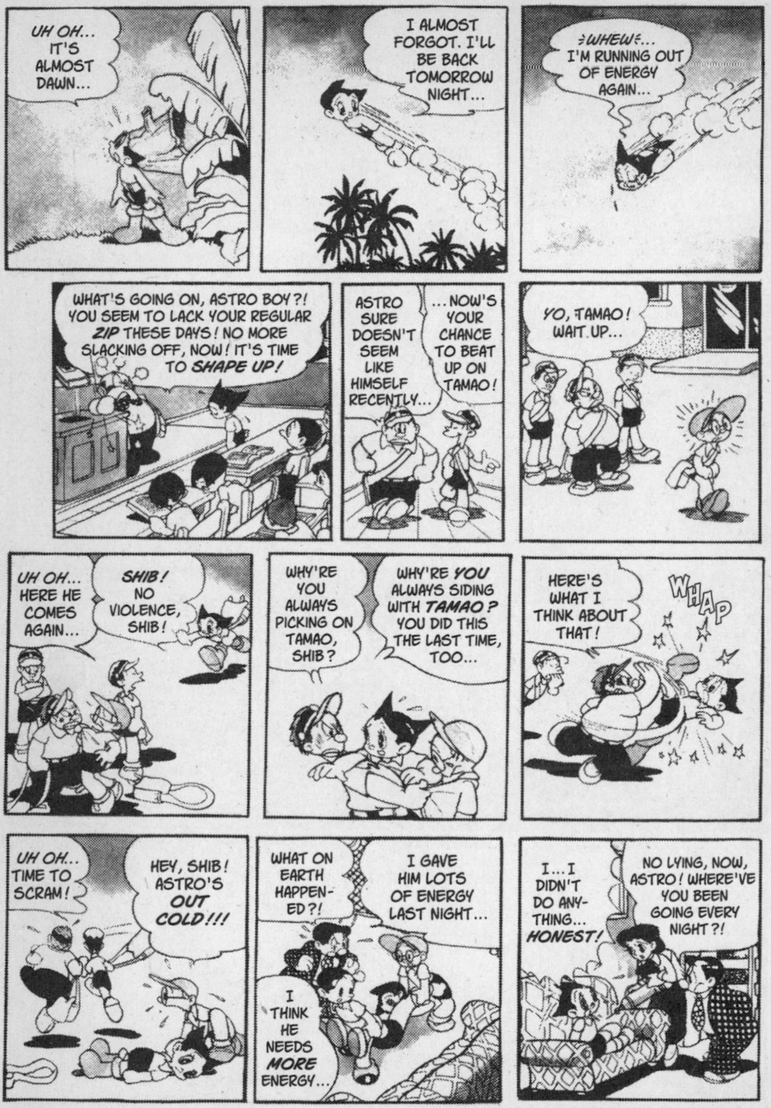
UH OH... IT'S ALMOST DAWN...
I ALMOST FORGOT. I'LL BE BACK TOMORROW NIGHT...
WHEW... I'M RUNNING OUT OF ENERGY AGAIN...
WHAT'S GOING ON, ASTRO BOY?! YOU SEEM TO LACK YOUR REGULAR ZIP THESE DAYS! NO MORE SLACKING OFF, NOW! IT'S TIME TO SHAPE UP!
ASTRO SURE DOESN'T SEEM LIKE HIMSELF RECENTLY...
...NOW'S YOUR CHANCE TO BEAT UP ON TAMAO!
YO, TAMAO! WAIT UP...
UH OH... HERE HE COMES AGAIN...
SHIB! NO VIOLENCE, SHIB!
WHY'RE YOU ALWAYS PICKING ON TAMAO, SHIB?
WHY'RE YOU ALWAYS SIDING WITH TAMAO? YOU DID THIS THE LAST TIME, TOO...
HERE'S WHAT I THINK ABOUT THAT!
WHAP
UH OH... TIME TO SCRAM!
HEY, SHIB! ASTRO'S OUT COLD!!!
WHAT ON EARTH HAPPENED?!
I GAVE HIM LOTS OF ENERGY LAST NIGHT...
I THINK HE NEEDS MORE ENERGY...
I... I DIDN'T DO ANYTHING... HONEST!
NO LYING, NOW, ASTRO! WHERE'VE YOU BEEN GOING EVERY NIGHT?!

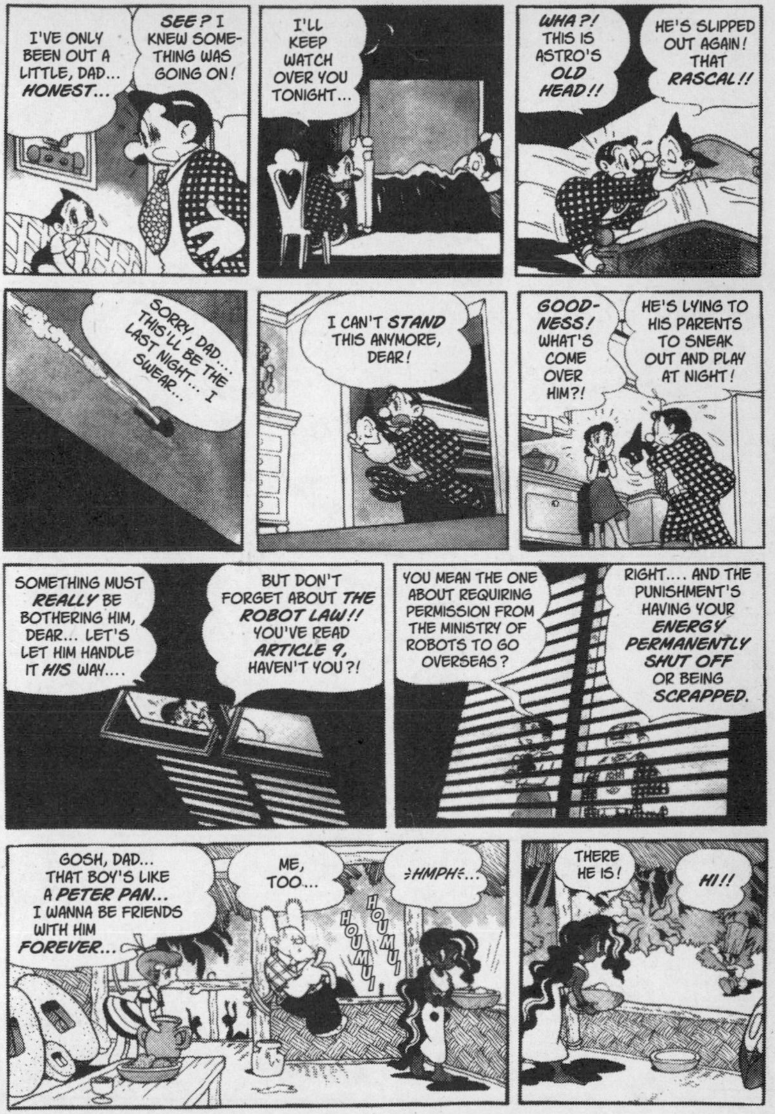

I'VE ONLY BEEN OUT A LITTLE, DAD... HONEST...
SEE? I KNEW SOMETHING WAS GOING ON!
I'LL KEEP WATCH OVER YOU TONIGHT...
WHA?! THIS IS ASTRO'S OLD HEAD!!
HE'S SLIPPED OUT AGAIN! THAT RASCAL!!
SORRY, DAD.... THIS'LL BE THE LAST NIGHT... I SWEAR...
I CAN'T STAND THIS ANYMORE, DEAR!
GOODNESS! WHAT'S COME OVER HIM?!
HE'S LYING TO HIS PARENTS TO SNEAK OUT AND PLAY AT NIGHT!
SOMETHING MUST REALLY BE BOTHERING HIM, DEAR... LET'S LET HIM HANDLE IT HIS WAY....
BUT DON'T FORGET ABOUT THE ROBOT LAW!! YOU'VE READ ARTICLE 9, HAVEN'T YOU?!
YOU MEAN THE ONE ABOUT REQUIRING PERMISSION FROM THE MINISTRY OF ROBOTS TO GO OVERSEAS?
RIGHT.... AND THE PUNISHMENT'S HAVING YOUR ENERGY PERMANENTLY SHUT OFF OR BEING SCRAPPED.
GOSH, DAD... THAT BOY'S LIKE A PETER PAN... I WANNA BE FRIENDS WITH HIM FOREVER...
ME, TOO...
HOUMUI
HOUMUI
≶HMPH≷...
THERE HE IS!
HI!!

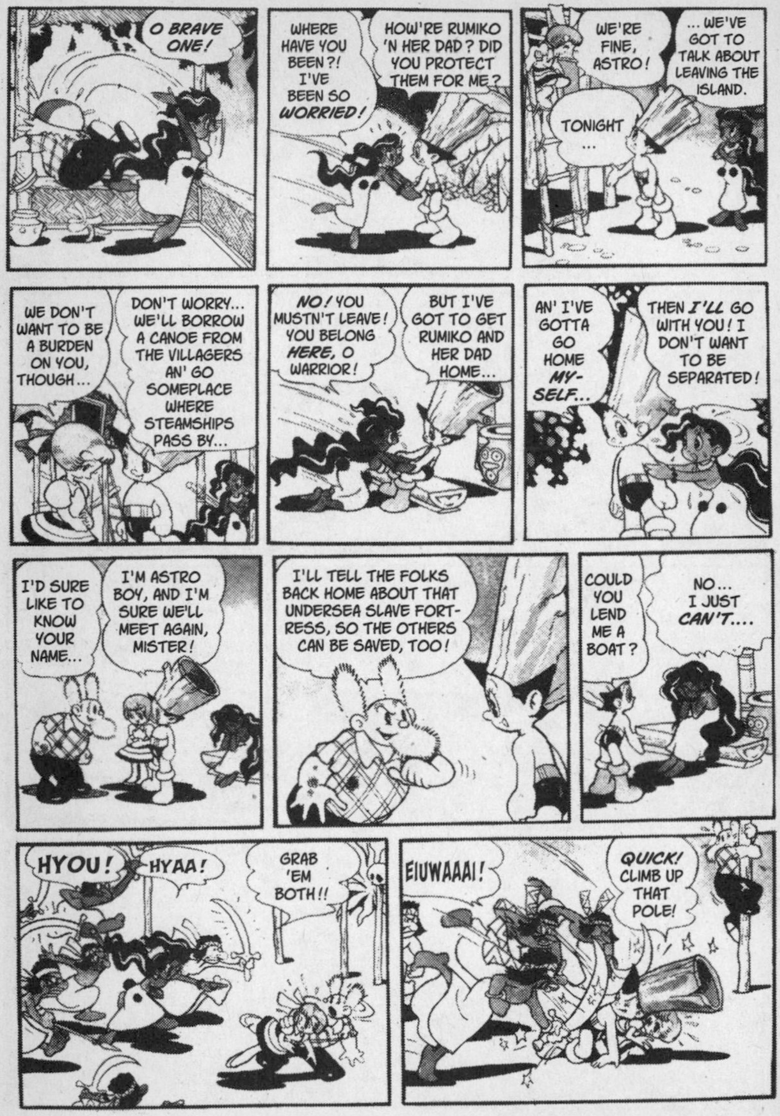
O BRAVE ONE!
WHERE HAVE YOU BEEN?! I'VE BEEN SO WORRIED!
HOW'RE RUMIKO 'N HER DAD? DID YOU PROTECT THEM FOR ME?
WE'RE FINE, ASTRO!
TONIGHT ...
... WE'VE GOT TO TALK ABOUT LEAVING THE ISLAND.
WE DON'T WANT TO BE A BURDEN ON YOU, THOUGH...
DON'T WORRY... WE'LL BORROW A CANOE FROM THE VILLAGERS AN' GO SOMEPLACE WHERE STEAMSHIPS PASS BY...
NO! YOU MUSTN'T LEAVE! YOU BELONG HERE, O WARRIOR!
BUT I'VE GOT TO GET RUMIKO AND HER DAD HOME...
AN' I'VE GOTTA GO HOME MY-SELF...
THEN I'LL GO WITH YOU! I DON'T WANT TO BE SEPARATED!
I'D SURE LIKE TO KNOW YOUR NAME...
I'M ASTRO BOY, AND I'M SURE WE'LL MEET AGAIN, MISTER!
I'LL TELL THE FOLKS BACK HOME ABOUT THAT UNDERSEA SLAVE FORT-RESS, SO THE OTHERS CAN BE SAVED, TOO!
COULD YOU LEND ME A BOAT?
NO... I JUST CAN'T....
HYOU!
HYAA!
GRAB 'EM BOTH!!
EIUWAAAI!
QUICK! CLIMB UP THAT POLE!

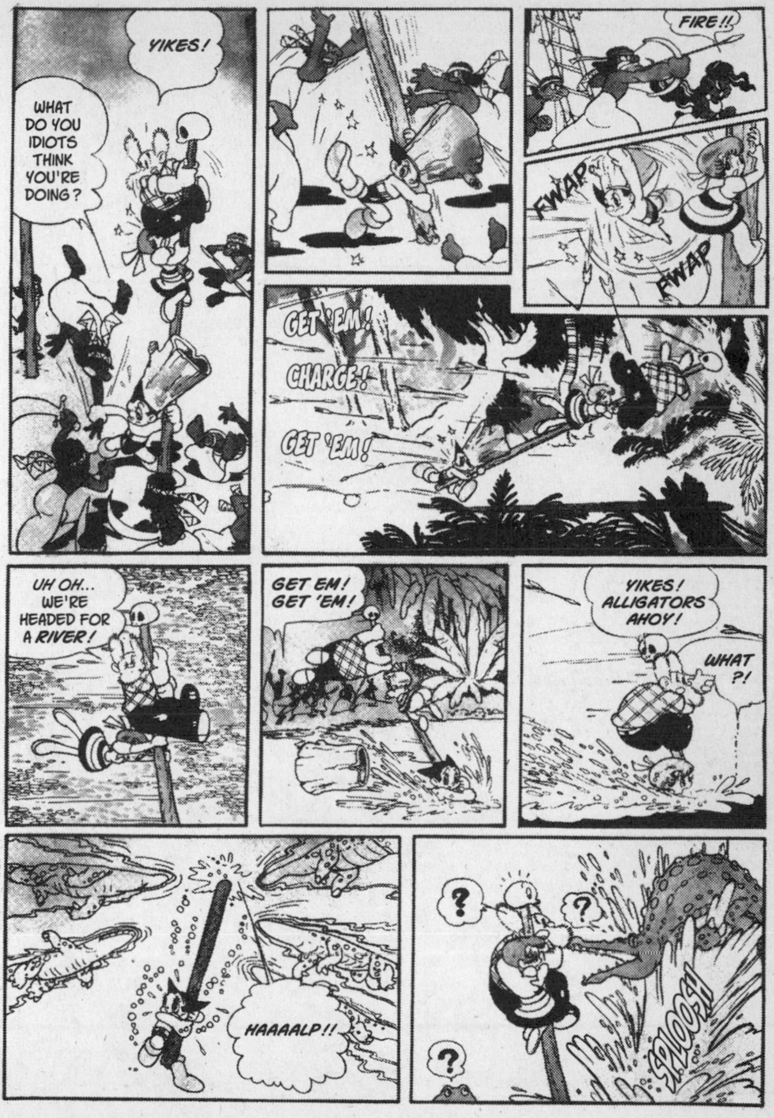
YIKES!
WHAT DO YOU IDIOTS THINK YOU'RE DOING?
FIRE!!
FWAP
FWAP
GET 'EM!
CHARGE!
GET 'EM!
UH OH... WE'RE HEADED FOR A RIVER!
GET EM! GET 'EM!
YIKES! ALLIGATORS AHOY!
WHAT ?!
HAAAALP!!
?
?
?
SPLOOSH

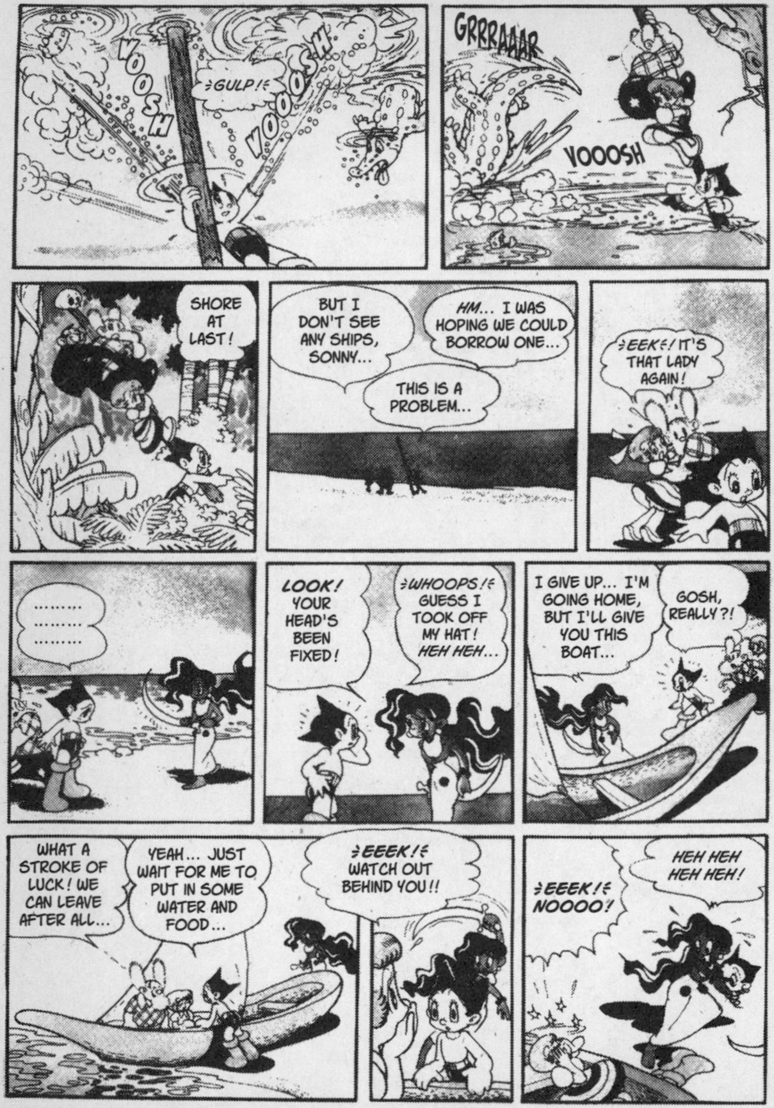
VOOSH
GULP!
VOOOSH
GRRRAAAR
VOOOSH
SHORE AT LAST!
BUT I DON'T SEE ANY SHIPS, SONNY...
HM... I WAS HOPING WE COULD BORROW ONE...
THIS IS A PROBLEM...
EEK! IT'S THAT LADY AGAIN!
....
....
....
LOOK! YOUR HEAD'S BEEN FIXED!
WHOOPS! GUESS I TOOK OFF MY HAT! HEH HEH...
I GIVE UP... I'M GOING HOME, BUT I'LL GIVE YOU THIS BOAT...
GOSH, REALLY?!
WHAT A STROKE OF LUCK! WE CAN LEAVE AFTER ALL...
YEAH... JUST WAIT FOR ME TO PUT IN SOME WATER AND FOOD...
EEEK! WATCH OUT BEHIND YOU!!
EEEK! NOOOO!
HEH HEH HEH HEH!

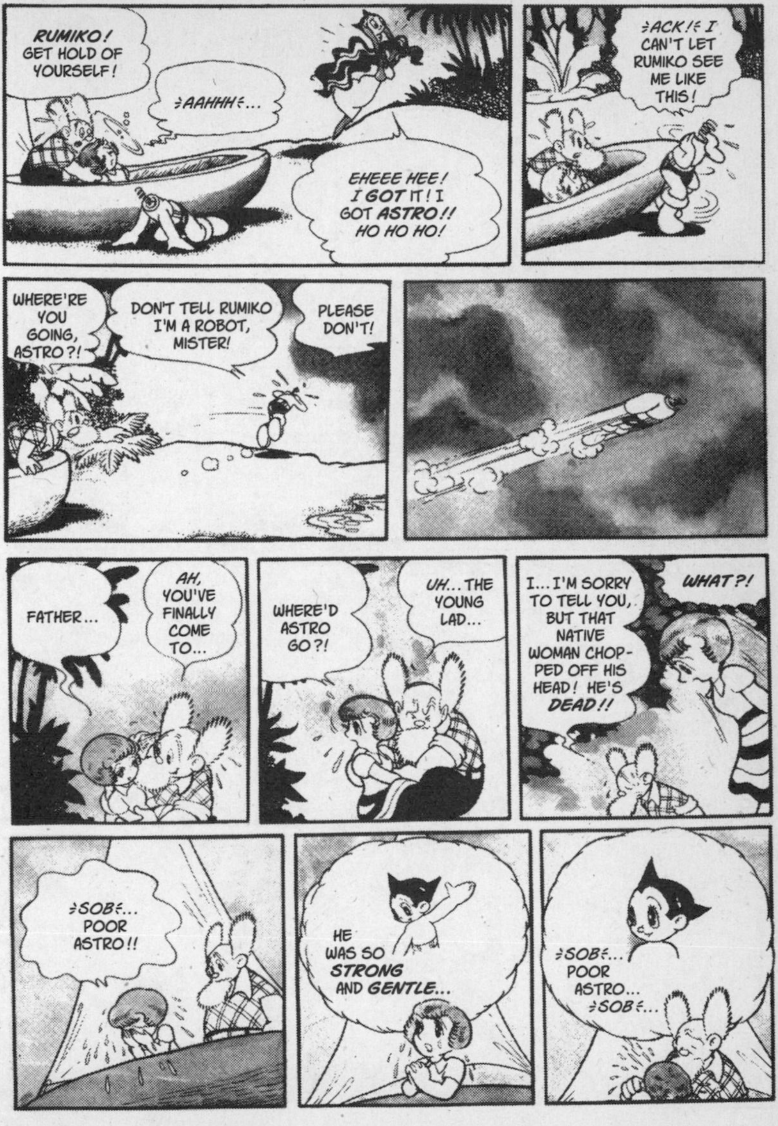
RUMIKO! GET HOLD OF YOURSELF!
≥AAHHH≤...
EHEEE HEE! I GOT IT! I GOT ASTRO!! HO HO HO!
≥ACK!≤ I CAN'T LET RUMIKO SEE ME LIKE THIS!
WHERE'RE YOU GOING, ASTRO?!
DON'T TELL RUMIKO I'M A ROBOT, MISTER!
PLEASE DON'T!
FATHER...
AH, YOU'VE FINALLY COME TO...
WHERE'D ASTRO GO?!
UH... THE YOUNG LAD...
I... I'M SORRY TO TELL YOU, BUT THAT NATIVE WOMAN CHOPPED OFF HIS HEAD! HE'S DEAD!!
WHAT?!
≥SOB≤... POOR ASTRO!!
HE WAS SO STRONG AND GENTLE...
≥SOB≤... POOR ASTRO... ≥SOB≤...

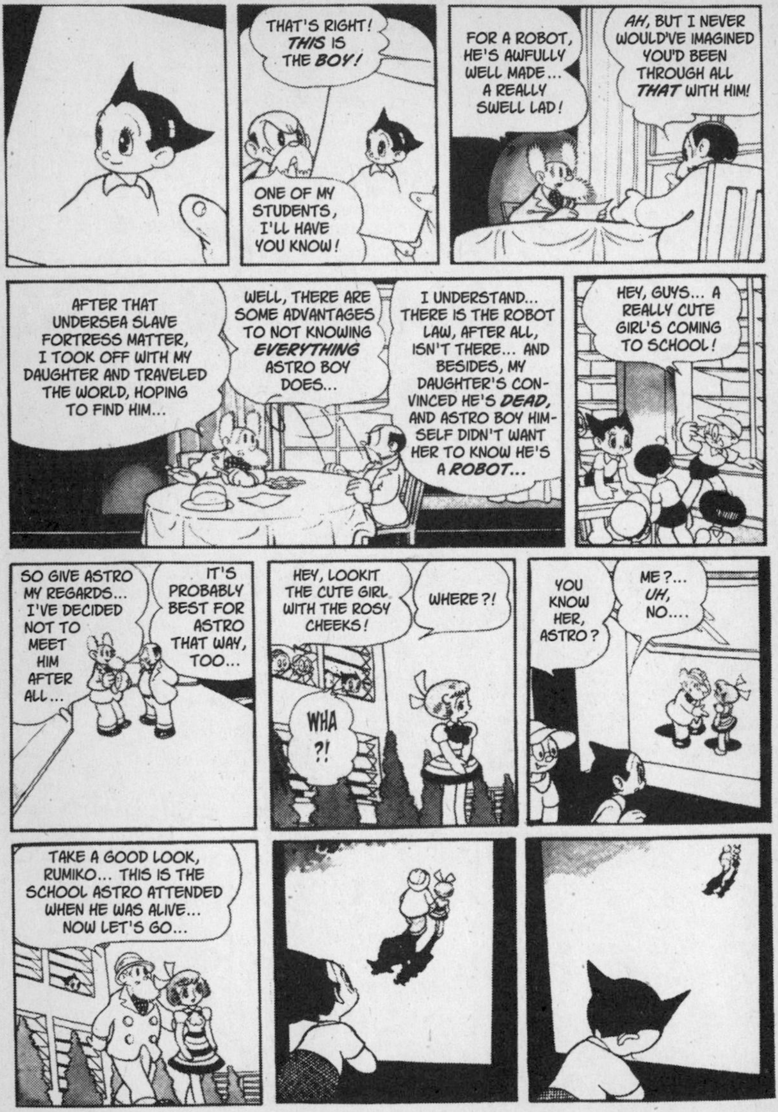
THAT'S RIGHT! THIS IS THE BOY!
ONE OF MY STUDENTS, I'LL HAVE YOU KNOW!
FOR A ROBOT, HE'S AWFULLY WELL MADE... A REALLY SWELL LAD!
AH, BUT I NEVER WOULD'VE IMAGINED YOU'D BEEN THROUGH ALL THAT WITH HIM!
AFTER THAT UNDERSEA SLAVE FORTRESS MATTER, I TOOK OFF WITH MY DAUGHTER AND TRAVELED THE WORLD, HOPING TO FIND HIM...
WELL, THERE ARE SOME ADVANTAGES TO NOT KNOWING EVERYTHING ASTRO BOY DOES...
I UNDERSTAND... THERE IS THE ROBOT LAW, AFTER ALL, ISN'T THERE... AND BESIDES, MY DAUGHTER'S CONVINCED HE'S DEAD, AND ASTRO BOY HIMSELF DIDN'T WANT HER TO KNOW HE'S A ROBOT...
HEY, GUYS... A REALLY CUTE GIRL'S COMING TO SCHOOL!
SO GIVE ASTRO MY REGARDS... I'VE DECIDED NOT TO MEET HIM AFTER ALL...
IT'S PROBABLY BEST FOR ASTRO THAT WAY, TOO...
HEY, LOOKIT THE CUTE GIRL WITH THE ROSY CHEEKS!
WHERE?!
WHA ?!
YOU KNOW HER, ASTRO?
ME?... UH, NO....
TAKE A GOOD LOOK, RUMIKO... THIS IS THE SCHOOL ASTRO ATTENDED WHEN HE WAS ALIVE... NOW LET'S GO...

FRANKENSTEIN

First serialized from November 1952 to April
1953 in *Shonen* magazine.

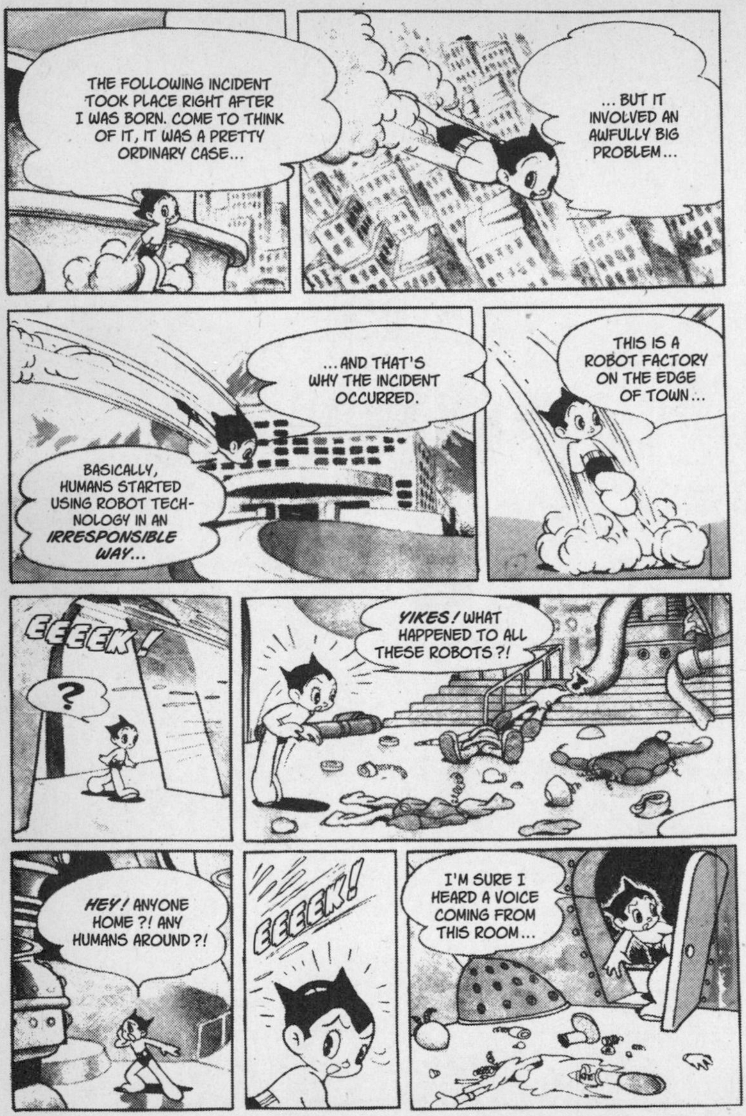
THE FOLLOWING INCIDENT TOOK PLACE RIGHT AFTER I WAS BORN. COME TO THINK OF IT, IT WAS A PRETTY ORDINARY CASE...
... BUT IT INVOLVED AN AWFULLY BIG PROBLEM...
BASICALLY, HUMANS STARTED USING ROBOT TECHNOLOGY IN AN IRRESPONSIBLE WAY...
...AND THAT'S WHY THE INCIDENT OCCURRED.
THIS IS A ROBOT FACTORY ON THE EDGE OF TOWN...
EEEEK!
?
YIKES! WHAT HAPPENED TO ALL THESE ROBOTS?!
HEY! ANYONE HOME?! ANY HUMANS AROUND?!
EEEEK!
I'M SURE I HEARD A VOICE COMING FROM THIS ROOM...

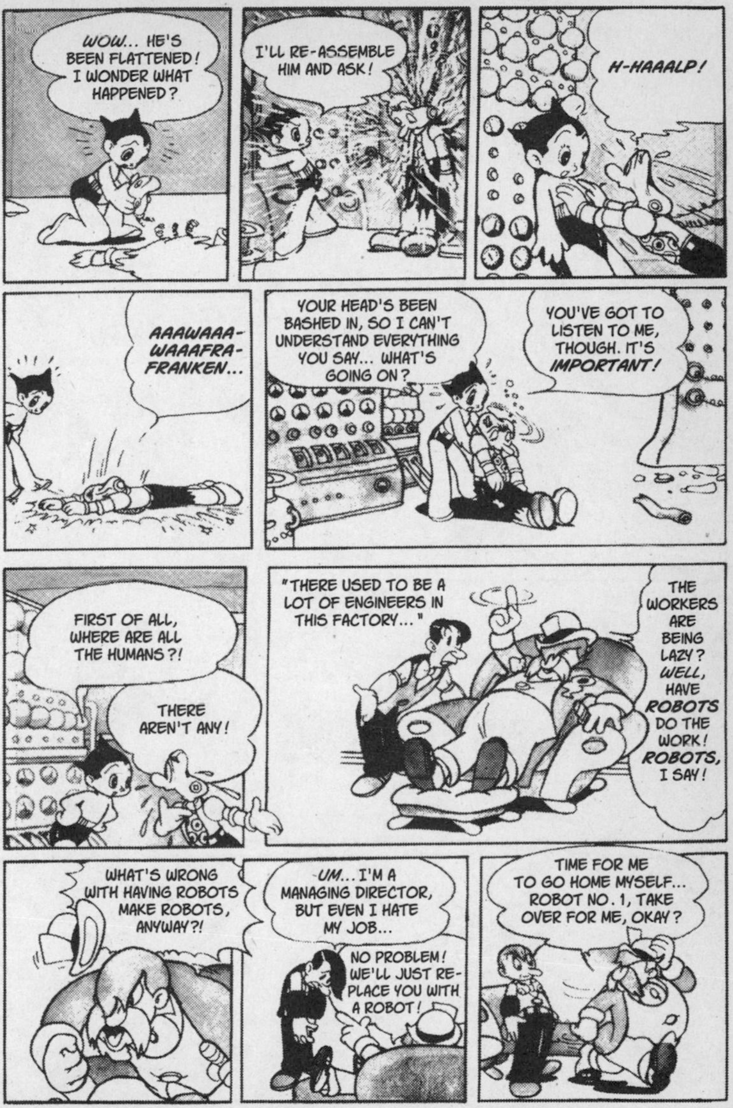
WOW... HE'S BEEN FLATTENED! I WONDER WHAT HAPPENED?
I'LL RE-ASSEMBLE HIM AND ASK!
H-HAAALP!
AAAWAAA-WAAAFRA-FRANKEN...
YOUR HEAD'S BEEN BASHED IN, SO I CAN'T UNDERSTAND EVERYTHING YOU SAY... WHAT'S GOING ON?
YOU'VE GOT TO LISTEN TO ME, THOUGH. IT'S IMPORTANT!
FIRST OF ALL, WHERE ARE ALL THE HUMANS?!
THERE AREN'T ANY!
"THERE USED TO BE A LOT OF ENGINEERS IN THIS FACTORY..."
THE WORKERS ARE BEING LAZY? WELL, HAVE ROBOTS DO THE WORK! ROBOTS, I SAY!
WHAT'S WRONG WITH HAVING ROBOTS MAKE ROBOTS, ANYWAY?!
UM... I'M A MANAGING DIRECTOR, BUT EVEN I HATE MY JOB...
NO PROBLEM! WE'LL JUST RE-PLACE YOU WITH A ROBOT!
TIME FOR ME TO GO HOME MYSELF... ROBOT NO. 1, TAKE OVER FOR ME, OKAY?

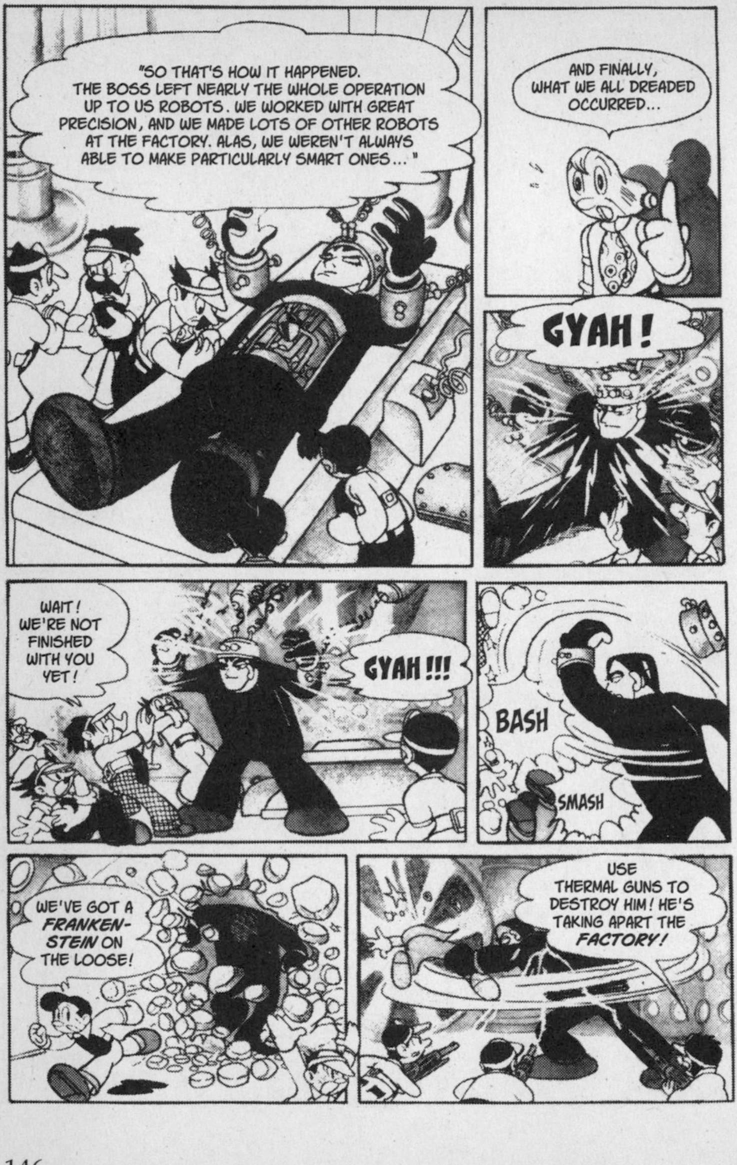
"SO THAT'S HOW IT HAPPENED. THE BOSS LEFT NEARLY THE WHOLE OPERATION UP TO US ROBOTS. WE WORKED WITH GREAT PRECISION, AND WE MADE LOTS OF OTHER ROBOTS AT THE FACTORY. ALAS, WE WEREN'T ALWAYS ABLE TO MAKE PARTICULARLY SMART ONES... "
AND FINALLY, WHAT WE ALL DREADED OCCURRED...
GYAH!
WAIT! WE'RE NOT FINISHED WITH YOU YET!
GYAH!!!
BASH
SMASH
WE'VE GOT A *FRANKEN-STEIN* ON THE LOOSE!
USE THERMAL GUNS TO DESTROY HIM! HE'S TAKING APART THE *FACTORY*!

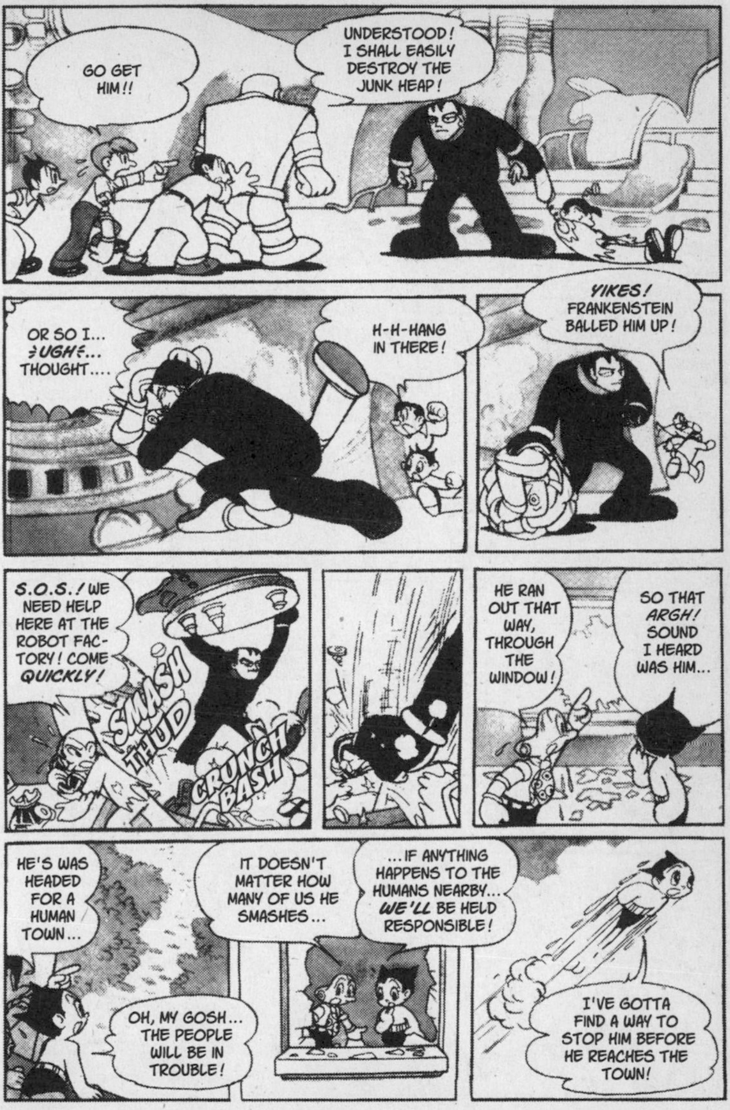
GO GET HIM!!
UNDERSTOOD! I SHALL EASILY DESTROY THE JUNK HEAP!
OR SO I... UGH... THOUGHT....
H-H-HANG IN THERE!
YIKES! FRANKENSTEIN BALLED HIM UP!
S.O.S.! WE NEED HELP HERE AT THE ROBOT FACTORY! COME QUICKLY!
SMASH
THUD
CRUNCH
BASH
HE RAN OUT THAT WAY, THROUGH THE WINDOW!
SO THAT ARGH! SOUND I HEARD WAS HIM...
HE'S WAS HEADED FOR A HUMAN TOWN...
OH, MY GOSH... THE PEOPLE WILL BE IN TROUBLE!
IT DOESN'T MATTER HOW MANY OF US HE SMASHES...
...IF ANYTHING HAPPENS TO THE HUMANS NEARBY... WE'LL BE HELD RESPONSIBLE!
I'VE GOTTA FIND A WAY TO STOP HIM BEFORE HE REACHES THE TOWN!

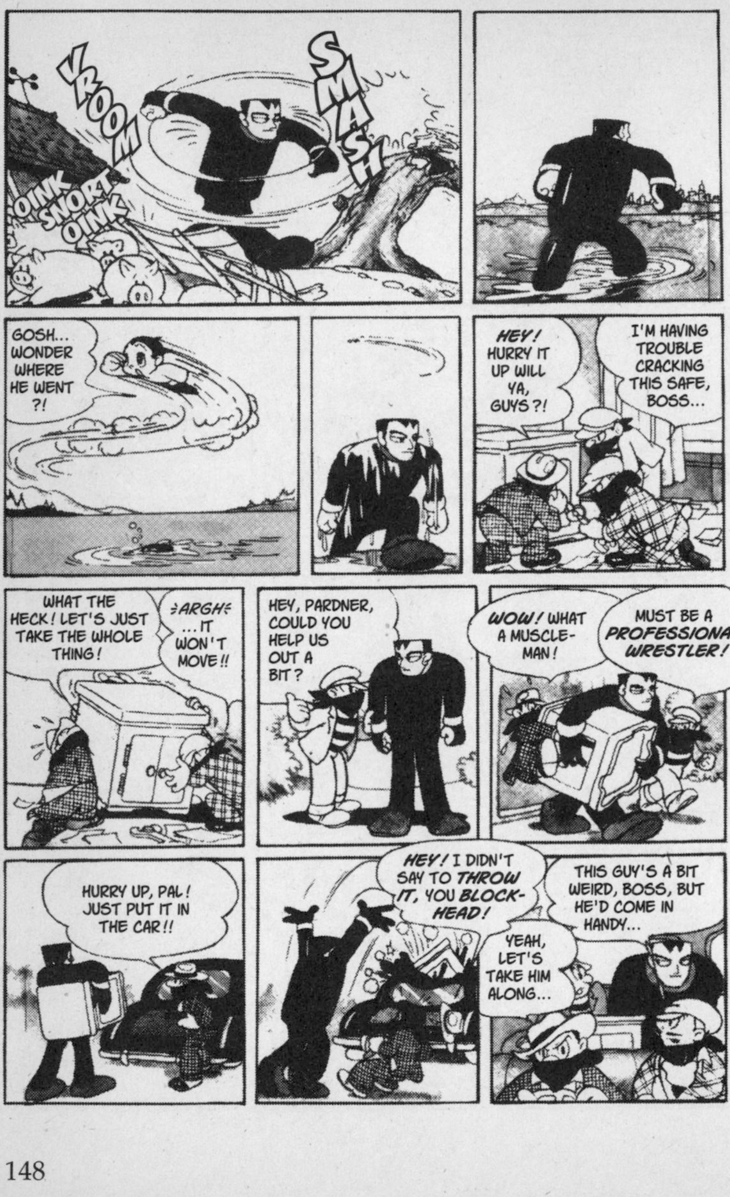
VROOM
SMASH
OINK SNORT OINK
GOSH... WONDER WHERE HE WENT ?!
HEY! HURRY IT UP WILL YA, GUYS ?!
I'M HAVING TROUBLE CRACKING THIS SAFE, BOSS...
WHAT THE HECK! LET'S JUST TAKE THE WHOLE THING!
ARGH ... IT WON'T MOVE!!
HEY, PARDNER, COULD YOU HELP US OUT A BIT ?
WOW! WHAT A MUSCLE-MAN!
MUST BE A PROFESSIONAL WRESTLER!
HURRY UP, PAL! JUST PUT IT IN THE CAR!!
HEY! I DIDN'T SAY TO THROW IT, YOU BLOCK-HEAD!
THIS GUY'S A BIT WEIRD, BOSS, BUT HE'D COME IN HANDY...
YEAH, LET'S TAKE HIM ALONG...

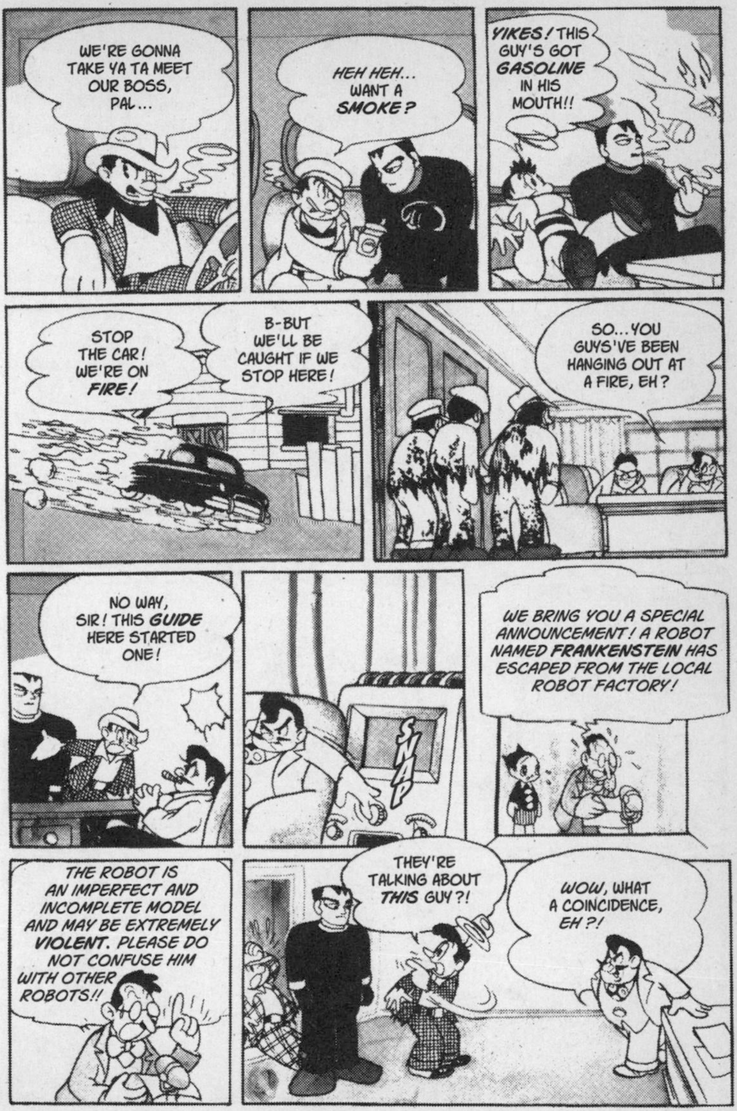
WE'RE GONNA TAKE YA TA MEET OUR BOSS, PAL...
HEH HEH... WANT A SMOKE?
YIKES! THIS GUY'S GOT GASOLINE IN HIS MOUTH!!
STOP THE CAR! WE'RE ON FIRE!
B-BUT WE'LL BE CAUGHT IF WE STOP HERE!
SO... YOU GUYS'VE BEEN HANGING OUT AT A FIRE, EH?
NO WAY, SIR! THIS GUIDE HERE STARTED ONE!
SNAP
WE BRING YOU A SPECIAL ANNOUNCEMENT! A ROBOT NAMED FRANKENSTEIN HAS ESCAPED FROM THE LOCAL ROBOT FACTORY!
THE ROBOT IS AN IMPERFECT AND INCOMPLETE MODEL AND MAY BE EXTREMELY VIOLENT. PLEASE DO NOT CONFUSE HIM WITH OTHER ROBOTS!!
THEY'RE TALKING ABOUT THIS GUY?!
WOW, WHAT A COINCIDENCE, EH?!

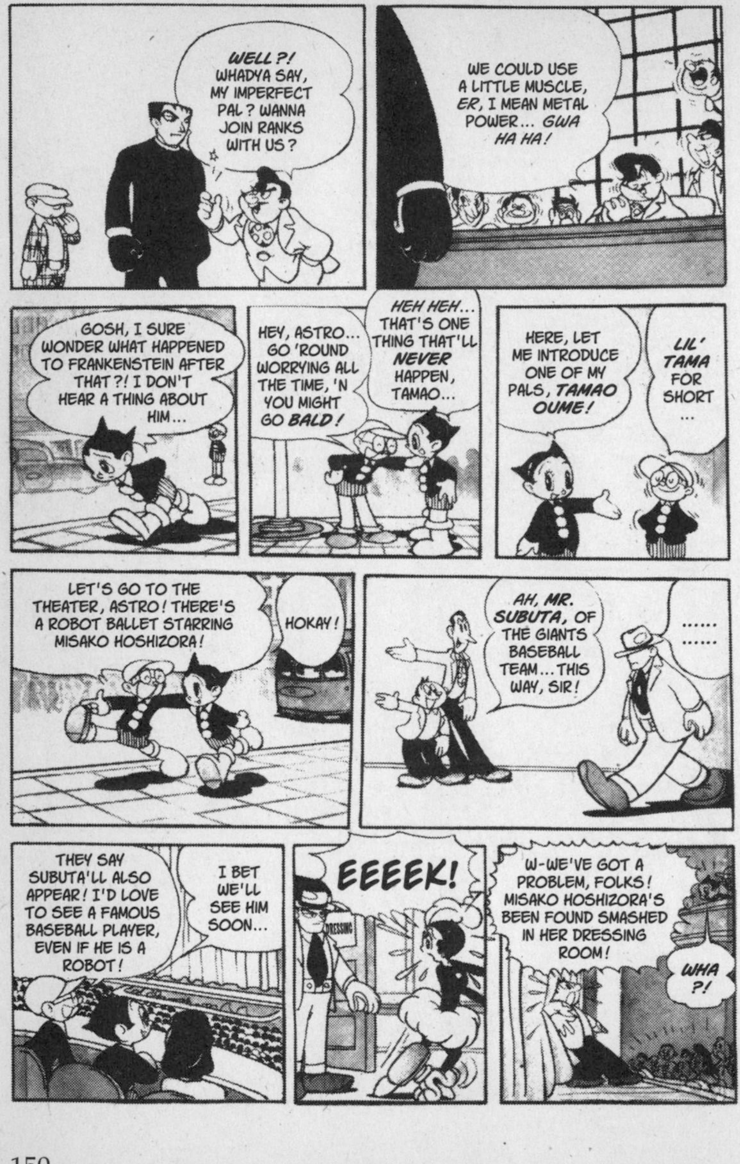

WELL?! WHADYA SAY, MY IMPERFECT PAL? WANNA JOIN RANKS WITH US?
WE COULD USE A LITTLE MUSCLE, *ER,* I MEAN METAL POWER... *GWA HA HA!*
GOSH, I SURE WONDER WHAT HAPPENED TO FRANKENSTEIN AFTER THAT?! I DON'T HEAR A THING ABOUT HIM...
HEY, ASTRO... GO 'ROUND WORRYING ALL THE TIME, 'N YOU MIGHT GO *BALD!*
HEH HEH... THAT'S ONE THING THAT'LL *NEVER* HAPPEN, TAMAO...
HERE, LET ME INTRODUCE ONE OF MY PALS, *TAMAO OUME!*
LIL' TAMA FOR SHORT ...
LET'S GO TO THE THEATER, ASTRO! THERE'S A ROBOT BALLET STARRING MISAKO HOSHIZORA!
HOKAY!
AH, MR. SUBUTA, OF THE GIANTS BASEBALL TEAM... THIS WAY, SIR!
....
THEY SAY SUBUTA'LL ALSO APPEAR! I'D LOVE TO SEE A FAMOUS BASEBALL PLAYER, EVEN IF HE IS A ROBOT!
I BET WE'LL SEE HIM SOON...
EEEEK!
DRESSING
W-WE'VE GOT A PROBLEM, FOLKS! MISAKO HOSHIZORA'S BEEN FOUND SMASHED IN HER DRESSING ROOM!
WHA ?!

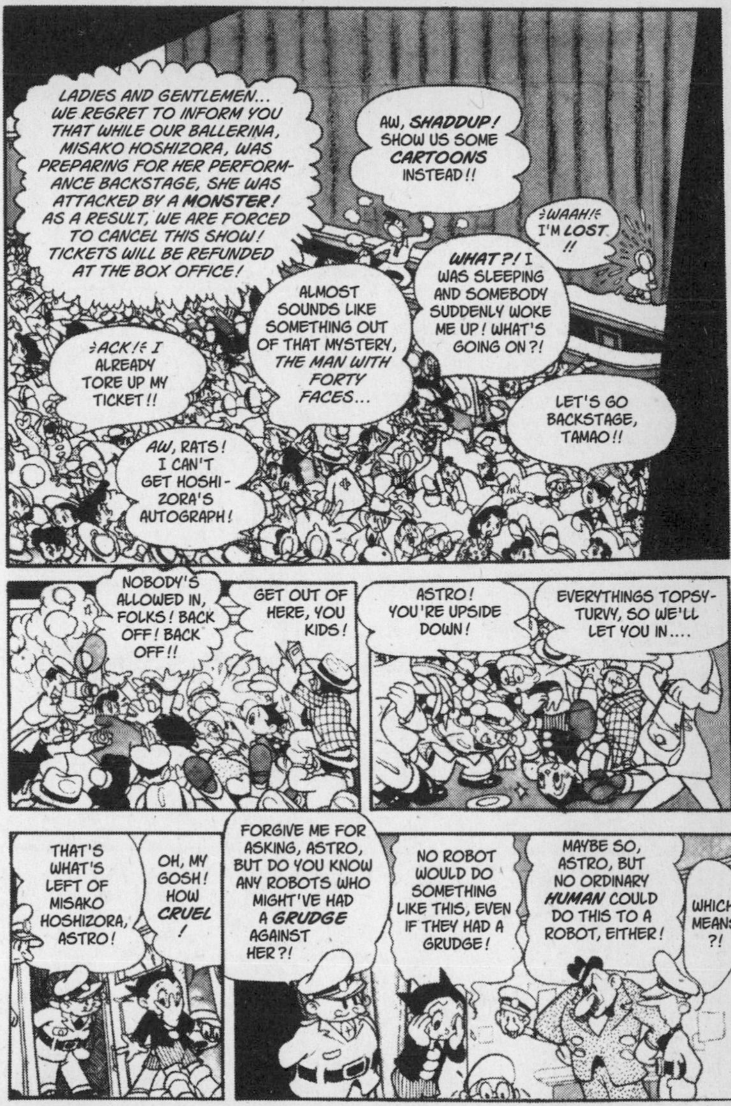

LADIES AND GENTLEMEN... WE REGRET TO INFORM YOU THAT WHILE OUR BALLERINA, MISAKO HOSHIZORA, WAS PREPARING FOR HER PERFORMANCE BACKSTAGE, SHE WAS ATTACKED BY A MONSTER! AS A RESULT, WE ARE FORCED TO CANCEL THIS SHOW! TICKETS WILL BE REFUNDED AT THE BOX OFFICE!
AW, SHADDUP! SHOW US SOME CARTOONS INSTEAD!!
WAAH! I'M LOST!!
WHAT?! I WAS SLEEPING AND SOMEBODY SUDDENLY WOKE ME UP! WHAT'S GOING ON?!
ALMOST SOUNDS LIKE SOMETHING OUT OF THAT MYSTERY, THE MAN WITH FORTY FACES...
ACK! I ALREADY TORE UP MY TICKET!!
LET'S GO BACKSTAGE, TAMAO!!
AW, RATS! I CAN'T GET HOSHIZORA'S AUTOGRAPH!
NOBODY'S ALLOWED IN, FOLKS! BACK OFF! BACK OFF!!
GET OUT OF HERE, YOU KIDS!
ASTRO! YOU'RE UPSIDE DOWN!
EVERYTHINGS TOPSY-TURVY, SO WE'LL LET YOU IN....
THAT'S WHAT'S LEFT OF MISAKO HOSHIZORA, ASTRO!
OH, MY GOSH! HOW CRUEL!
FORGIVE ME FOR ASKING, ASTRO, BUT DO YOU KNOW ANY ROBOTS WHO MIGHT'VE HAD A GRUDGE AGAINST HER?!
NO ROBOT WOULD DO SOMETHING LIKE THIS, EVEN IF THEY HAD A GRUDGE!
MAYBE SO, ASTRO, BUT NO ORDINARY HUMAN COULD DO THIS TO A ROBOT, EITHER!
WHICH MEANS?!

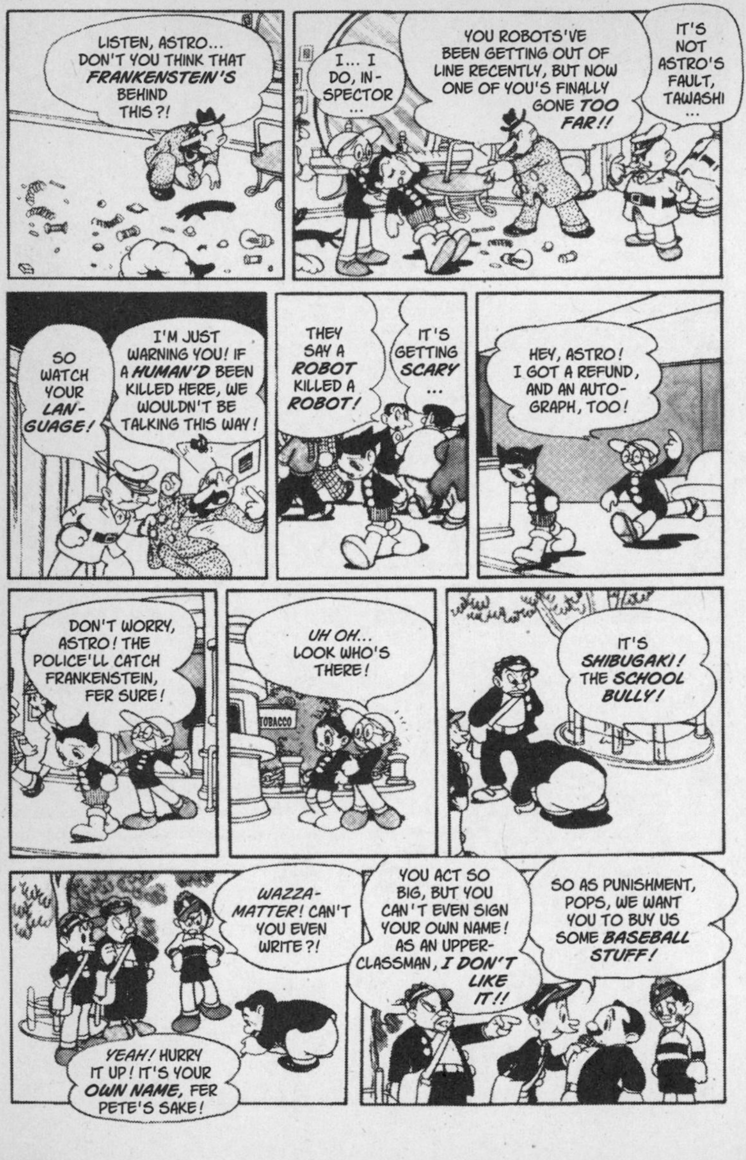
LISTEN, ASTRO... DON'T YOU THINK THAT FRANKENSTEIN'S BEHIND THIS?!
I... I DO, IN-SPECTOR...
YOU ROBOTS'VE BEEN GETTING OUT OF LINE RECENTLY, BUT NOW ONE OF YOU'S FINALLY GONE TOO FAR!!
IT'S NOT ASTRO'S FAULT, TAWASHI...
SO WATCH YOUR LAN-GUAGE!
I'M JUST WARNING YOU! IF A HUMAN'D BEEN KILLED HERE, WE WOULDN'T BE TALKING THIS WAY!
THEY SAY A ROBOT KILLED A ROBOT!
IT'S GETTING SCARY...
HEY, ASTRO! I GOT A REFUND, AND AN AUTO-GRAPH, TOO!
DON'T WORRY, ASTRO! THE POLICE'LL CATCH FRANKENSTEIN, FER SURE!
UH OH... LOOK WHO'S THERE!
TOBACCO
IT'S SHIBUGAKI! THE SCHOOL BULLY!
WAZZA-MATTER! CAN'T YOU EVEN WRITE?!
YEAH! HURRY IT UP! IT'S YOUR OWN NAME, FER PETE'S SAKE!
YOU ACT SO BIG, BUT YOU CAN'T EVEN SIGN YOUR OWN NAME! AS AN UPPER-CLASSMAN, I DON'T LIKE IT!!
SO AS PUNISHMENT, POPS, WE WANT YOU TO BUY US SOME BASEBALL STUFF!

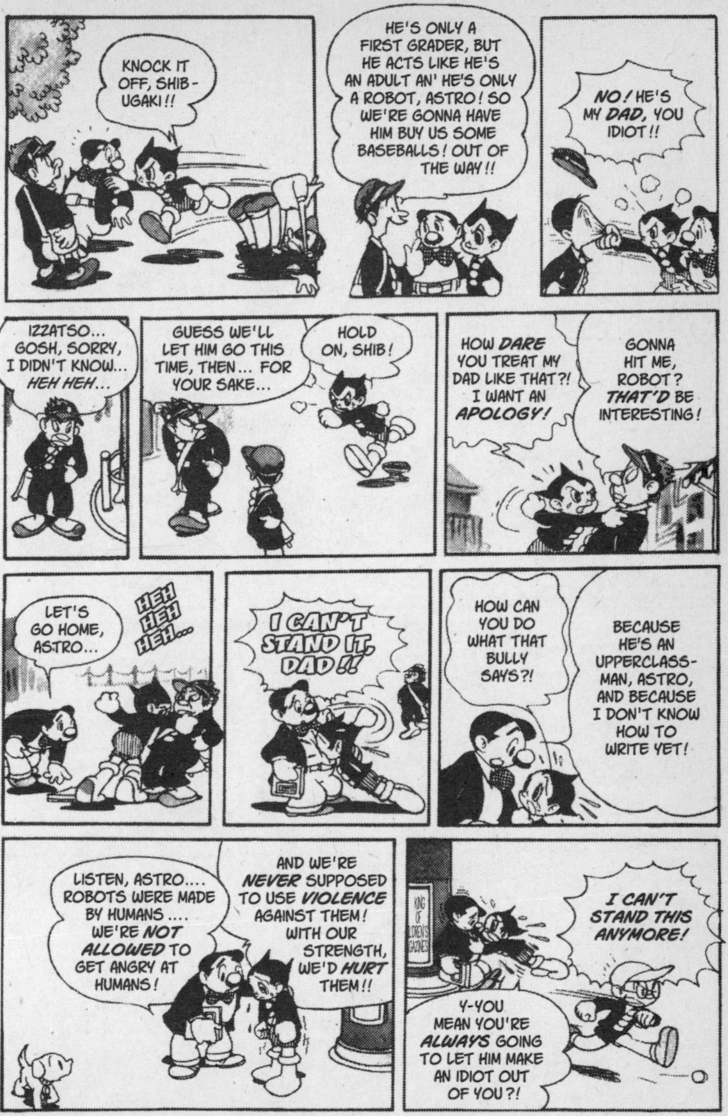
KNOCK IT OFF, SHIB-UGAKI!!
HE'S ONLY A FIRST GRADER, BUT HE ACTS LIKE HE'S AN ADULT AN' HE'S ONLY A ROBOT, ASTRO! SO WE'RE GONNA HAVE HIM BUY US SOME BASEBALLS! OUT OF THE WAY!!
NO! HE'S MY DAD, YOU IDIOT!!
IZZATSO... GOSH, SORRY, I DIDN'T KNOW... HEH HEH...
GUESS WE'LL LET HIM GO THIS TIME, THEN... FOR YOUR SAKE...
HOLD ON, SHIB!
HOW DARE YOU TREAT MY DAD LIKE THAT?! I WANT AN APOLOGY!
GONNA HIT ME, ROBOT? THAT'D BE INTERESTING!
LET'S GO HOME, ASTRO...
HEH HEH HEH...
I CAN'T STAND IT, DAD!!
HOW CAN YOU DO WHAT THAT BULLY SAYS?!
BECAUSE HE'S AN UPPERCLASS-MAN, ASTRO, AND BECAUSE I DON'T KNOW HOW TO WRITE YET!
LISTEN, ASTRO.... ROBOTS WERE MADE BY HUMANS .... WE'RE NOT ALLOWED TO GET ANGRY AT HUMANS!
AND WE'RE NEVER SUPPOSED TO USE VIOLENCE AGAINST THEM! WITH OUR STRENGTH, WE'D HURT THEM!!
I CAN'T STAND THIS ANYMORE!
Y-YOU MEAN YOU'RE ALWAYS GOING TO LET HIM MAKE AN IDIOT OUT OF YOU?!

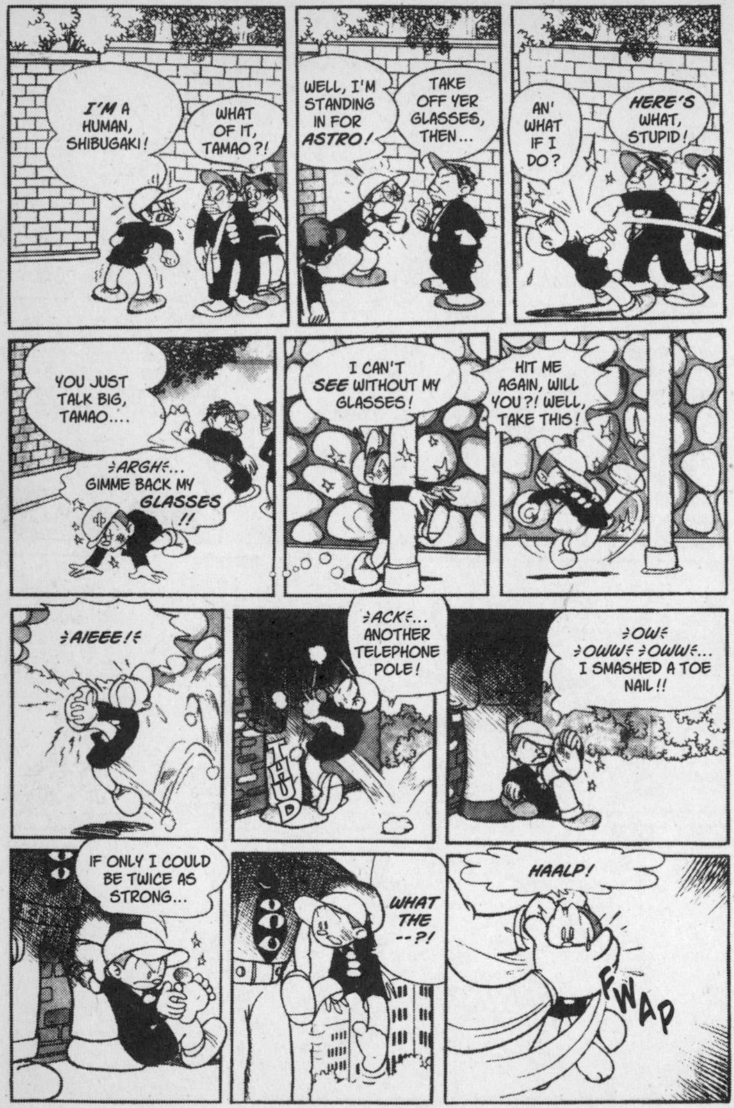
I'M A HUMAN, SHIBUGAKI!
WHAT OF IT, TAMAO?!
WELL, I'M STANDING IN FOR ASTRO!
TAKE OFF YER GLASSES, THEN...
AN' WHAT IF I DO?
HERE'S WHAT, STUPID!
YOU JUST TALK BIG, TAMAO....
ARGH... GIMME BACK MY GLASSES!!
I CAN'T SEE WITHOUT MY GLASSES!
HIT ME AGAIN, WILL YOU?! WELL, TAKE THIS!
AIEEE!
ACK... ANOTHER TELEPHONE POLE!
THUD
OW OWW OWW... I SMASHED A TOE NAIL!!
IF ONLY I COULD BE TWICE AS STRONG...
WHAT THE --?!
HAALP!
FWAP

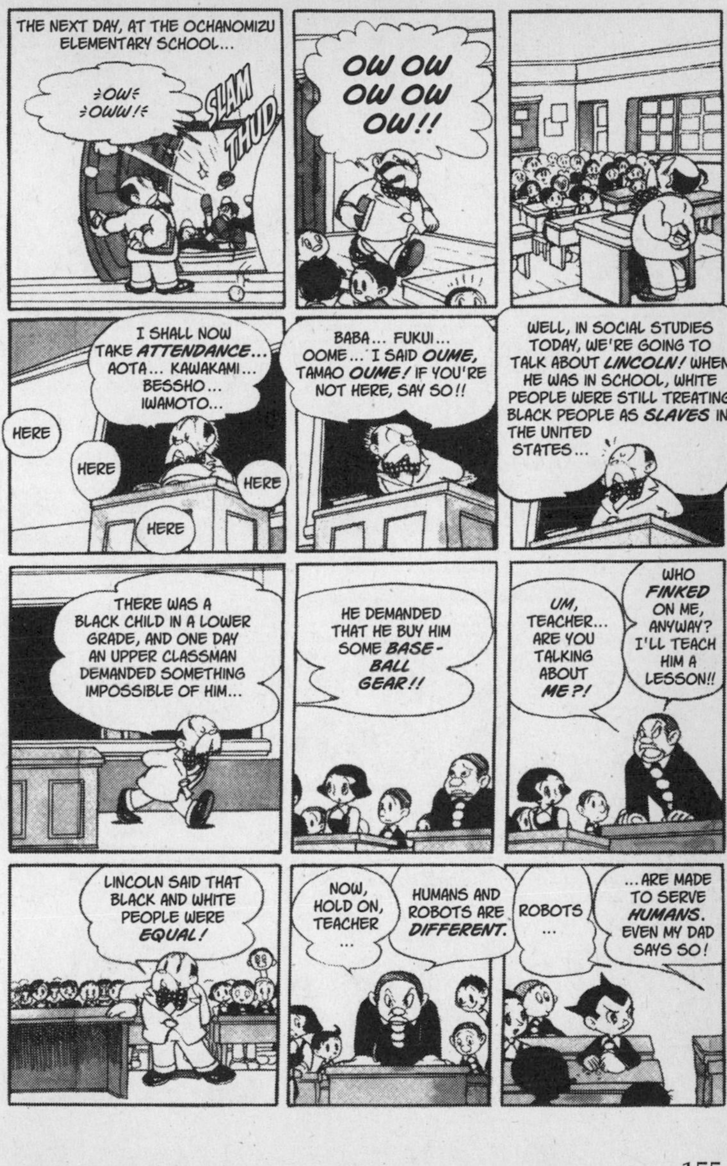

THE NEXT DAY, AT THE OCHANOMIZU ELEMENTARY SCHOOL...
OW OWW!
SLAM
THUD
OW OW OW OW OW!!
I SHALL NOW TAKE ATTENDANCE... AOTA... KAWAKAMI... BESSHO... IWAMOTO...
HERE
HERE
HERE
HERE
BABA... FUKUI... OOME... I SAID OUME, TAMAO OUME! IF YOU'RE NOT HERE, SAY SO!!
WELL, IN SOCIAL STUDIES TODAY, WE'RE GOING TO TALK ABOUT LINCOLN! WHEN HE WAS IN SCHOOL, WHITE PEOPLE WERE STILL TREATING BLACK PEOPLE AS SLAVES IN THE UNITED STATES...
THERE WAS A BLACK CHILD IN A LOWER GRADE, AND ONE DAY AN UPPER CLASSMAN DEMANDED SOMETHING IMPOSSIBLE OF HIM...
HE DEMANDED THAT HE BUY HIM SOME BASE-BALL GEAR!!
UM, TEACHER... ARE YOU TALKING ABOUT ME?!
WHO FINKED ON ME, ANYWAY? I'LL TEACH HIM A LESSON!!
LINCOLN SAID THAT BLACK AND WHITE PEOPLE WERE EQUAL!
NOW, HOLD ON, TEACHER ...
HUMANS AND ROBOTS ARE DIFFERENT.
ROBOTS ...
...ARE MADE TO SERVE HUMANS. EVEN MY DAD SAYS SO!

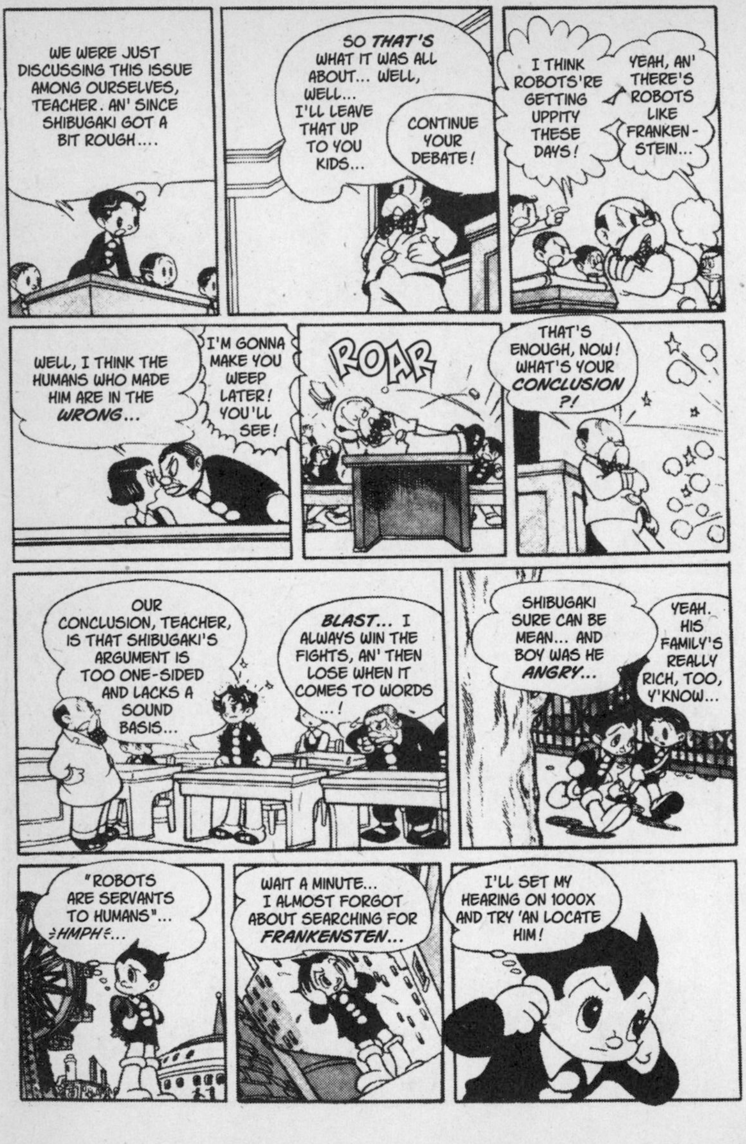
WE WERE JUST DISCUSSING THIS ISSUE AMONG OURSELVES, TEACHER. AN' SINCE SHIBUGAKI GOT A BIT ROUGH....
SO THAT'S WHAT IT WAS ALL ABOUT... WELL, WELL... I'LL LEAVE THAT UP TO YOU KIDS...
CONTINUE YOUR DEBATE!
I THINK ROBOTS'RE GETTING UPPITY THESE DAYS!
YEAH, AN' THERE'S ROBOTS LIKE FRANKEN-STEIN...
WELL, I THINK THE HUMANS WHO MADE HIM ARE IN THE WRONG...
I'M GONNA MAKE YOU WEEP LATER! YOU'LL SEE!
ROAR
THAT'S ENOUGH, NOW! WHAT'S YOUR CONCLUSION ?!
OUR CONCLUSION, TEACHER, IS THAT SHIBUGAKI'S ARGUMENT IS TOO ONE-SIDED AND LACKS A SOUND BASIS...
BLAST... I ALWAYS WIN THE FIGHTS, AN' THEN LOSE WHEN IT COMES TO WORDS ...!
SHIBUGAKI SURE CAN BE MEAN... AND BOY WAS HE ANGRY...
YEAH. HIS FAMILY'S REALLY RICH, TOO, Y'KNOW...
"ROBOTS ARE SERVANTS TO HUMANS"... HMPH...
WAIT A MINUTE... I ALMOST FORGOT ABOUT SEARCHING FOR FRANKENSTEN...
I'LL SET MY HEARING ON 1000X AND TRY 'AN LOCATE HIM!

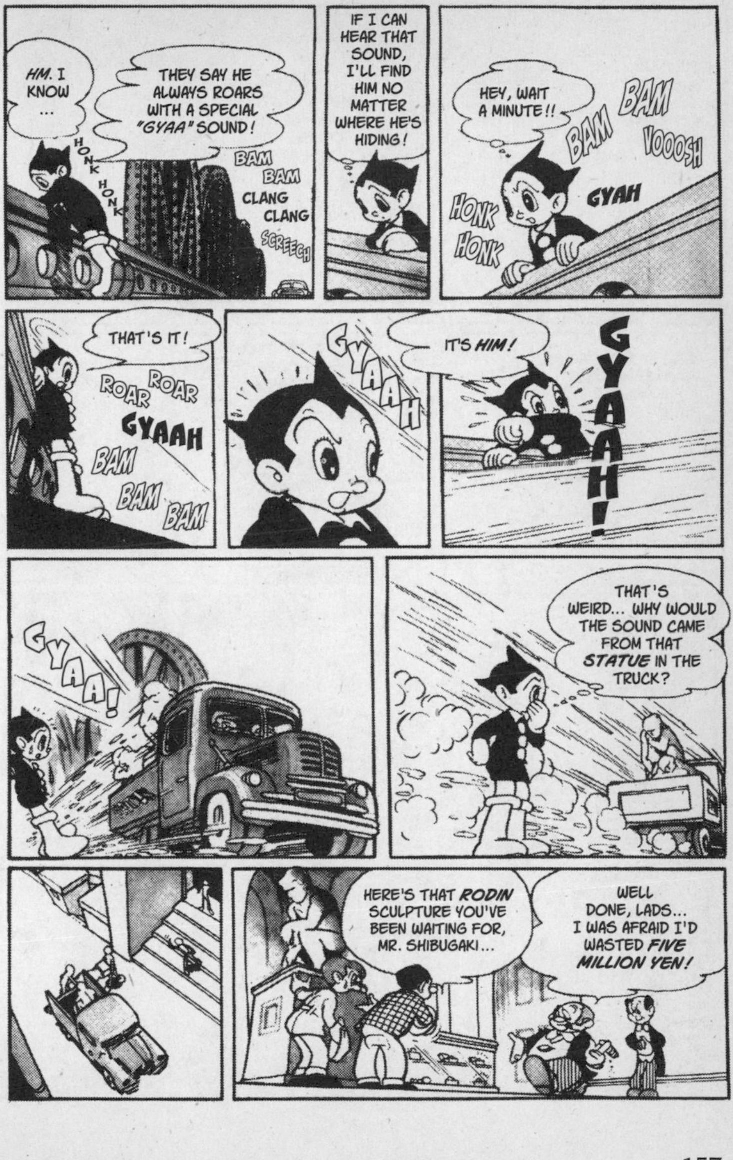
HM. I KNOW ...
THEY SAY HE ALWAYS ROARS WITH A SPECIAL "GYAA" SOUND!
HONK HONK
BAM BAM
CLANG CLANG
SCREECH
IF I CAN HEAR THAT SOUND, I'LL FIND HIM NO MATTER WHERE HE'S HIDING!
HEY, WAIT A MINUTE!!
BAM BAM
VOOOSH
GYAH
HONK HONK
THAT'S IT!
ROAR ROAR
GYAAH
BAM BAM BAM
GYAAAH
IT'S HIM!
GYAAAH!
GYAAA!
THAT'S WEIRD... WHY WOULD THE SOUND CAME FROM THAT STATUE IN THE TRUCK?
HERE'S THAT RODIN SCULPTURE YOU'VE BEEN WAITING FOR, MR. SHIBUGAKI...
WELL DONE, LADS... I WAS AFRAID I'D WASTED FIVE MILLION YEN!

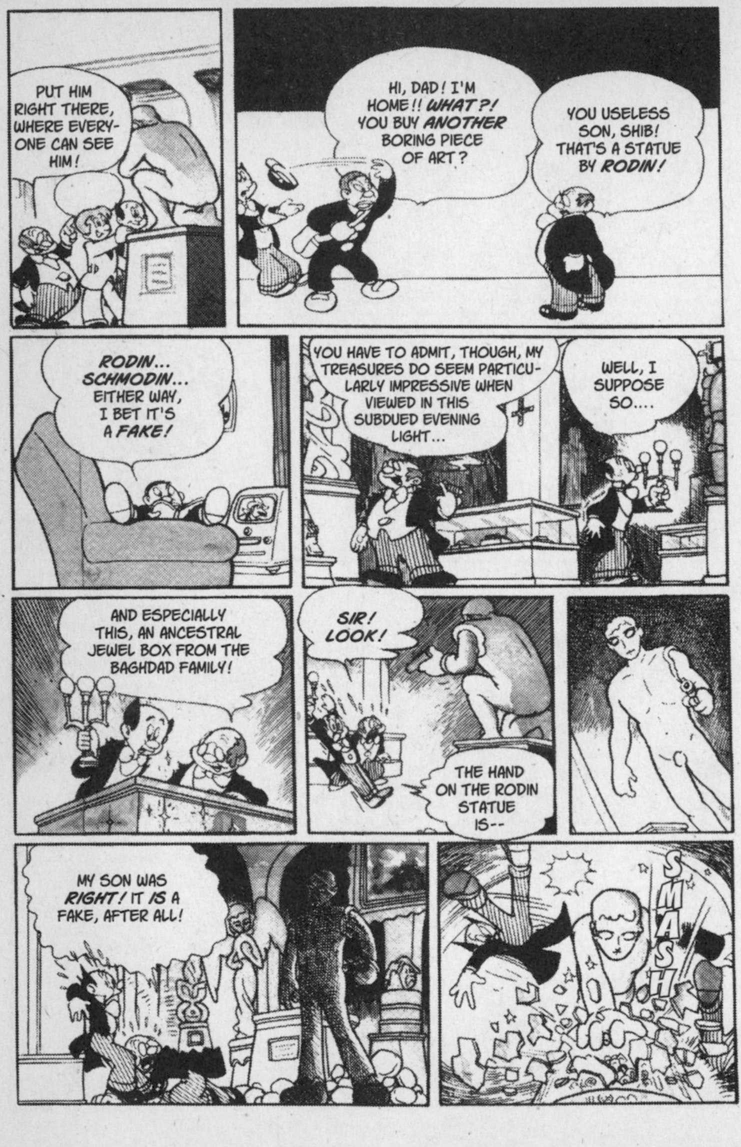
PUT HIM RIGHT THERE, WHERE EVERY-ONE CAN SEE HIM!
HI, DAD! I'M HOME!! WHAT?! YOU BUY ANOTHER BORING PIECE OF ART?
YOU USELESS SON, SHIB! THAT'S A STATUE BY RODIN!
RODIN... SCHMODIN... EITHER WAY, I BET IT'S A FAKE!
YOU HAVE TO ADMIT, THOUGH, MY TREASURES DO SEEM PARTICU-LARLY IMPRESSIVE WHEN VIEWED IN THIS SUBDUED EVENING LIGHT...
WELL, I SUPPOSE SO....
AND ESPECIALLY THIS, AN ANCESTRAL JEWEL BOX FROM THE BAGHDAD FAMILY!
SIR! LOOK!
THE HAND ON THE RODIN STATUE IS--
MY SON WAS RIGHT! IT IS A FAKE, AFTER ALL!
SMASH

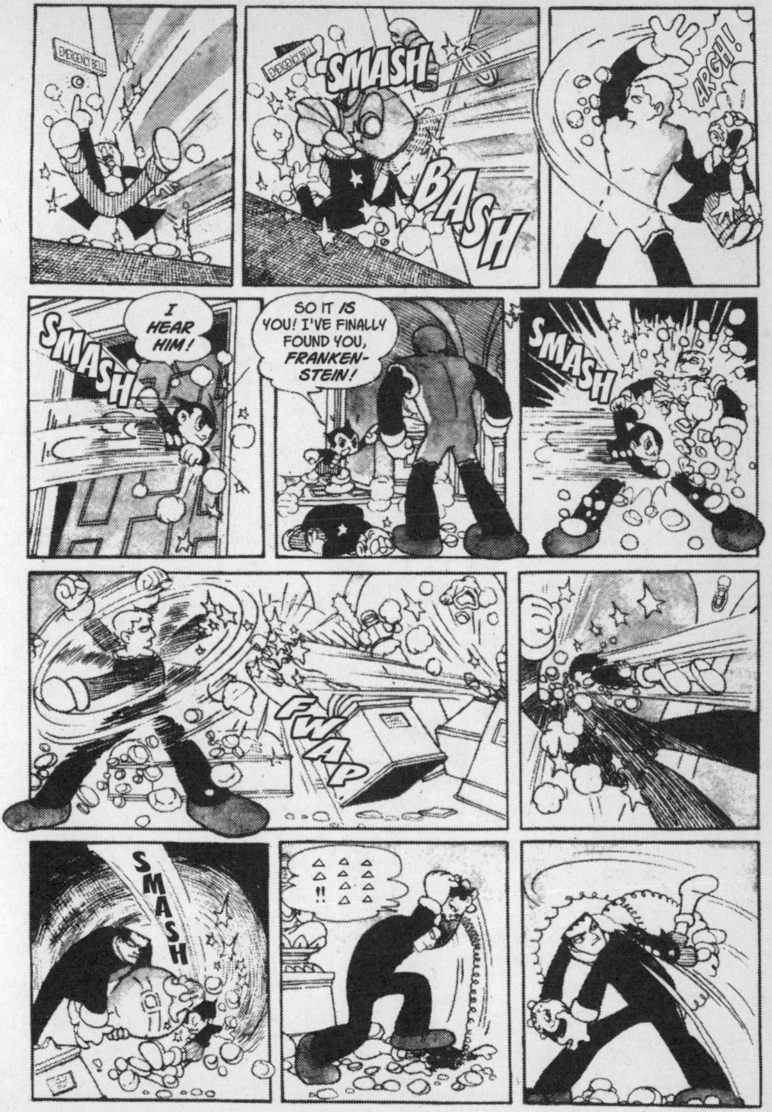
EMERGENCY BELL
EMERGENCY BELL
SMASH
BASH
ARGH!
SMASH
I HEAR HIM!
SO IT IS YOU! I'VE FINALLY FOUND YOU, FRANKENSTEIN!
SMASH
FWAP
SMASH
!!

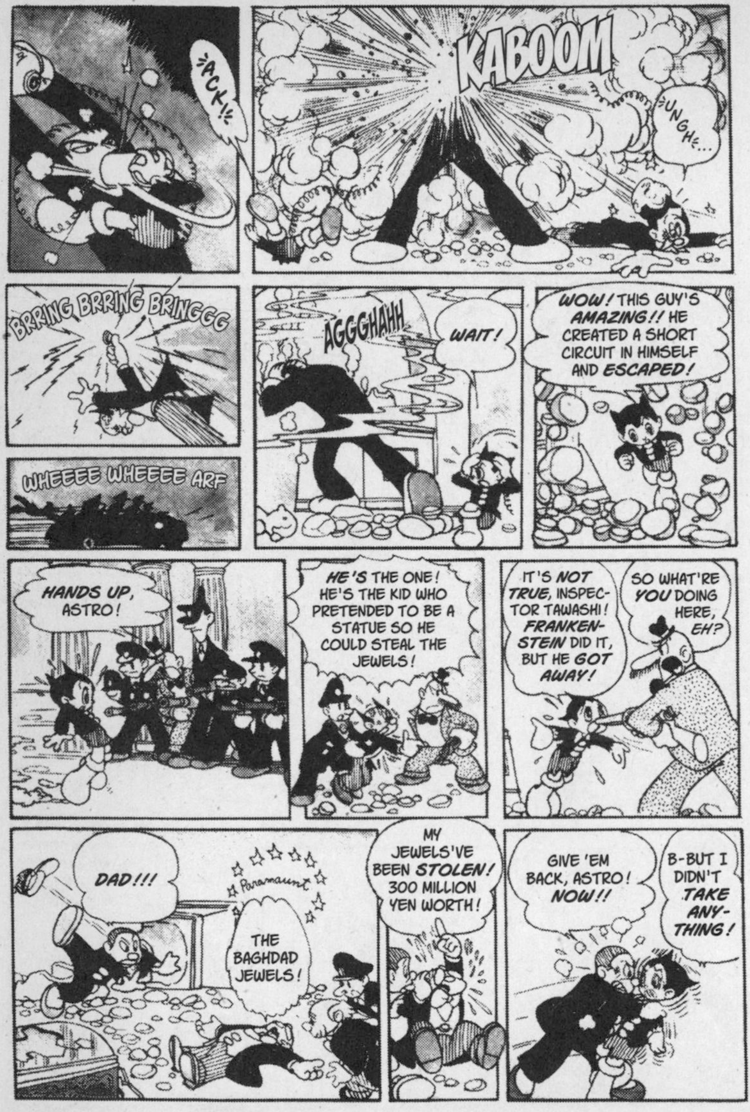
ACK!
KABOOM
UNGH...
BRRING BRRING BRINGGG
WHEEEE WHEEEE ARF
AGGGHAHH
WAIT!
WOW! THIS GUY'S AMAZING!! HE CREATED A SHORT CIRCUIT IN HIMSELF AND ESCAPED!
HANDS UP, ASTRO!
HE'S THE ONE! HE'S THE KID WHO PRETENDED TO BE A STATUE SO HE COULD STEAL THE JEWELS!
IT'S NOT TRUE, INSPECTOR TAWASHI! FRANKENSTEIN DID IT, BUT HE GOT AWAY!
SO WHAT'RE YOU DOING HERE, EH?
DAD!!!
Paramount
THE BAGHDAD JEWELS!
MY JEWELS'VE BEEN STOLEN! 300 MILLION YEN WORTH!
GIVE 'EM BACK, ASTRO! NOW!!
B-BUT I DIDN'T TAKE ANYTHING!

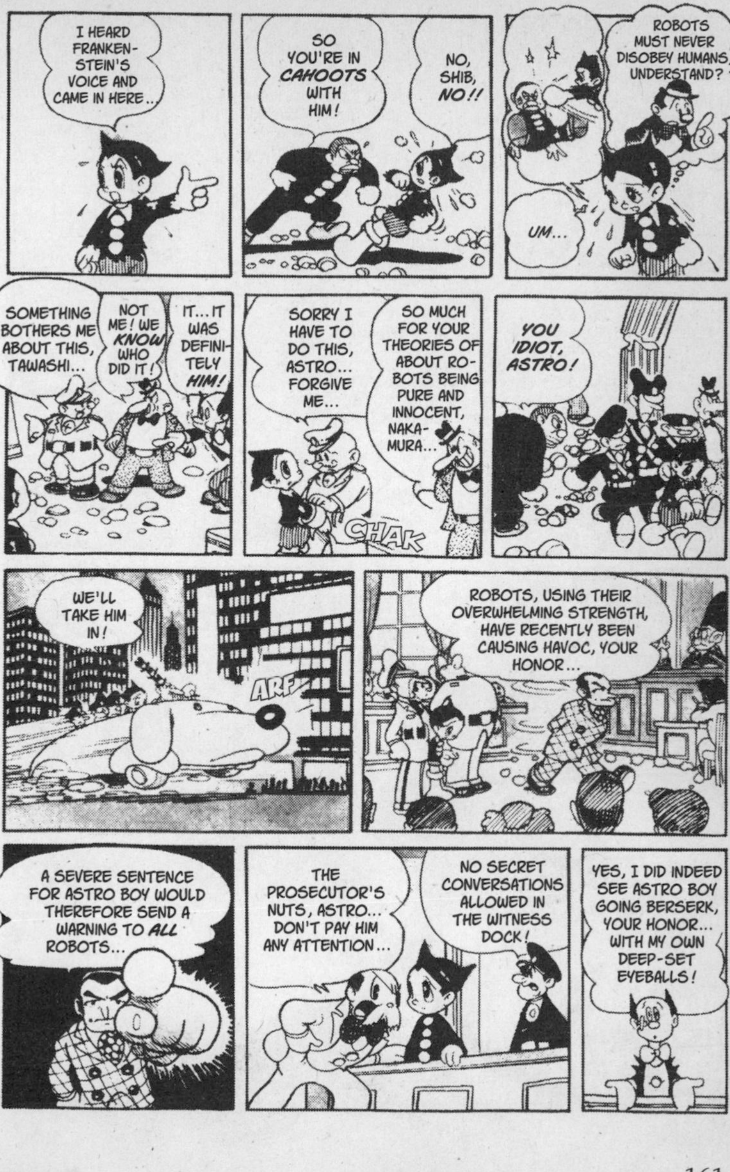
I HEARD FRANKEN-STEIN'S VOICE AND CAME IN HERE...
SO YOU'RE IN CAHOOTS WITH HIM!
NO, SHIB, NO!!
ROBOTS MUST NEVER DISOBEY HUMANS, UNDERSTAND?
UM...
SOMETHING BOTHERS ME ABOUT THIS, TAWASHI...
NOT ME! WE KNOW WHO DID IT!
IT... IT WAS DEFINI-TELY HIM!
SORRY I HAVE TO DO THIS, ASTRO... FORGIVE ME...
SO MUCH FOR YOUR THEORIES OF ABOUT RO-BOTS BEING PURE AND INNOCENT, NAKA-MURA...
CHAK
YOU IDIOT, ASTRO!
WE'LL TAKE HIM IN!
ARF
ROBOTS, USING THEIR OVERWHELMING STRENGTH, HAVE RECENTLY BEEN CAUSING HAVOC, YOUR HONOR...
A SEVERE SENTENCE FOR ASTRO BOY WOULD THEREFORE SEND A WARNING TO ALL ROBOTS...
THE PROSECUTOR'S NUTS, ASTRO... DON'T PAY HIM ANY ATTENTION...
NO SECRET CONVERSATIONS ALLOWED IN THE WITNESS DOCK!
YES, I DID INDEED SEE ASTRO BOY GOING BERSERK, YOUR HONOR... WITH MY OWN DEEP-SET EYEBALLS!

I HAD A FIGHT WITH ASTRO THE PREVIOUS DAY, Y'R HONOR, AND HE THREATENED TO GET *REVENGE* THEN...

I DON'T CARE WHO THE CRIMINAL IS, YOUR HONOR! I JUST WANT MY *JEWELS* BACK!! ≶WAAAH!≶

YOUR HONORS... WE ARE... I MEAN... I AM, SIR, AN *AMATEUR DETECTIVE* AS WELL AS A *LAWYER* AND A *SCHOOL TEACHER*... AND THE NAME'S *MUSTACHIO*!!

WHILE LISTENING TO THESE "WIT-NESSES," YOU'VE OVERLOOKED A *VERY IMPOR-TANT POINT!*

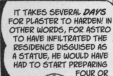

IT TAKES SEVERAL *DAYS* FOR PLASTER TO HARDEN! IN OTHER WORDS, FOR ASTRO TO HAVE INFILTRATED THE RESIDENCE DISGUISED AS A STATUE, HE WOULD HAVE HAD TO START PREPARING FOUR OR FIVE DAYS IN *AD-VANCE!*

...THE IDEA THAT HE WAS IN CAHOOTS WITH FRANKENSTEIN IS ALSO ABSURD! ASTRO BOY'S DESIGNED SO THAT HE *CAN'T* GET ALONG WITH *BAD PEOPLE!*

THE COURT SHALL NOW READ ITS VERDICT...

HANG IN THERE, ASTRO!

ASTRO BOY IS RELEASED FOR LACK OF EVIDENCE!

WE DID IT, ASTRO! WE *DID* IT! NOW, LET'S GO HOME!

THANKS, TEACHER! IT'S ALL 'CUZ OF YOU!

EVERYBODY IN THE STATION CHIPPED IN AND BOUGHT THIS FOR YOU, ASTRO! LET'S *CELEBRATE!*

HA HA... YOU THINK A ROBOT CAN EAT *ROASTED SWEET POTATOES?*

ACTUALLY, HE *LOVES* 'EM... THE ALCOHOL IN 'EM'S GOOD FOR HIS SYSTEM...

SO, ASTRO... ≶MUNCH≶... WHAT DO YOU PLAN TO DO NOW?

I'M GONNA KEEP SEARCHING FOR FRANKENSTEIN AND PROVE I'M *INNOCENT!*

THAT'S GOOD, BUT WE ALSO NEED YOUR HELP, BECAUSE *TAMAO'S BEEN KIDNAPPED!*

You've got to come and help me, Astro... I'm being held against my will! Wait on the train platform at Tokyo's Ichigaya station tomorrow at noon. Make sure you're alone...

162

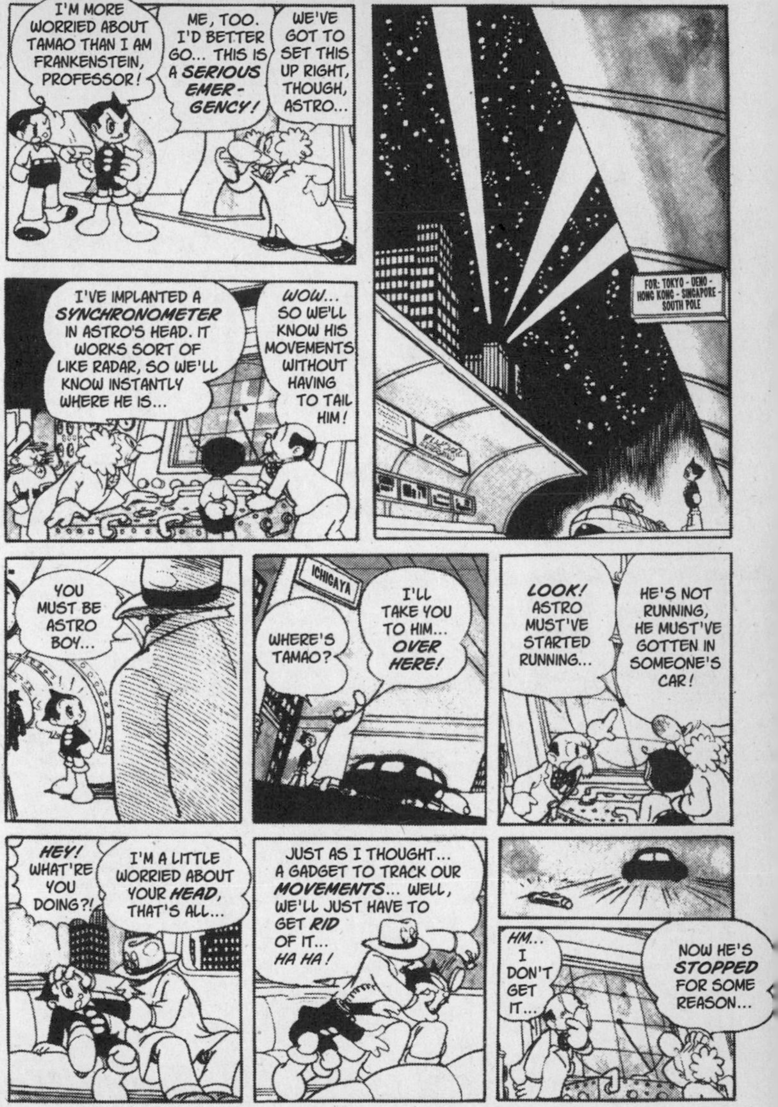
I'M MORE WORRIED ABOUT TAMAO THAN I AM FRANKENSTEIN, PROFESSOR!
ME, TOO. I'D BETTER GO... THIS IS A SERIOUS EMER-GENCY!
WE'VE GOT TO SET THIS UP RIGHT, THOUGH, ASTRO...
I'VE IMPLANTED A SYNCHRONOMETER IN ASTRO'S HEAD. IT WORKS SORT OF LIKE RADAR, SO WE'LL KNOW INSTANTLY WHERE HE IS...
WOW... SO WE'LL KNOW HIS MOVEMENTS WITHOUT HAVING TO TAIL HIM!
FOR: TOKYO - UENO - HONG KONG - SINGAPORE - SOUTH POLE
YOU MUST BE ASTRO BOY...
ICHIGAYA
WHERE'S TAMAO?
I'LL TAKE YOU TO HIM... OVER HERE!
LOOK! ASTRO MUST'VE STARTED RUNNING...
HE'S NOT RUNNING, HE MUST'VE GOTTEN IN SOMEONE'S CAR!
HEY! WHAT'RE YOU DOING?!
I'M A LITTLE WORRIED ABOUT YOUR HEAD, THAT'S ALL...
JUST AS I THOUGHT... A GADGET TO TRACK OUR MOVEMENTS... WELL, WE'LL JUST HAVE TO GET RID OF IT... HA HA!
HM... I DON'T GET IT...
NOW HE'S STOPPED FOR SOME REASON...

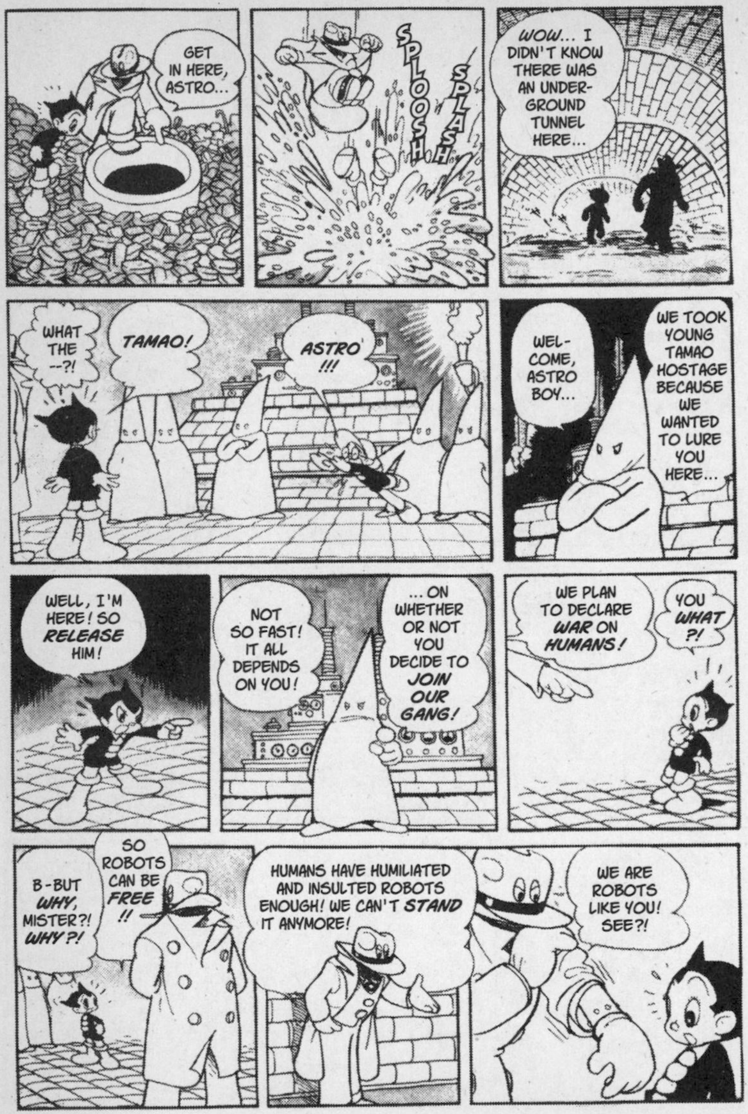
GET IN HERE, ASTRO...
SPLOOSH
SPLASH
WOW... I DIDN'T KNOW THERE WAS AN UNDER-GROUND TUNNEL HERE...
WHAT THE --?!
TAMAO!
ASTRO !!!
WEL-COME, ASTRO BOY...
WE TOOK YOUNG TAMAO HOSTAGE BECAUSE WE WANTED TO LURE YOU HERE...
WELL, I'M HERE! SO RELEASE HIM!
NOT SO FAST! IT ALL DEPENDS ON YOU!
...ON WHETHER OR NOT YOU DECIDE TO JOIN OUR GANG!
WE PLAN TO DECLARE WAR ON HUMANS!
YOU WHAT ?!
B-BUT WHY, MISTER?! WHY?!
SO ROBOTS CAN BE FREE !!
HUMANS HAVE HUMILIATED AND INSULTED ROBOTS ENOUGH! WE CAN'T STAND IT ANYMORE!
WE ARE ROBOTS LIKE YOU! SEE?!

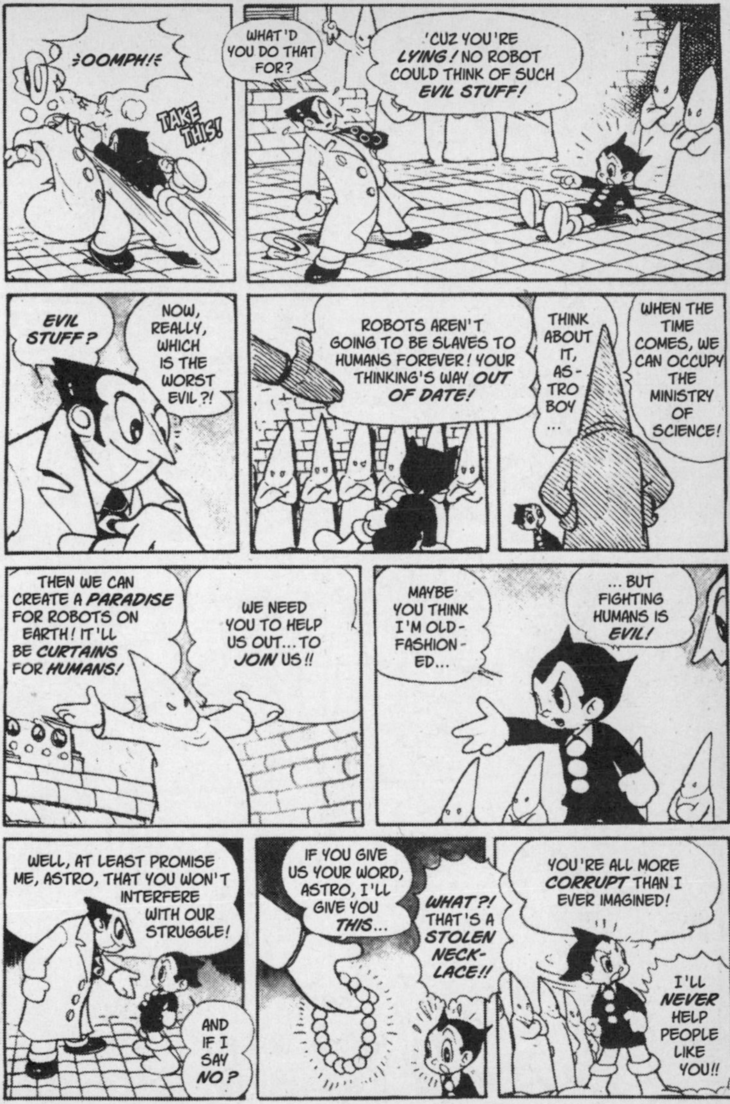
OOMPH!
TAKE THIS!
WHAT'D YOU DO THAT FOR?
'CUZ YOU'RE LYING! NO ROBOT COULD THINK OF SUCH EVIL STUFF!
EVIL STUFF?
NOW, REALLY, WHICH IS THE WORST EVIL?!
ROBOTS AREN'T GOING TO BE SLAVES TO HUMANS FOREVER! YOUR THINKING'S WAY OUT OF DATE!
THINK ABOUT IT, ASTRO BOY...
WHEN THE TIME COMES, WE CAN OCCUPY THE MINISTRY OF SCIENCE!
THEN WE CAN CREATE A PARADISE FOR ROBOTS ON EARTH! IT'LL BE CURTAINS FOR HUMANS!
WE NEED YOU TO HELP US OUT...TO JOIN US!!
MAYBE YOU THINK I'M OLD-FASHIONED...
... BUT FIGHTING HUMANS IS EVIL!
WELL, AT LEAST PROMISE ME, ASTRO, THAT YOU WON'T INTERFERE WITH OUR STRUGGLE!
AND IF I SAY NO?
IF YOU GIVE US YOUR WORD, ASTRO, I'LL GIVE YOU THIS...
WHAT?! THAT'S A STOLEN NECKLACE!!
YOU'RE ALL MORE CORRUPT THAN I EVER IMAGINED!
I'LL NEVER HELP PEOPLE LIKE YOU!!

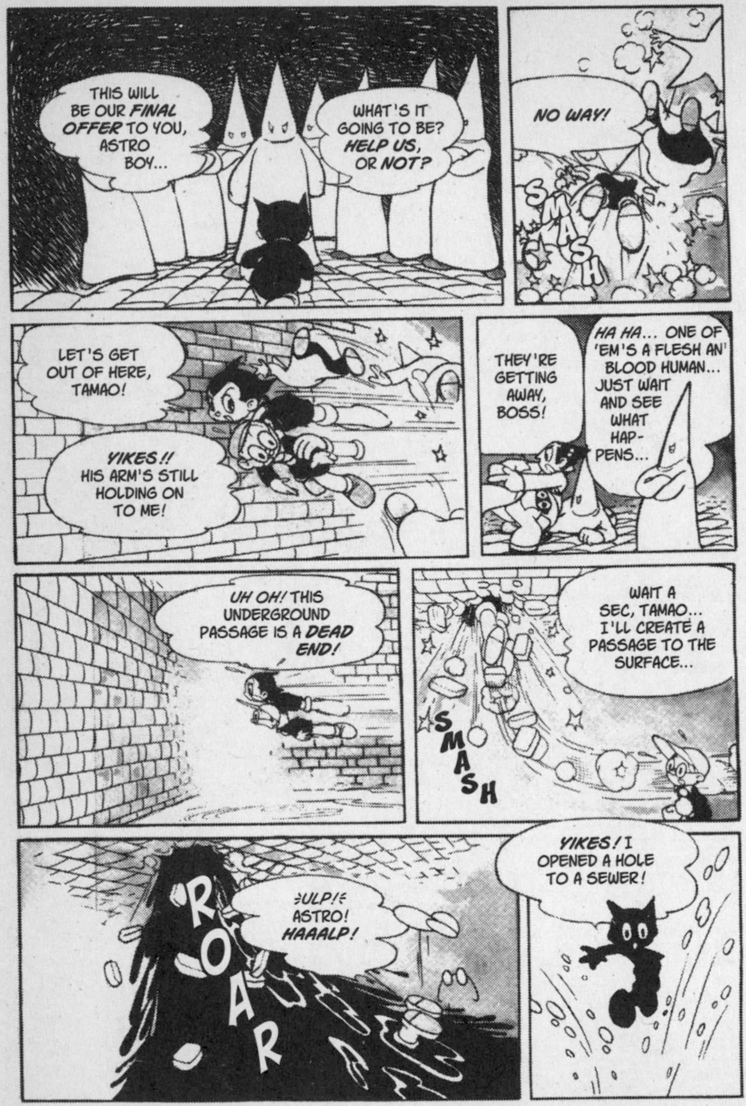
THIS WILL BE OUR FINAL OFFER TO YOU, ASTRO BOY...
WHAT'S IT GOING TO BE? HELP US, OR NOT?
NO WAY!
SMASH
LET'S GET OUT OF HERE, TAMAO!
YIKES!! HIS ARM'S STILL HOLDING ON TO ME!
THEY'RE GETTING AWAY, BOSS!
HA HA... ONE OF 'EM'S A FLESH AN' BLOOD HUMAN... JUST WAIT AND SEE WHAT HAP-PENS...
UH OH! THIS UNDERGROUND PASSAGE IS A DEAD END!
WAIT A SEC, TAMAO... I'LL CREATE A PASSAGE TO THE SURFACE...
SMASH
ROAR
GULP! ASTRO! HAAALP!
YIKES! I OPENED A HOLE TO A SEWER!

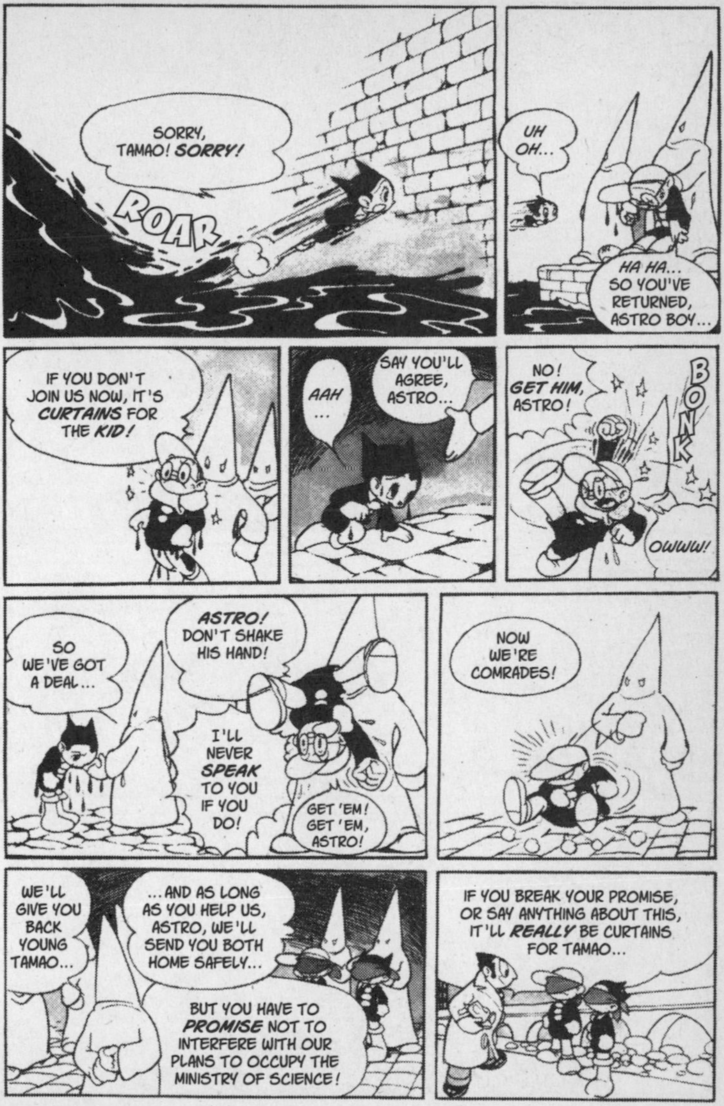
SORRY, TAMAO! SORRY!
ROAR
UH OH...
HA HA... SO YOU'VE RETURNED, ASTRO BOY...
IF YOU DON'T JOIN US NOW, IT'S CURTAINS FOR THE KID!
AAH ...
SAY YOU'LL AGREE, ASTRO...
NO! GET HIM, ASTRO!
BONK
OWWW!
SO WE'VE GOT A DEAL...
ASTRO! DON'T SHAKE HIS HAND!
I'LL NEVER SPEAK TO YOU IF YOU DO!
GET 'EM! GET 'EM, ASTRO!
NOW WE'RE COMRADES!
WE'LL GIVE YOU BACK YOUNG TAMAO...
...AND AS LONG AS YOU HELP US, ASTRO, WE'LL SEND YOU BOTH HOME SAFELY...
BUT YOU HAVE TO PROMISE NOT TO INTERFERE WITH OUR PLANS TO OCCUPY THE MINISTRY OF SCIENCE!
IF YOU BREAK YOUR PROMISE, OR SAY ANYTHING ABOUT THIS, IT'LL REALLY BE CURTAINS FOR TAMAO...

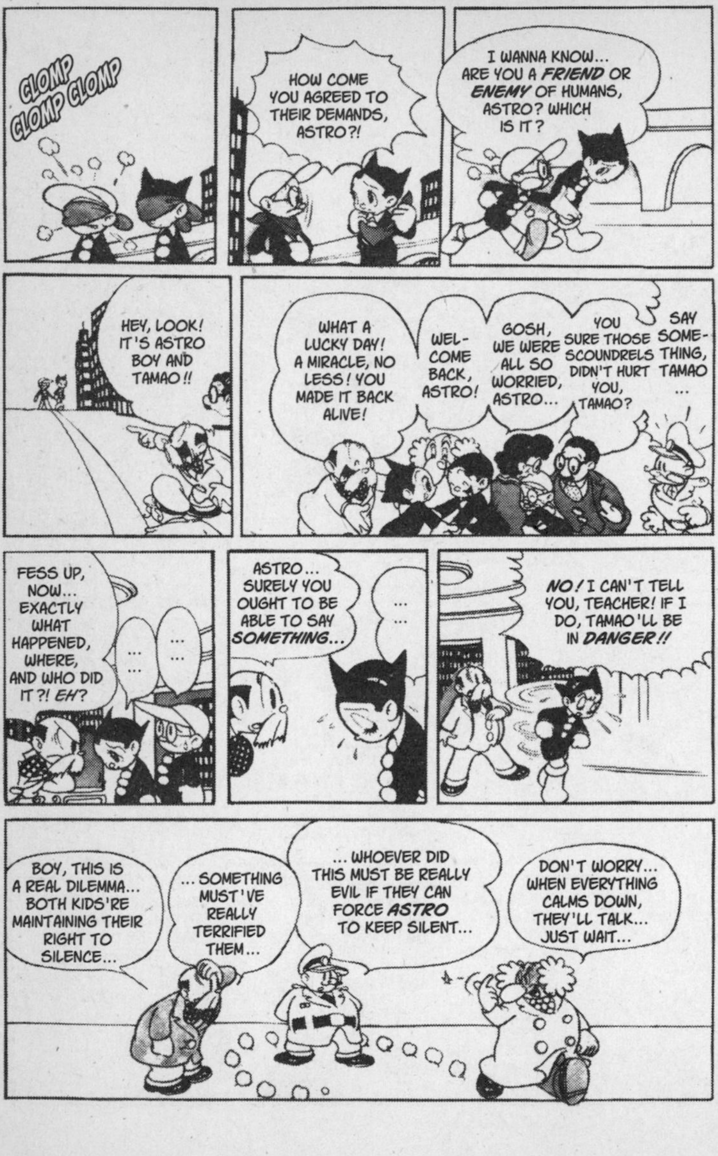
CLOMP CLOMP CLOMP
HOW COME YOU AGREED TO THEIR DEMANDS, ASTRO?!
I WANNA KNOW... ARE YOU A FRIEND OR ENEMY OF HUMANS, ASTRO? WHICH IS IT?
HEY, LOOK! IT'S ASTRO BOY AND TAMAO!!
WHAT A LUCKY DAY! A MIRACLE, NO LESS! YOU MADE IT BACK ALIVE!
WEL-COME BACK, ASTRO!
GOSH, WE WERE ALL SO WORRIED, ASTRO...
YOU SURE THOSE SCOUNDRELS DIDN'T HURT YOU, TAMAO?
SAY SOME-THING, TAMAO ...
FESS UP, NOW... EXACTLY WHAT HAPPENED, WHERE, AND WHO DID IT?! EH?
... ...
... ...
ASTRO... SURELY YOU OUGHT TO BE ABLE TO SAY SOMETHING...
... ...
NO! I CAN'T TELL YOU, TEACHER! IF I DO, TAMAO'LL BE IN DANGER!!
BOY, THIS IS A REAL DILEMMA... BOTH KIDS'RE MAINTAINING THEIR RIGHT TO SILENCE...
... SOMETHING MUST'VE REALLY TERRIFIED THEM...
... WHOEVER DID THIS MUST BE REALLY EVIL IF THEY CAN FORCE ASTRO TO KEEP SILENT...
DON'T WORRY... WHEN EVERYTHING CALMS DOWN, THEY'LL TALK... JUST WAIT...

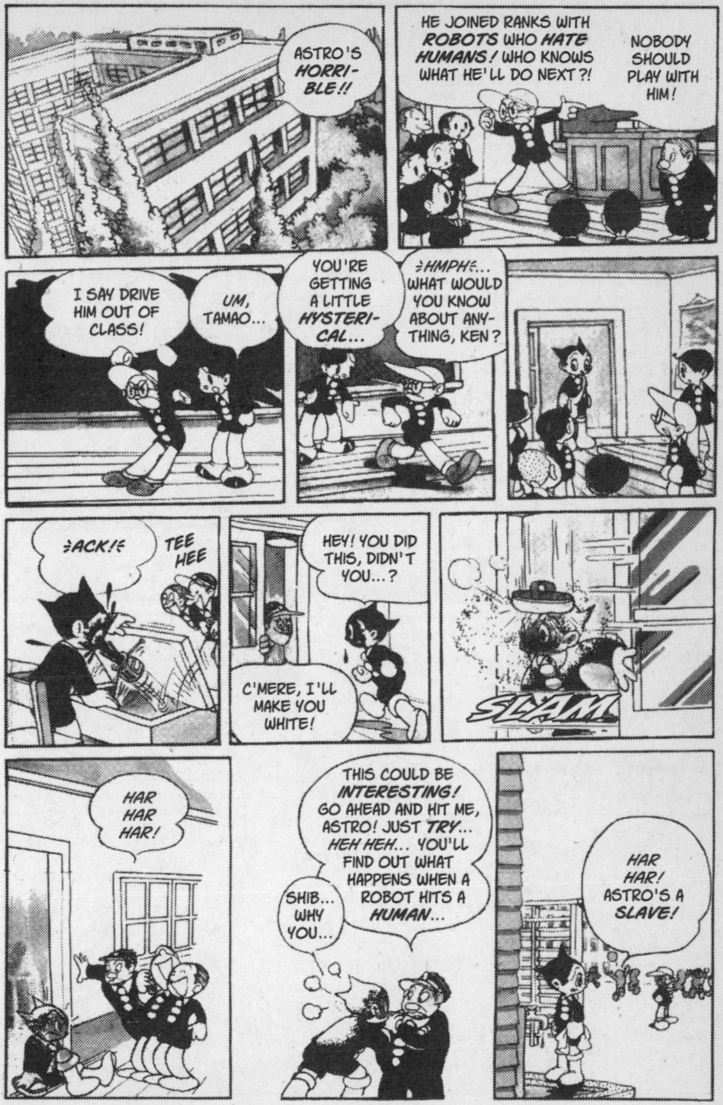
ASTRO'S HORRIBLE!!
HE JOINED RANKS WITH ROBOTS WHO HATE HUMANS! WHO KNOWS WHAT HE'LL DO NEXT?!
NOBODY SHOULD PLAY WITH HIM!
I SAY DRIVE HIM OUT OF CLASS!
UM, TAMAO...
YOU'RE GETTING A LITTLE HYSTERICAL...
HMPH... WHAT WOULD YOU KNOW ABOUT ANYTHING, KEN?
ACK!
TEE HEE
HEY! YOU DID THIS, DIDN'T YOU...?
C'MERE, I'LL MAKE YOU WHITE!
SLAM
HAR HAR HAR!
THIS COULD BE INTERESTING! GO AHEAD AND HIT ME, ASTRO! JUST TRY... HEH HEH... YOU'LL FIND OUT WHAT HAPPENS WHEN A ROBOT HITS A HUMAN...
SHIB... WHY YOU...
HAR HAR! ASTRO'S A SLAVE!

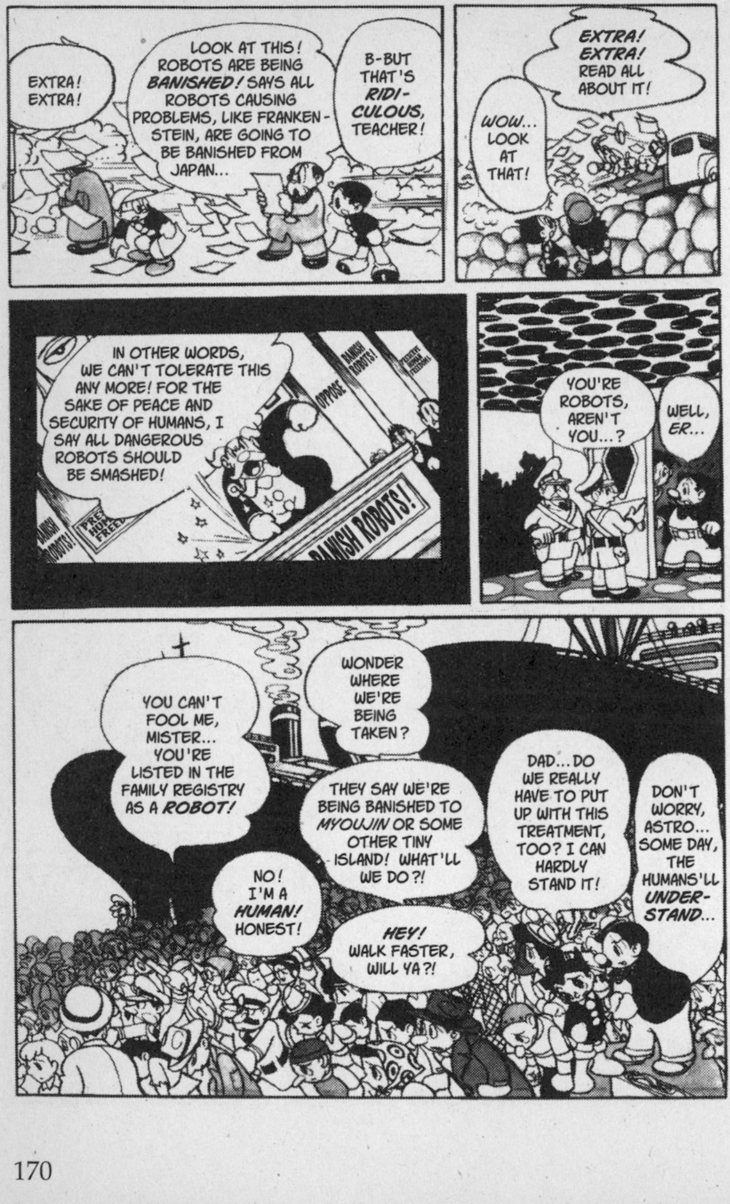
EXTRA! EXTRA!
LOOK AT THIS! ROBOTS ARE BEING BANISHED! SAYS ALL ROBOTS CAUSING PROBLEMS, LIKE FRANKEN-STEIN, ARE GOING TO BE BANISHED FROM JAPAN...
B-BUT THAT'S RIDI-CULOUS, TEACHER!
EXTRA! EXTRA! READ ALL ABOUT IT!
WOW... LOOK AT THAT!
IN OTHER WORDS, WE CAN'T TOLERATE THIS ANY MORE! FOR THE SAKE OF PEACE AND SECURITY OF HUMANS, I SAY ALL DANGEROUS ROBOTS SHOULD BE SMASHED!
OPPOSE
BANISH ROBOTS!
YOU'RE ROBOTS, AREN'T YOU...?
WELL, ER...
YOU CAN'T FOOL ME, MISTER... YOU'RE LISTED IN THE FAMILY REGISTRY AS A ROBOT!
WONDER WHERE WE'RE BEING TAKEN?
THEY SAY WE'RE BEING BANISHED TO MYOUJIN OR SOME OTHER TINY ISLAND! WHAT'LL WE DO?!
NO! I'M A HUMAN! HONEST!
DAD... DO WE REALLY HAVE TO PUT UP WITH THIS TREATMENT, TOO? I CAN HARDLY STAND IT!
DON'T WORRY, ASTRO... SOME DAY, THE HUMANS'LL UNDER-STAND...
HEY! WALK FASTER, WILL YA?!

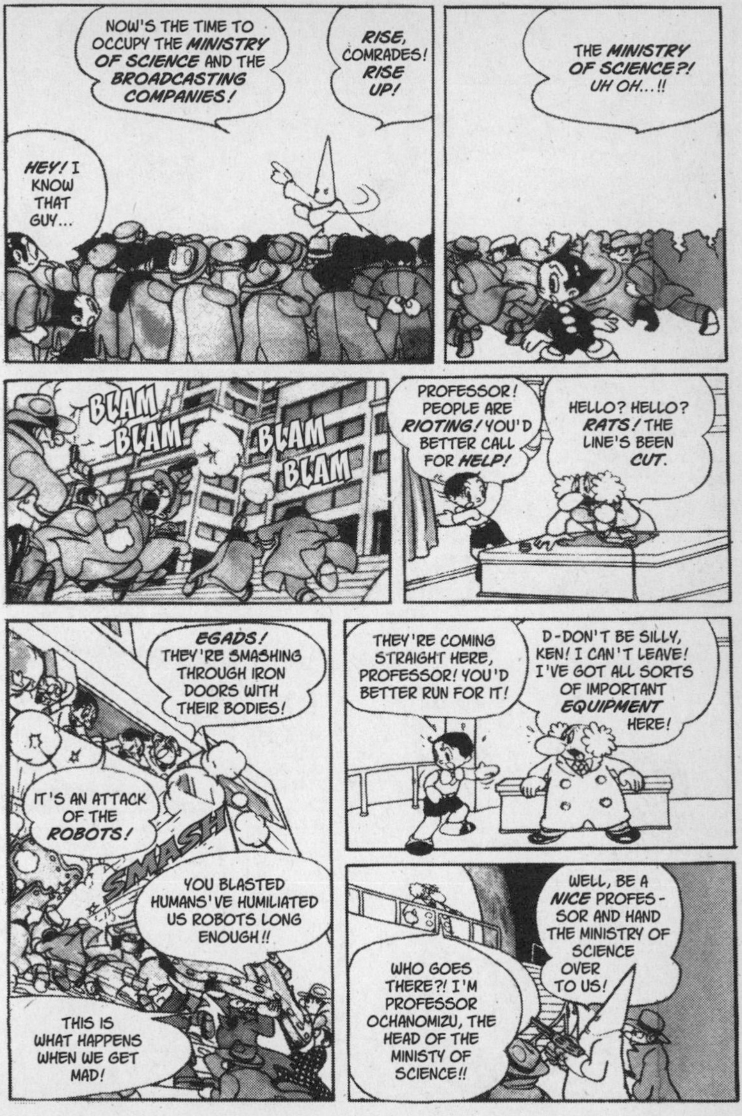
NOW'S THE TIME TO OCCUPY THE MINISTRY OF SCIENCE AND THE BROADCASTING COMPANIES!
RISE, COMRADES! RISE UP!
HEY! I KNOW THAT GUY...
THE MINISTRY OF SCIENCE?! UH OH...!!
BLAM BLAM
BLAM BLAM
PROFESSOR! PEOPLE ARE RIOTING! YOU'D BETTER CALL FOR HELP!
HELLO? HELLO? RATS! THE LINE'S BEEN CUT.
EGADS! THEY'RE SMASHING THROUGH IRON DOORS WITH THEIR BODIES!
IT'S AN ATTACK OF THE ROBOTS!
SMASH
YOU BLASTED HUMANS'VE HUMILIATED US ROBOTS LONG ENOUGH!!
THIS IS WHAT HAPPENS WHEN WE GET MAD!
THEY'RE COMING STRAIGHT HERE, PROFESSOR! YOU'D BETTER RUN FOR IT!
D-DON'T BE SILLY, KEN! I CAN'T LEAVE! I'VE GOT ALL SORTS OF IMPORTANT EQUIPMENT HERE!
WELL, BE A NICE PROFES-SOR AND HAND THE MINISTRY OF SCIENCE OVER TO US!
WHO GOES THERE?! I'M PROFESSOR OCHANOMIZU, THE HEAD OF THE MINISTY OF SCIENCE!!

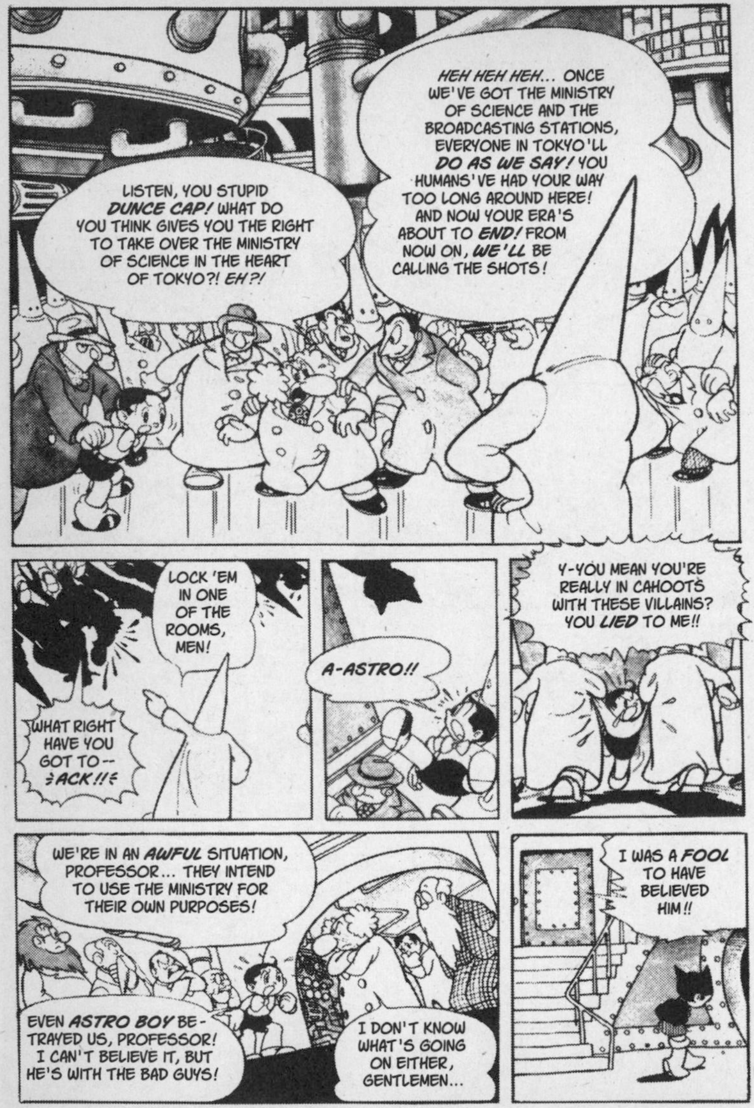
LISTEN, YOU STUPID DUNCE CAP! WHAT DO YOU THINK GIVES YOU THE RIGHT TO TAKE OVER THE MINISTRY OF SCIENCE IN THE HEART OF TOKYO?! EH?!
HEH HEH HEH... ONCE WE'VE GOT THE MINISTRY OF SCIENCE AND THE BROADCASTING STATIONS, EVERYONE IN TOKYO'LL DO AS WE SAY! YOU HUMANS'VE HAD YOUR WAY TOO LONG AROUND HERE! AND NOW YOUR ERA'S ABOUT TO END! FROM NOW ON, WE'LL BE CALLING THE SHOTS!
LOCK 'EM IN ONE OF THE ROOMS, MEN!
WHAT RIGHT HAVE YOU GOT TO-- ACK!!
A-ASTRO!!
Y-YOU MEAN YOU'RE REALLY IN CAHOOTS WITH THESE VILLAINS? YOU LIED TO ME!!
WE'RE IN AN AWFUL SITUATION, PROFESSOR... THEY INTEND TO USE THE MINISTRY FOR THEIR OWN PURPOSES!
EVEN ASTRO BOY BE-TRAYED US, PROFESSOR! I CAN'T BELIEVE IT, BUT HE'S WITH THE BAD GUYS!
I DON'T KNOW WHAT'S GOING ON EITHER, GENTLEMEN...
I WAS A FOOL TO HAVE BELIEVED HIM!!

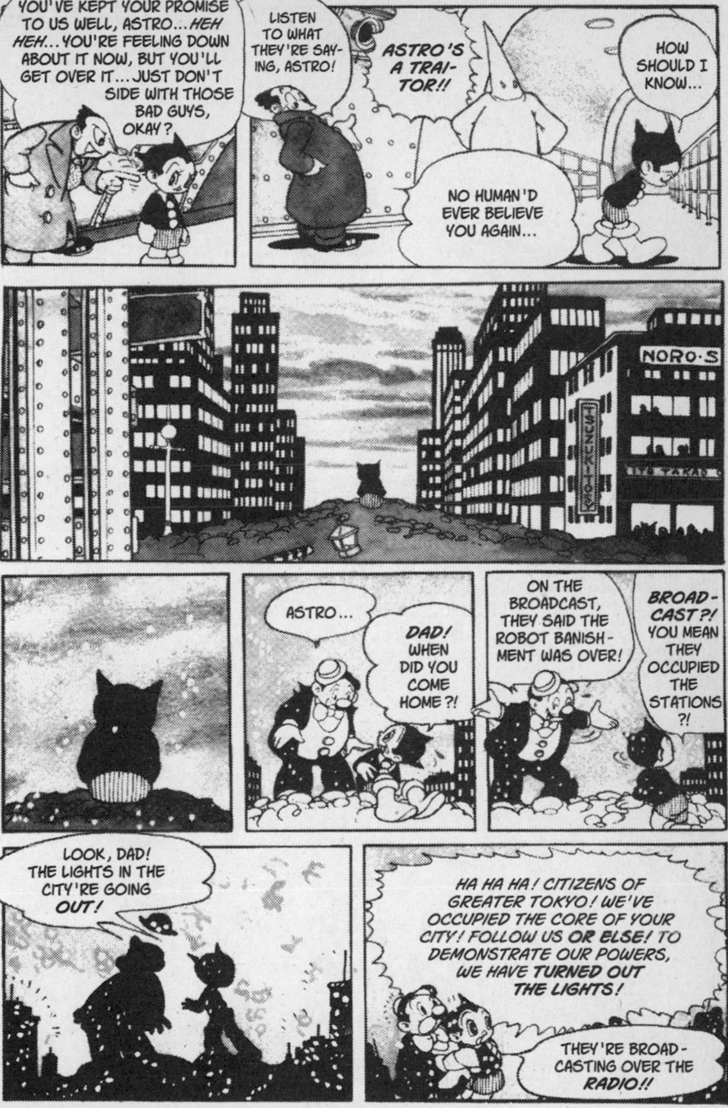
YOU'VE KEPT YOUR PROMISE TO US WELL, ASTRO... *HEH HEH*... YOU'RE FEELING DOWN ABOUT IT NOW, BUT YOU'LL GET OVER IT... JUST DON'T SIDE WITH THOSE BAD GUYS, OKAY?
LISTEN TO WHAT THEY'RE SAYING, ASTRO!
ASTRO'S A TRAITOR!!
NO HUMAN'D EVER BELIEVE YOU AGAIN...
HOW SHOULD I KNOW...
NORO·S
ASTRO...
DAD! WHEN DID YOU COME HOME?!
ON THE BROADCAST, THEY SAID THE ROBOT BANISHMENT WAS OVER!
BROADCAST?! YOU MEAN THEY OCCUPIED THE STATIONS?!
LOOK, DAD! THE LIGHTS IN THE CITY'RE GOING *OUT!*
*HA HA HA! CITIZENS OF GREATER TOKYO! WE'VE OCCUPIED THE CORE OF YOUR CITY! FOLLOW US **OR ELSE!** TO DEMONSTRATE OUR POWERS, WE HAVE **TURNED OUT THE LIGHTS!***
THEY'RE BROADCASTING OVER THE *RADIO!!*

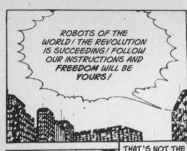

ROBOTS OF THE WORLD! THE REVOLUTION IS SUCCEEDING! FOLLOW OUR INSTRUCTIONS AND FREEDOM WILL BE YOURS!

A NEW CENTURY HAS BEGUN! GO BACK TO YOUR HOMES AND TO YOUR JOBS! THIS IS THE BROADCAST DIVISION OF YOUR REVOLUTIONARY GROUP!

DAD, I'M CONFUSED... SHOULD I SIDE WITH THE ROBOTS OR THE HUMANS?!

THAT'S NOT THE QUESTION, ASTRO. THE QUESTION IS, WHY AREN'T YOU SEARCHING FOR FRANKENSTEIN?!!

GET FRANKENSTEIN, AND EVERYTHING'LL BE BETTER!

OKAY, DAD...

I'LL DO AS YOU SAY!

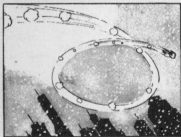

HEAD FOR THE MINISTRY OF SCIENCE! ON THE DOUBLE!

WHEEE WHEEE

WHEEEE WHEEEE

DISPERSE, MEN!

ALL RIGHT, YOU SCOUNDRELS IN THE MINISTRY OF SCIENCE! SURRENDER NOW OR FACE THE CONSEQUENCES!

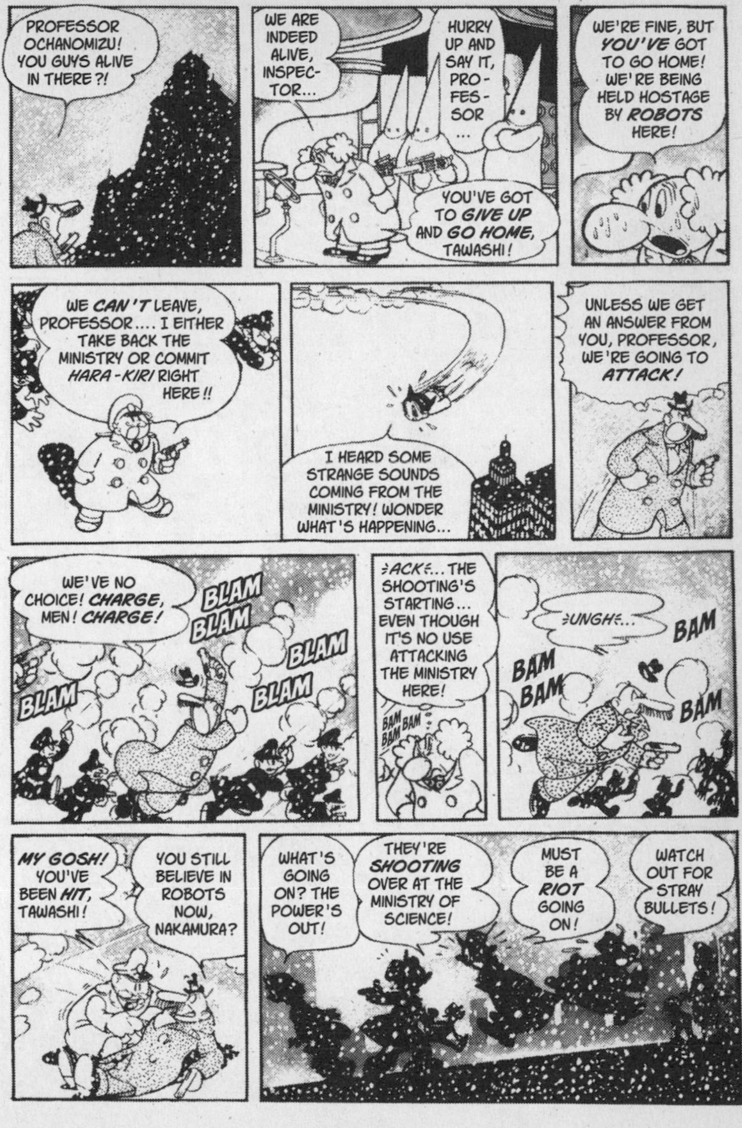
PROFESSOR OCHANOMIZU! YOU GUYS ALIVE IN THERE?!
WE ARE INDEED ALIVE, INSPECTOR...
HURRY UP AND SAY IT, PRO- FES- SOR ...
YOU'VE GOT TO GIVE UP AND GO HOME, TAWASHI!
WE'RE FINE, BUT YOU'VE GOT TO GO HOME! WE'RE BEING HELD HOSTAGE BY ROBOTS HERE!
WE CAN'T LEAVE, PROFESSOR.... I EITHER TAKE BACK THE MINISTRY OR COMMIT HARA-KIRI RIGHT HERE!!
I HEARD SOME STRANGE SOUNDS COMING FROM THE MINISTRY! WONDER WHAT'S HAPPENING...
UNLESS WE GET AN ANSWER FROM YOU, PROFESSOR, WE'RE GOING TO ATTACK!
WE'VE NO CHOICE! CHARGE, MEN! CHARGE!
BLAM BLAM
BLAM
BLAM
BLAM
ACK... THE SHOOTING'S STARTING... EVEN THOUGH IT'S NO USE ATTACKING THE MINISTRY HERE!
BAM BAM BAM
UNGH...
BAM
BAM BAM
BAM
MY GOSH! YOU'VE BEEN HIT, TAWASHI!
YOU STILL BELIEVE IN ROBOTS NOW, NAKAMURA?
WHAT'S GOING ON? THE POWER'S OUT!
THEY'RE SHOOTING OVER AT THE MINISTRY OF SCIENCE!
MUST BE A RIOT GOING ON!
WATCH OUT FOR STRAY BULLETS!

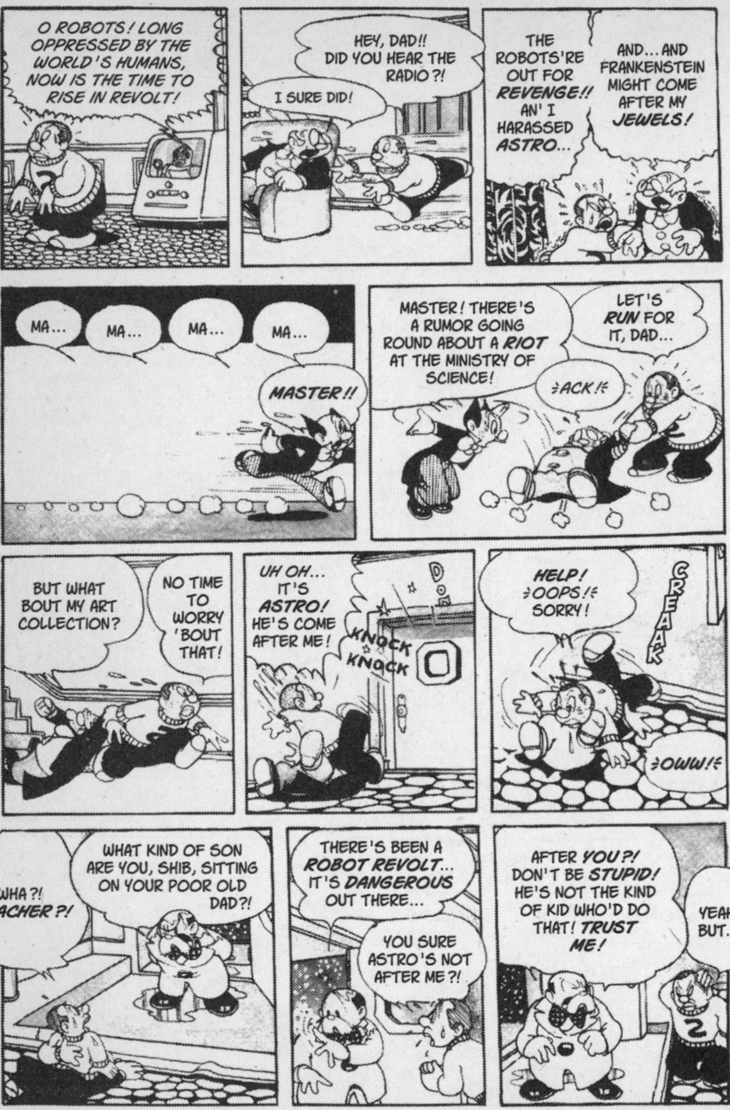

O ROBOTS! LONG OPPRESSED BY THE WORLD'S HUMANS, NOW IS THE TIME TO RISE IN REVOLT!
HEY, DAD!! DID YOU HEAR THE RADIO?!
I SURE DID!
THE ROBOTS'RE OUT FOR REVENGE!! AN' I HARASSED ASTRO...
AND... AND FRANKENSTEIN MIGHT COME AFTER MY JEWELS!
MA...
MA...
MA...
MA...
MASTER!!
MASTER! THERE'S A RUMOR GOING ROUND ABOUT A RIOT AT THE MINISTRY OF SCIENCE!
LET'S RUN FOR IT, DAD...
ACK!
BUT WHAT BOUT MY ART COLLECTION?
NO TIME TO WORRY 'BOUT THAT!
UH OH... IT'S ASTRO! HE'S COME AFTER ME!
KNOCK KNOCK
HELP! OOPS! SORRY!
CREAAK
OWW!
WHA?! TEACHER?!
WHAT KIND OF SON ARE YOU, SHIB, SITTING ON YOUR POOR OLD DAD?!
THERE'S BEEN A ROBOT REVOLT... IT'S DANGEROUS OUT THERE...
YOU SURE ASTRO'S NOT AFTER ME?!
AFTER YOU?! DON'T BE STUPID! HE'S NOT THE KIND OF KID WHO'D DO THAT! TRUST ME!
YEAH, BUT...

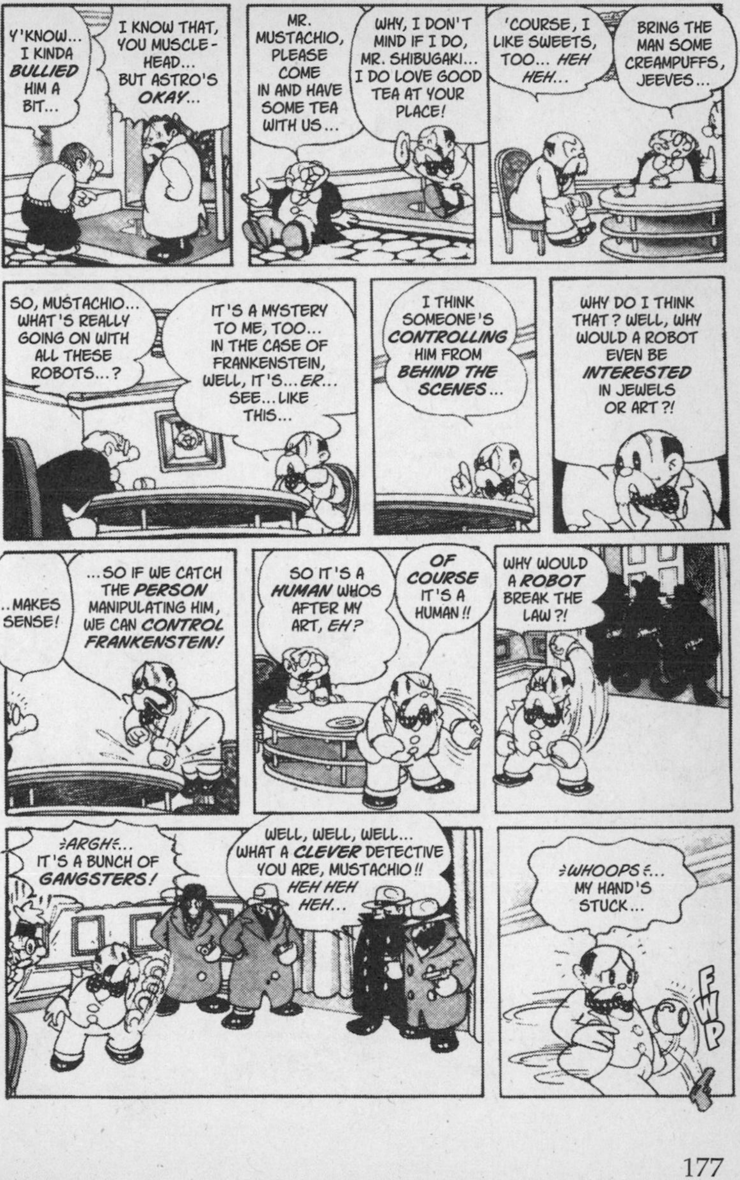
Y'KNOW... I KINDA BULLIED HIM A BIT...
I KNOW THAT, YOU MUSCLE-HEAD... BUT ASTRO'S OKAY...
MR. MUSTACHIO, PLEASE COME IN AND HAVE SOME TEA WITH US...
WHY, I DON'T MIND IF I DO, MR. SHIBUGAKI... I DO LOVE GOOD TEA AT YOUR PLACE!
'COURSE, I LIKE SWEETS, TOO... HEH HEH...
BRING THE MAN SOME CREAMPUFFS, JEEVES...
SO, MUSTACHIO... WHAT'S REALLY GOING ON WITH ALL THESE ROBOTS...?
IT'S A MYSTERY TO ME, TOO... IN THE CASE OF FRANKENSTEIN, WELL, IT'S... ER... SEE... LIKE THIS...
I THINK SOMEONE'S CONTROLLING HIM FROM BEHIND THE SCENES...
WHY DO I THINK THAT? WELL, WHY WOULD A ROBOT EVEN BE INTERESTED IN JEWELS OR ART?!
...MAKES SENSE!
...SO IF WE CATCH THE PERSON MANIPULATING HIM, WE CAN CONTROL FRANKENSTEIN!
SO IT'S A HUMAN WHOS AFTER MY ART, EH?
OF COURSE IT'S A HUMAN!!
WHY WOULD A ROBOT BREAK THE LAW?!
ARGH... IT'S A BUNCH OF GANGSTERS!
WELL, WELL, WELL... WHAT A CLEVER DETECTIVE YOU ARE, MUSTACHIO!! HEH HEH HEH...
WHOOPS... MY HAND'S STUCK...
FWP

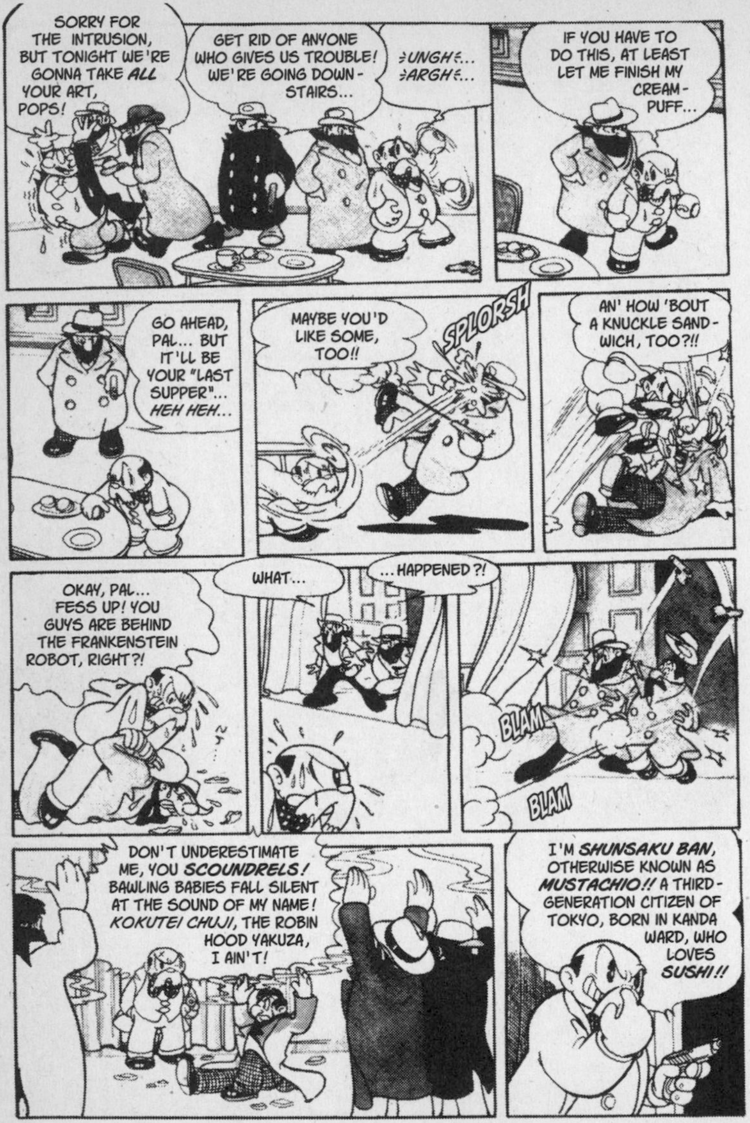
SORRY FOR THE INTRUSION, BUT TONIGHT WE'RE GONNA TAKE ALL YOUR ART, POPS!
GET RID OF ANYONE WHO GIVES US TROUBLE! WE'RE GOING DOWN-STAIRS...
UNGH... ARGH...
IF YOU HAVE TO DO THIS, AT LEAST LET ME FINISH MY CREAM-PUFF...
GO AHEAD, PAL... BUT IT'LL BE YOUR "LAST SUPPER"... HEH HEH...
MAYBE YOU'D LIKE SOME, TOO!!
SPLORSH
AN' HOW 'BOUT A KNUCKLE SAND-WICH, TOO?!!
OKAY, PAL... FESS UP! YOU GUYS ARE BEHIND THE FRANKENSTEIN ROBOT, RIGHT?!
WHAT...
...HAPPENED?!
BLAM
BLAM
DON'T UNDERESTIMATE ME, YOU SCOUNDRELS! BAWLING BABIES FALL SILENT AT THE SOUND OF MY NAME! KOKUTEI CHUJI, THE ROBIN HOOD YAKUZA, I AIN'T!
I'M SHUNSAKU BAN, OTHERWISE KNOWN AS MUSTACHIO!! A THIRD-GENERATION CITIZEN OF TOKYO, BORN IN KANDA WARD, WHO LOVES SUSHI!!

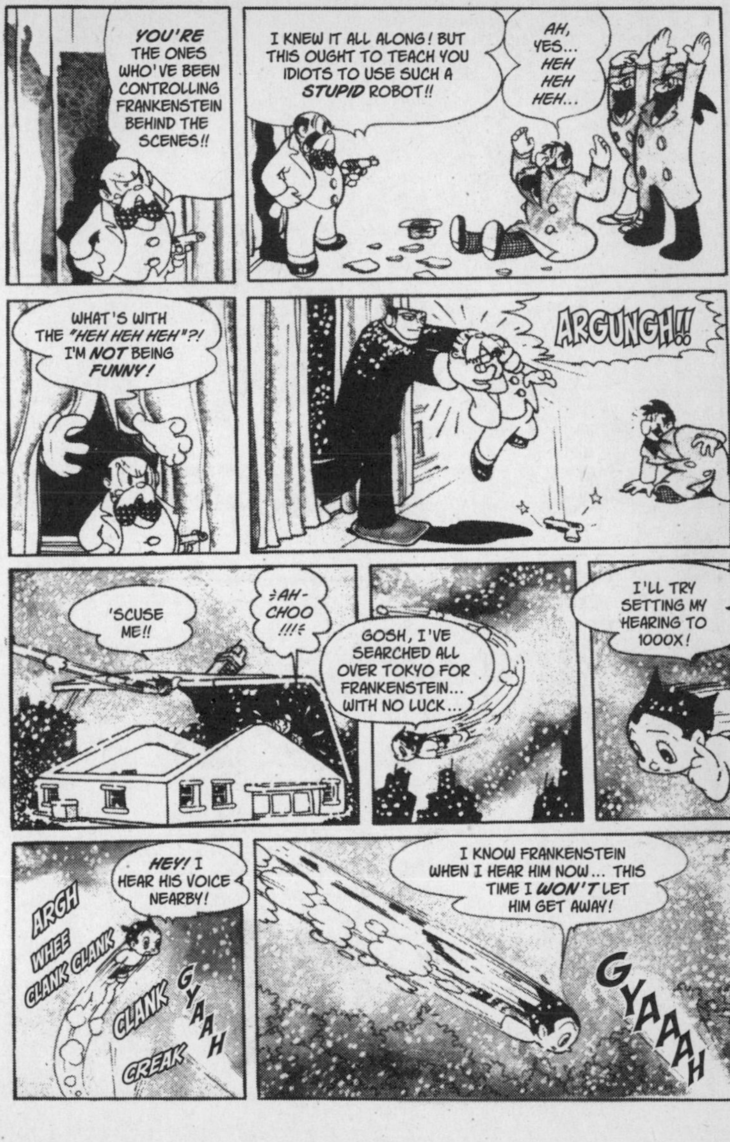
YOU'RE THE ONES WHO'VE BEEN CONTROLLING FRANKENSTEIN BEHIND THE SCENES!!
I KNEW IT ALL ALONG! BUT THIS OUGHT TO TEACH YOU IDIOTS TO USE SUCH A STUPID ROBOT!!
AH, YES... HEH HEH HEH...
WHAT'S WITH THE "HEH HEH HEH"?! I'M NOT BEING FUNNY!
ARGUNGH!!
'SCUSE ME!!
AH-CHOO!!!
GOSH, I'VE SEARCHED ALL OVER TOKYO FOR FRANKENSTEIN... WITH NO LUCK...
I'LL TRY SETTING MY HEARING TO 1000X!
HEY! I HEAR HIS VOICE NEARBY!
ARGH
WHEE
CLANK CLANK
CLANK
GYAAH
CREAK
I KNOW FRANKENSTEIN WHEN I HEAR HIM NOW... THIS TIME I WON'T LET HIM GET AWAY!
GYAAAH

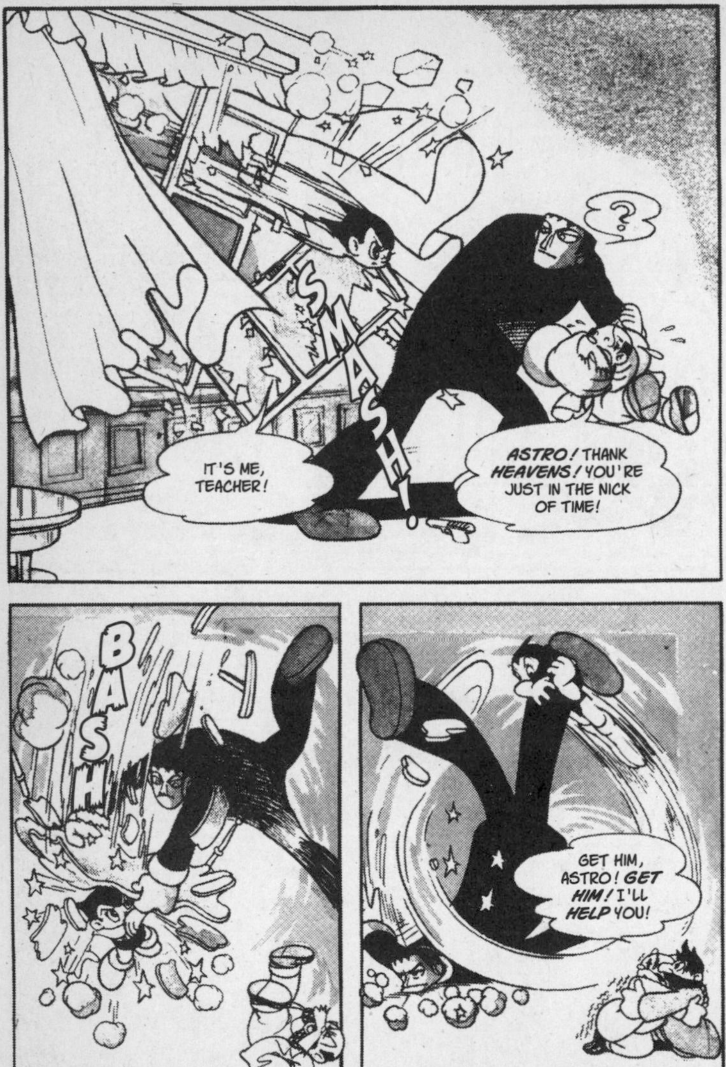
?
SMASH!
IT'S ME, TEACHER!
ASTRO! THANK HEAVENS! YOU'RE JUST IN THE NICK OF TIME!
BASH
GET HIM, ASTRO! GET HIM! I'LL HELP YOU!

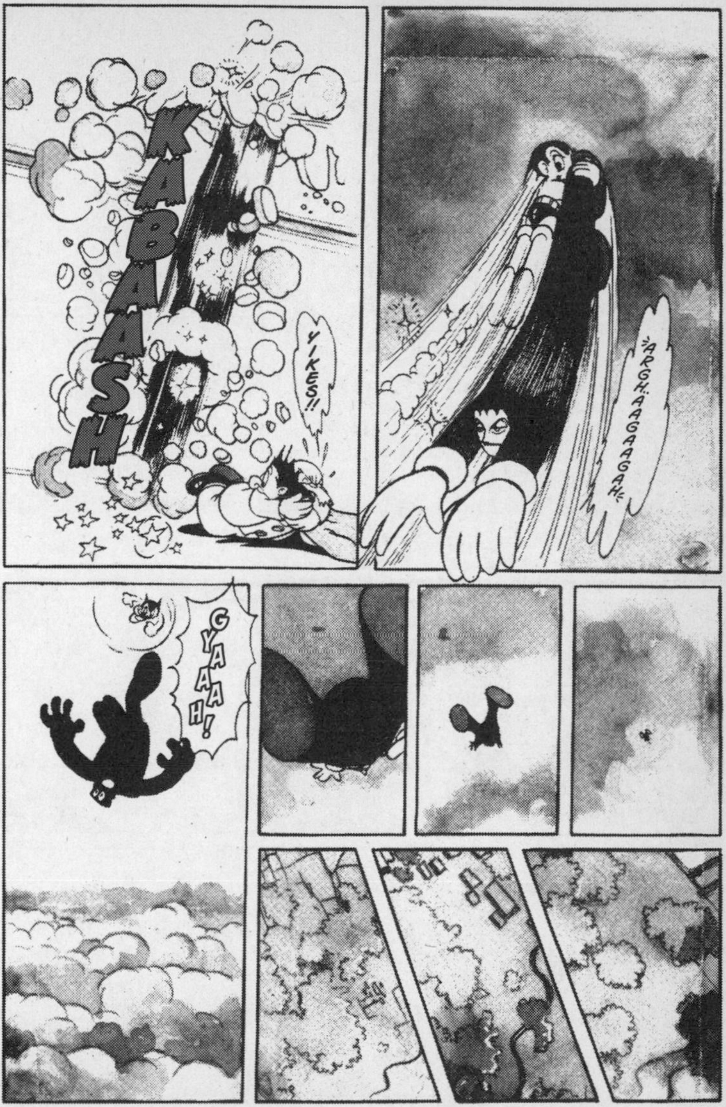
KABAAASH
YIKES!!
ARGH...AAGAAGAH
GYAAAH!

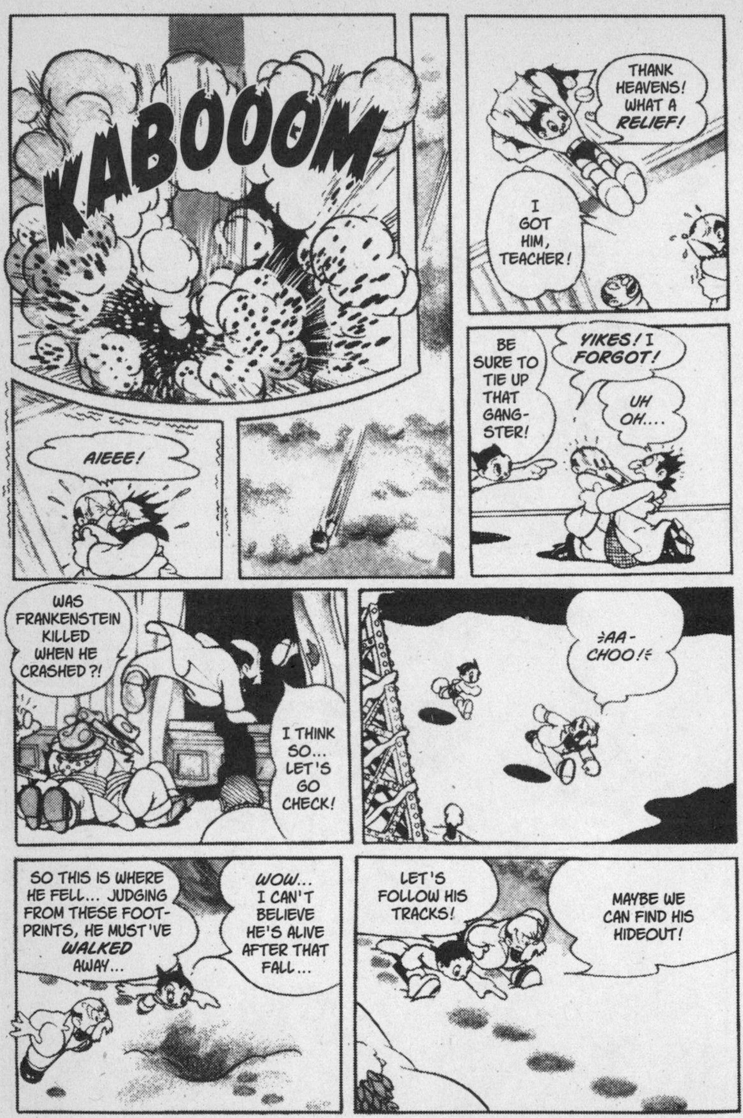
KABOOOM
THANK HEAVENS! WHAT A RELIEF!
I GOT HIM, TEACHER!
AIEEE!
BE SURE TO TIE UP THAT GANG-STER!
YIKES! I FORGOT!
UH OH....
WAS FRANKENSTEIN KILLED WHEN HE CRASHED?!
I THINK SO... LET'S GO CHECK!
AA-CHOO!
SO THIS IS WHERE HE FELL... JUDGING FROM THESE FOOT-PRINTS, HE MUST'VE WALKED AWAY...
WOW... I CAN'T BELIEVE HE'S ALIVE AFTER THAT FALL...
LET'S FOLLOW HIS TRACKS!
MAYBE WE CAN FIND HIS HIDEOUT!

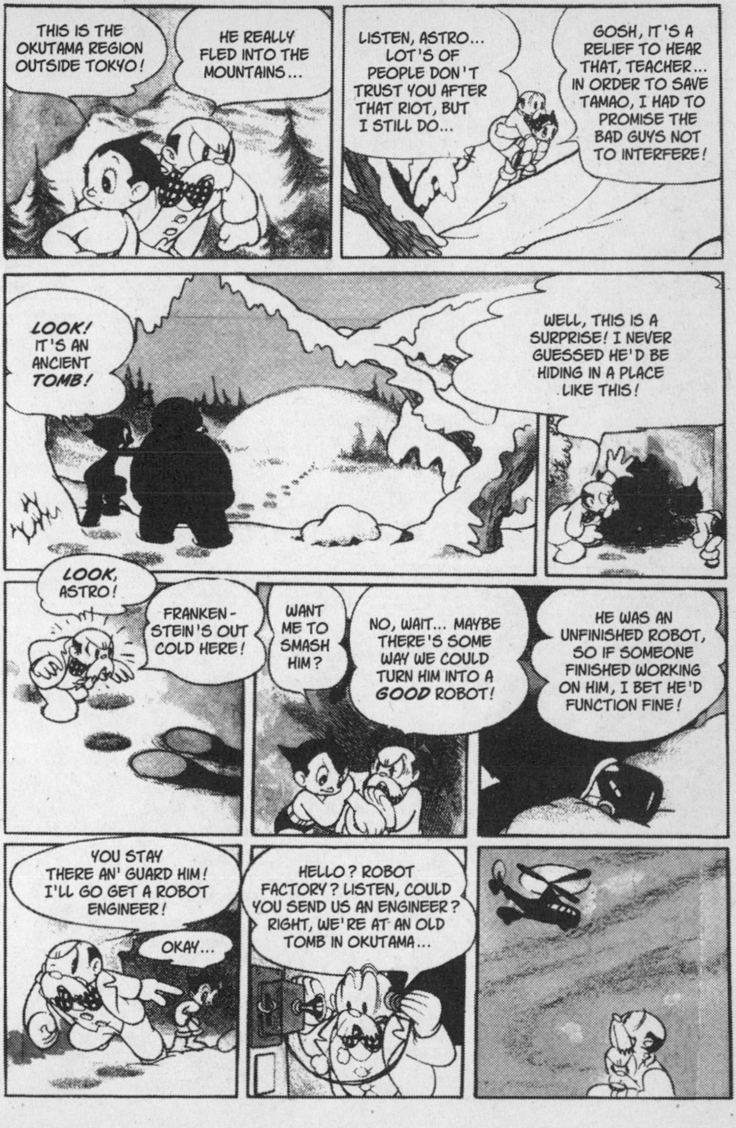
THIS IS THE OKUTAMA REGION OUTSIDE TOKYO!
HE REALLY FLED INTO THE MOUNTAINS...
LISTEN, ASTRO... LOT'S OF PEOPLE DON'T TRUST YOU AFTER THAT RIOT, BUT I STILL DO...
GOSH, IT'S A RELIEF TO HEAR THAT, TEACHER... IN ORDER TO SAVE TAMAO, I HAD TO PROMISE THE BAD GUYS NOT TO INTERFERE!
LOOK! IT'S AN ANCIENT TOMB!
WELL, THIS IS A SURPRISE! I NEVER GUESSED HE'D BE HIDING IN A PLACE LIKE THIS!
LOOK, ASTRO!
FRANKEN-STEIN'S OUT COLD HERE!
WANT ME TO SMASH HIM?
NO, WAIT... MAYBE THERE'S SOME WAY WE COULD TURN HIM INTO A GOOD ROBOT!
HE WAS AN UNFINISHED ROBOT, SO IF SOMEONE FINISHED WORKING ON HIM, I BET HE'D FUNCTION FINE!
YOU STAY THERE AN' GUARD HIM! I'LL GO GET A ROBOT ENGINEER!
OKAY...
HELLO? ROBOT FACTORY? LISTEN, COULD YOU SEND US AN ENGINEER? RIGHT, WE'RE AT AN OLD TOMB IN OKUTAMA...

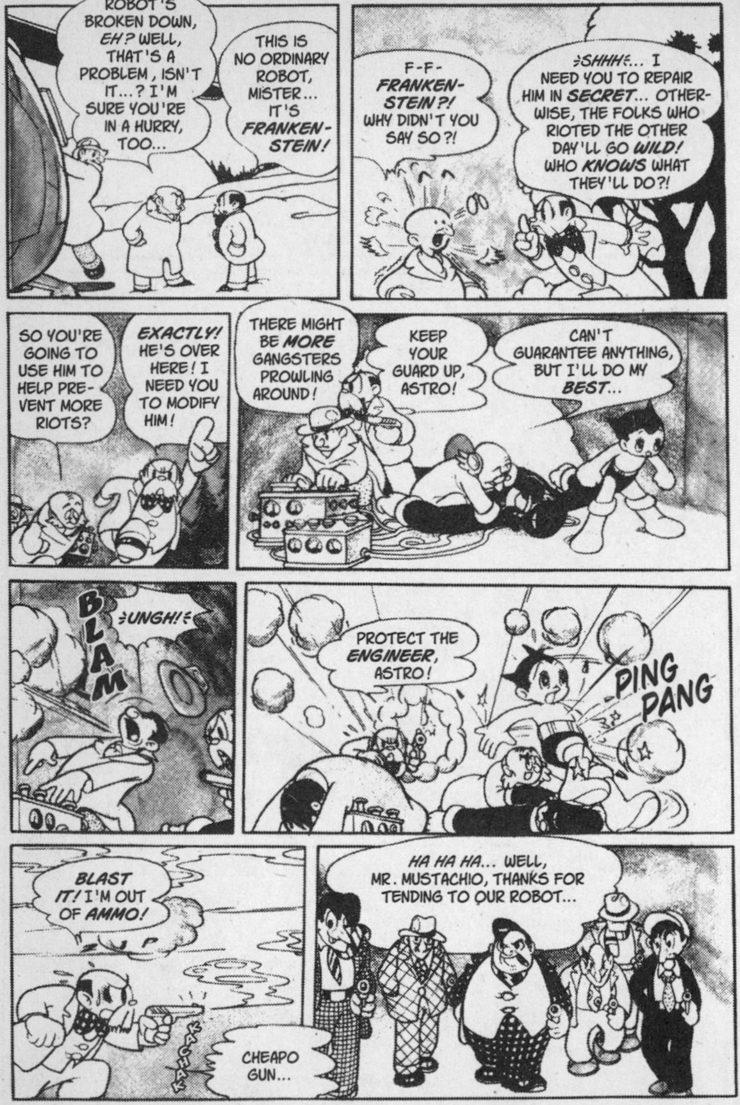
ROBOT'S BROKEN DOWN, EH? WELL, THAT'S A PROBLEM, ISN'T IT...? I'M SURE YOU'RE IN A HURRY, TOO...
THIS IS NO ORDINARY ROBOT, MISTER... IT'S FRANKEN-STEIN!
F-F-FRANKEN-STEIN?! WHY DIDN'T YOU SAY SO?!
SHHH... I NEED YOU TO REPAIR HIM IN SECRET... OTHER-WISE, THE FOLKS WHO RIOTED THE OTHER DAY'LL GO WILD! WHO KNOWS WHAT THEY'LL DO?!
SO YOU'RE GOING TO USE HIM TO HELP PRE-VENT MORE RIOTS?
EXACTLY! HE'S OVER HERE! I NEED YOU TO MODIFY HIM!
THERE MIGHT BE MORE GANGSTERS PROWLING AROUND!
KEEP YOUR GUARD UP, ASTRO!
CAN'T GUARANTEE ANYTHING, BUT I'LL DO MY BEST...
BLAM
UNGH!
PROTECT THE ENGINEER, ASTRO!
PING PANG
BLAST IT! I'M OUT OF AMMO!
KACHAK
CHEAPO GUN...
HA HA HA... WELL, MR. MUSTACHIO, THANKS FOR TENDING TO OUR ROBOT...

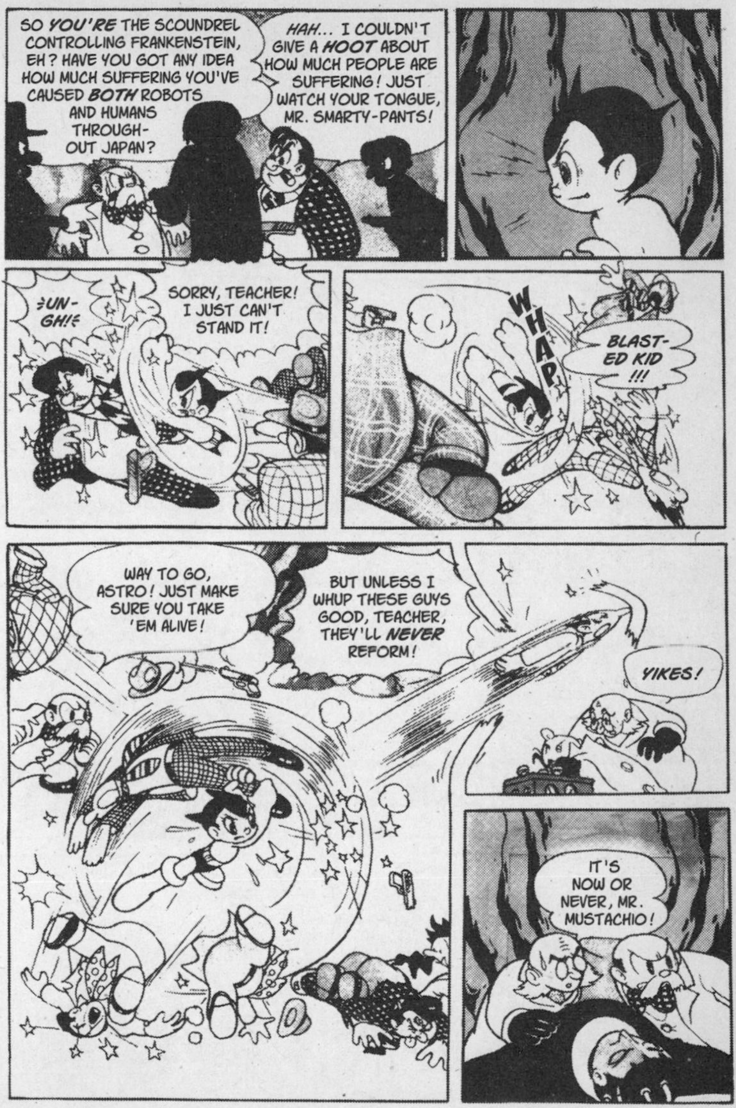

SO *YOU'RE* THE SCOUNDREL CONTROLLING FRANKENSTEIN, EH? HAVE YOU GOT ANY IDEA HOW MUCH SUFFERING YOU'VE CAUSED *BOTH* ROBOTS AND HUMANS THROUGH-OUT JAPAN?
HAH... I COULDN'T GIVE A *HOOT* ABOUT HOW MUCH PEOPLE ARE SUFFERING! JUST WATCH YOUR TONGUE, MR. SMARTY-PANTS!
UN-GH!
SORRY, TEACHER! I JUST CAN'T STAND IT!
WHAP
BLAST-ED KID !!!
WAY TO GO, ASTRO! JUST MAKE SURE YOU TAKE 'EM ALIVE!
BUT UNLESS I WHUP THESE GUYS GOOD, TEACHER, THEY'LL *NEVER* REFORM!
YIKES!
IT'S NOW OR NEVER, MR. MUSTACHIO!

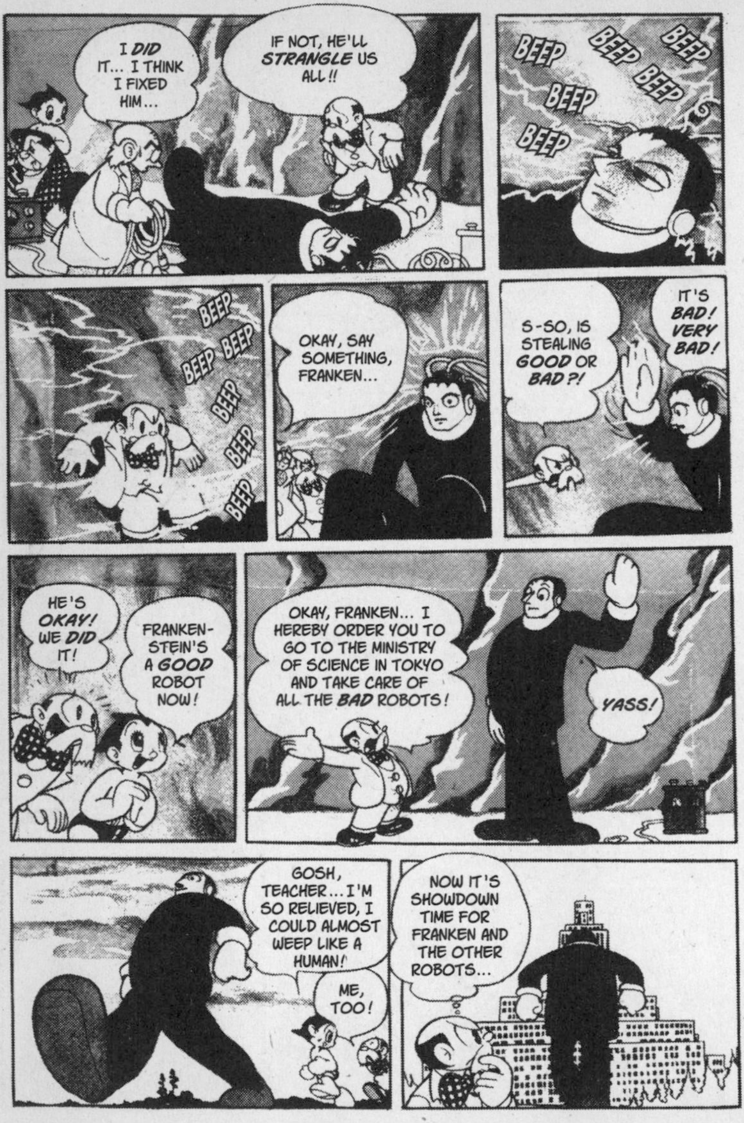
I DID IT... I THINK I FIXED HIM...
IF NOT, HE'LL STRANGLE US ALL!!
BEEP BEEP BEEP BEEP BEEP BEEP
BEEP BEEP BEEP BEEP BEEP BEEP
OKAY, SAY SOMETHING, FRANKEN...
S-SO, IS STEALING GOOD OR BAD?!
IT'S BAD! VERY BAD!
HE'S OKAY! WE DID IT!
FRANKEN-STEIN'S A GOOD ROBOT NOW!
OKAY, FRANKEN... I HEREBY ORDER YOU TO GO TO THE MINISTRY OF SCIENCE IN TOKYO AND TAKE CARE OF ALL THE BAD ROBOTS!
YASS!
GOSH, TEACHER... I'M SO RELIEVED, I COULD ALMOST WEEP LIKE A HUMAN!
ME, TOO!
NOW IT'S SHOWDOWN TIME FOR FRANKEN AND THE OTHER ROBOTS...

YIKES! IT'S FRANKEN-STEIN!

IT'S FRANKEN-STEIN!

‡ARGH!‡

HAALP!

A MONSTER'S AFTER US!

WE SUR-RENDER! WE SUR-RENDER!

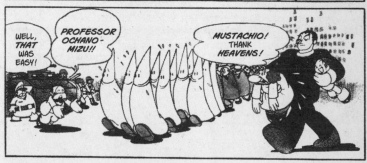

WELL, THAT WAS EASY!

PROFESSOR OCHANO-MIZU!!

MUSTACHIO! THANK HEAVENS!

NOW WE'D BETTER TAKE THESE ROBOTS APART AND FIND OUT WHY THEY DEVELOPED SUCH EVIL MINDS!

WE CONFESS... ACTUALLY, WE'RE NOT ROBOTS!

WHAT?! HUMANS?!

YOU SCOUN-DRELS!!

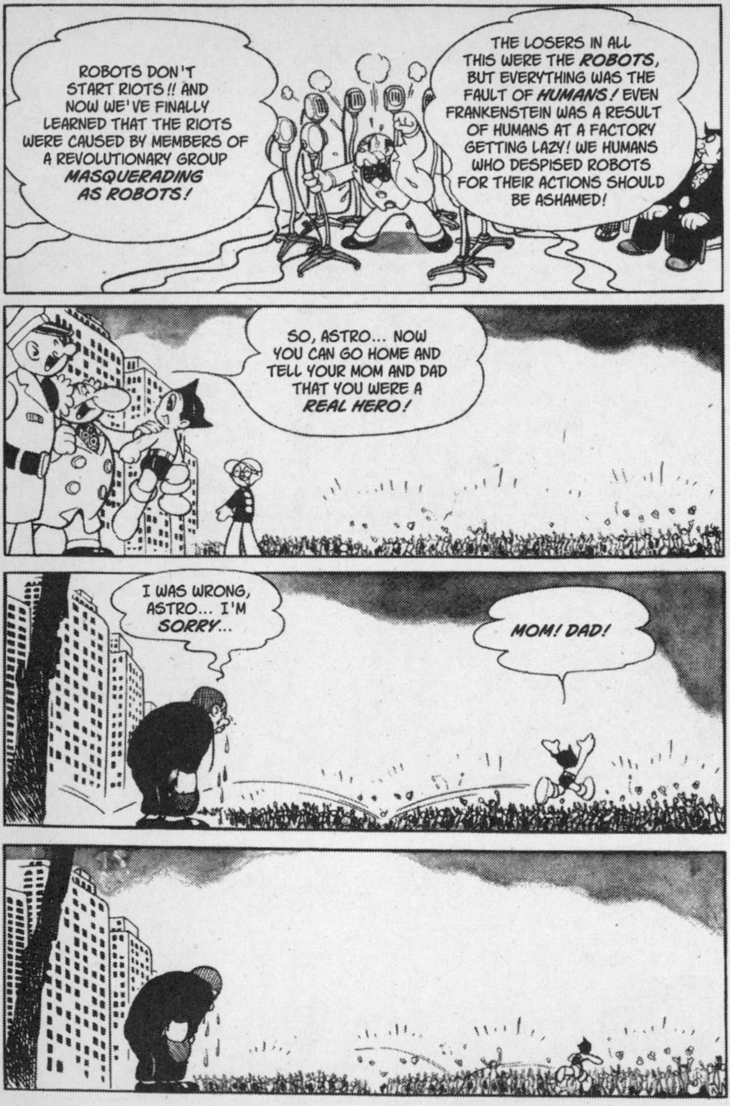
ROBOTS DON'T START RIOTS!! AND NOW WE'VE FINALLY LEARNED THAT THE RIOTS WERE CAUSED BY MEMBERS OF A REVOLUTIONARY GROUP MASQUERADING AS ROBOTS!
THE LOSERS IN ALL THIS WERE THE ROBOTS, BUT EVERYTHING WAS THE FAULT OF HUMANS! EVEN FRANKENSTEIN WAS A RESULT OF HUMANS AT A FACTORY GETTING LAZY! WE HUMANS WHO DESPISED ROBOTS FOR THEIR ACTIONS SHOULD BE ASHAMED!
SO, ASTRO... NOW YOU CAN GO HOME AND TELL YOUR MOM AND DAD THAT YOU WERE A REAL HERO!
I WAS WRONG, ASTRO... I'M SORRY...
MOM! DAD!

THE CORAL REEF ADVENTURE

First appeared in the 1954 expanded summer edition of *Shonen* magazine.

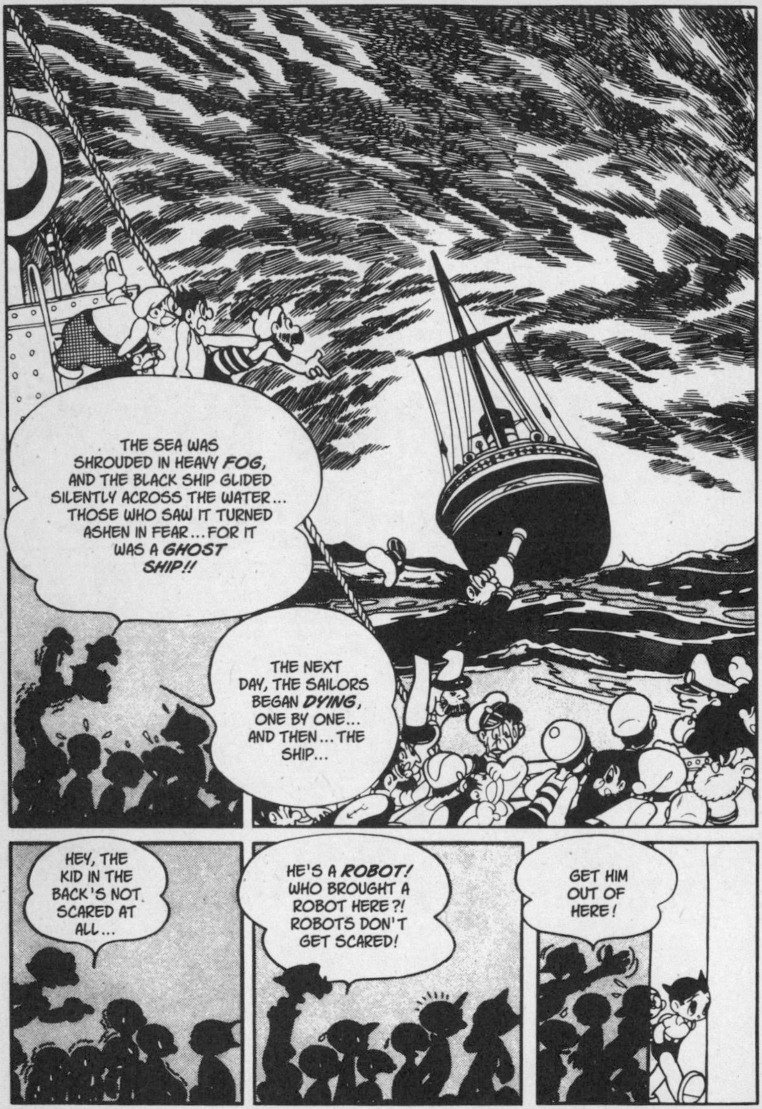
THE SEA WAS SHROUDED IN HEAVY FOG, AND THE BLACK SHIP GLIDED SILENTLY ACROSS THE WATER... THOSE WHO SAW IT TURNED ASHEN IN FEAR...FOR IT WAS A GHOST SHIP!!
THE NEXT DAY, THE SAILORS BEGAN DYING, ONE BY ONE... AND THEN... THE SHIP...
HEY, THE KID IN THE BACK'S NOT SCARED AT ALL...
HE'S A ROBOT! WHO BROUGHT A ROBOT HERE?! ROBOTS DON'T GET SCARED!
GET HIM OUT OF HERE!

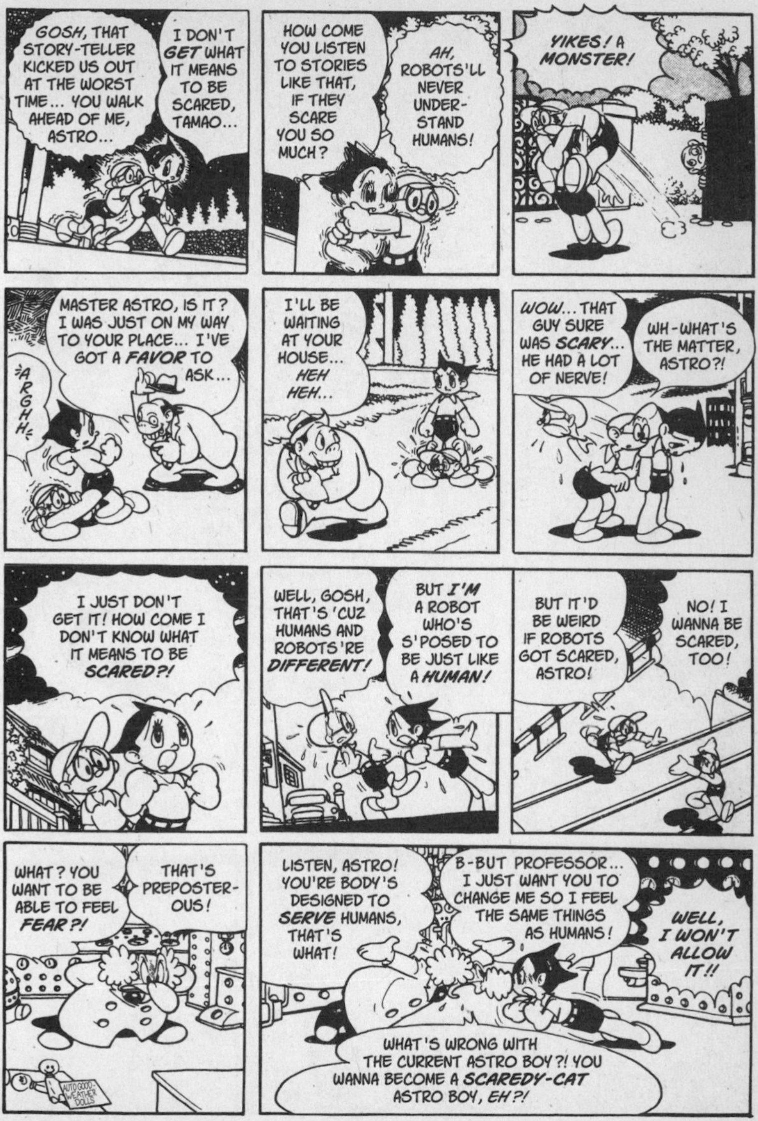
GOSH, THAT STORY-TELLER KICKED US OUT AT THE WORST TIME... YOU WALK AHEAD OF ME, ASTRO...
I DON'T GET WHAT IT MEANS TO BE SCARED, TAMAO...
HOW COME YOU LISTEN TO STORIES LIKE THAT, IF THEY SCARE YOU SO MUCH?
AH, ROBOTS'LL NEVER UNDER-STAND HUMANS!
YIKES! A MONSTER!
MASTER ASTRO, IS IT? I WAS JUST ON MY WAY TO YOUR PLACE... I'VE GOT A FAVOR TO ASK...
ARGHH
I'LL BE WAITING AT YOUR HOUSE... HEH HEH...
WOW... THAT GUY SURE WAS SCARY... HE HAD A LOT OF NERVE!
WH-WHAT'S THE MATTER, ASTRO?!
I JUST DON'T GET IT! HOW COME I DON'T KNOW WHAT IT MEANS TO BE SCARED?!
WELL, GOSH, THAT'S 'CUZ HUMANS AND ROBOTS'RE DIFFERENT!
BUT I'M A ROBOT WHO'S S'POSED TO BE JUST LIKE A HUMAN!
BUT IT'D BE WEIRD IF ROBOTS GOT SCARED, ASTRO!
NO! I WANNA BE SCARED, TOO!
WHAT? YOU WANT TO BE ABLE TO FEEL FEAR?!
THAT'S PREPOSTER-OUS!
AUTO GOOD-WEATHER DOLLS
LISTEN, ASTRO! YOU'RE BODY'S DESIGNED TO SERVE HUMANS, THAT'S WHAT!
B-BUT PROFESSOR... I JUST WANT YOU TO CHANGE ME SO I FEEL THE SAME THINGS AS HUMANS!
WELL, I WON'T ALLOW IT!!
WHAT'S WRONG WITH THE CURRENT ASTRO BOY?! YOU WANNA BECOME A SCAREDY-CAT ASTRO BOY, EH?!

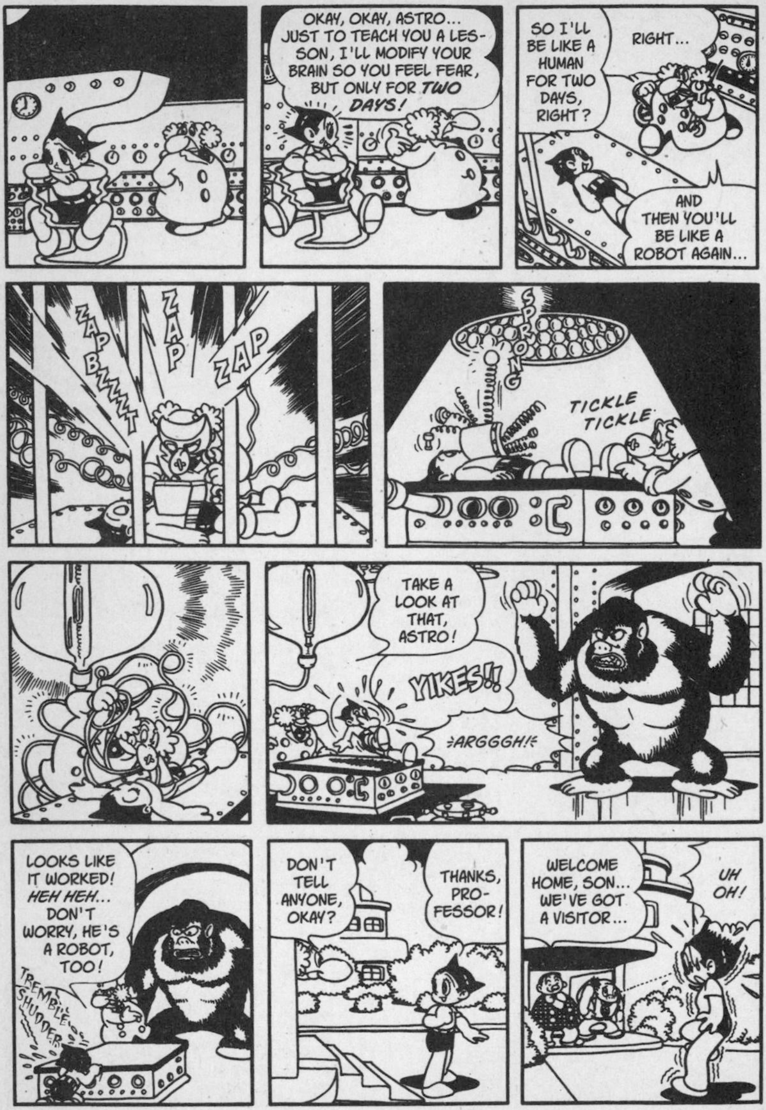
OKAY, OKAY, ASTRO... JUST TO TEACH YOU A LES-SON, I'LL MODIFY YOUR BRAIN SO YOU FEEL FEAR, BUT ONLY FOR TWO DAYS!
SO I'LL BE LIKE A HUMAN FOR TWO DAYS, RIGHT?
RIGHT...
AND THEN YOU'LL BE LIKE A ROBOT AGAIN...
ZAP
BZZZT
ZAP
ZAP
SPRONG
TICKLE TICKLE
TAKE A LOOK AT THAT, ASTRO!
YIKES!!
ARGGGH!
LOOKS LIKE IT WORKED! HEH HEH... DON'T WORRY, HE'S A ROBOT, TOO!
TREMBLE
SHUDDER
DON'T TELL ANYONE, OKAY?
THANKS, PRO-FESSOR!
WELCOME HOME, SON... WE'VE GOT A VISITOR...
UH OH!

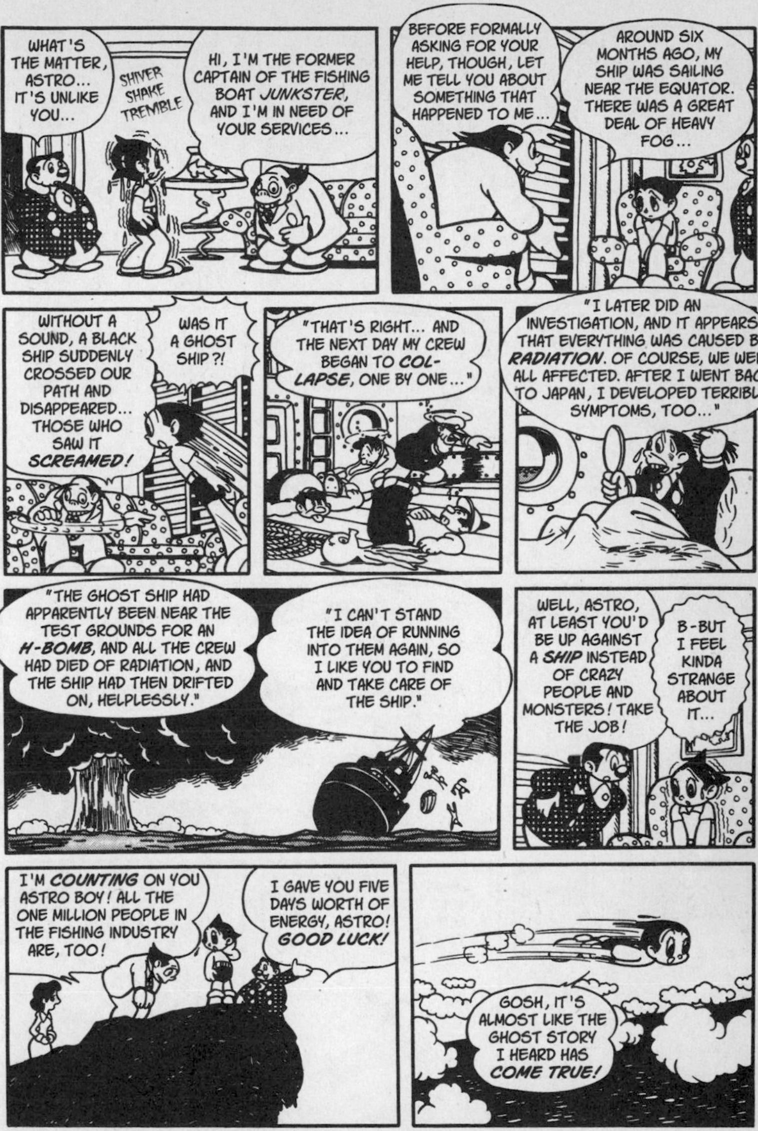
WHAT'S THE MATTER, ASTRO... IT'S UNLIKE YOU...
SHIVER SHAKE TREMBLE
HI, I'M THE FORMER CAPTAIN OF THE FISHING BOAT JUNKSTER, AND I'M IN NEED OF YOUR SERVICES...
BEFORE FORMALLY ASKING FOR YOUR HELP, THOUGH, LET ME TELL YOU ABOUT SOMETHING THAT HAPPENED TO ME...
AROUND SIX MONTHS AGO, MY SHIP WAS SAILING NEAR THE EQUATOR. THERE WAS A GREAT DEAL OF HEAVY FOG...
WITHOUT A SOUND, A BLACK SHIP SUDDENLY CROSSED OUR PATH AND DISAPPEARED... THOSE WHO SAW IT SCREAMED!
WAS IT A GHOST SHIP?!
"THAT'S RIGHT... AND THE NEXT DAY MY CREW BEGAN TO COL-LAPSE, ONE BY ONE..."
"I LATER DID AN INVESTIGATION, AND IT APPEARS THAT EVERYTHING WAS CAUSED BY RADIATION. OF COURSE, WE WERE ALL AFFECTED. AFTER I WENT BACK TO JAPAN, I DEVELOPED TERRIBLE SYMPTOMS, TOO..."
"THE GHOST SHIP HAD APPARENTLY BEEN NEAR THE TEST GROUNDS FOR AN H-BOMB, AND ALL THE CREW HAD DIED OF RADIATION, AND THE SHIP HAD THEN DRIFTED ON, HELPLESSLY."
"I CAN'T STAND THE IDEA OF RUNNING INTO THEM AGAIN, SO I LIKE YOU TO FIND AND TAKE CARE OF THE SHIP."
WELL, ASTRO, AT LEAST YOU'D BE UP AGAINST A SHIP INSTEAD OF CRAZY PEOPLE AND MONSTERS! TAKE THE JOB!
B-BUT I FEEL KINDA STRANGE ABOUT IT...
I'M COUNTING ON YOU ASTRO BOY! ALL THE ONE MILLION PEOPLE IN THE FISHING INDUSTRY ARE, TOO!
I GAVE YOU FIVE DAYS WORTH OF ENERGY, ASTRO! GOOD LUCK!
GOSH, IT'S ALMOST LIKE THE GHOST STORY I HEARD HAS COME TRUE!

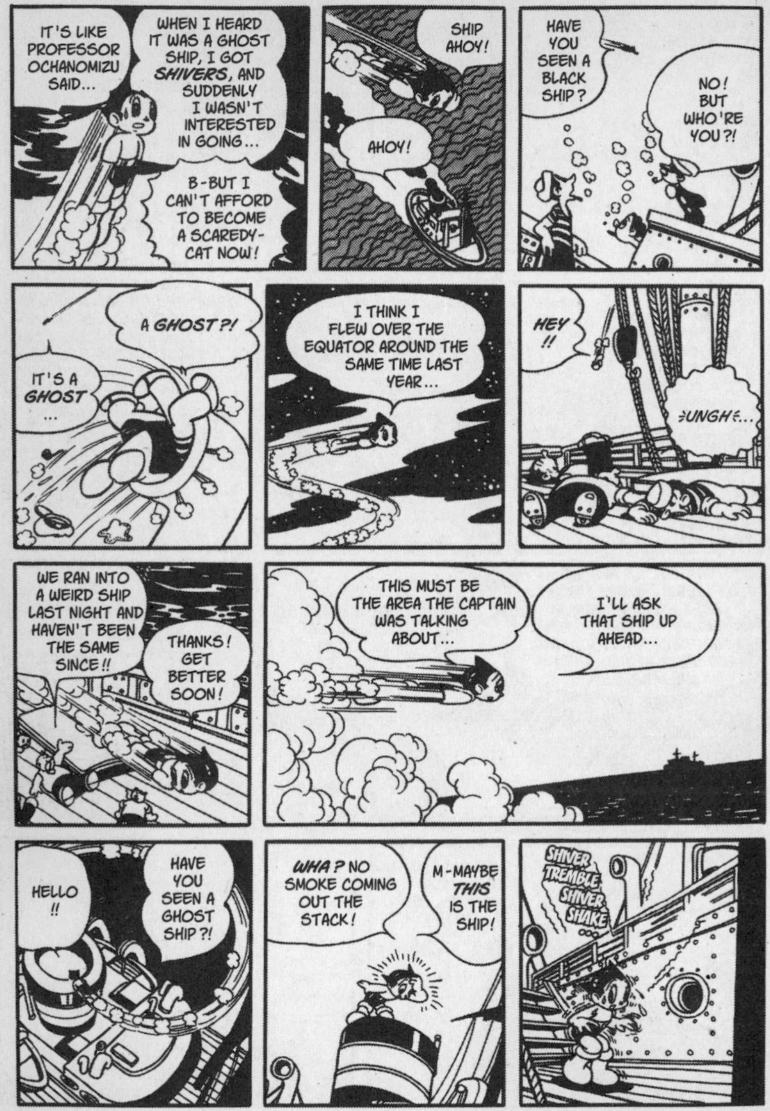
IT'S LIKE PROFESSOR OCHANOMIZU SAID...
WHEN I HEARD IT WAS A GHOST SHIP, I GOT SHIVERS, AND SUDDENLY I WASN'T INTERESTED IN GOING...
B-BUT I CAN'T AFFORD TO BECOME A SCAREDY-CAT NOW!
SHIP AHOY!
AHOY!
HAVE YOU SEEN A BLACK SHIP?
NO! BUT WHO'RE YOU?!
A GHOST?!
IT'S A GHOST...
I THINK I FLEW OVER THE EQUATOR AROUND THE SAME TIME LAST YEAR...
HEY!!
UNGH...
WE RAN INTO A WEIRD SHIP LAST NIGHT AND HAVEN'T BEEN THE SAME SINCE!!
THANKS! GET BETTER SOON!
THIS MUST BE THE AREA THE CAPTAIN WAS TALKING ABOUT...
I'LL ASK THAT SHIP UP AHEAD...
HELLO!!
HAVE YOU SEEN A GHOST SHIP?!
WHA? NO SMOKE COMING OUT THE STACK!
M-MAYBE THIS IS THE SHIP!
SHIVER
TREMBLE
SHIVER
SHAKE

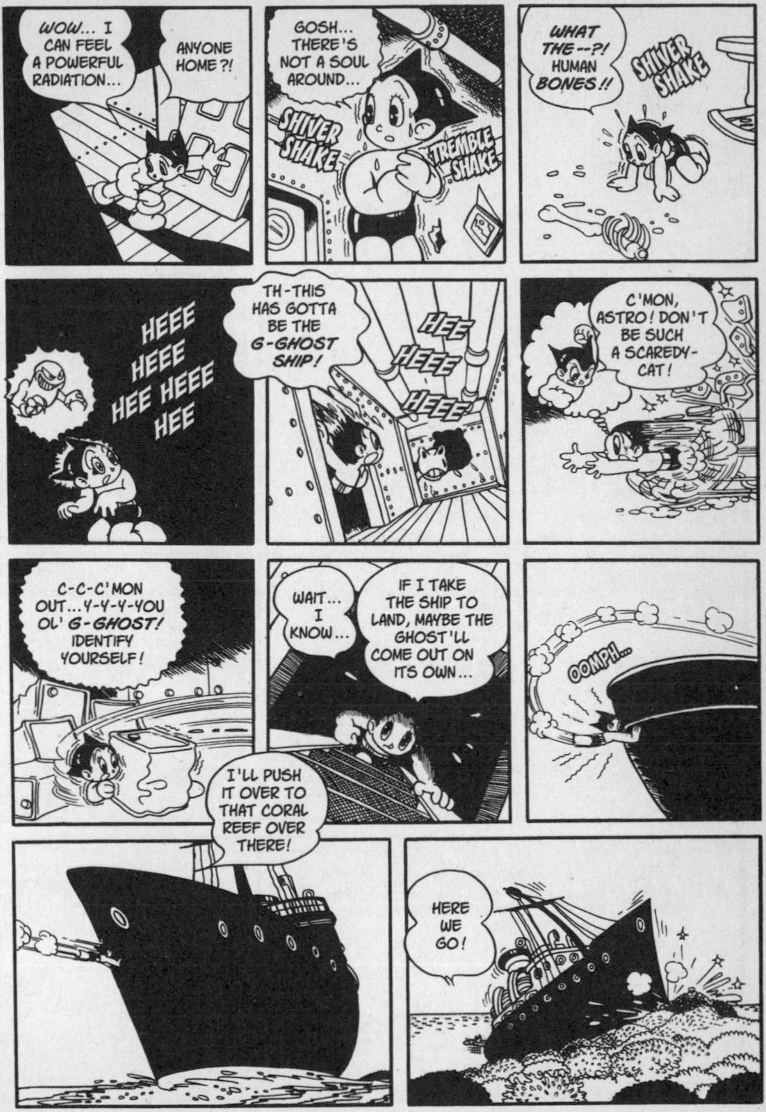

WOW... I CAN FEEL A POWERFUL RADIATION...
ANYONE HOME?!
GOSH... THERE'S NOT A SOUL AROUND...
SHIVER SHAKE
TREMBLE SHAKE
WHAT THE--?! HUMAN BONES!!
SHIVER SHAKE
HEEE HEEE HEE HEEE HEE
TH-THIS HAS GOTTA BE THE G-GHOST SHIP!
HEE HEEE HEEE
C'MON, ASTRO! DON'T BE SUCH A SCAREDY-CAT!
C-C-C'MON OUT...Y-Y-Y-YOU OL' G-GHOST! IDENTIFY YOURSELF!
WAIT... I KNOW...
IF I TAKE THE SHIP TO LAND, MAYBE THE GHOST'LL COME OUT ON ITS OWN...
OOMPH...
I'LL PUSH IT OVER TO THAT CORAL REEF OVER THERE!
HERE WE GO!

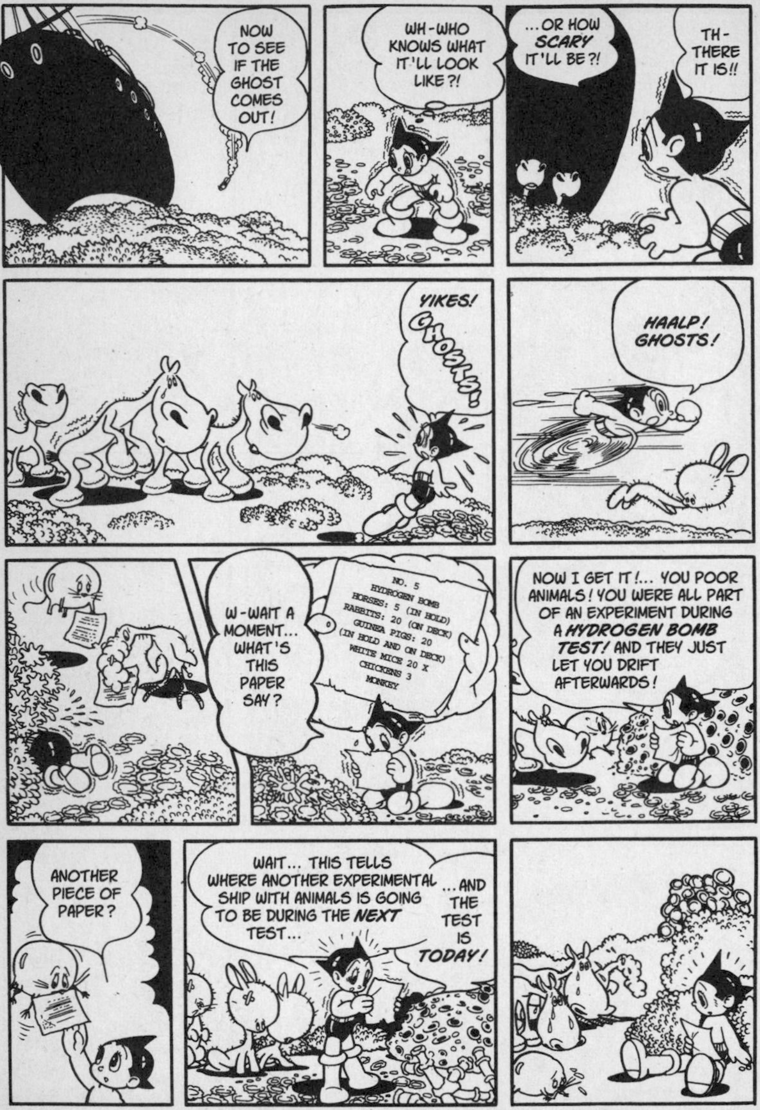
NOW TO SEE IF THE GHOST COMES OUT!
WH-WHO KNOWS WHAT IT'LL LOOK LIKE?!
...OR HOW SCARY IT'LL BE?!
TH-THERE IT IS!!
YIKES! GHOSTS!
HAALP! GHOSTS!
W-WAIT A MOMENT... WHAT'S THIS PAPER SAY?
NO. 5
HYDROGEN BOMB
HORSES: 5 (IN HOLD)
RABBITS: 20 (ON DECK)
GUINEA PIGS: 20
(IN HOLD AND ON DECK)
WHITE MICE 20 X
CHICKENS 3
MONKEY
NOW I GET IT!... YOU POOR ANIMALS! YOU WERE ALL PART OF AN EXPERIMENT DURING A HYDROGEN BOMB TEST! AND THEY JUST LET YOU DRIFT AFTERWARDS!
ANOTHER PIECE OF PAPER?
WAIT... THIS TELLS WHERE ANOTHER EXPERIMENTAL SHIP WITH ANIMALS IS GOING TO BE DURING THE NEXT TEST...
...AND THE TEST IS TODAY!

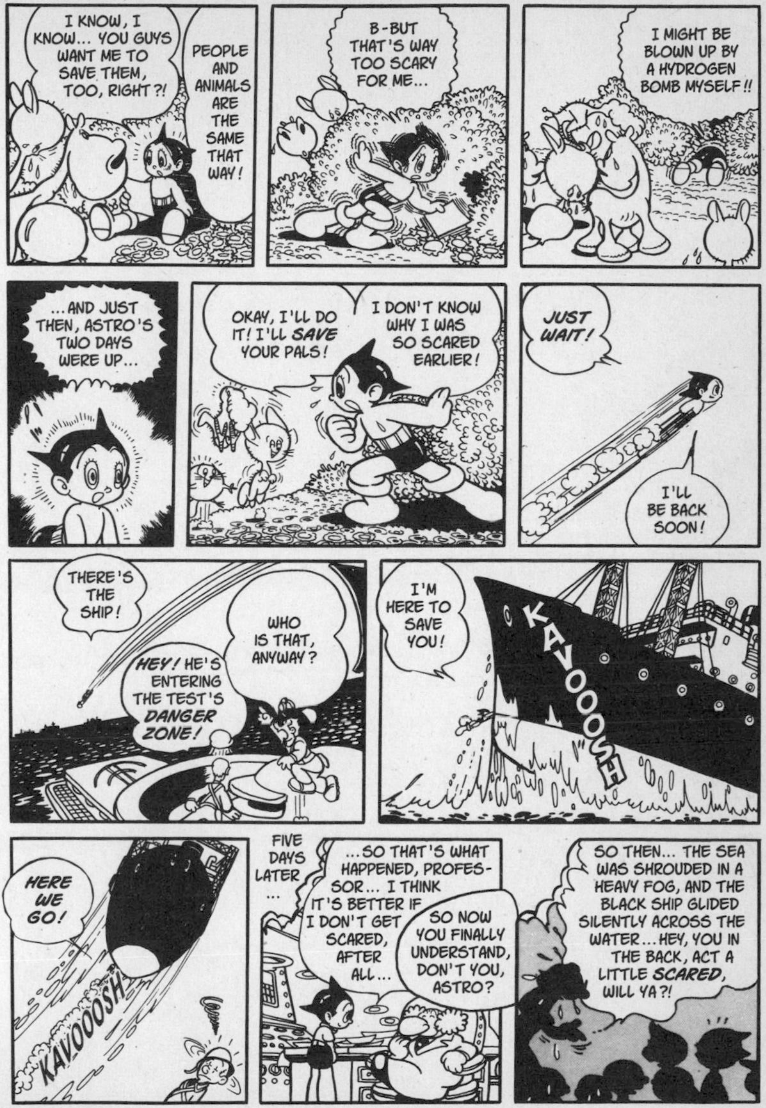
I KNOW, I KNOW... YOU GUYS WANT ME TO SAVE THEM, TOO, RIGHT?!
PEOPLE AND ANIMALS ARE THE SAME THAT WAY!
B-BUT THAT'S WAY TOO SCARY FOR ME...
I MIGHT BE BLOWN UP BY A HYDROGEN BOMB MYSELF!!
...AND JUST THEN, ASTRO'S TWO DAYS WERE UP...
OKAY, I'LL DO IT! I'LL SAVE YOUR PALS!
I DON'T KNOW WHY I WAS SO SCARED EARLIER!
JUST WAIT!
I'LL BE BACK SOON!
THERE'S THE SHIP!
WHO IS THAT, ANYWAY?
HEY! HE'S ENTERING THE TEST'S DANGER ZONE!
I'M HERE TO SAVE YOU!
KAVOOOSH
HERE WE GO!
KAVOOOSH
FIVE DAYS LATER ...
...SO THAT'S WHAT HAPPENED, PROFESSOR... I THINK IT'S BETTER IF I DON'T GET SCARED, AFTER ALL...
SO NOW YOU FINALLY UNDERSTAND, DON'T YOU, ASTRO?
SO THEN... THE SEA WAS SHROUDED IN A HEAVY FOG, AND THE BLACK SHIP GLIDED SILENTLY ACROSS THE WATER... HEY, YOU IN THE BACK, ACT A LITTLE SCARED, WILL YA?!

THE TEST PILOT

First appeared in the September 1956
supplement of *Shonen* magazine.

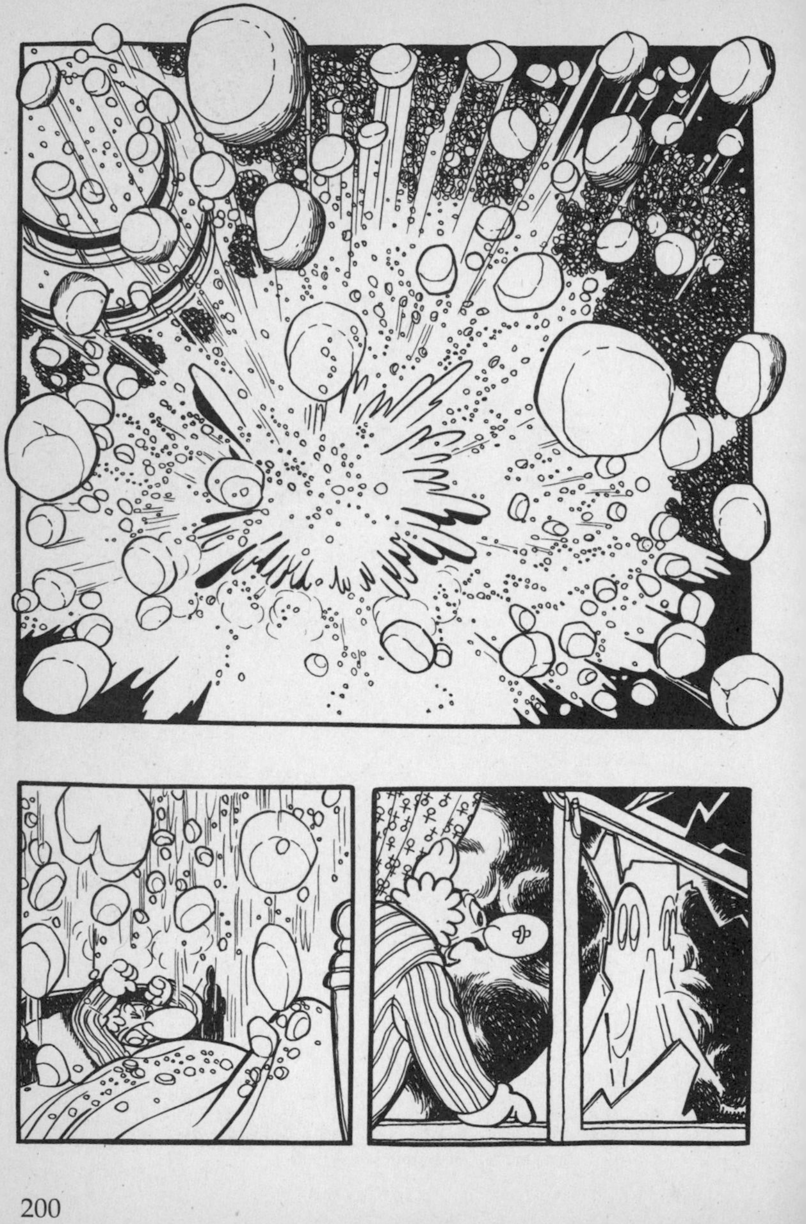

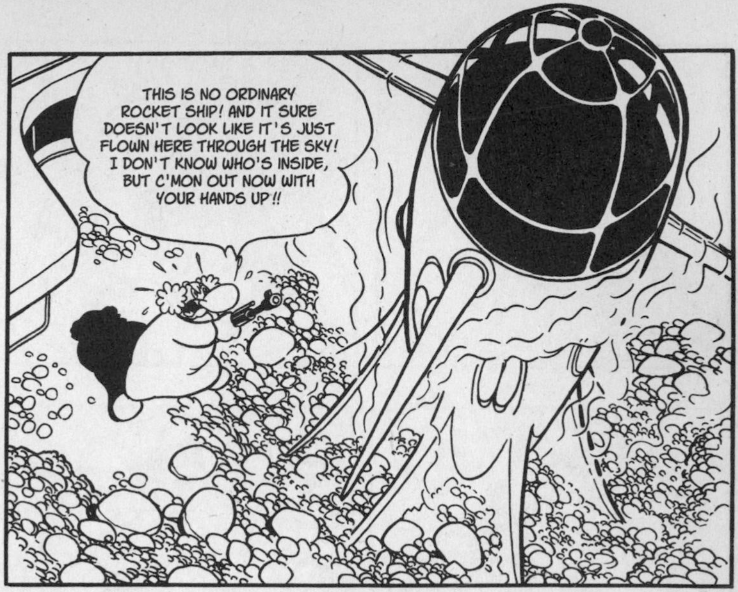
THIS IS NO ORDINARY ROCKET SHIP! AND IT SURE DOESN'T LOOK LIKE IT'S JUST FLOWN HERE THROUGH THE SKY! I DON'T KNOW WHO'S INSIDE, BUT C'MON OUT NOW WITH YOUR HANDS UP!!

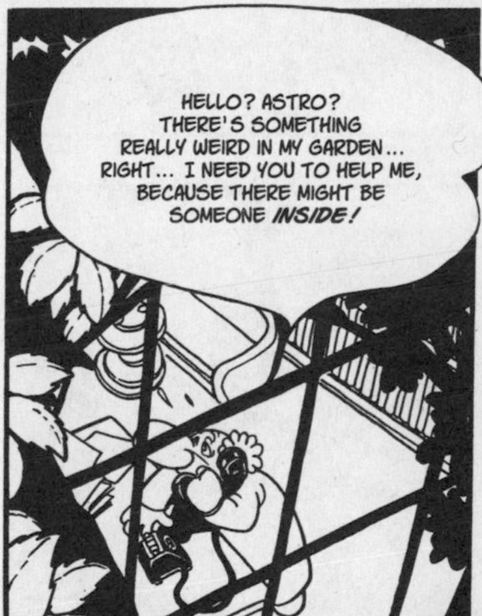
HELLO? ASTRO? THERE'S SOMETHING REALLY WEIRD IN MY GARDEN... RIGHT... I NEED YOU TO HELP ME, BECAUSE THERE MIGHT BE SOMEONE *INSIDE!*

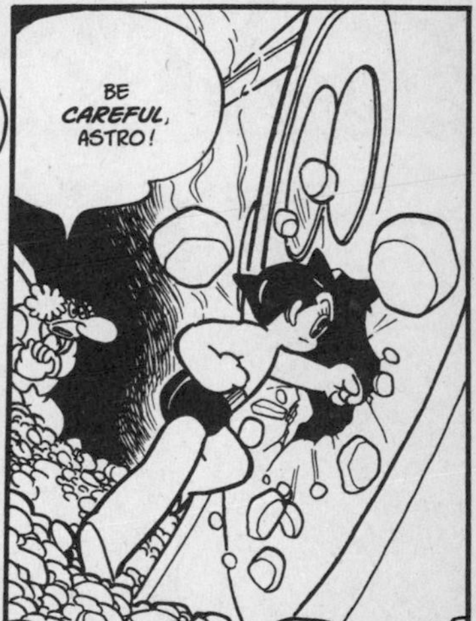
BE *CAREFUL*, ASTRO!

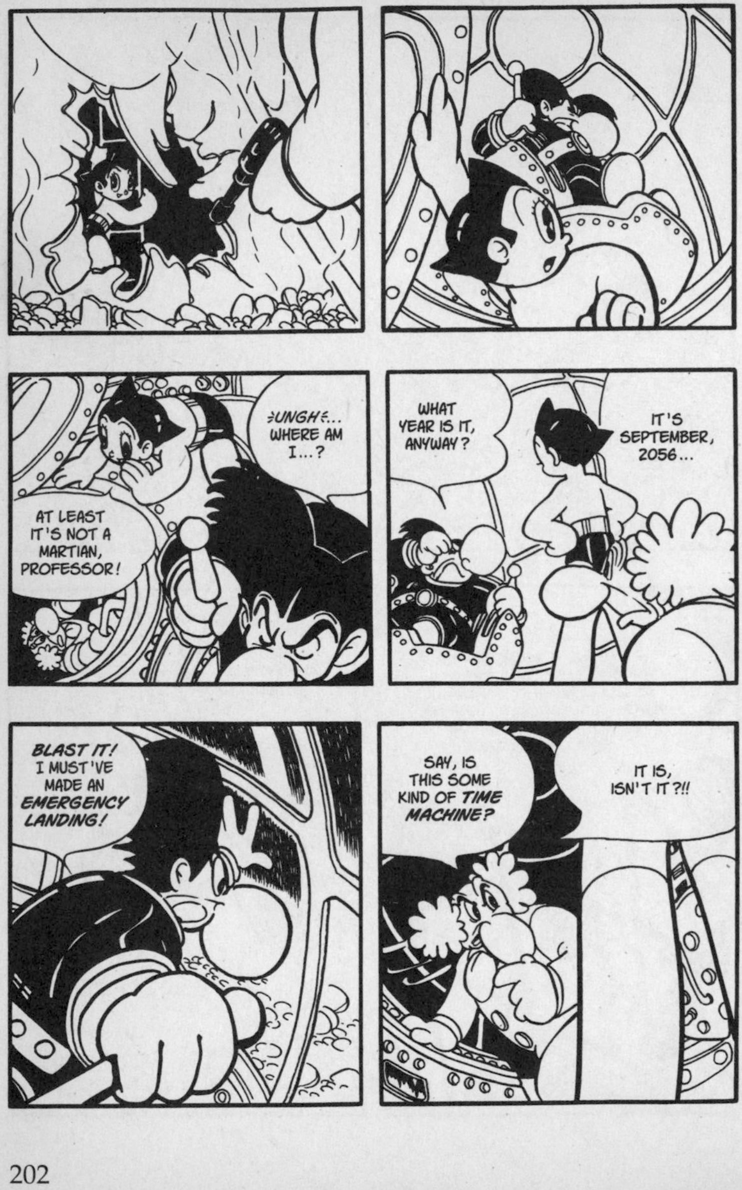

≶UNGH≷... WHERE AM I...?
AT LEAST IT'S NOT A MARTIAN, PROFESSOR!
WHAT YEAR IS IT, ANYWAY?
IT'S SEPTEMBER, 2056...
BLAST IT! I MUST'VE MADE AN *EMERGENCY LANDING!*
SAY, IS THIS SOME KIND OF *TIME MACHINE?*
IT IS, ISN'T IT?!!

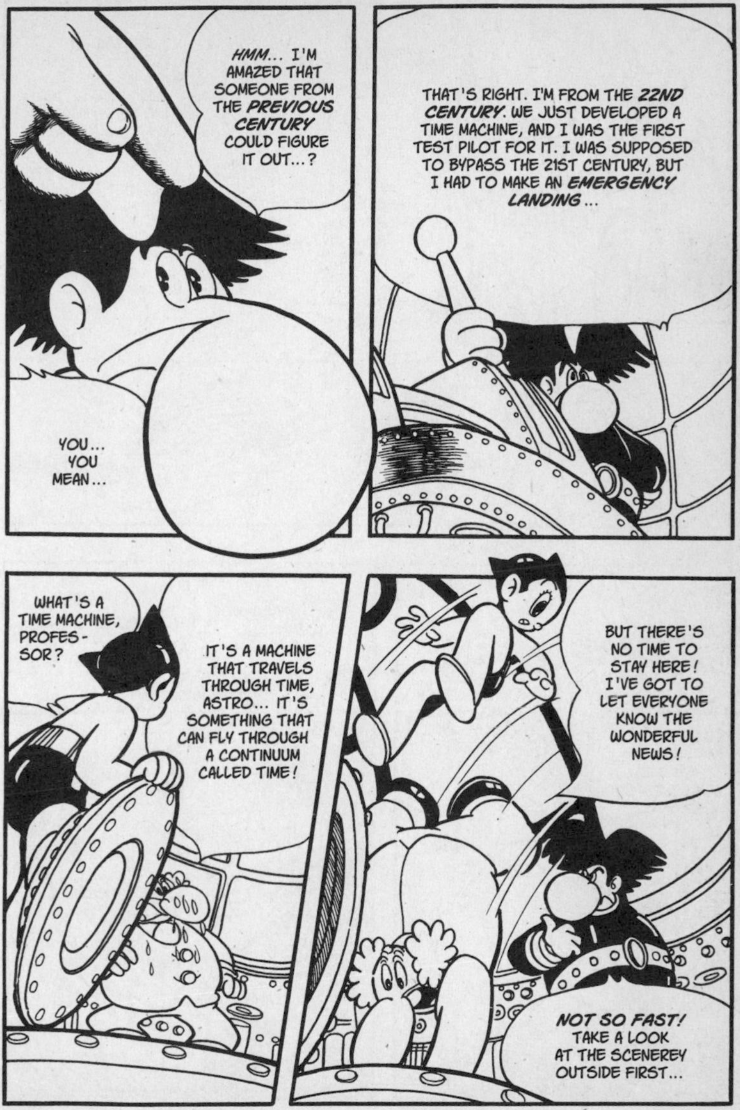
HMM... I'M AMAZED THAT SOMEONE FROM THE PREVIOUS CENTURY COULD FIGURE IT OUT...?
YOU... YOU MEAN...
THAT'S RIGHT. I'M FROM THE 22ND CENTURY. WE JUST DEVELOPED A TIME MACHINE, AND I WAS THE FIRST TEST PILOT FOR IT. I WAS SUPPOSED TO BYPASS THE 21ST CENTURY, BUT I HAD TO MAKE AN EMERGENCY LANDING...
WHAT'S A TIME MACHINE, PROFES-SOR?
IT'S A MACHINE THAT TRAVELS THROUGH TIME, ASTRO... IT'S SOMETHING THAT CAN FLY THROUGH A CONTINUUM CALLED TIME!
BUT THERE'S NO TIME TO STAY HERE! I'VE GOT TO LET EVERYONE KNOW THE WONDERFUL NEWS!
NOT SO FAST! TAKE A LOOK AT THE SCENEREY OUTSIDE FIRST...

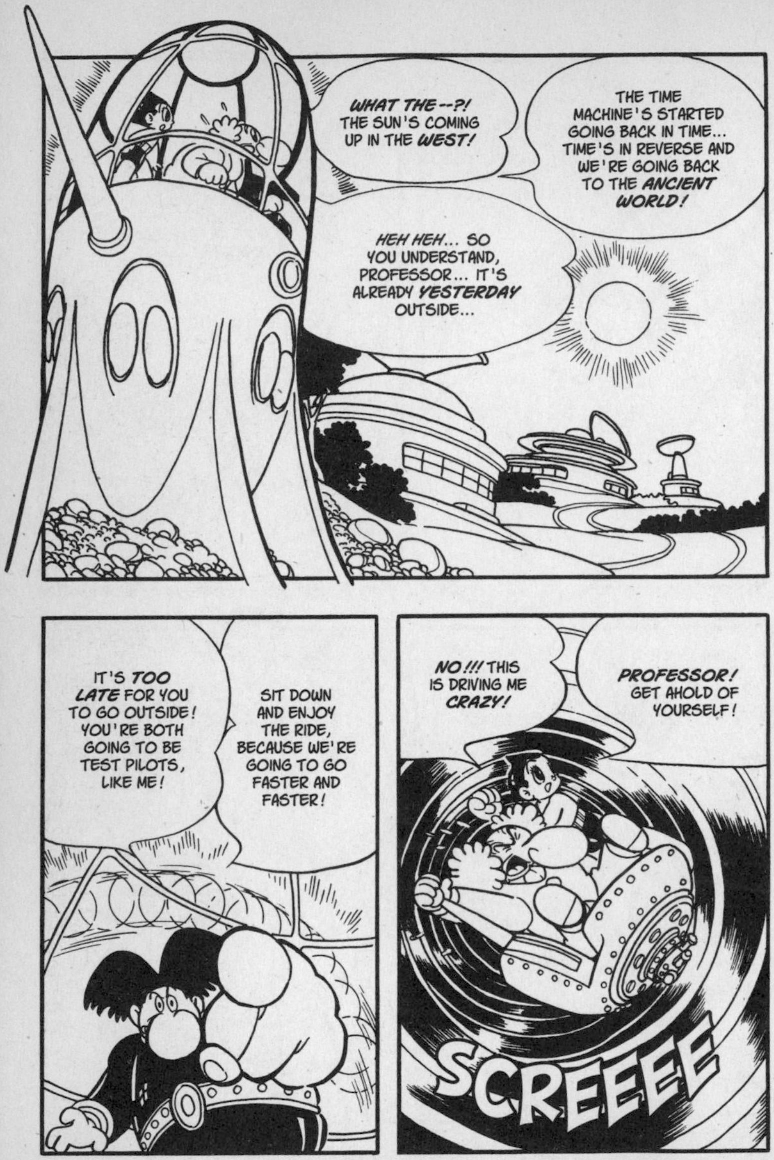
WHAT THE--?! THE SUN'S COMING UP IN THE WEST!
THE TIME MACHINE'S STARTED GOING BACK IN TIME... TIME'S IN REVERSE AND WE'RE GOING BACK TO THE ANCIENT WORLD!
HEH HEH... SO YOU UNDERSTAND, PROFESSOR... IT'S ALREADY YESTERDAY OUTSIDE...
IT'S TOO LATE FOR YOU TO GO OUTSIDE! YOU'RE BOTH GOING TO BE TEST PILOTS, LIKE ME!
SIT DOWN AND ENJOY THE RIDE, BECAUSE WE'RE GOING TO GO FASTER AND FASTER!
NO!!! THIS IS DRIVING ME CRAZY!
PROFESSOR! GET AHOLD OF YOURSELF!
SCREEEE

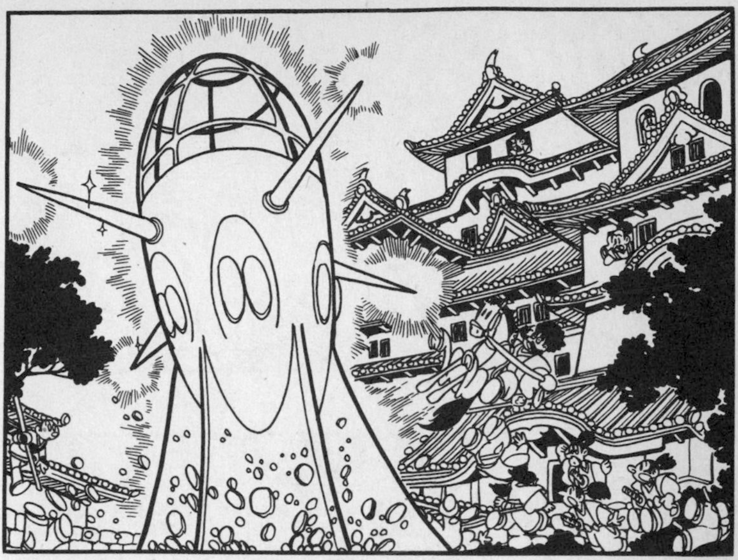

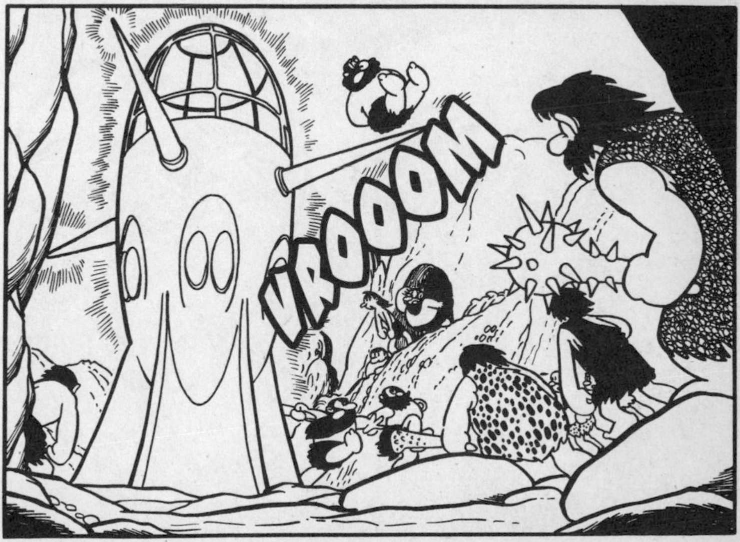
VROOOM

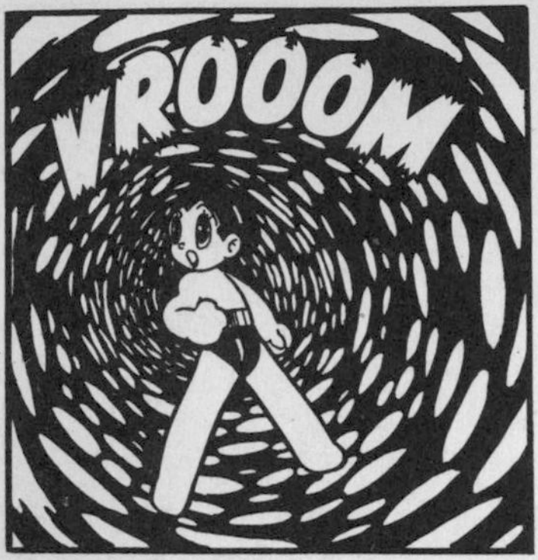
VROOOM

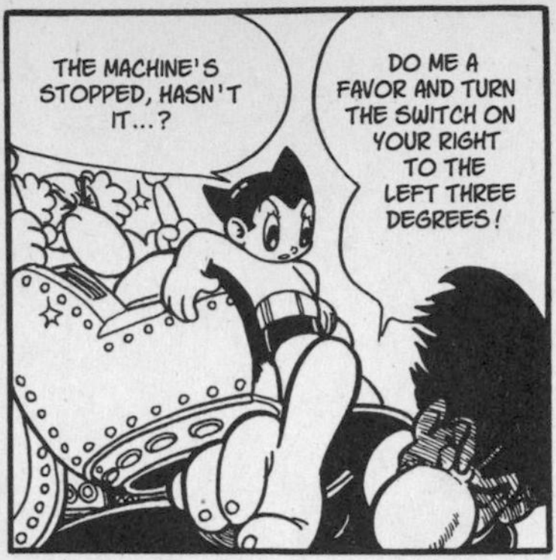
THE MACHINE'S STOPPED, HASN'T IT...?
DO ME A FAVOR AND TURN THE SWITCH ON YOUR RIGHT TO THE LEFT THREE DEGREES!

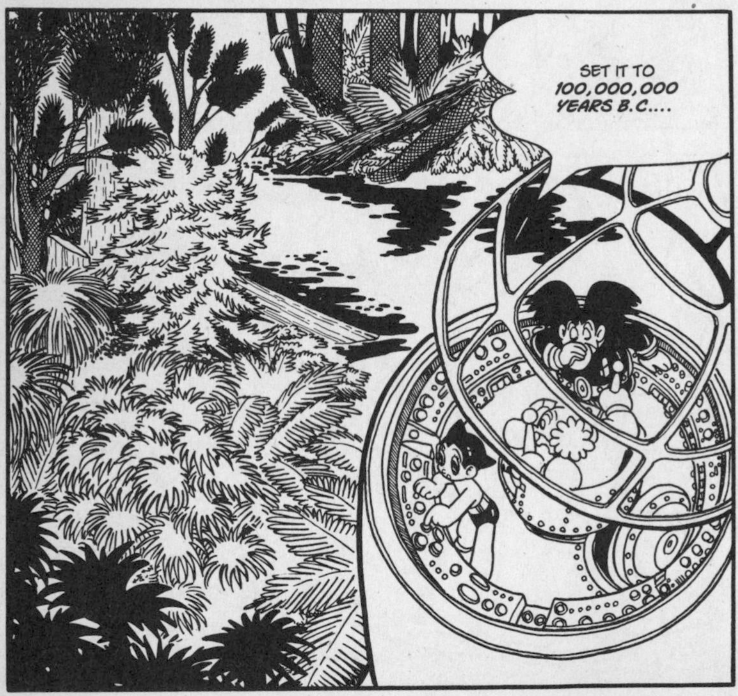
SET IT TO 100,000,000 YEARS B.C....

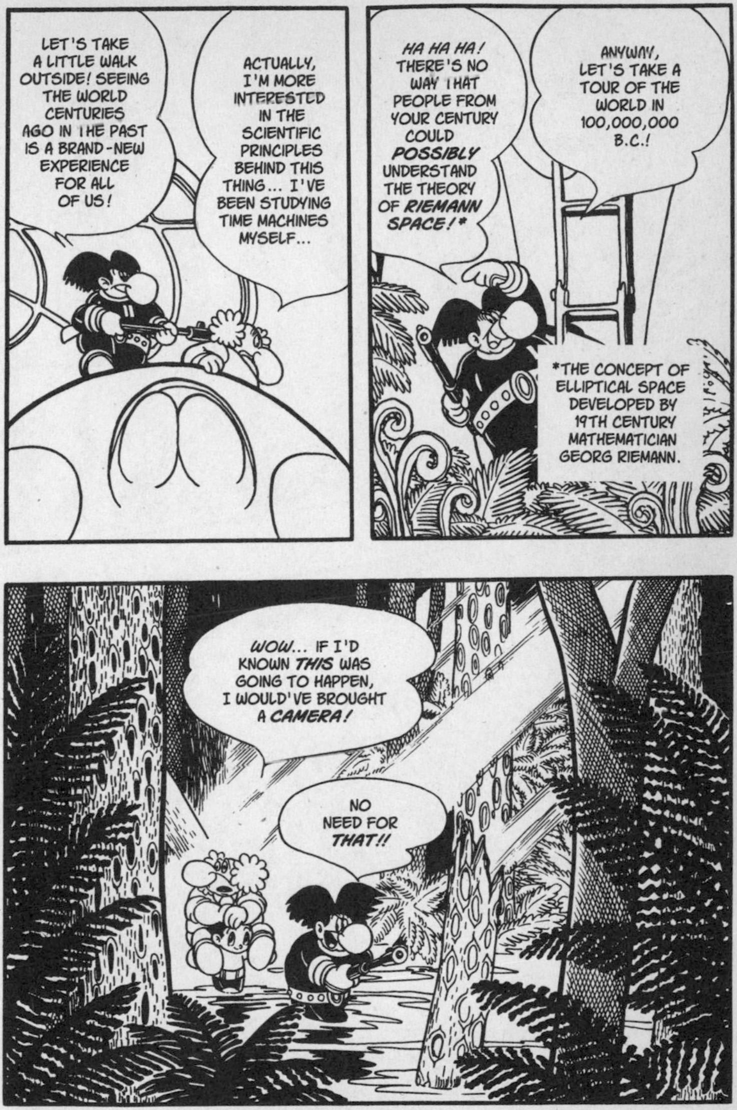
LET'S TAKE A LITTLE WALK OUTSIDE! SEEING THE WORLD CENTURIES AGO IN THE PAST IS A BRAND-NEW EXPERIENCE FOR ALL OF US!
ACTUALLY, I'M MORE INTERESTED IN THE SCIENTIFIC PRINCIPLES BEHIND THIS THING... I'VE BEEN STUDYING TIME MACHINES MYSELF...
HA HA HA! THERE'S NO WAY THAT PEOPLE FROM YOUR CENTURY COULD POSSIBLY UNDERSTAND THE THEORY OF RIEMANN SPACE!*
ANYWAY, LET'S TAKE A TOUR OF THE WORLD IN 100,000,000 B.C.!
*THE CONCEPT OF ELLIPTICAL SPACE DEVELOPED BY 19TH CENTURY MATHEMATICIAN GEORG RIEMANN.
WOW... IF I'D KNOWN THIS WAS GOING TO HAPPEN, I WOULD'VE BROUGHT A CAMERA!
NO NEED FOR THAT!!

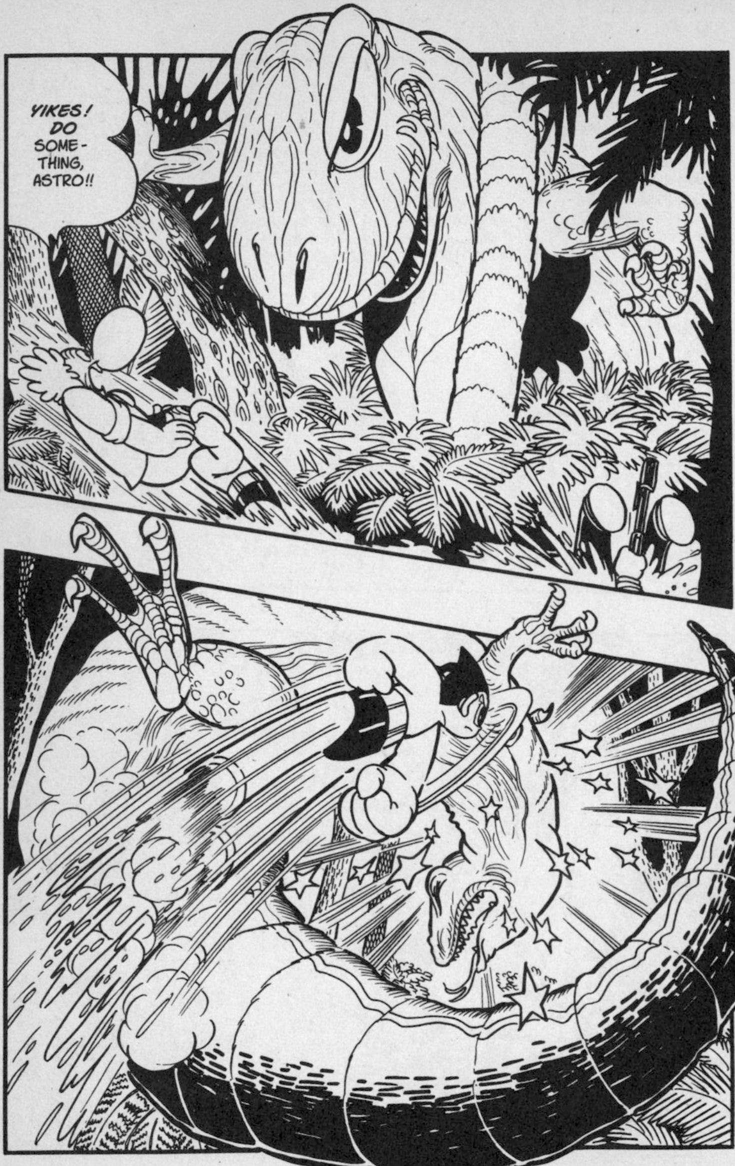
YIKES! DO SOME-THING, ASTRO!!

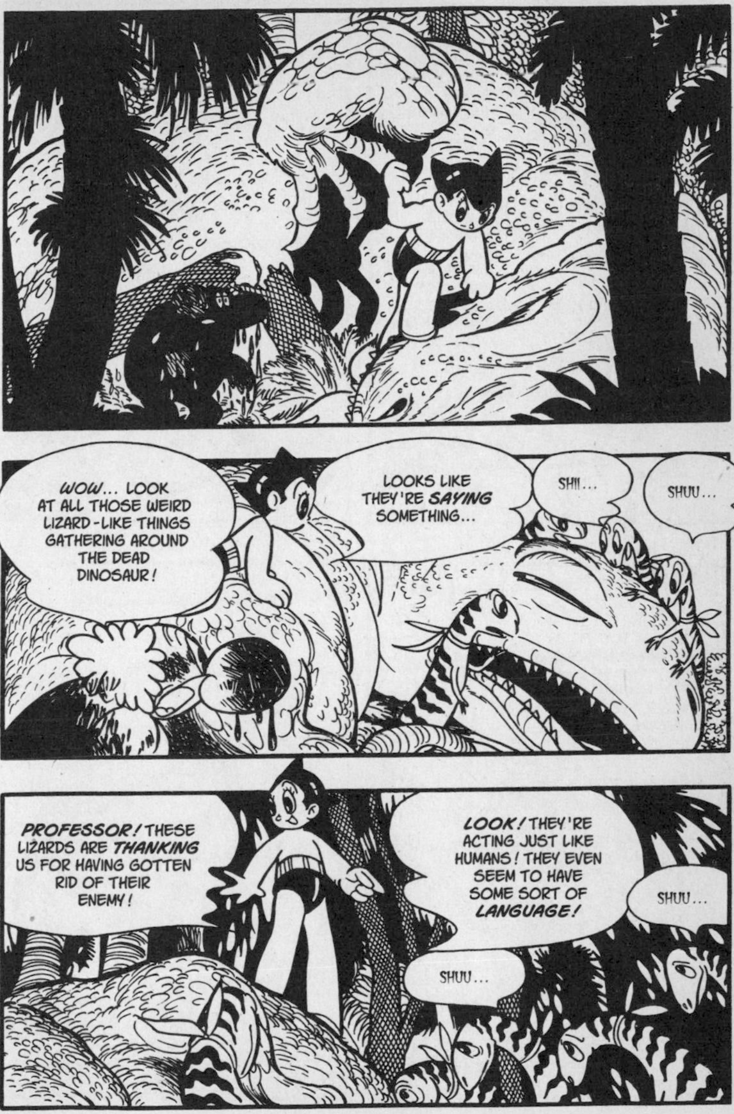
WOW... LOOK AT ALL THOSE WEIRD LIZARD-LIKE THINGS GATHERING AROUND THE DEAD DINOSAUR!
LOOKS LIKE THEY'RE SAYING SOMETHING...
SHII...
SHUU...
PROFESSOR! THESE LIZARDS ARE THANKING US FOR HAVING GOTTEN RID OF THEIR ENEMY!
LOOK! THEY'RE ACTING JUST LIKE HUMANS! THEY EVEN SEEM TO HAVE SOME SORT OF LANGUAGE!
SHUU...
SHUU...

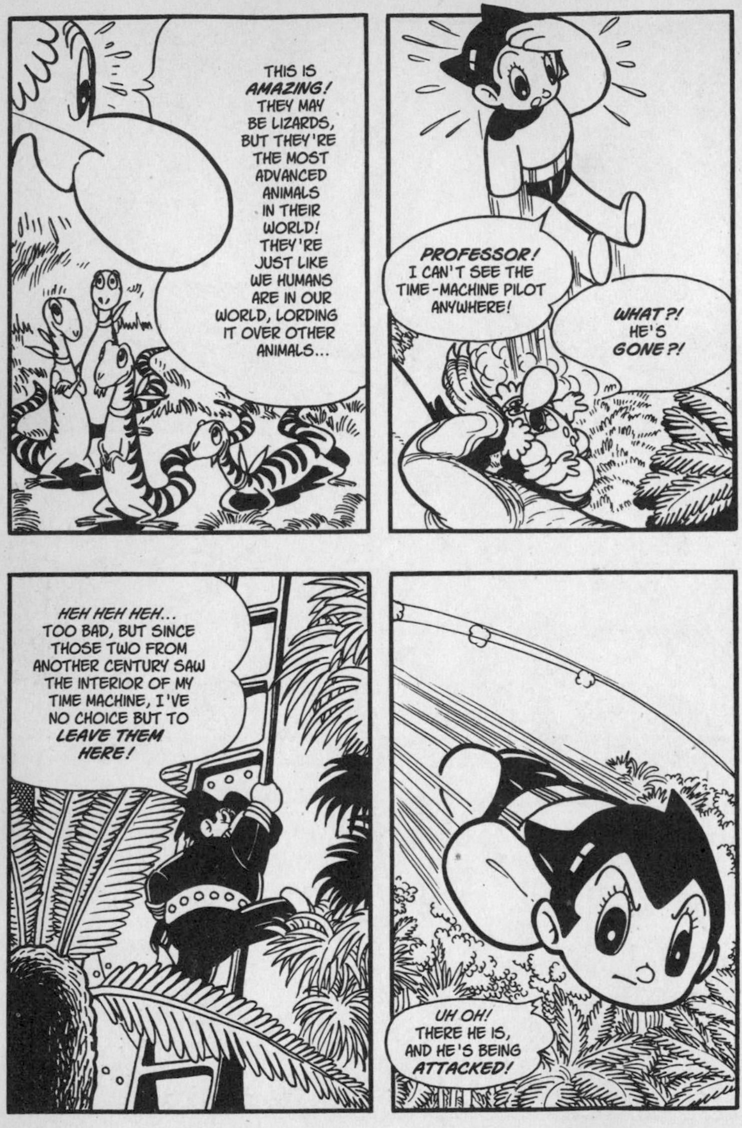
THIS IS AMAZING! THEY MAY BE LIZARDS, BUT THEY'RE THE MOST ADVANCED ANIMALS IN THEIR WORLD! THEY'RE JUST LIKE WE HUMANS ARE IN OUR WORLD, LORDING IT OVER OTHER ANIMALS...
PROFESSOR! I CAN'T SEE THE TIME-MACHINE PILOT ANYWHERE!
WHAT?! HE'S GONE?!
HEH HEH HEH... TOO BAD, BUT SINCE THOSE TWO FROM ANOTHER CENTURY SAW THE INTERIOR OF MY TIME MACHINE, I'VE NO CHOICE BUT TO LEAVE THEM HERE!
UH OH! THERE HE IS, AND HE'S BEING ATTACKED!

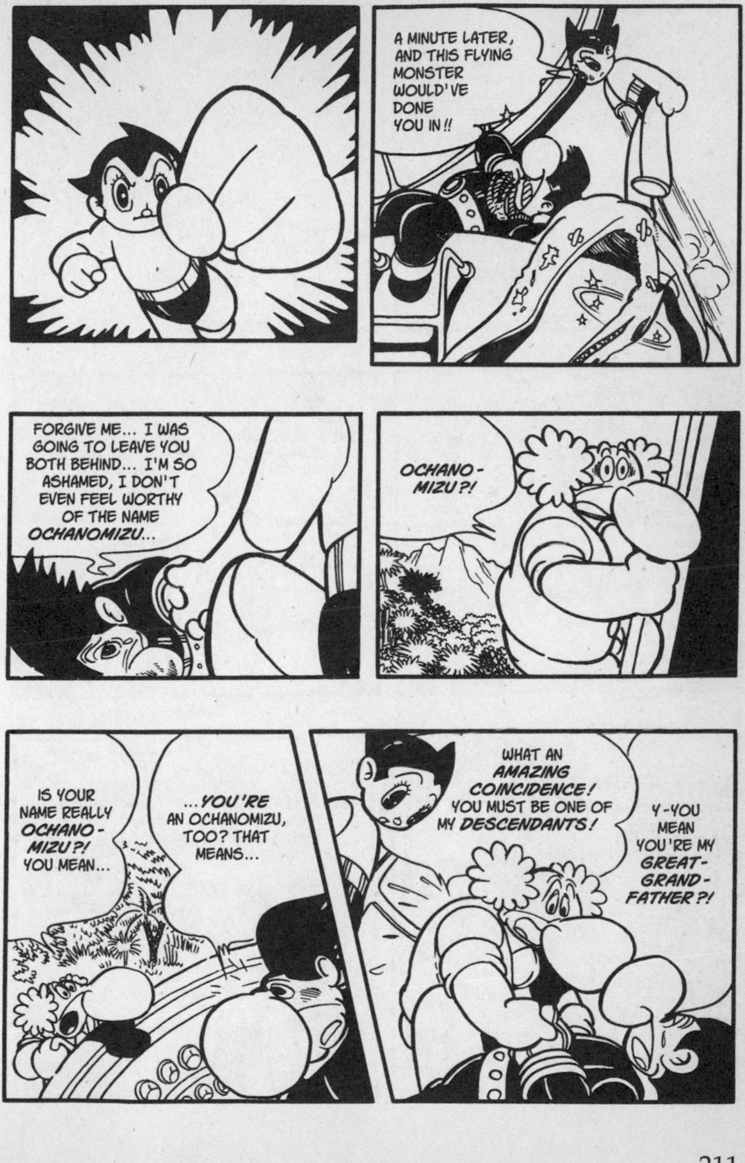

A MINUTE LATER, AND THIS FLYING MONSTER WOULD'VE DONE YOU IN!!
FORGIVE ME... I WAS GOING TO LEAVE YOU BOTH BEHIND... I'M SO ASHAMED, I DON'T EVEN FEEL WORTHY OF THE NAME OCHANOMIZU...
OCHANO-MIZU?!
IS YOUR NAME REALLY OCHANO-MIZU?! YOU MEAN...
...YOU'RE AN OCHANOMIZU, TOO? THAT MEANS...
WHAT AN AMAZING COINCIDENCE! YOU MUST BE ONE OF MY DESCENDANTS!
Y-YOU MEAN YOU'RE MY GREAT-GRAND-FATHER?!

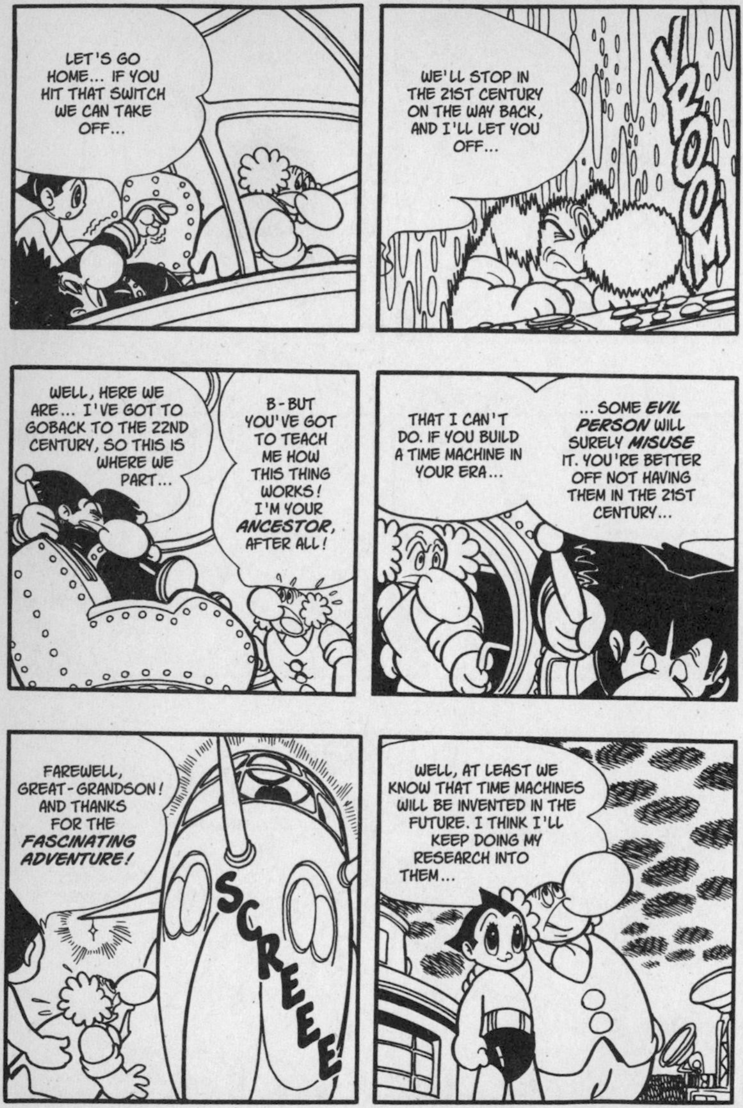

LET'S GO HOME... IF YOU HIT THAT SWITCH WE CAN TAKE OFF...
WE'LL STOP IN THE 21ST CENTURY ON THE WAY BACK, AND I'LL LET YOU OFF...
VROOM
WELL, HERE WE ARE... I'VE GOT TO GOBACK TO THE 22ND CENTURY, SO THIS IS WHERE WE PART...
B-BUT YOU'VE GOT TO TEACH ME HOW THIS THING WORKS! I'M YOUR *ANCESTOR*, AFTER ALL!
THAT I CAN'T DO. IF YOU BUILD A TIME MACHINE IN YOUR ERA...
...SOME *EVIL PERSON* WILL SURELY *MISUSE* IT. YOU'RE BETTER OFF NOT HAVING THEM IN THE 21ST CENTURY...
FAREWELL, GREAT-GRANDSON! AND THANKS FOR THE *FASCINATING ADVENTURE!*
SCREEEE!
WELL, AT LEAST WE KNOW THAT TIME MACHINES WILL BE INVENTED IN THE FUTURE. I THINK I'LL KEEP DOING MY RESEARCH INTO THEM...

SUPER CYCLONE

First appeared in the December 1956
supplement of *Shonen* magazine.

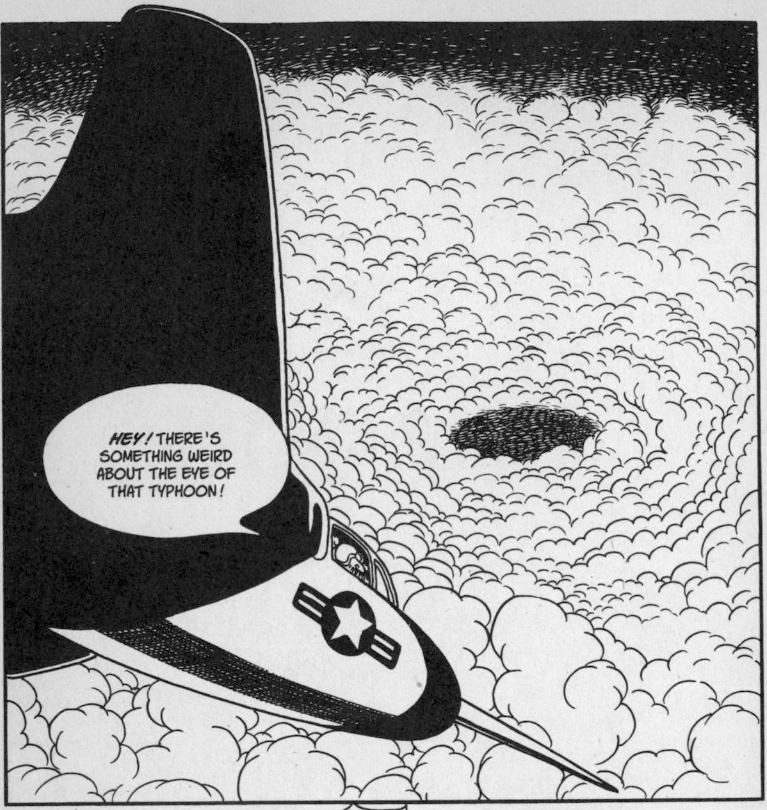
HEY! THERE'S SOMETHING WEIRD ABOUT THE EYE OF THAT TYPHOON!
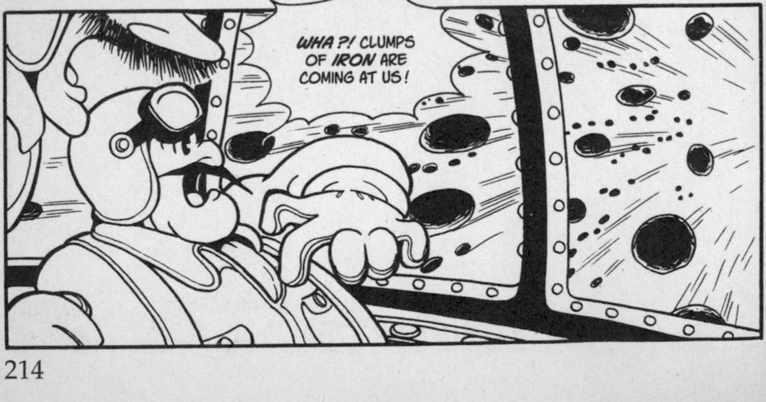
WHA?! CLUMPS OF IRON ARE COMING AT US!

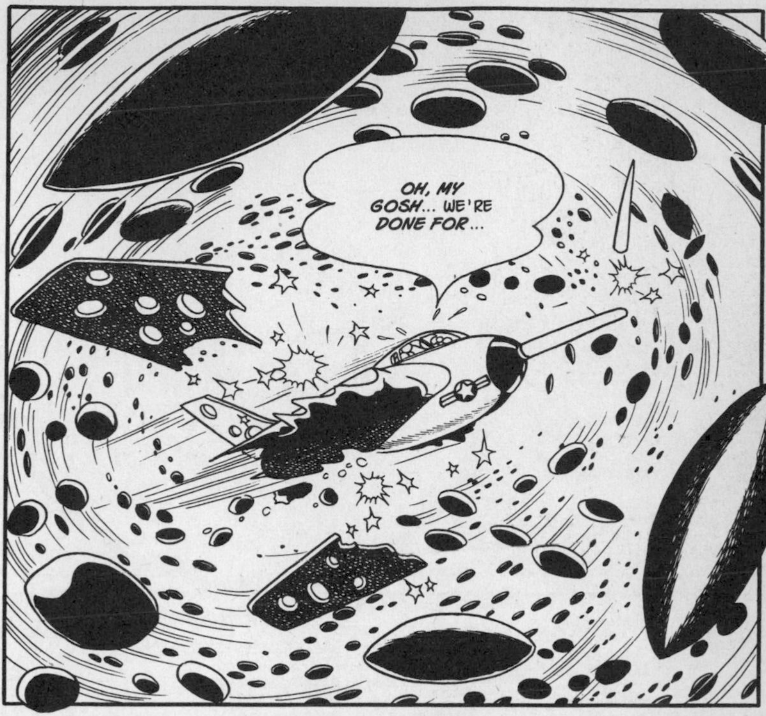
OH, MY GOSH... WE'RE DONE FOR...

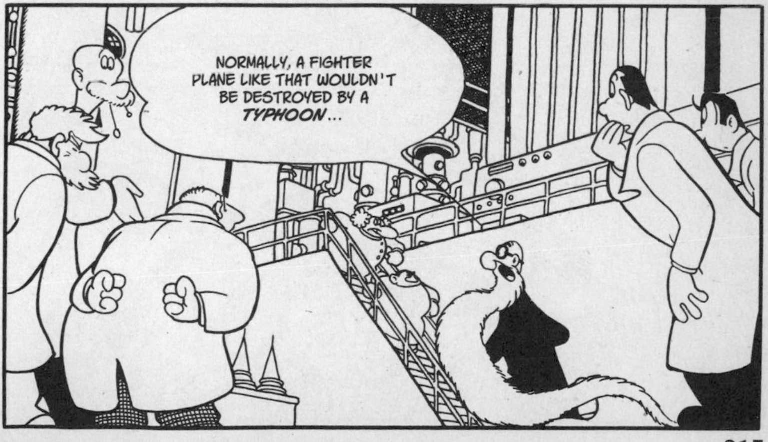
NORMALLY, A FIGHTER PLANE LIKE THAT WOULDN'T BE DESTROYED BY A TYPHOON...

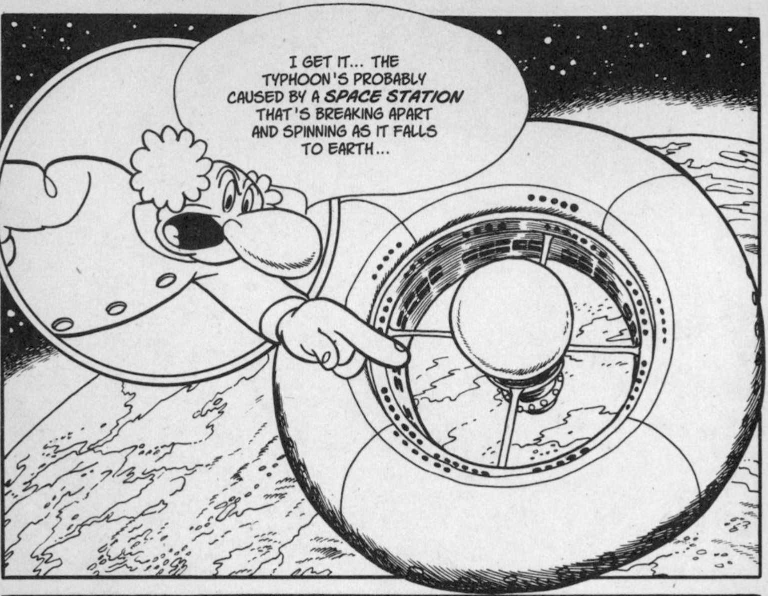
I GET IT... THE TYPHOON'S PROBABLY CAUSED BY A SPACE STATION THAT'S BREAKING APART AND SPINNING AS IT FALLS TO EARTH...

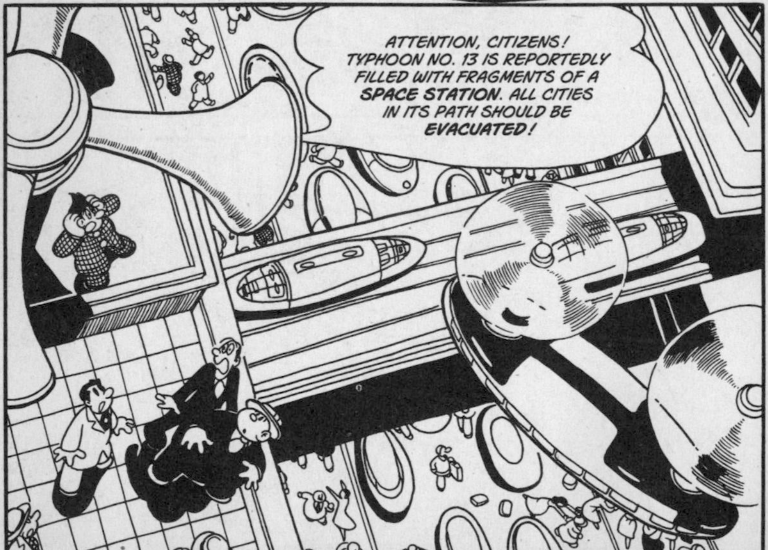
ATTENTION, CITIZENS! TYPHOON NO. 13 IS REPORTEDLY FILLED WITH FRAGMENTS OF A SPACE STATION. ALL CITIES IN ITS PATH SHOULD BE EVACUATED!

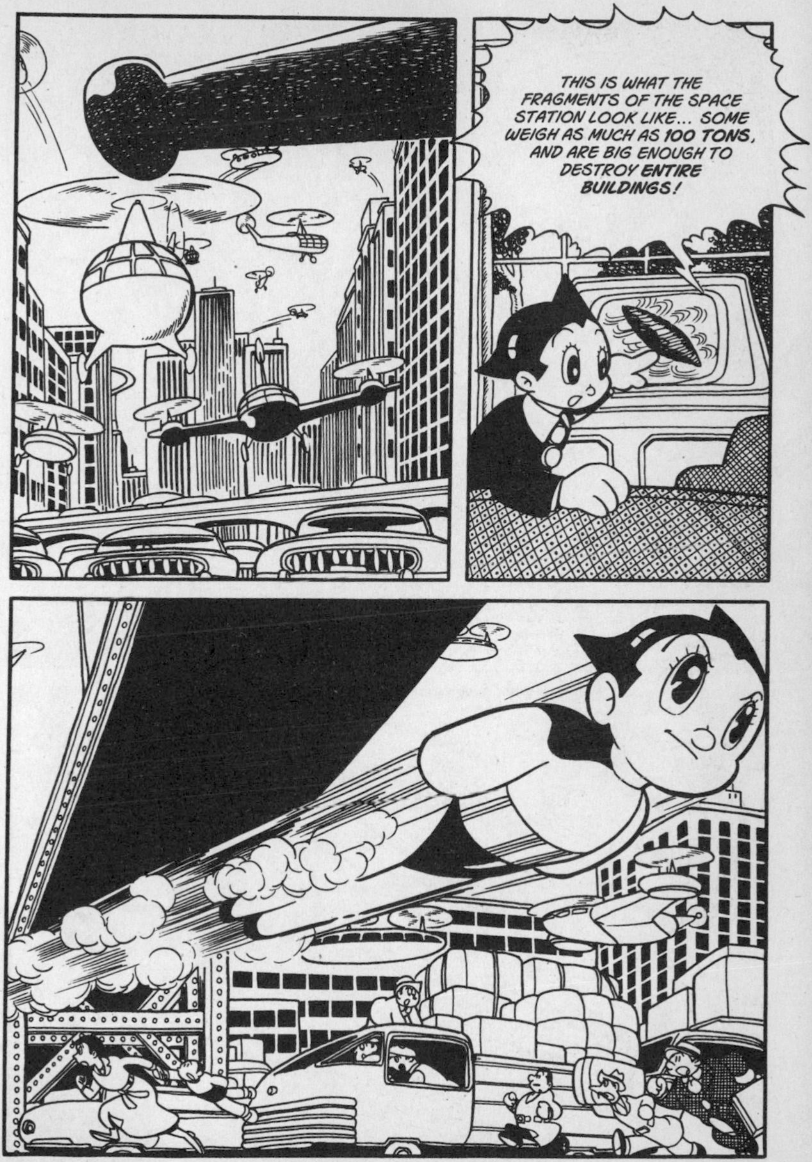
THIS IS WHAT THE FRAGMENTS OF THE SPACE STATION LOOK LIKE... SOME WEIGH AS MUCH AS 100 TONS, AND ARE BIG ENOUGH TO DESTROY ENTIRE BUILDINGS!

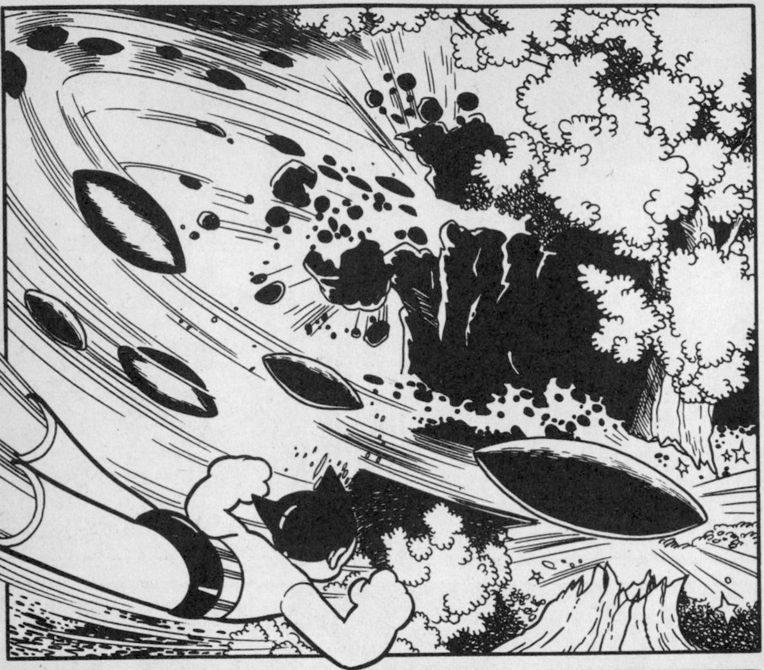

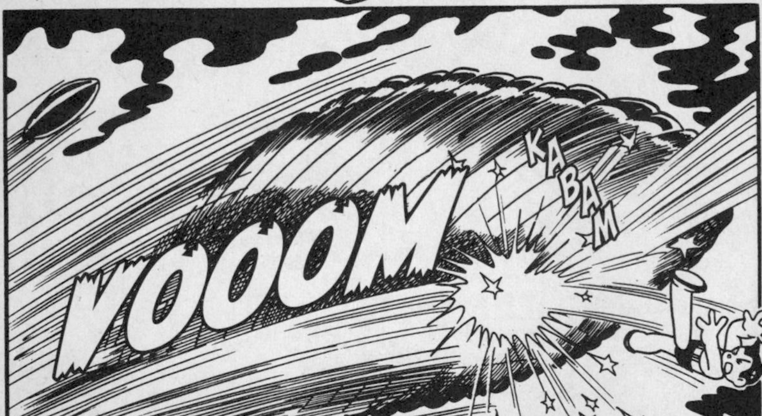
VOOOM
KABAM

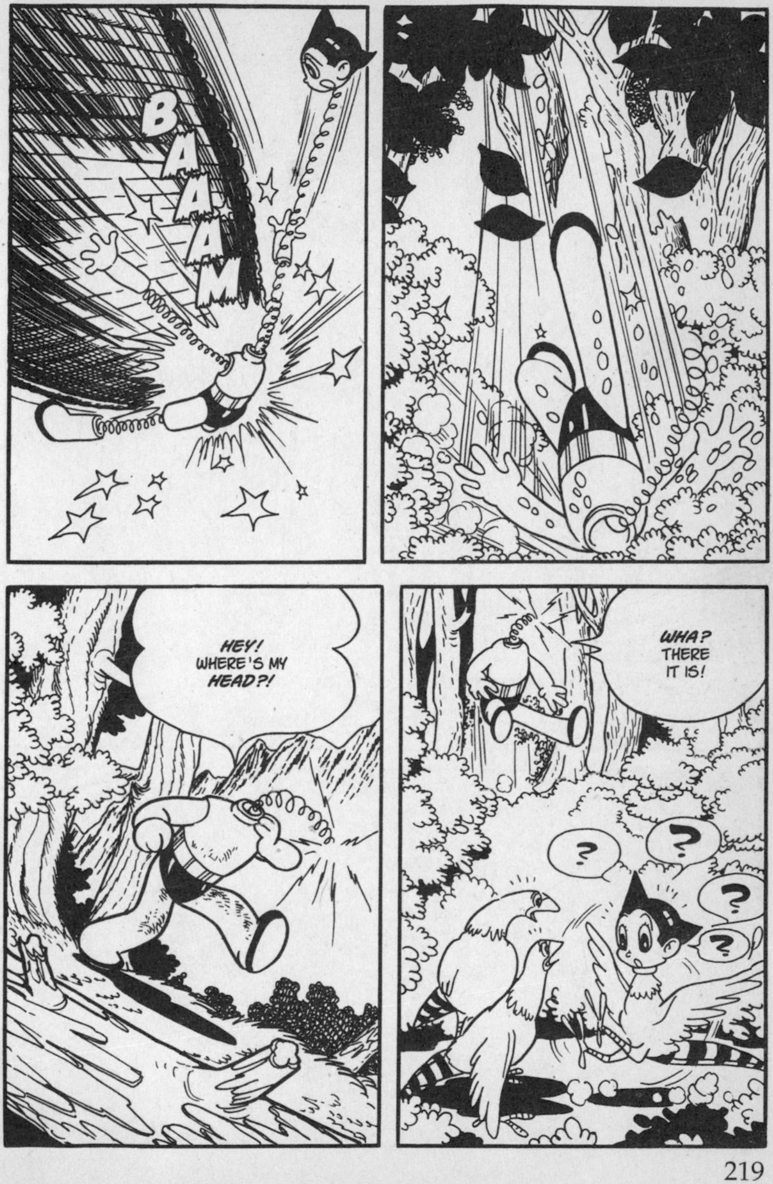
BAAAAM
HEY! WHERE'S MY HEAD?!
WHA? THERE IT IS!
?
?
?
?

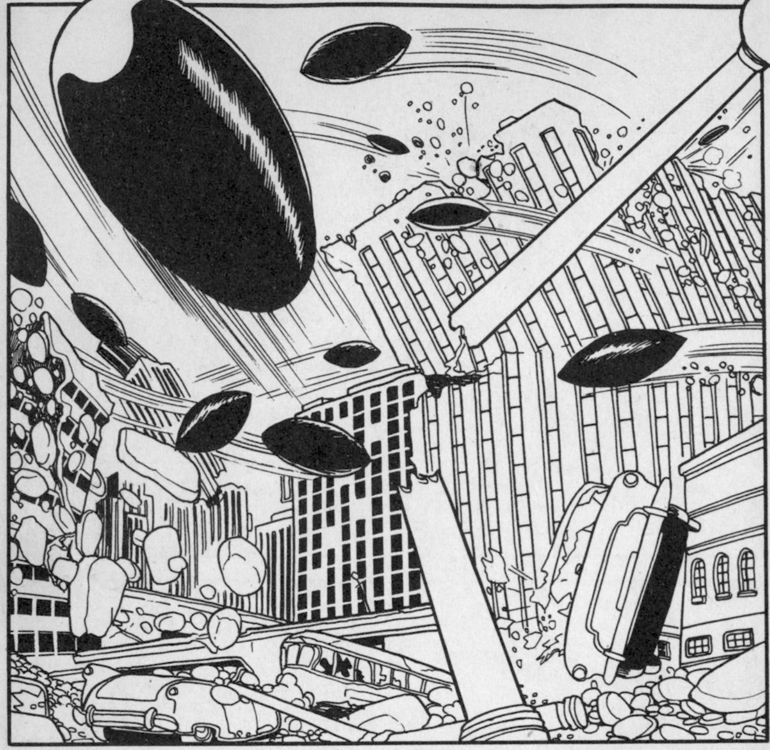

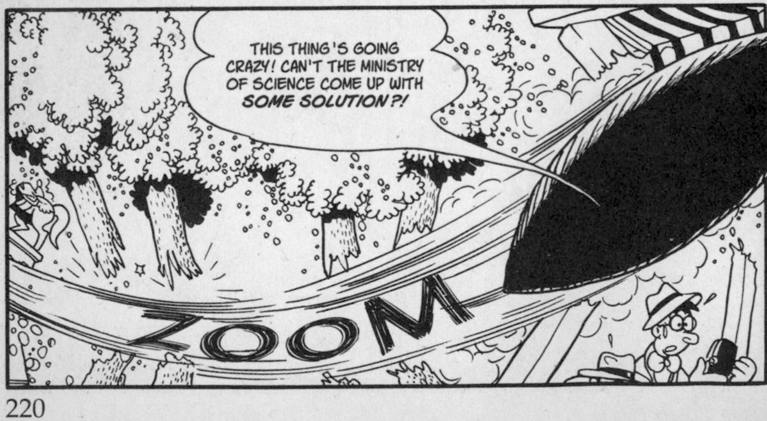
THIS THING'S GOING CRAZY! CAN'T THE MINISTRY OF SCIENCE COME UP WITH SOME SOLUTION?!
ZOOM

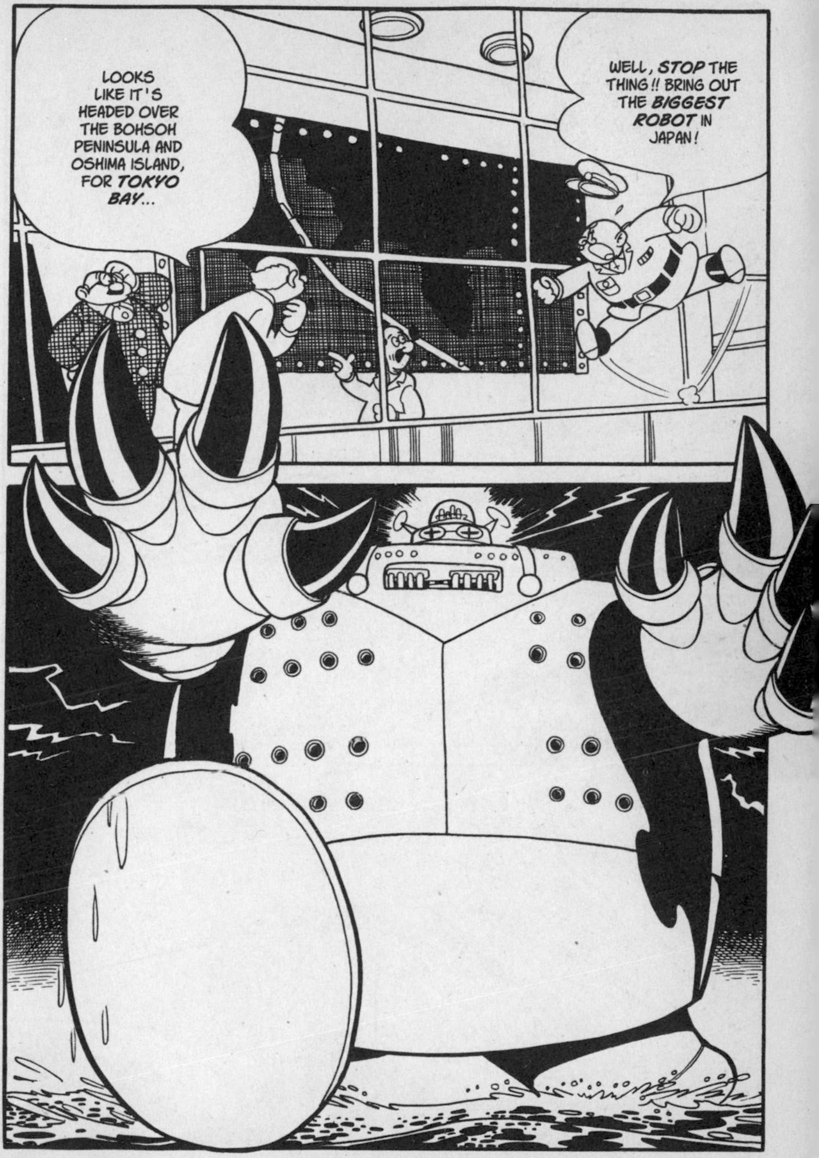
LOOKS LIKE IT'S HEADED OVER THE BOHSOH PENINSULA AND OSHIMA ISLAND, FOR *TOKYO BAY*...
WELL, *STOP* THE THING!! BRING OUT THE *BIGGEST ROBOT* IN JAPAN!

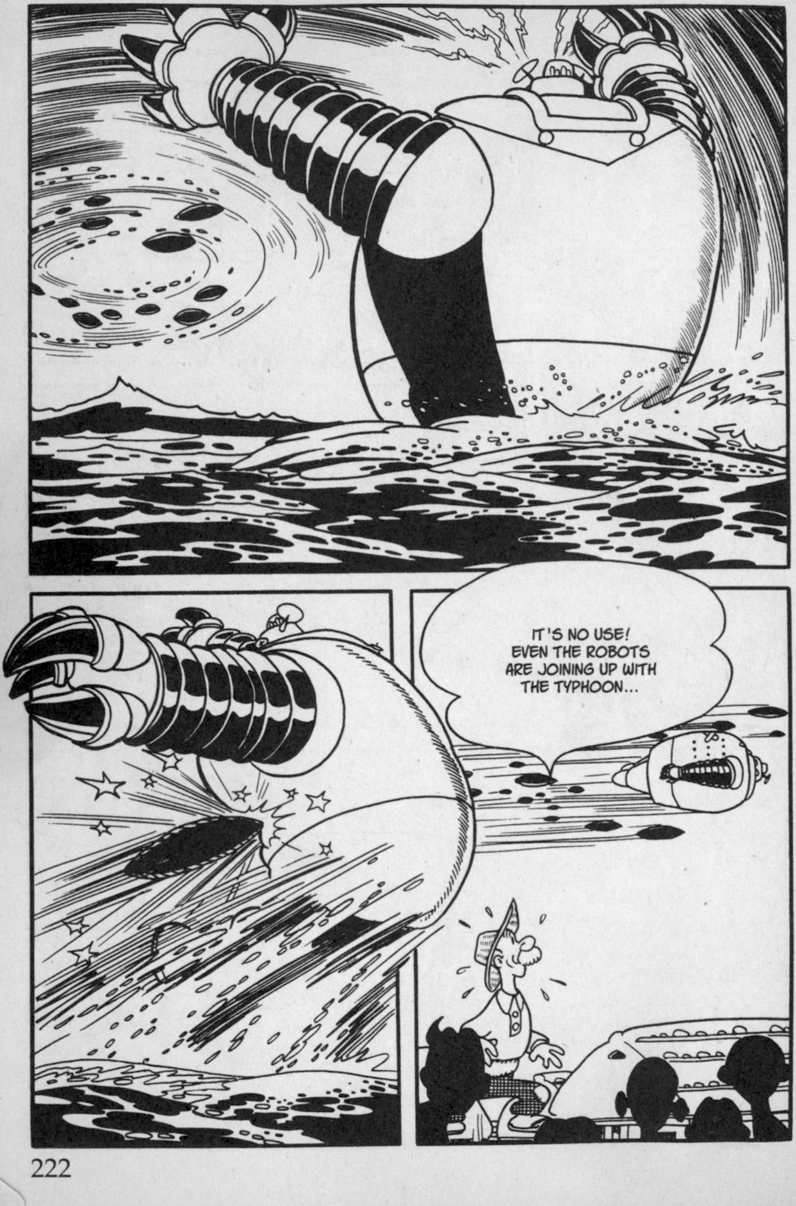
IT'S NO USE! EVEN THE ROBOTS ARE JOINING UP WITH THE TYPHOON...

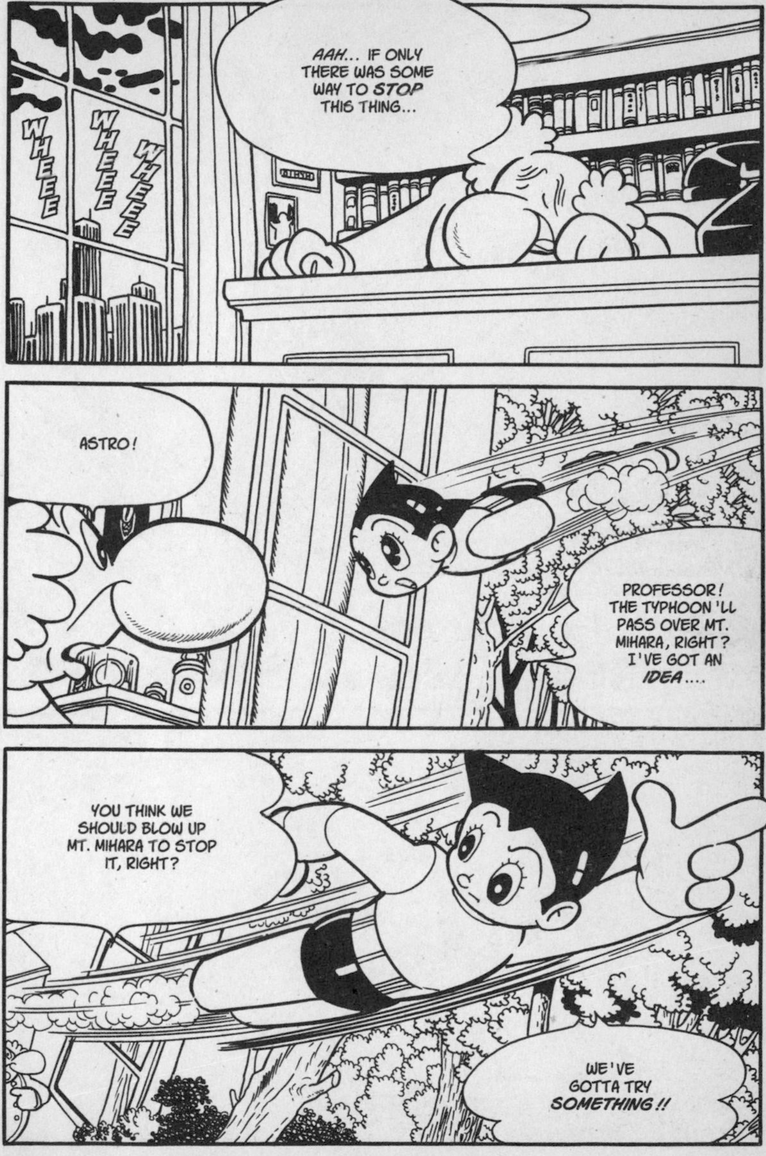
WHEEE
WHEEE
WHEEEE
AAH... IF ONLY THERE WAS SOME WAY TO STOP THIS THING...
ASTRO!
PROFESSOR! THE TYPHOON'LL PASS OVER MT. MIHARA, RIGHT? I'VE GOT AN IDEA....
YOU THINK WE SHOULD BLOW UP MT. MIHARA TO STOP IT, RIGHT?
WE'VE GOTTA TRY SOMETHING!!

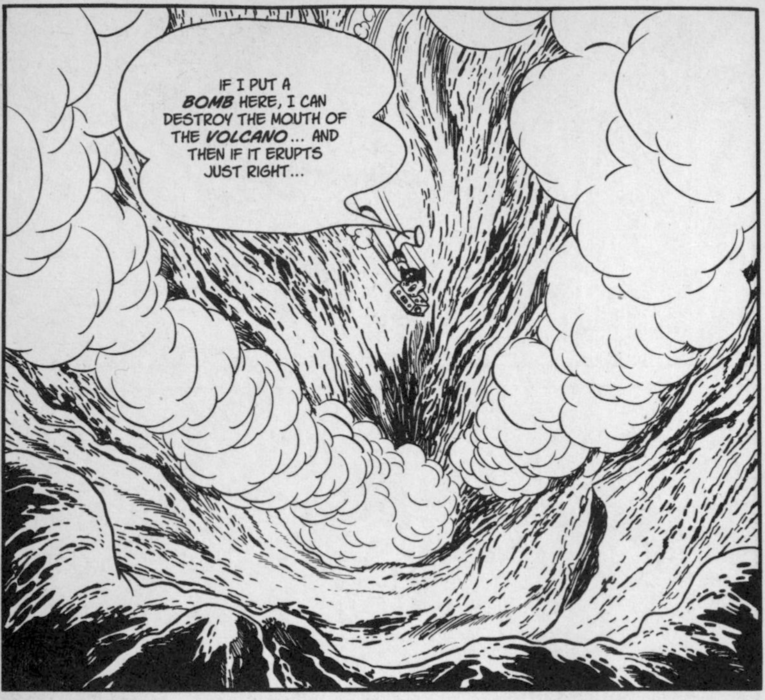
IF I PUT A BOMB HERE, I CAN DESTROY THE MOUTH OF THE VOLCANO... AND THEN IF IT ERUPTS JUST RIGHT...

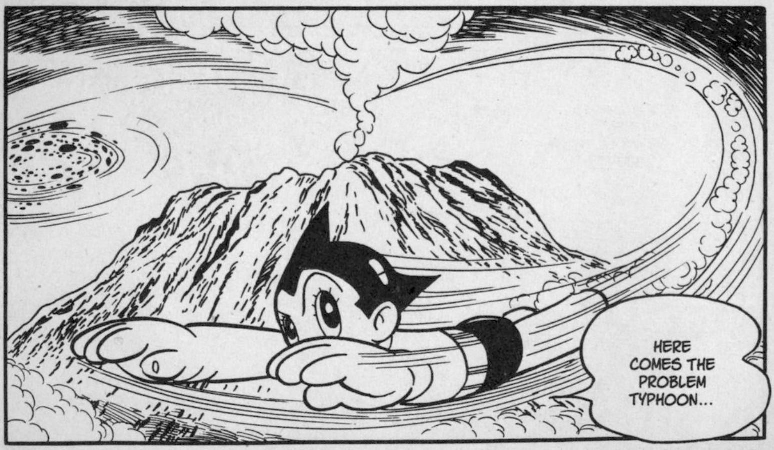
HERE COMES THE PROBLEM TYPHOON...

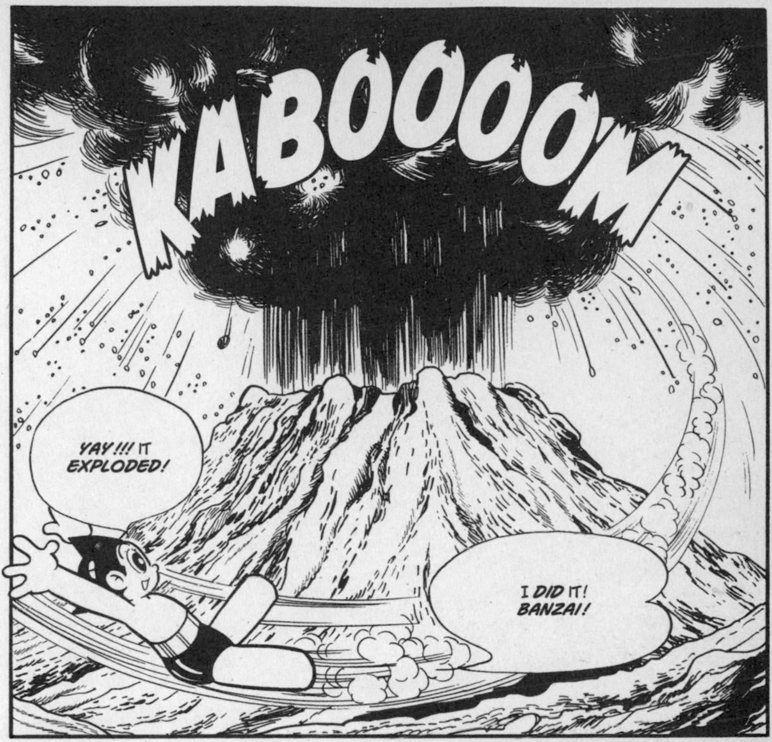
KABOOOOM
YAY!!! IT EXPLODED!
I DID IT! BANZAI!

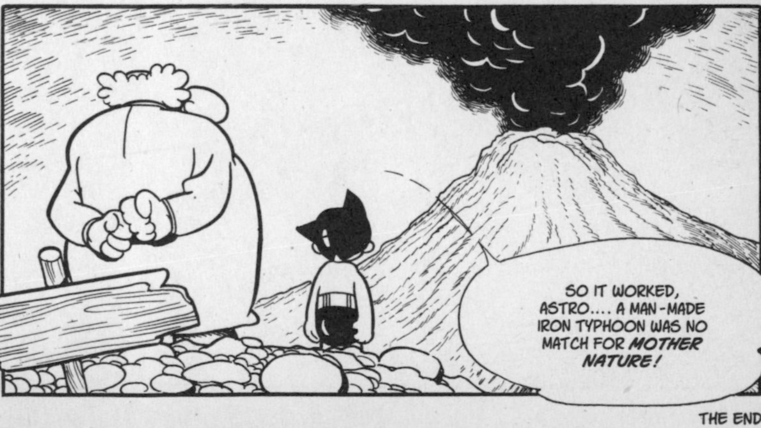
SO IT WORKED, ASTRO.... A MAN-MADE IRON TYPHOON WAS NO MATCH FOR MOTHER NATURE!

THE END

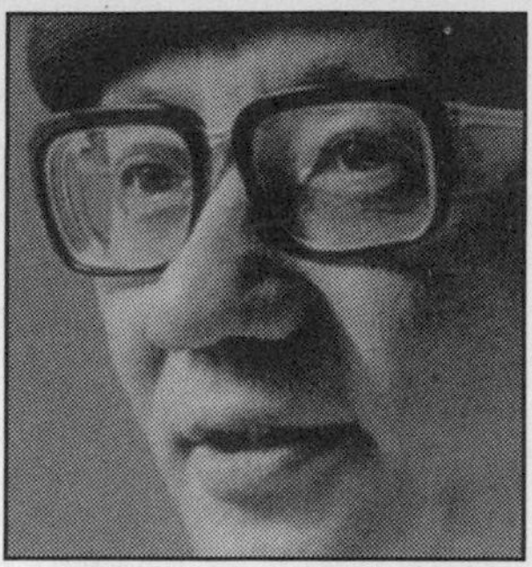

Osamu Tezuka was born in the city of Toyonaka, in Osaka, Japan, on November 3, 1928, and raised in Takarazuka, in Hyogo prefecture. He graduated from the Medical Department of Osaka University and was later awarded a Doctorate of Medicine.

In 1946 Tezuka made his debut as a manga artist with the work *Ma-chan's Diary*, and in 1947 he had his first big hit with *New Treasure Island*. In over forty years as a cartoonist, Tezuka produced in excess of an astounding 150,000 pages of manga, including the creation of *Metropolis*, *Mighty Atom* (a.k.a. *Astro Boy*), *Jungle Emperor* (a.k.a. *Kimba the White Lion*), *Black Jack*, *Phoenix*, *Buddha*, and many more.

Tezuka's fascination with Disney cartoons led him to begin his own animation studio, creating the first serialized Japanese cartoon series, which was later exported to America as *Astro Boy* in 1963. Tezuka Productions went on to create animated versions of *Kimba the White Lion* (*Jungle Emperor*) and *Phoenix*, among others.

He received numerous awards during his life, including the Bungei Shunju Manga Award, the Kodansha Manga Award, the Shogakukan Manga Award, and the Japan Cartoonists' Association Special Award for Excellence. He also served a variety of organizations. He was a director of the Japan Cartoonists' Association, the chairman of the Japan Animation Association, and a member of the Manga Group, Japan Pen Club, and the Japan SF Authors' Club, among others. Tezuka became Japan's "comics ambassador," taking Japan's comics culture to the world. In 1980, he toured and lectured in America, including a speech at the United Nations.

Regarded as a national treasure, Osamu Tezuka died on February 9, 1989 at the age of 60. In April 1994, the Osamu Tezuka Manga Museum opened in the city of Takarazuka, where he was raised. His creations remain hugely popular in Japan and are printed in many languages throughout the world, where he is acclaimed as one of the true giants of comics and animation, his work as vital and influential today as it was half a century ago.

"Comics are an international language," Tezuka said. "They can cross boundaries and generations. Comics are a bridge between all cultures."

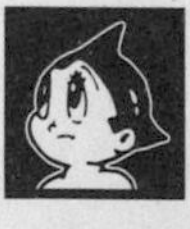

MORE EXCITING MANGA FROM OSAMU TEZUKA AND DARK HORSE COMICS!

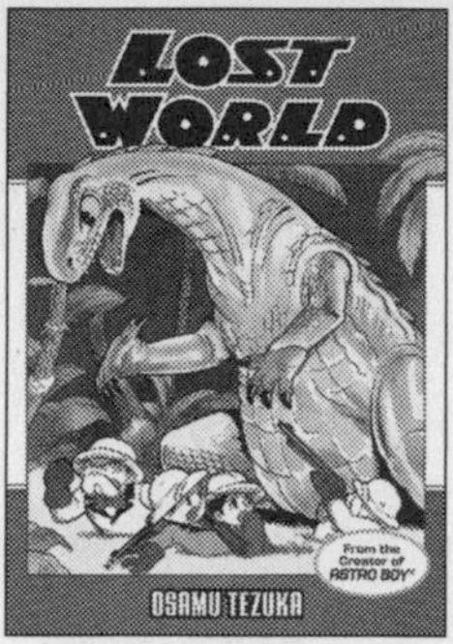
LOST WORLD
From the Creator of ASTRO BOY
OSAMU TEZUKA

Lost World
ISBN: 1-56971-865-2
$14.95

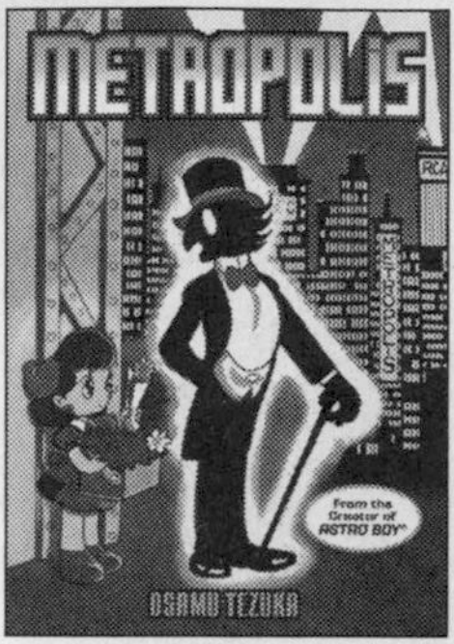
METROPOLIS
From the Creator of ASTRO BOY
OSAMU TEZUKA

Metropolis
ISBN: 1-56971-864-4
$13.95

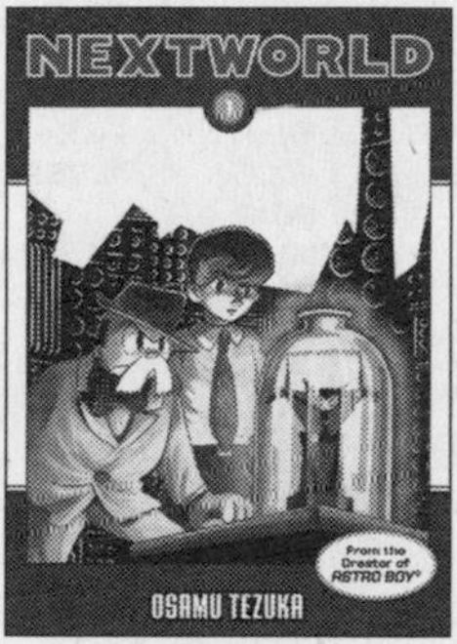
NEXTWORLD
From the Creator of ASTRO BOY
OSAMU TEZUKA

Nextworld Volume 1
ISBN: 1-56971-866-0
$13.95

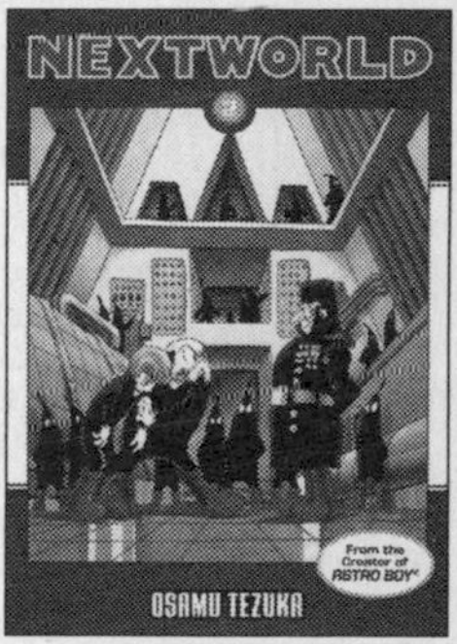
NEXTWORLD
From the Creator of ASTRO BOY
OSAMU TEZUKA

Nextworld Volume 2
ISBN: 1-56971-867-9
$13.95

DARK HORSE MANGA
darkhorse.com

AVAILABLE AT YOUR LOCAL COMICS SHOP
OR BOOKSTORE
To find a comics shop in your area, call 1-888-266-4226
For more information or to order direct visit
darkhorse.com or call 1-800-862-0052
Mon.-Sat. 9 A.M. to 5 P.M. Pacific Time
*Prices and availability subject to change without notice

STUDIO PROTEUS
studioproteus.com

AKIRA
Katsuhiro Otomo
BOOK 1
ISBN: 1-56971-498-3 $24.95
BOOK 2
ISBN: 1-56971-499-1 $24.95
BOOK 3
ISBN: 1-56971-525-4 $24.95
BOOK 4
ISBN: 1-56971-526-2 $27.95
BOOK 5
ISBN: 1-56971-527-0 $27.95
BOOK 6
ISBN: 1-56971-528-9 $29.95

APPLESEED
Masamune Shirow
BOOK ONE
ISBN: 1-56971-070-8 $16.95
BOOK TWO
ISBN: 1-56971-071-6 $16.95
BOOK THREE
ISBN: 1-56971-072-4 $17.95
BOOK FOUR
ISBN: 1-56971-074-0 $17.95

BLACK MAGIC
Masamune Shirow
ISBN: 1-56971-360-X $16.95

BLADE OF THE IMMORTAL
Hiroaki Samura
BLOOD OF A THOUSAND
ISBN: 1-56971-239-5 $14.95
CRY OF THE WORM
ISBN: 1-56971-300-6 $14.95
DREAMSONG
ISBN: 1-56971-357-X $14.95
ON SILENT WINGS
ISBN: 1-56971-412-6 $14.95
ON SILENT WINGS II
ISBN: 1-56971-444-4 $14.95
DARK SHADOWS
ISBN: 1-56971-469-X $14.95
HEART OF DARKNESS
ISBN: 1-56971-531-9 $16.95
THE GATHERING
ISBN: 1-56971-546-7 $15.95
THE GATHERING II
ISBN: 1-56971-560-2 $15.95
BEASTS
ISBN: 1-56971-741-9 $14.95

BUBBLEGUM CRISIS
Adam Warren • Toren Smith
GRAND MAL
ISBN: 1-56971-120-8 $14.95

CANNON GOD EXAXXION
Kenichi Sonoda
VOLUME 1
ISBN: 1-56971-745-1 $15.95

CARAVAN KIDD
Johji Manabe
VOLUME 1
ISBN: 1-56971-260-3 $19.95
VOLUME 2
ISBN: 1-56971-324-3 $19.95
VOLUME 3
ISBN: 1-56971-338-3 $19.95

THE DIRTY PAIR
Adam Warren • Toren Smith
BIOHAZARDS
ISBN: 1-56971-339-1 $12.95
DANGEROUS ACQUAINTANCES
ISBN: 1-56971-227-1 $12.95
A PLAGUE OF ANGELS
ISBN: 1-56971-029-5 $12.95
SIM HELL
ISBN: 1-56971-742-7 $13.95
FATAL BUT NOT SERIOUS
ISBN: 1-56971-172-0 $14.95

DOMINION
Masamune Shirow
ISBN: 1-56971-488-6 $16.95

DOMU: A CHILD'S DREAM
Katsuhiro Otomo
ISBN: 1-56971-611-0 $17.95

GHOST IN THE SHELL
Masamune Shirow
ISBN: 1-56971-081-3 $24.95

GUNSMITH CATS
Kenichi Sonoda
BONNIE AND CLYDE
ISBN: 1-56971-215-8 $13.95

MISFIRE
ISBN: 1-56971-253-0 $14.95
THE RETURN OF GRAY
ISBN: 1-56971-299-9 $17.95
GOLDIE VS. MISTY
ISBN: 1-56971-371-5 $15.95
BAD TRIP
ISBN: 1-56971-442-8 $13.95
BEAN BANDIT
ISBN: 1-56971-453-3 $16.95
KIDNAPPED
ISBN: 1-56971-529-7 $16.95
MR. V
ISBN: 1-56971-550-5 $18.95
MISTY'S RUN
ISBN: 1-56971-684-6 $14.95

INTRON DEPOT
Masamune Shirow
INTRON DEPOT 1
ISBN: 1-56971-085-6 $39.95
INTRON DEPOT 2: BLADES
ISBN: 1-56971-382-0 $39.95

LONE WOLF AND CUB
Kazuo Koike & Goseki Kojima
VOLUME 1: THE ASSASSIN'S ROAD
ISBN: 1-56971-502-5 $9.95
VOLUME 2: THE GATELESS BARRIER
ISBN: 1-56971-503-3 $9.95
VOLUME 3: THE FLUTE OF THE FALLEN TIGER
ISBN: 1-56971-504-1 $9.95
VOLUME 4: THE BELL WARDEN
ISBN: 1-56971-505-X $9.95
VOLUME 5: BLACK WIND
ISBN: 1-5671-506-8 $9.95
VOLUME 6: LANTERNS FOR THE DEAD
ISBN: 1-56971-507-6 $9.95
VOLUME 7: CLOUD DRAGON, WIND TIGER
ISBN: 1-56971-508-4 $9.95
VOLUME 8: CHAINS OF DEATH
ISBN: 1-56971-509-2 $9.95
VOLUME 9: ECHO OF THE ASSASSIN
ISBN: 1-56971-510-6 $9.95
VOLUME 10: HOSTAGE CHILD
ISBN: 1-56971-511-4 $9.95